TOKYO GHOUL

TOKYO GHOUL

SUI ISHIDA

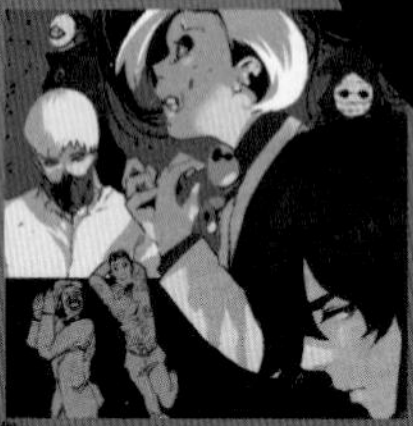

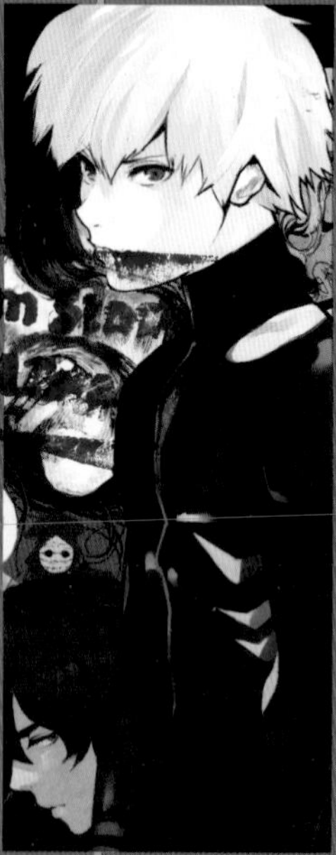

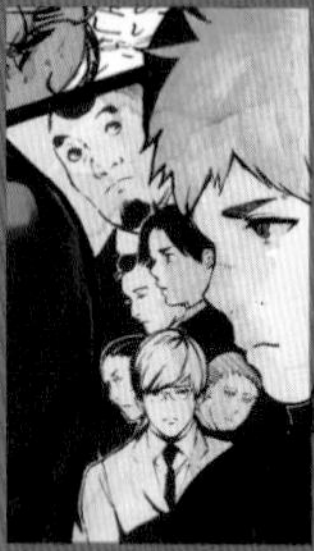

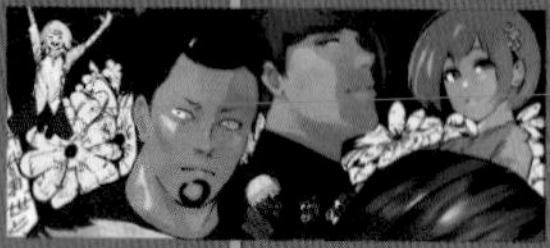

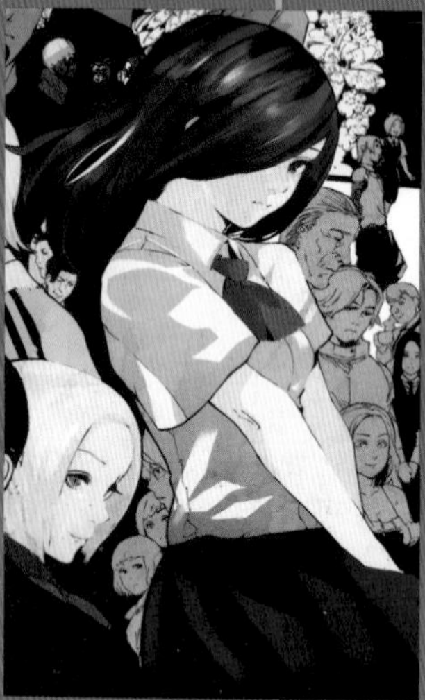

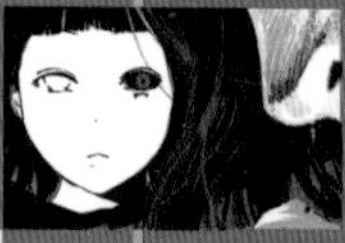

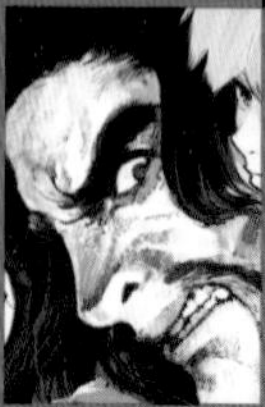

TOKYO GHOUL

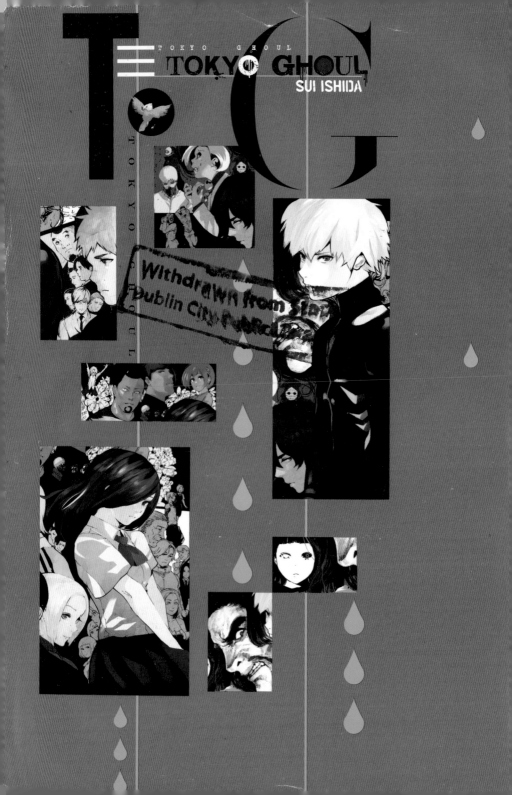

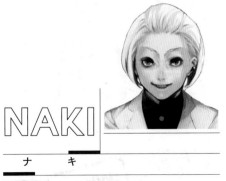

NAKI

ナ キ

BORN January 28th Aquarius

Cochlea Rate S Detainee

BLOOD-TYPE: B

Size: 173 cm 65 kg FEET 26.0 CM

Likes: TORTURE, Mob films, errands

Respects: Yamori (Godly Bro)

Rc Type: Kokaku

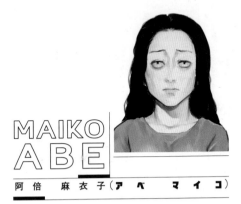

MAIKO ABE

阿倍 麻衣子(アベ マイコ)

BORN May 15th Taurus

Madame A

BLOOD-TYPE: A

Size: 160cm 56kg FEET 23.0cm

Likes: Expensive items, celebrities, parties

Respects: Big Madame

Rc Type: -

SUI ISHIDA was born in Fukuoka, Japan. He is the author of ***Tokyo Ghoul*** and several ***Tokyo Ghoul*** one-shots, including one that won him second place in the *Weekly Young Jump* 113th Grand Prix award in 2010. ***Tokyo Ghoul*** began serialization in *Weekly Young Jump* in 2011 and was adapted into an anime series in 2014.

東京喰種

TOKYO GHOUL

10

TOKYO

TOKYO GHOUL

TOKYO GHOUL

SUI ISHIDA

TOKYO GHOUL

sui ishida

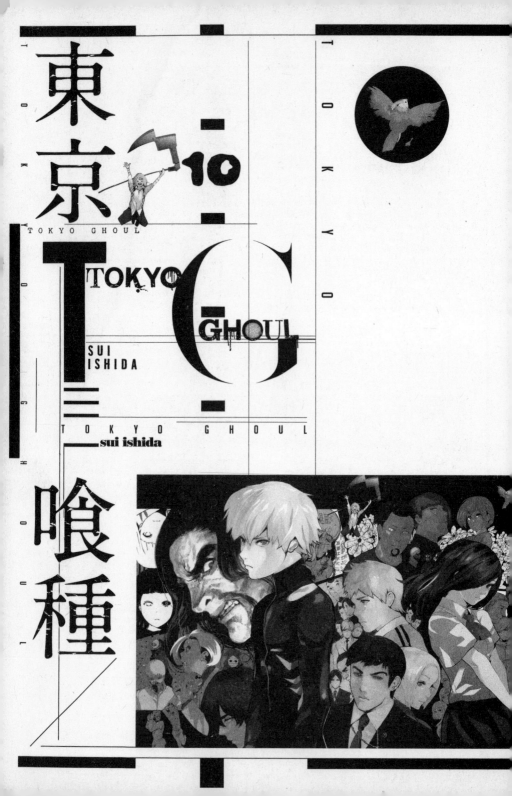

TOKYO GHOUL SO FAR

喰 GHOULS 種

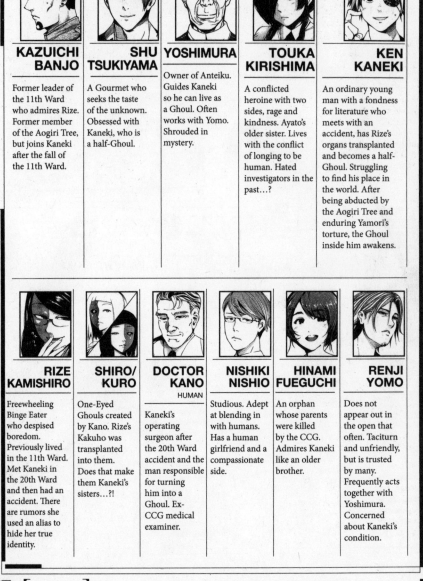

KAZUICHI BANJO

Former leader of the 11th Ward who admires Rize. Former member of the Aogiri Tree, but joins Kaneki after the fall of the 11th Ward.

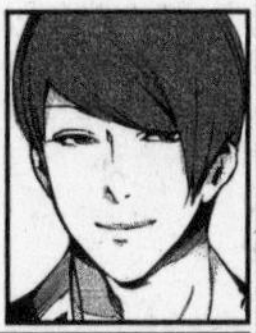

SHU TSUKIYAMA

A Gourmet who seeks the taste of the unknown. Obsessed with Kaneki, who is a half-Ghoul.

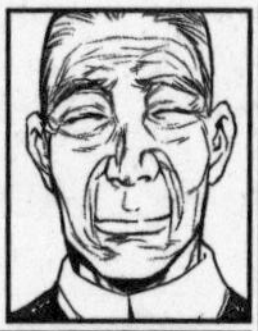

YOSHIMURA

Owner of Anteiku. Guides Kaneki so he can live as a Ghoul. Often works with Yomo. Shrouded in mystery.

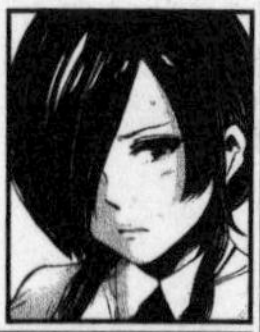

TOUKA KIRISHIMA

A conflicted heroine with two sides, rage and kindness. Ayato's older sister. Lives with the conflict of longing to be human. Hated investigators in the past…?

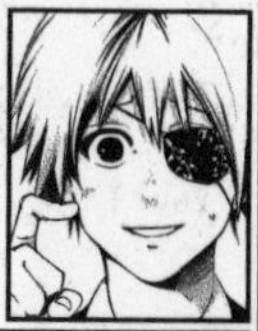

KEN KANEKI

An ordinary young man with a fondness for literature who meets with an accident, has Rize's organs transplanted and becomes a half-Ghoul. Struggling to find his place in the world. After being abducted by the Aogiri Tree and enduring Yamori's torture, the Ghoul inside him awakens.

RIZE KAMISHIRO

Freewheeling Binge Eater who despised boredom. Previously lived in the 11th Ward. Met Kaneki in the 20th Ward and then had an accident. There are rumors she used an alias to hide her true identity.

SHIRO/ KURO

One-Eyed Ghouls created by Kano. Rize's Kakuho was transplanted into them. Does that make them Kaneki's sisters…?!

DOCTOR KANO

HUMAN

Kaneki's operating surgeon after the 20th Ward accident and the man responsible for turning him into a Ghoul. Ex-CCG medical examiner.

NISHIKI NISHIO

Studious. Adept at blending in with humans. Has a human girlfriend and a compassionate side.

HINAMI FUEGUCHI

An orphan whose parents were killed by the CCG. Admires Kaneki like an older brother.

RENJI YOMO

Does not appear out in the open that often. Taciturn and unfriendly, but is trusted by many. Frequently acts together with Yoshimura. Concerned about Kaneki's condition.

[GHOUL]

A creature that appears human yet consumes humans. The top of the food chain. Finds anything other than humans and coffee unpleasant. Releases a highly lethal natural weapon unique to Ghouls, known as Kagune, from their body to prey on humans. Can be cannibalistic. Only sustains damage from Kagune or Quinques that are made from Kagune.

T O K Y O G H O U L

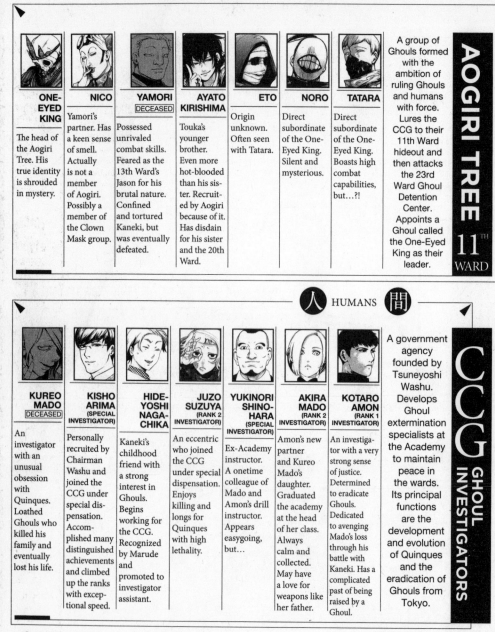

AOGIRI TREE 11TH WARD

A group of Ghouls formed with the ambition of ruling Ghouls and humans with force. Lures the CCG to their 11th Ward hideout and then attacks the 23rd Ward Ghoul Detention Center. Appoints a Ghoul called the One-Eyed King as their leader.

ONE-EYED KING
The head of the Aogiri Tree. His true identity is shrouded in mystery.

NICO
Yamori's partner. Has a keen sense of smell. Actually is not a member of Aogiri. Possibly a member of the Clown Mask group.

YAMORI [DECEASED]
Possessed unrivaled combat skills. Feared as the 13th Ward's Jason for his brutal nature. Confined and tortured Kaneki, but was eventually defeated.

AYATO KIRISHIMA
Touka's younger brother. Even more hot-blooded than his sister. Recruited by Aogiri because of it. Has disdain for his sister and the 20th Ward.

ETO
Origin unknown. Often seen with Tatara.

NORO
Direct subordinate of the One-Eyed King. Silent and mysterious.

TATARA
Direct subordinate of the One-Eyed King. Boasts high combat capabilities, but…?!

人 HUMANS 間

CCG GHOUL INVESTIGATORS

A government agency founded by Tsuneyoshi Washu. Develops Ghoul extermination specialists at the Academy to maintain peace in the wards. Its principal functions are the development and evolution of Quinques and the eradication of Ghouls from Tokyo.

KUREO MADO [DECEASED]
An investigator with an unusual obsession with Quinques. Loathed Ghouls who killed his family and eventually lost his life.

KISHO ARIMA (SPECIAL INVESTIGATOR)
Personally recruited by Chairman Washu and joined the CCG under special dispensation. Accomplished many distinguished achievements and climbed up the ranks with exceptional speed.

HIDEYOSHI NAGACHIKA
Kaneki's childhood friend with a strong interest in Ghouls. Begins working for the CCG. Recognized by Marude and promoted to investigator assistant.

JUZO SUZUYA (RANK 2 INVESTIGATOR)
An eccentric who joined the CCG under special dispensation. Enjoys killing and longs for Quinques with high lethality.

YUKINORI SHINOHARA (SPECIAL INVESTIGATOR)
Ex-Academy instructor. A onetime colleague of Mado and Amon's drill instructor. Appears easygoing, but…

AKIRA MADO (RANK 2 INVESTIGATOR)
Amon's new partner and Kureo Mado's daughter. Graduated the academy at the head of her class. Always calm and collected. May have a love for weapons like her father.

KOTARO AMON (RANK 1 INVESTIGATOR)
An investigator with a very strong sense of justice. Determined to eradicate Ghouls. Dedicated to avenging Mado's loss through his battle with Kaneki. Has a complicated past of being raised by a Ghoul.

Summary

Kaneki, an average college student, is fated to live as a Ghoul when Rize's organs are transplanted into him. While questioning and struggling with the existence of creatures that take human lives to survive, he searches for how the world should be. One day while at Anteiku, he is abducted by the Aogiri Tree. While being held captive and viciously tortured by Yamori, he accepts that he is a Ghoul. He escapes from the Aogiri Tree with help from members of Anteiku. The Aogiri Tree's 11th Ward hideout is taken down by the CCG, and Kaneki, with Tsukiyama and Banjo, heads to the 6th Ward. They search for Kano, the doctor who turned Kaneki into a Ghoul, by retracing Rize's steps.

東

京

喰

種

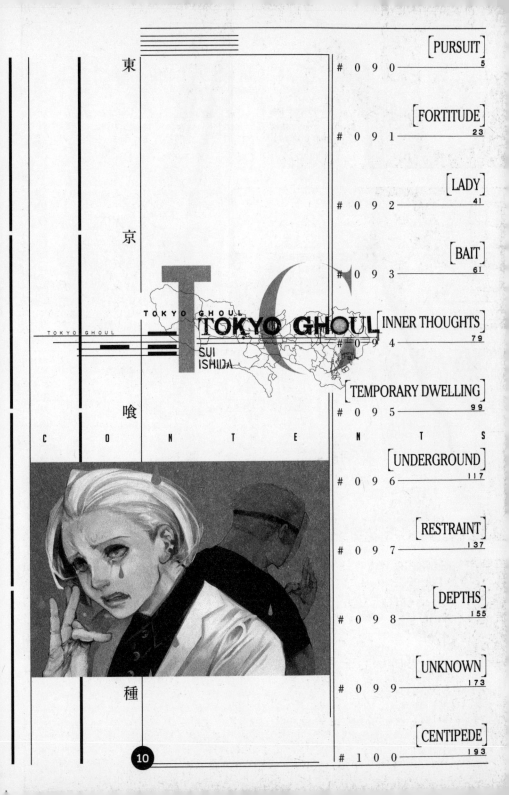

TOKYO GHOUL

SUI ISHIDA

C O N T E N T S

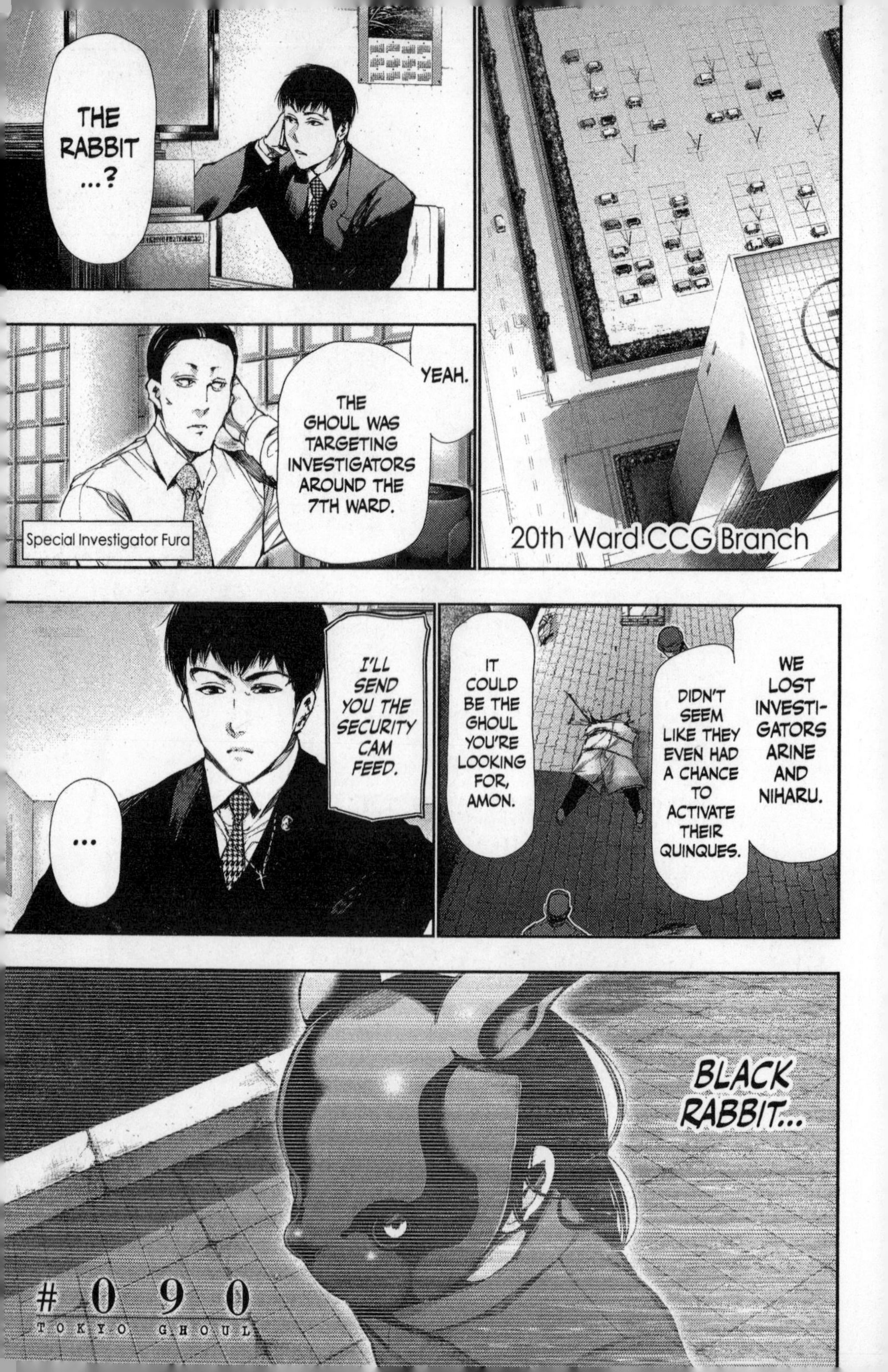
20th Ward CCG Branch
THE RABBIT ...?
YEAH.
THE GHOUL WAS TARGETING INVESTIGATORS AROUND THE 7TH WARD.
Special Investigator Fura
WE LOST INVESTI-GATORS ARINE AND NIHARU.
DIDN'T SEEM LIKE THEY EVEN HAD A CHANCE TO ACTIVATE THEIR QUINQUES.
IT COULD BE THE GHOUL YOU'RE LOOKING FOR, AMON.
I'LL SEND YOU THE SECURITY CAM FEED.
...
BLACK RABBIT...
#090
TOKYO GHOUL

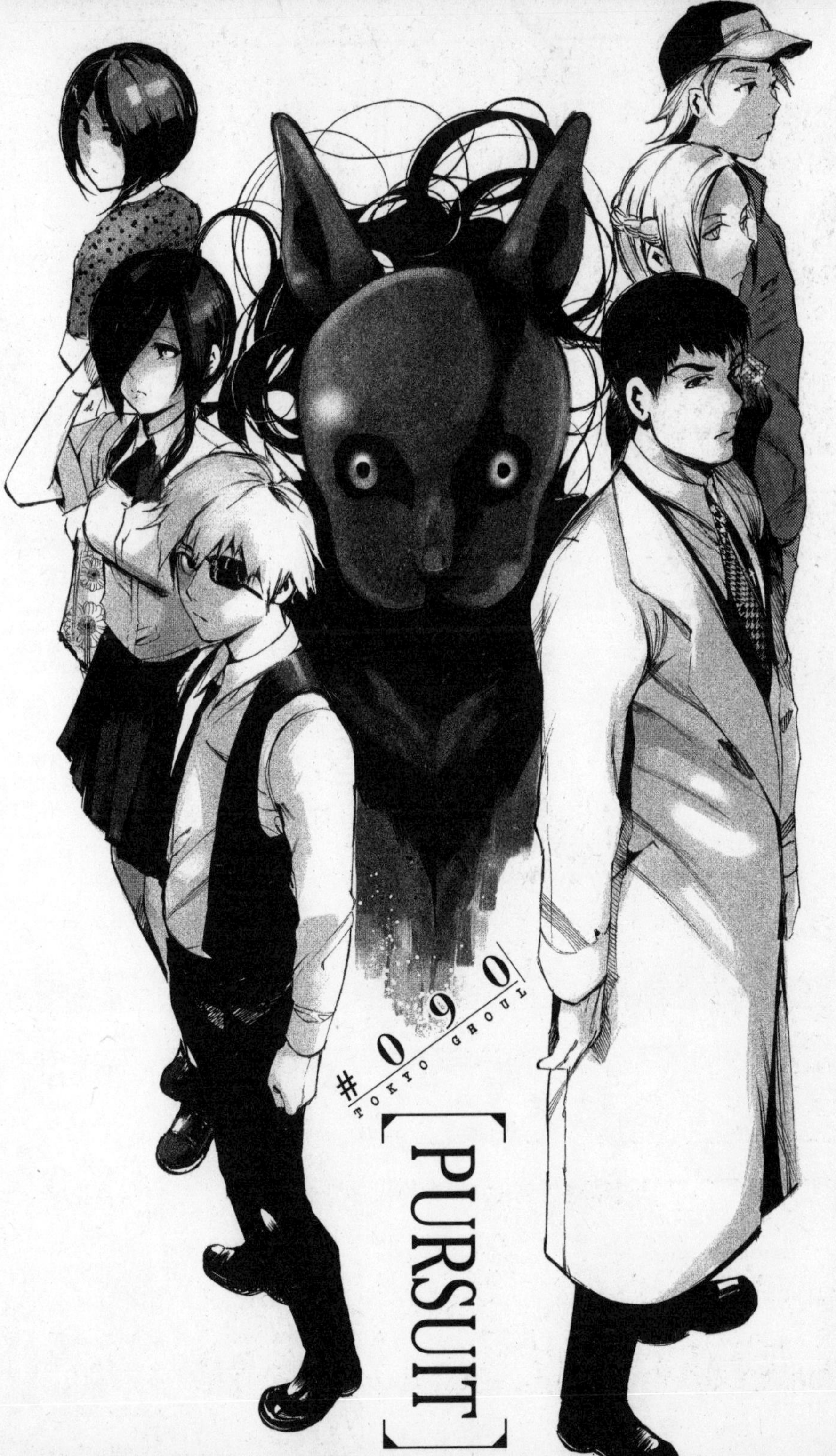
#090
TOKYO GHOUL
[PURSUIT]

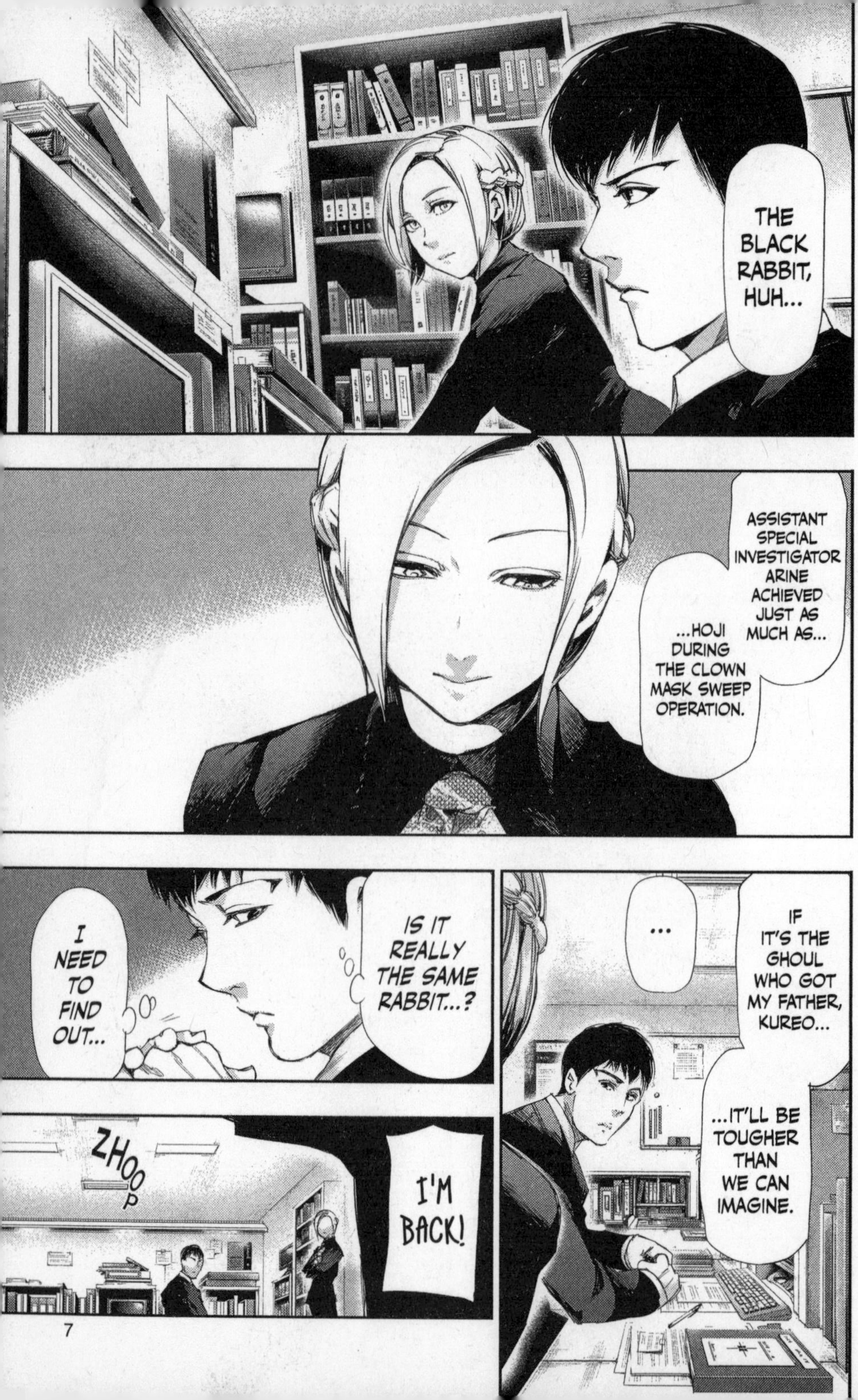
THE BLACK RABBIT, HUH...
ASSISTANT SPECIAL INVESTIGATOR ARINE ACHIEVED JUST AS MUCH AS...
...HOJI DURING THE CLOWN MASK SWEEP OPERATION.
...
IF IT'S THE GHOUL WHO GOT MY FATHER, KUREO...
...IT'LL BE TOUGHER THAN WE CAN IMAGINE.
IS IT REALLY THE SAME RABBIT...?
I NEED TO FIND OUT...
I'M BACK!
ZHOOP

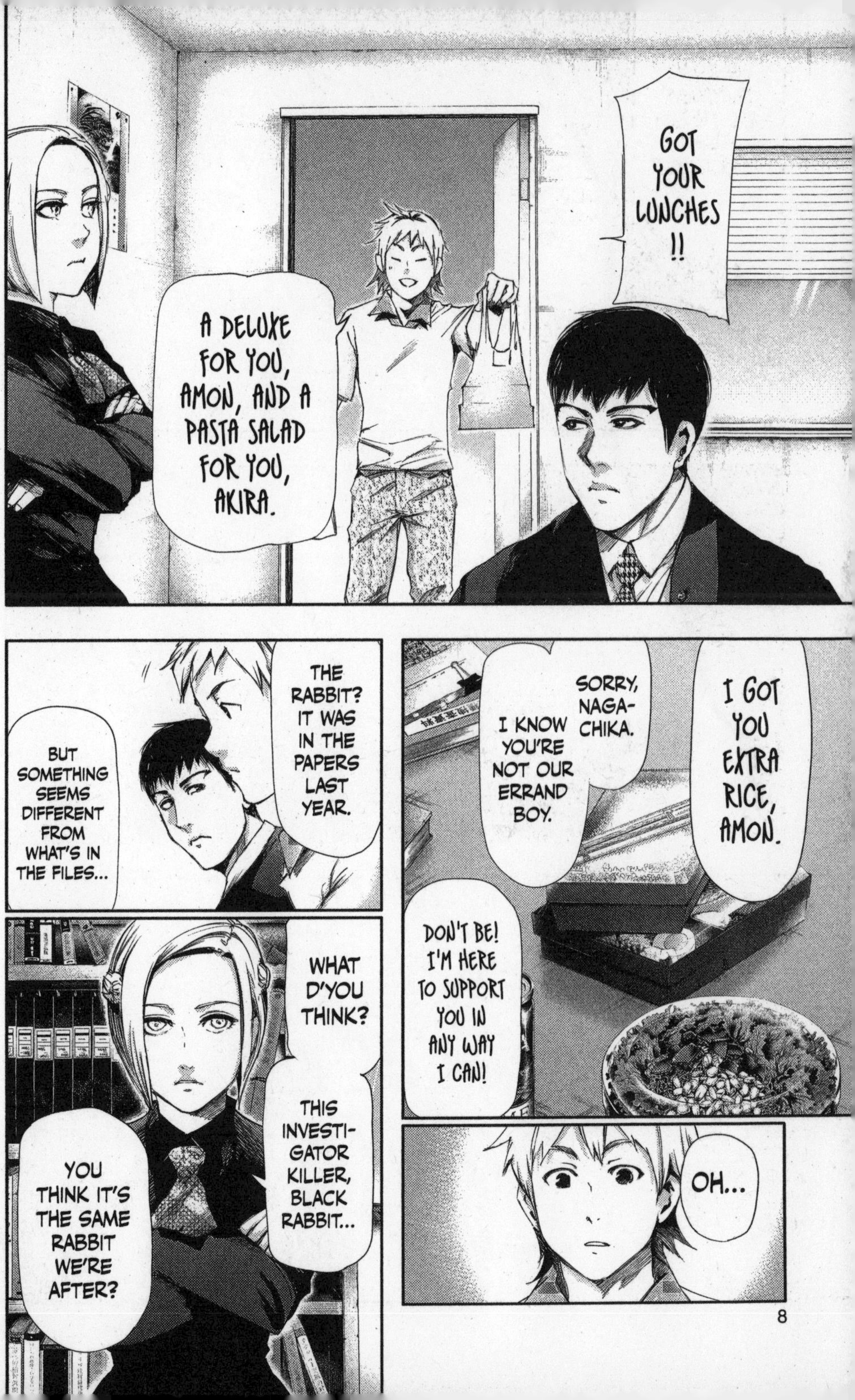
GOT YOUR LUNCHES !!
A DELUXE FOR YOU, AMON, AND A PASTA SALAD FOR YOU, AKIRA.
I GOT YOU EXTRA RICE, AMON.
SORRY, NAGA-CHIKA.
I KNOW YOU'RE NOT OUR ERRAND BOY.
DON'T BE! I'M HERE TO SUPPORT YOU IN ANY WAY I CAN!
OH...
THE RABBIT? IT WAS IN THE PAPERS LAST YEAR.
BUT SOMETHING SEEMS DIFFERENT FROM WHAT'S IN THE FILES...
WHAT D'YOU THINK?
THIS INVESTI-GATOR KILLER, BLACK RABBIT...
YOU THINK IT'S THE SAME RABBIT WE'RE AFTER?

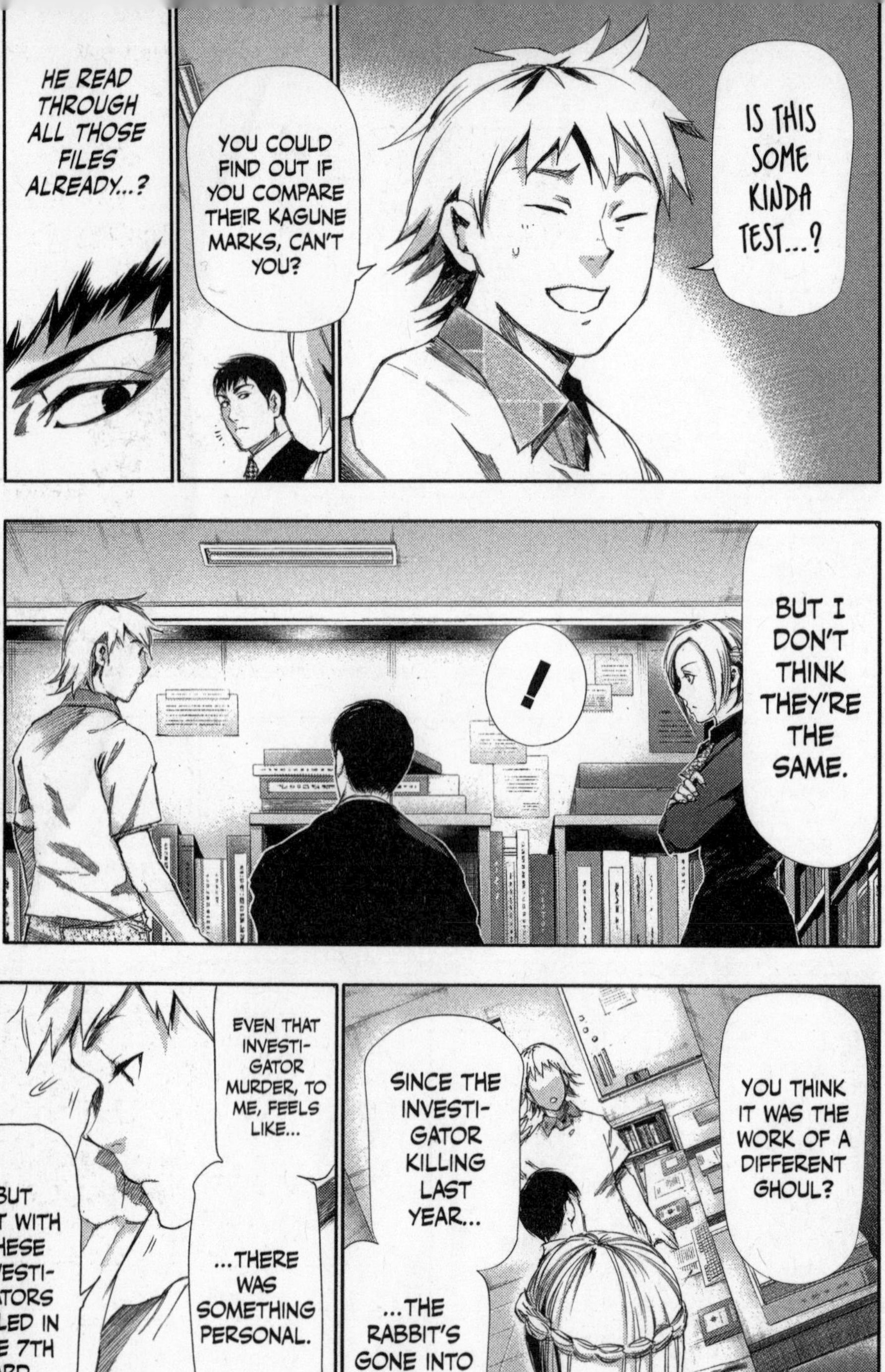
IS THIS SOME KINDA TEST...?
YOU COULD FIND OUT IF YOU COMPARE THEIR KAGUNE MARKS, CAN'T YOU?
HE READ THROUGH ALL THOSE FILES ALREADY...?
BUT I DON'T THINK THEY'RE THE SAME.
!
YOU THINK IT WAS THE WORK OF A DIFFERENT GHOUL?
SINCE THE INVESTI-GATOR KILLING LAST YEAR...
...THE RABBIT'S GONE INTO HIDING, RIGHT?
EVEN THAT INVESTI-GATOR MURDER, TO ME, FEELS LIKE...
...THERE WAS SOMETHING PERSONAL.
BUT NOT WITH THESE INVESTI-GATORS KILLED IN THE 7TH WARD...

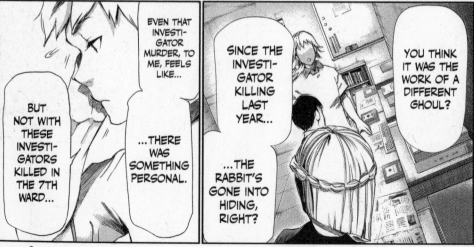

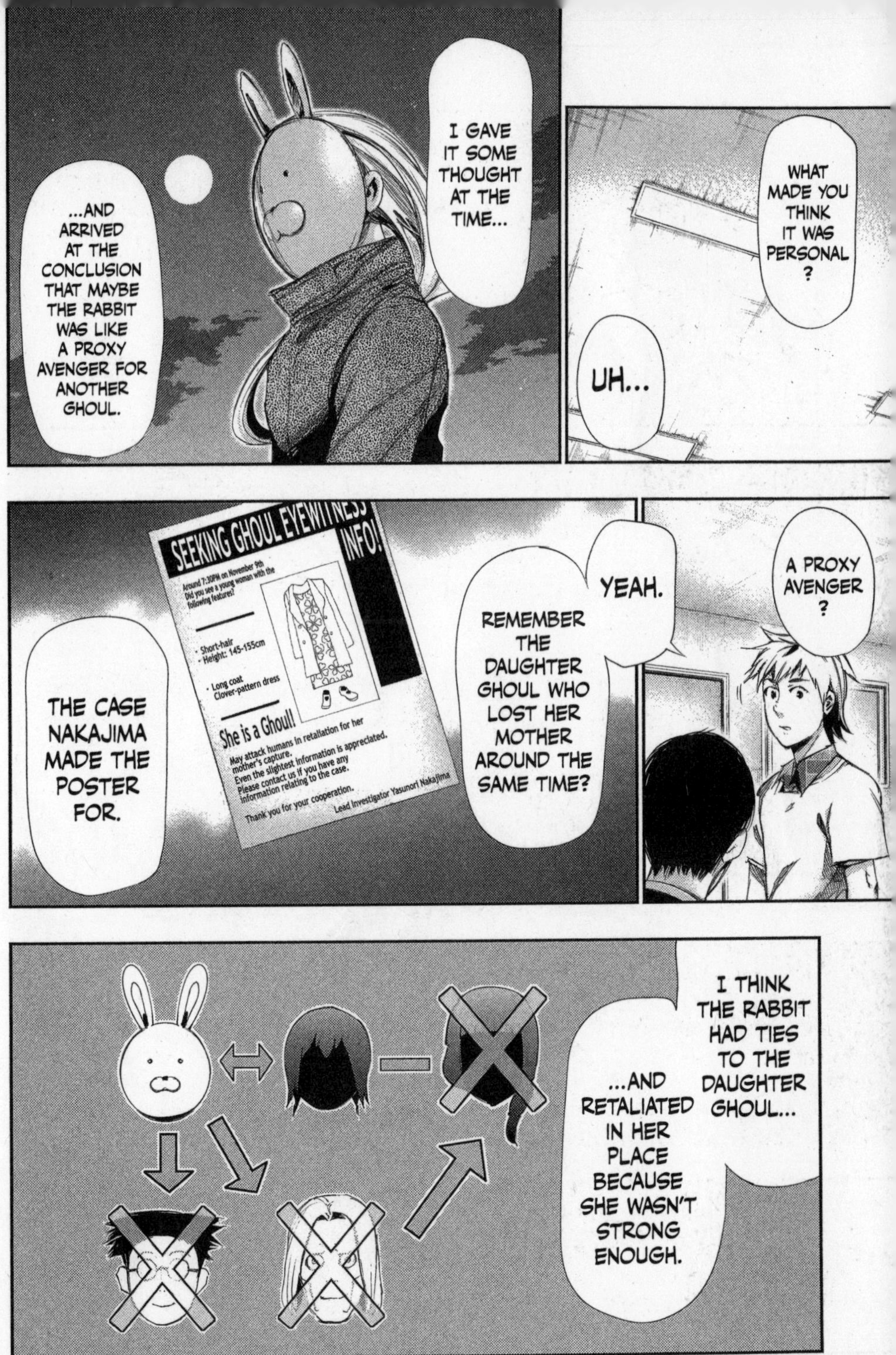
WHAT MADE YOU THINK IT WAS PERSONAL?
UH...
I GAVE IT SOME THOUGHT AT THE TIME...
...AND ARRIVED AT THE CONCLUSION THAT MAYBE THE RABBIT WAS LIKE A PROXY AVENGER FOR ANOTHER GHOUL.
A PROXY AVENGER?
YEAH.
REMEMBER THE DAUGHTER GHOUL WHO LOST HER MOTHER AROUND THE SAME TIME?
SEEKING GHOUL EYEWITNESS INFO!
Around 7:30PM on November 9th Did you see a young woman with the following features?
· Short-hair
· Height: 145-155cm
· Long coat Clover-pattern dress
She is a Ghoul!
May attack humans in retaliation for her mother's capture.
Even the slightest information is appreciated.
Please contact us if you have any information relating to the case.
Thank you for your cooperation.
Lead Investigator Yasunori Nakajima
THE CASE NAKAJIMA MADE THE POSTER FOR.
I THINK THE RABBIT HAD TIES TO THE DAUGHTER GHOUL...
...AND RETALIATED IN HER PLACE BECAUSE SHE WASN'T STRONG ENOUGH.

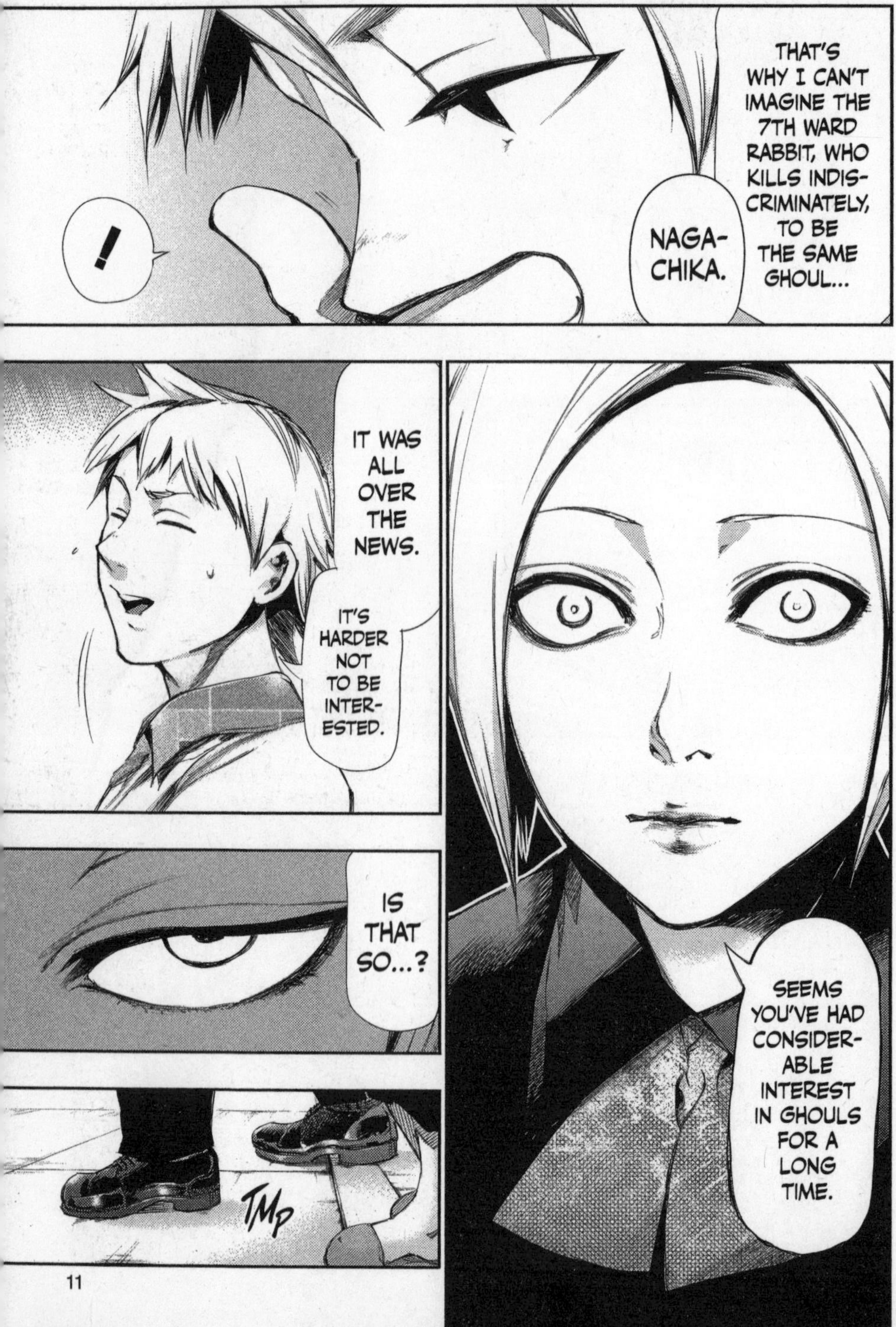
THAT'S WHY I CAN'T IMAGINE THE 7TH WARD RABBIT, WHO KILLS INDIS-CRIMINATELY, TO BE THE SAME GHOUL...
NAGA-CHIKA.
!
SEEMS YOU'VE HAD CONSIDER-ABLE INTEREST IN GHOULS FOR A LONG TIME.
IT WAS ALL OVER THE NEWS.
IT'S HARDER NOT TO BE INTER-ESTED.
IS THAT SO...?
TMP

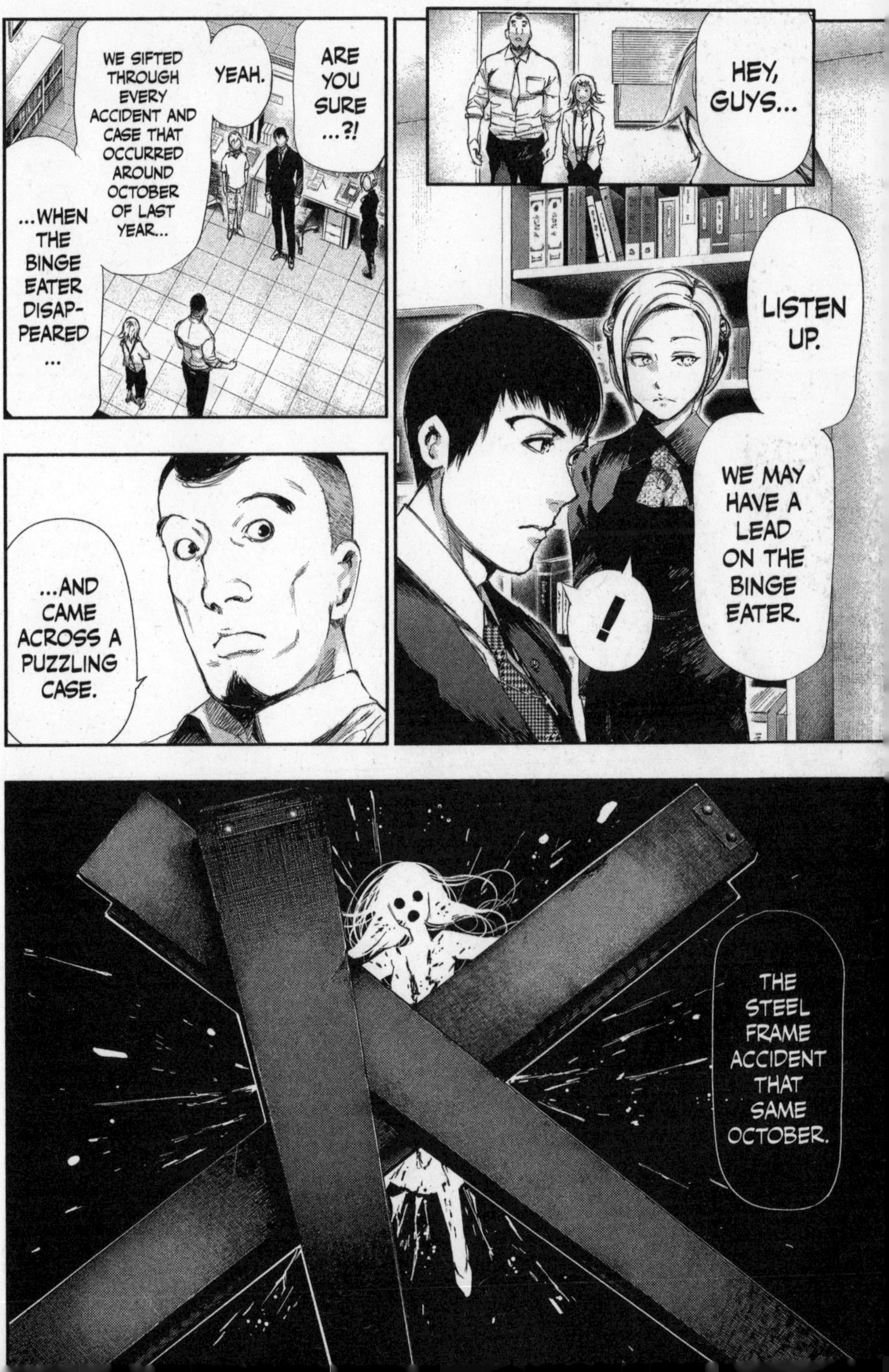
HEY, GUYS...
LISTEN UP.
WE MAY HAVE A LEAD ON THE BINGE EATER.
!
ARE YOU SURE ...?!
YEAH.
WE SIFTED THROUGH EVERY ACCIDENT AND CASE THAT OCCURRED AROUND OCTOBER OF LAST YEAR...
...WHEN THE BINGE EATER DISAPPEARED ...
...AND CAME ACROSS A PUZZLING CASE.
THE STEEL FRAME ACCIDENT THAT SAME OCTOBER.

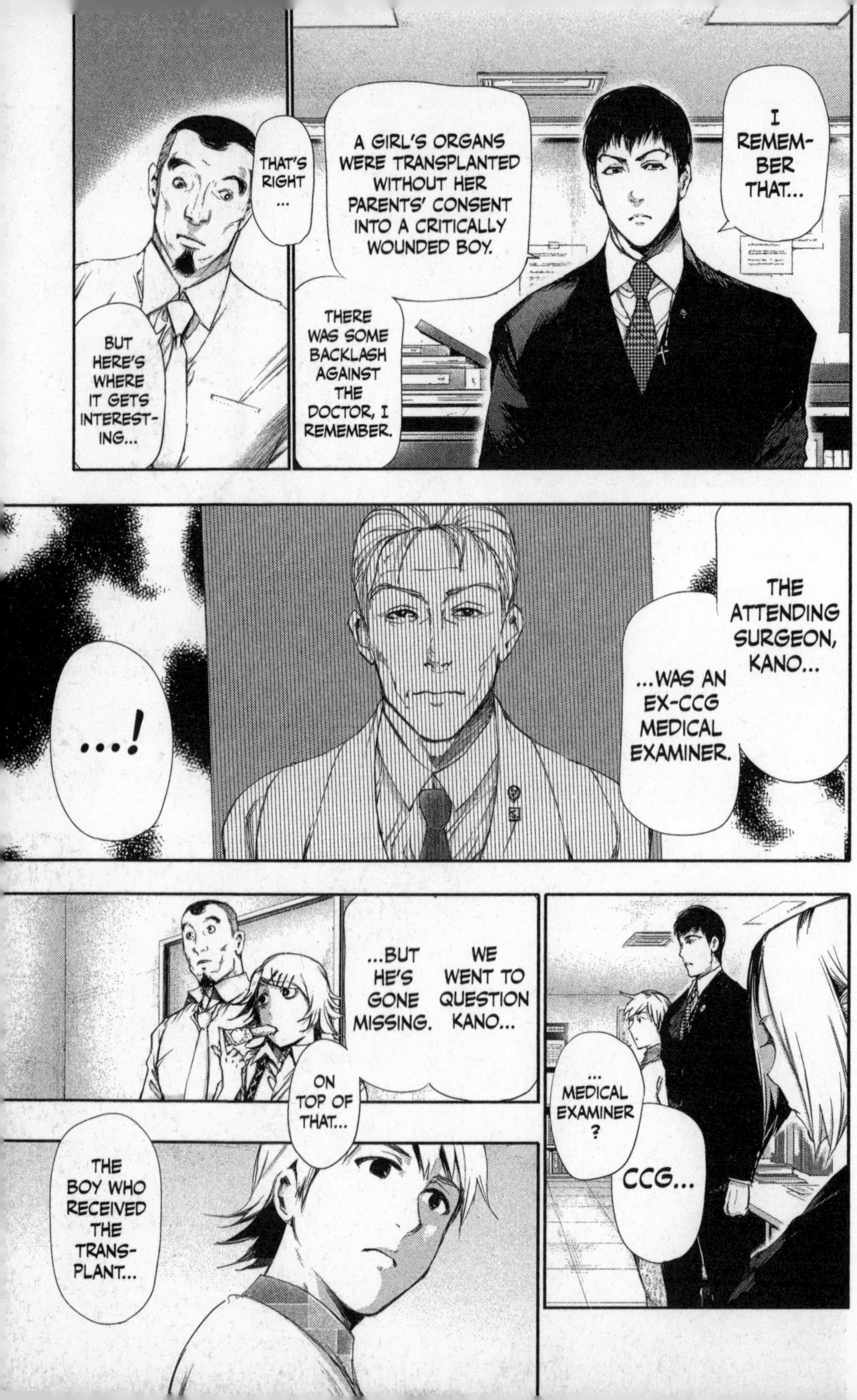
I REMEMBER THAT...
A GIRL'S ORGANS WERE TRANSPLANTED WITHOUT HER PARENTS' CONSENT INTO A CRITICALLY WOUNDED BOY.
THERE WAS SOME BACKLASH AGAINST THE DOCTOR, I REMEMBER.
THAT'S RIGHT...
BUT HERE'S WHERE IT GETS INTERESTING...
THE ATTENDING SURGEON, KANO...
...WAS AN EX-CCG MEDICAL EXAMINER.
...!
...MEDICAL EXAMINER?
CCG...
WE WENT TO QUESTION KANO...
...BUT HE'S GONE MISSING.
ON TOP OF THAT...
THE BOY WHO RECEIVED THE TRANSPLANT...

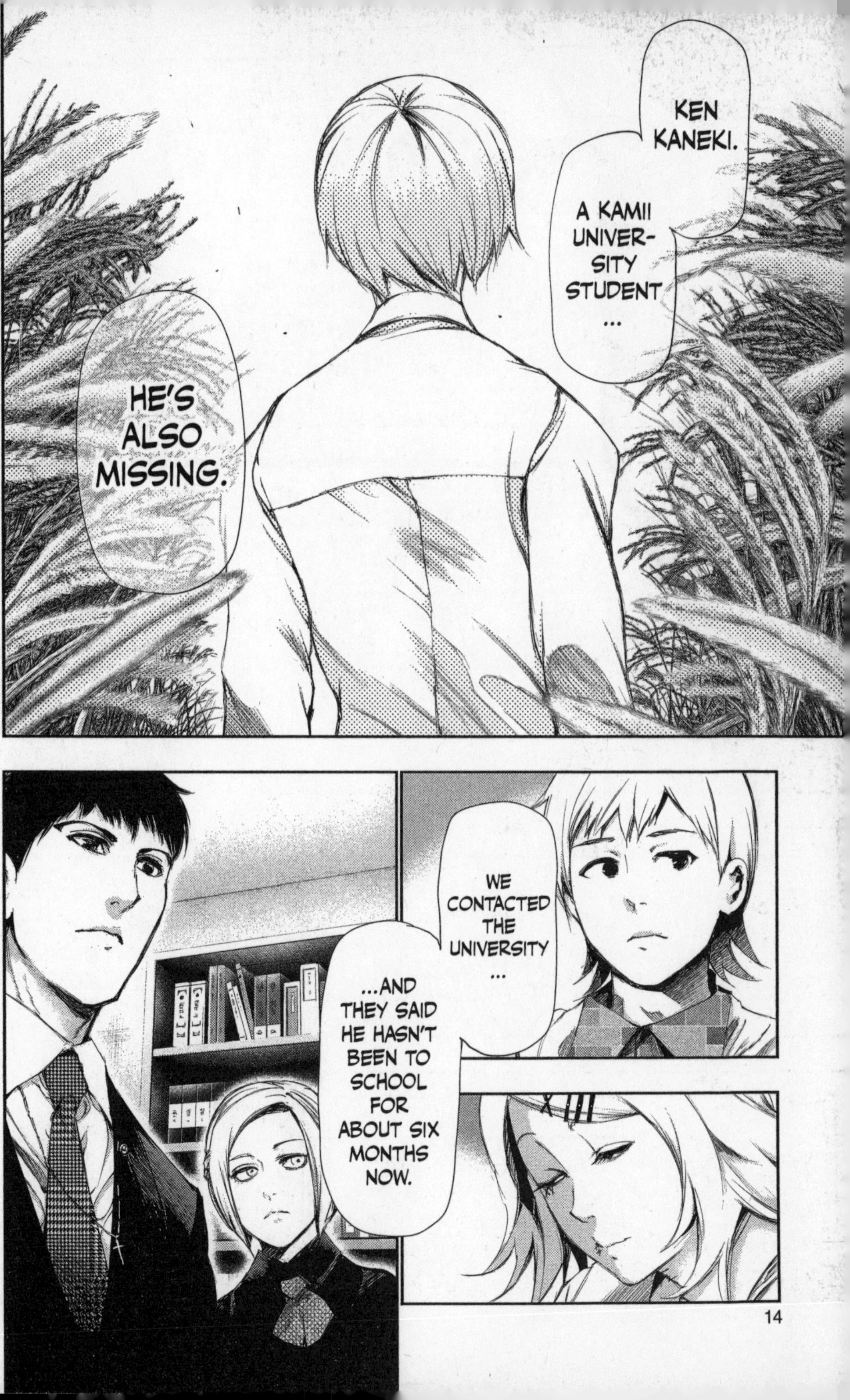
KEN KANEKI.
A KAMII UNIVER-SITY STUDENT ...
HE'S ALSO MISSING.
WE CONTACTED THE UNIVERSITY ...
...AND THEY SAID HE HASN'T BEEN TO SCHOOL FOR ABOUT SIX MONTHS NOW.

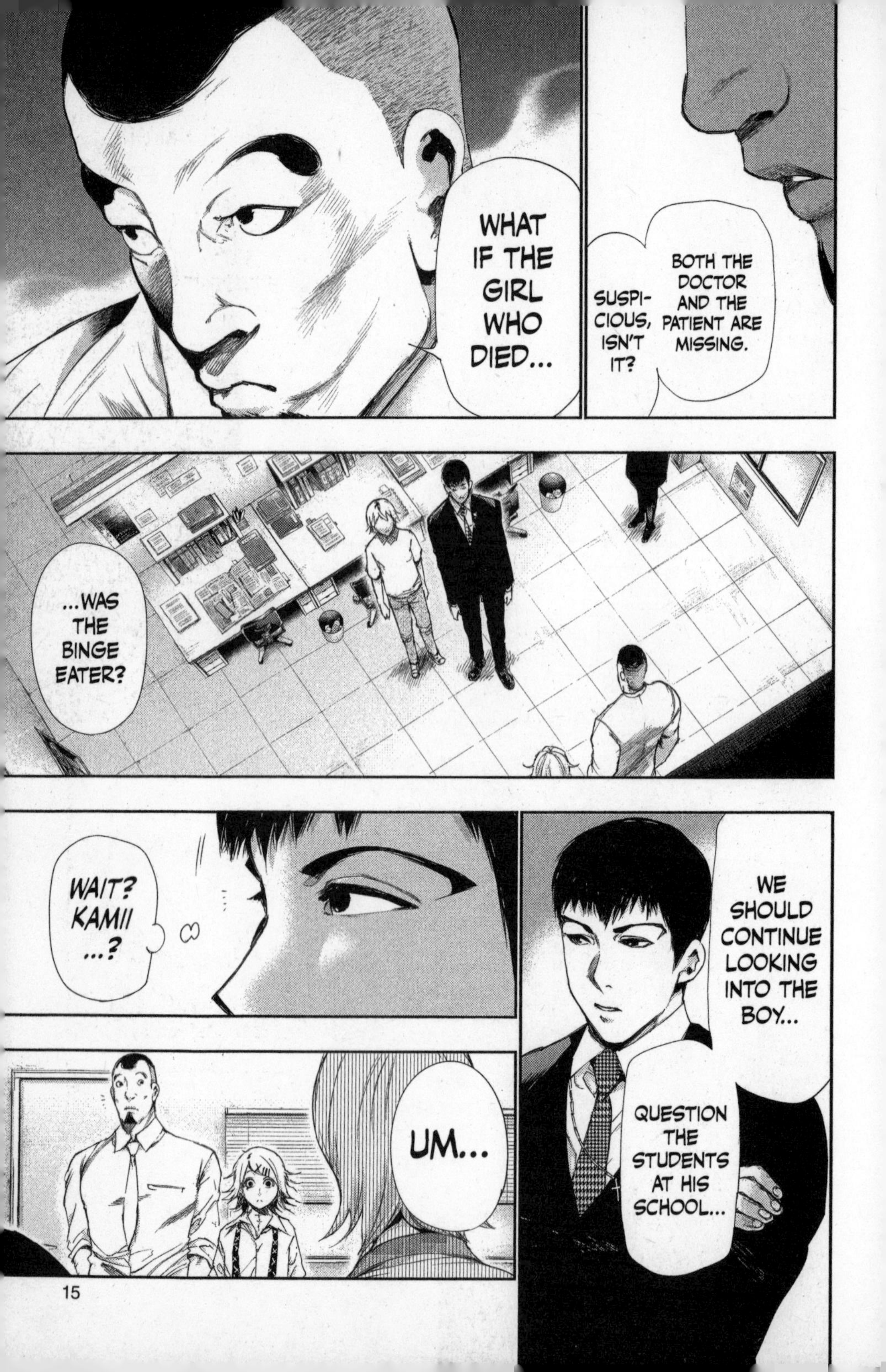
BOTH THE DOCTOR AND THE PATIENT ARE MISSING.
SUSPICIOUS, ISN'T IT?
WHAT IF THE GIRL WHO DIED...
...WAS THE BINGE EATER?
WE SHOULD CONTINUE LOOKING INTO THE BOY...
QUESTION THE STUDENTS AT HIS SCHOOL...
WAIT? KAMII ...?
UM...

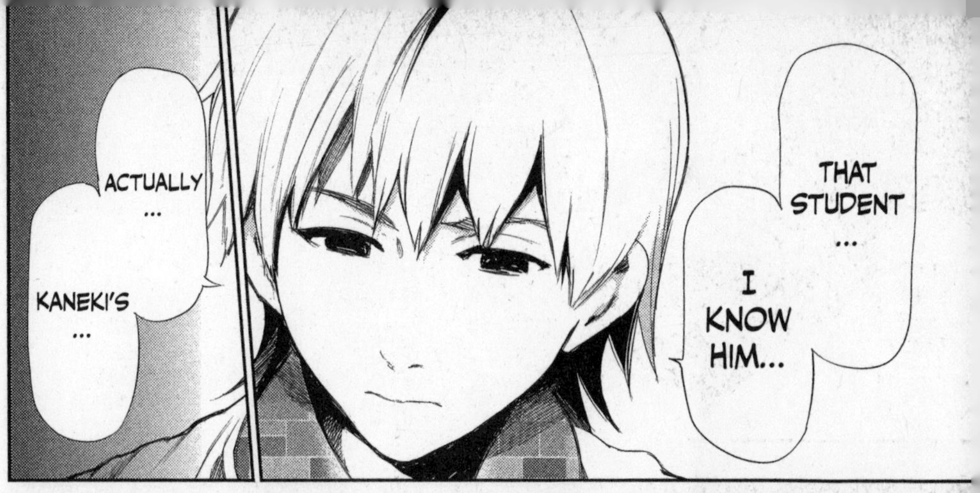
THAT STUDENT ...
I KNOW HIM...
ACTUALLY ...
KANEKI'S ...
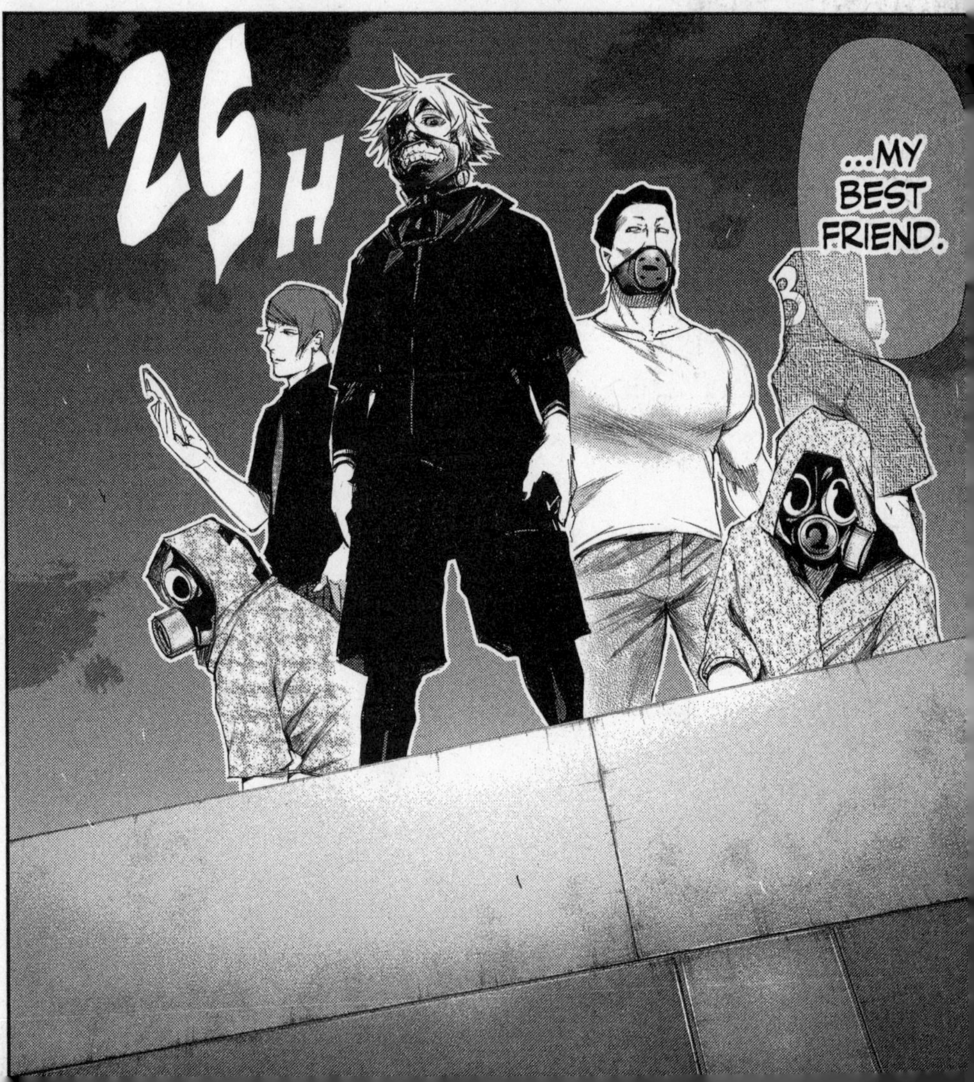
...MY BEST FRIEND.
ZSH

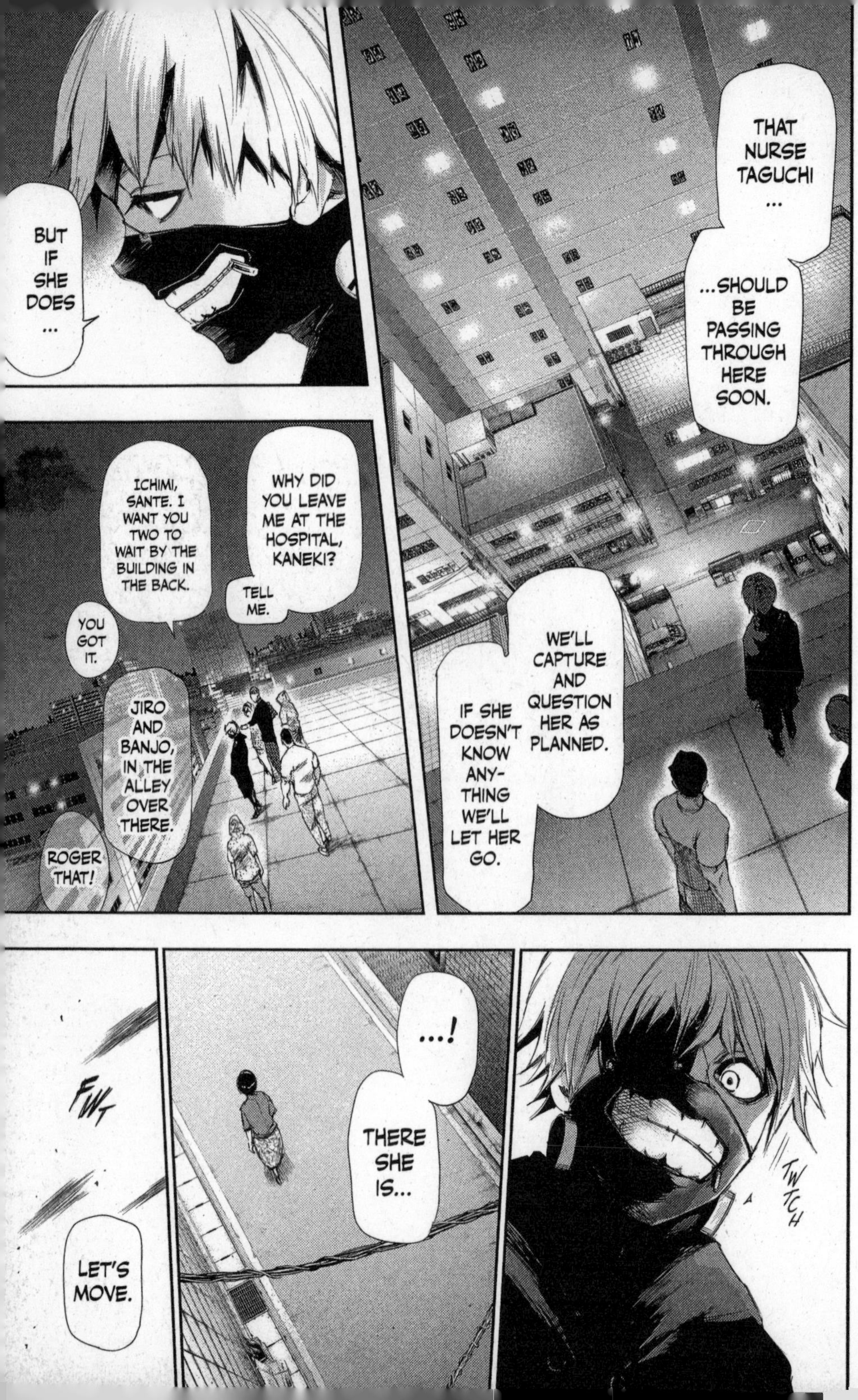
THAT NURSE TAGUCHI ...
...SHOULD BE PASSING THROUGH HERE SOON.
BUT IF SHE DOES ...
WE'LL CAPTURE AND QUESTION HER AS PLANNED.
IF SHE DOESN'T KNOW ANY-THING WE'LL LET HER GO.
WHY DID YOU LEAVE ME AT THE HOSPITAL, KANEKI?
TELL ME.
ICHIMI, SANTE. I WANT YOU TWO TO WAIT BY THE BUILDING IN THE BACK.
YOU GOT IT.
JIRO AND BANJO, IN THE ALLEY OVER THERE.
ROGER THAT!
TWITCH
...!
THERE SHE IS...
FWT
LET'S MOVE.

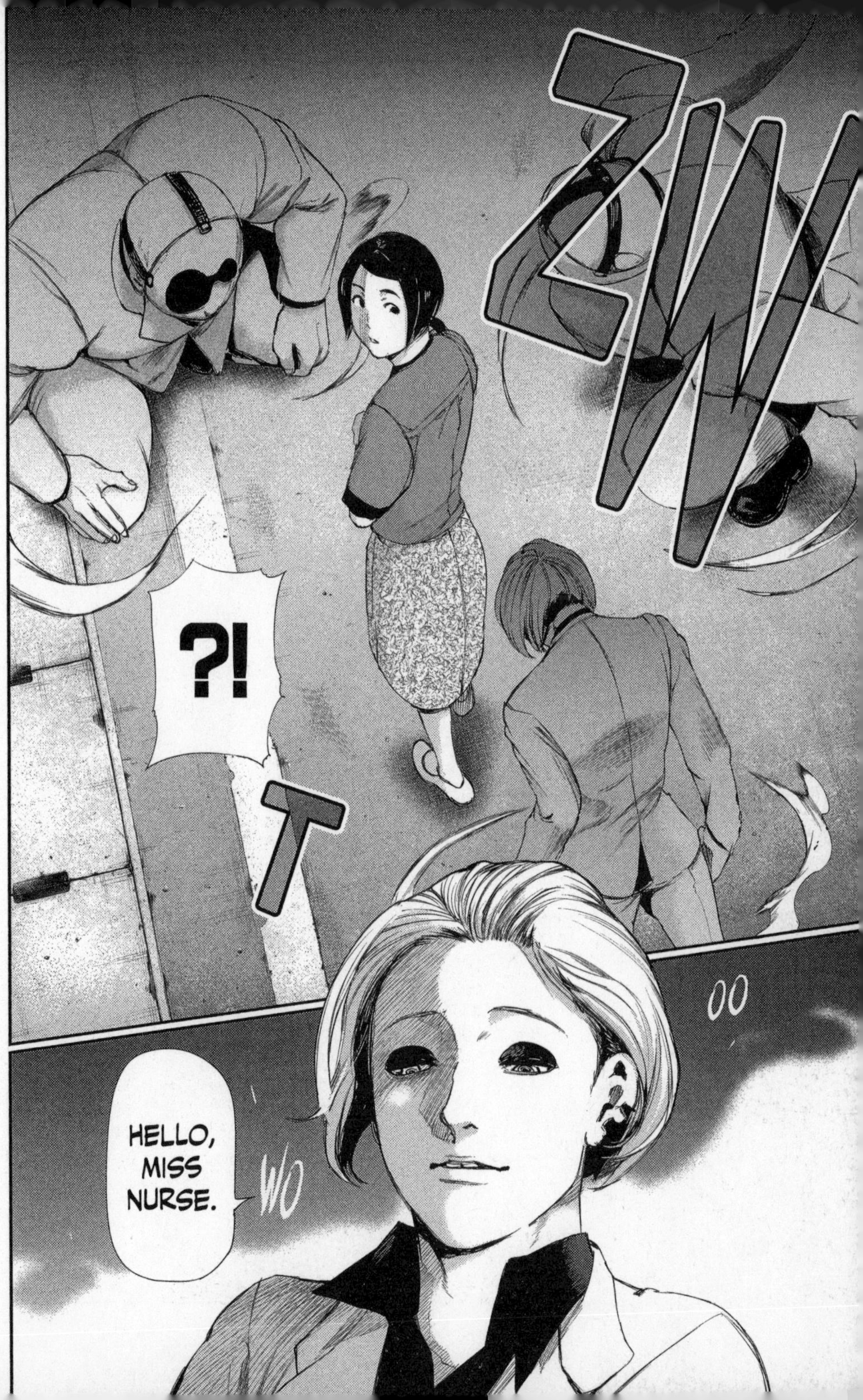
ZWN
?!
T
HELLO, MISS NURSE.
OO
WO

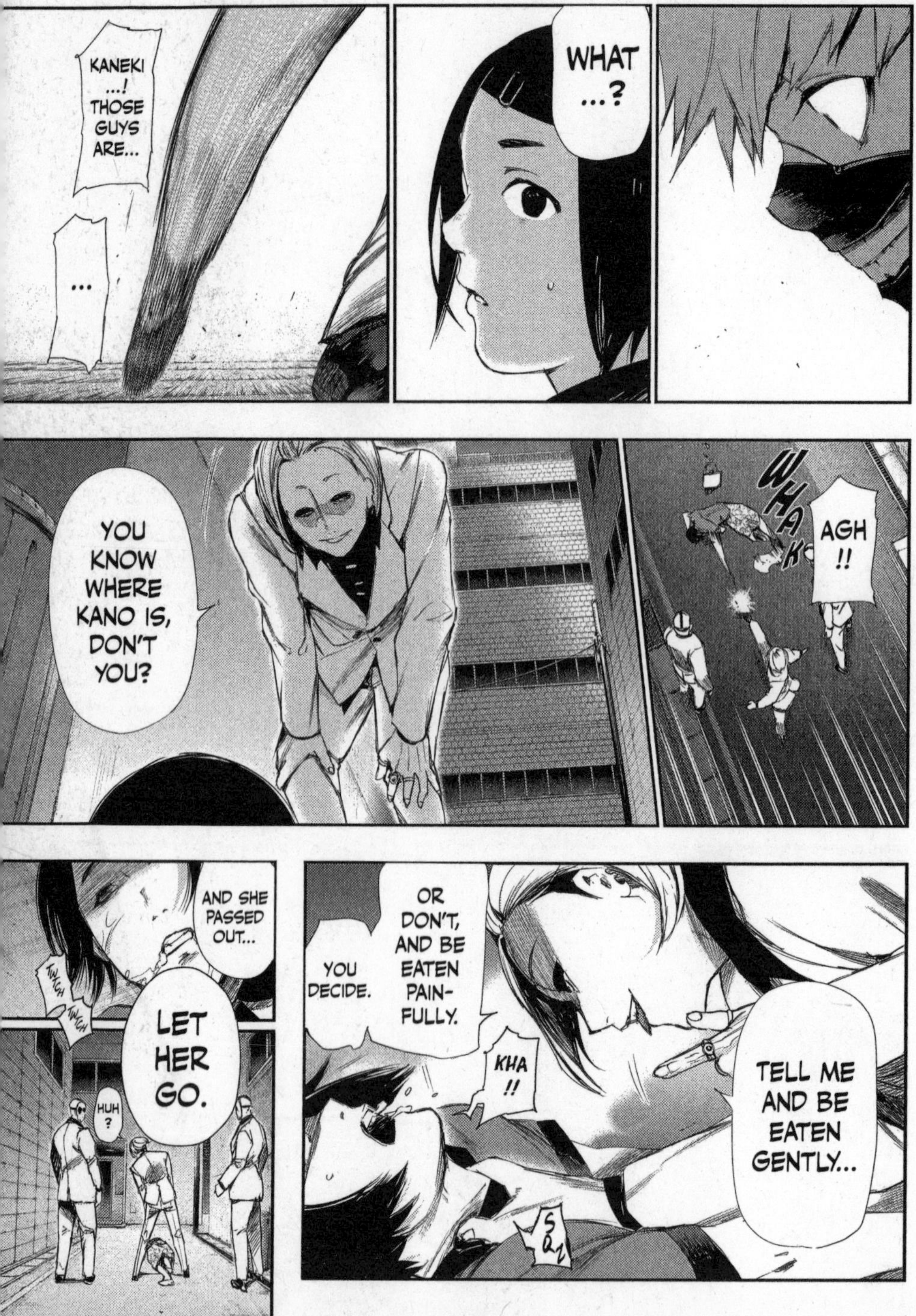
WHAT ...?
KANEKI ...! THOSE GUYS ARE...
...
WHAK
AGH !!
YOU KNOW WHERE KANO IS, DON'T YOU?
TELL ME AND BE EATEN GENTLY...
OR DON'T, AND BE EATEN PAIN-FULLY.
YOU DECIDE.
KHA !!
SQZ
AND SHE PASSED OUT...
TWITCH
TWITCH
LET HER GO.
HUH ?

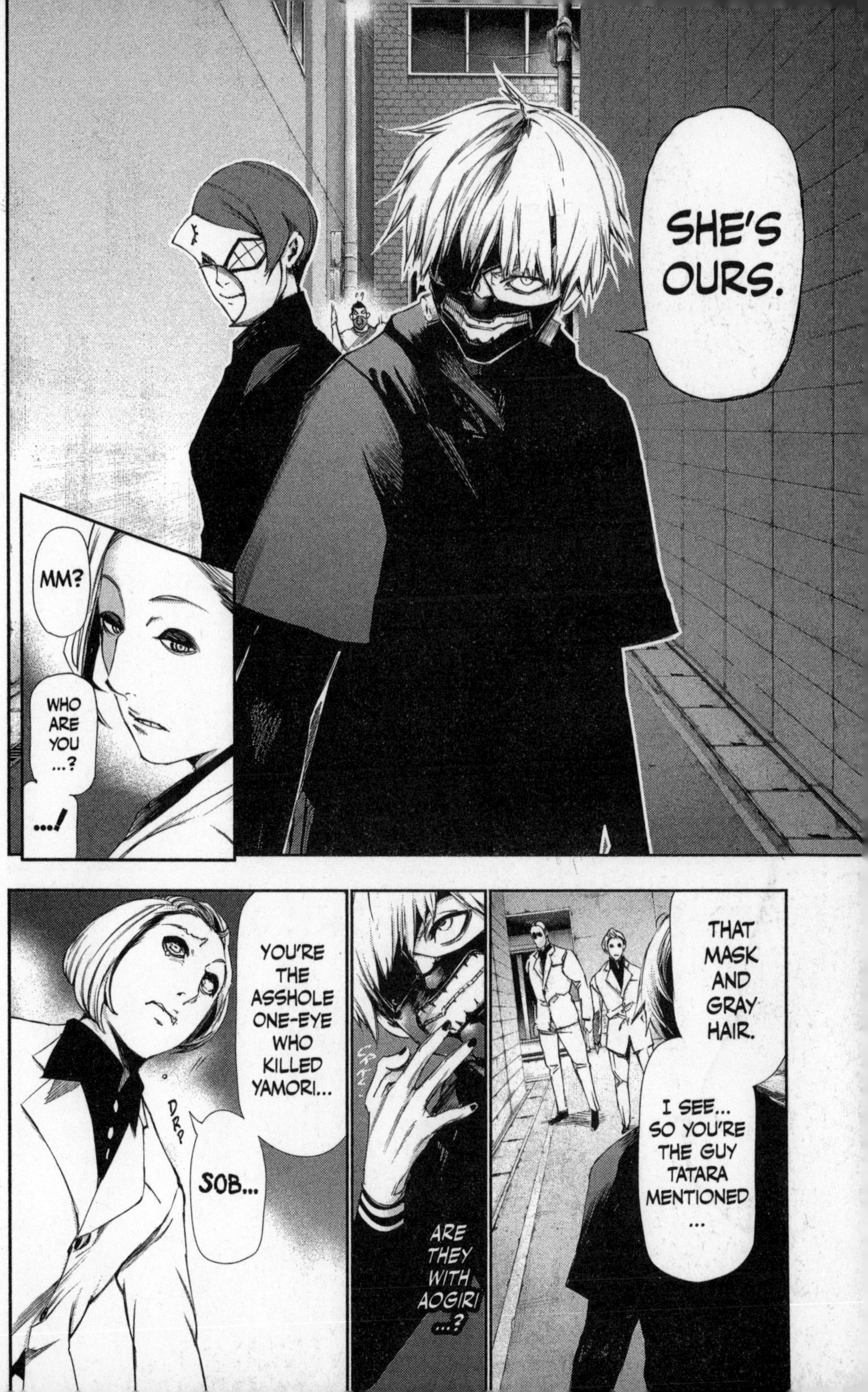
SHE'S OURS.
MM?
WHO ARE YOU ...?
...!
THAT MASK AND GRAY HAIR.
I SEE... SO YOU'RE THE GUY TATARA MENTIONED ...
ARE THEY WITH AOGIRI ...?
YOU'RE THE ASSHOLE ONE-EYE WHO KILLED YAMORI...
DRP
SOB...

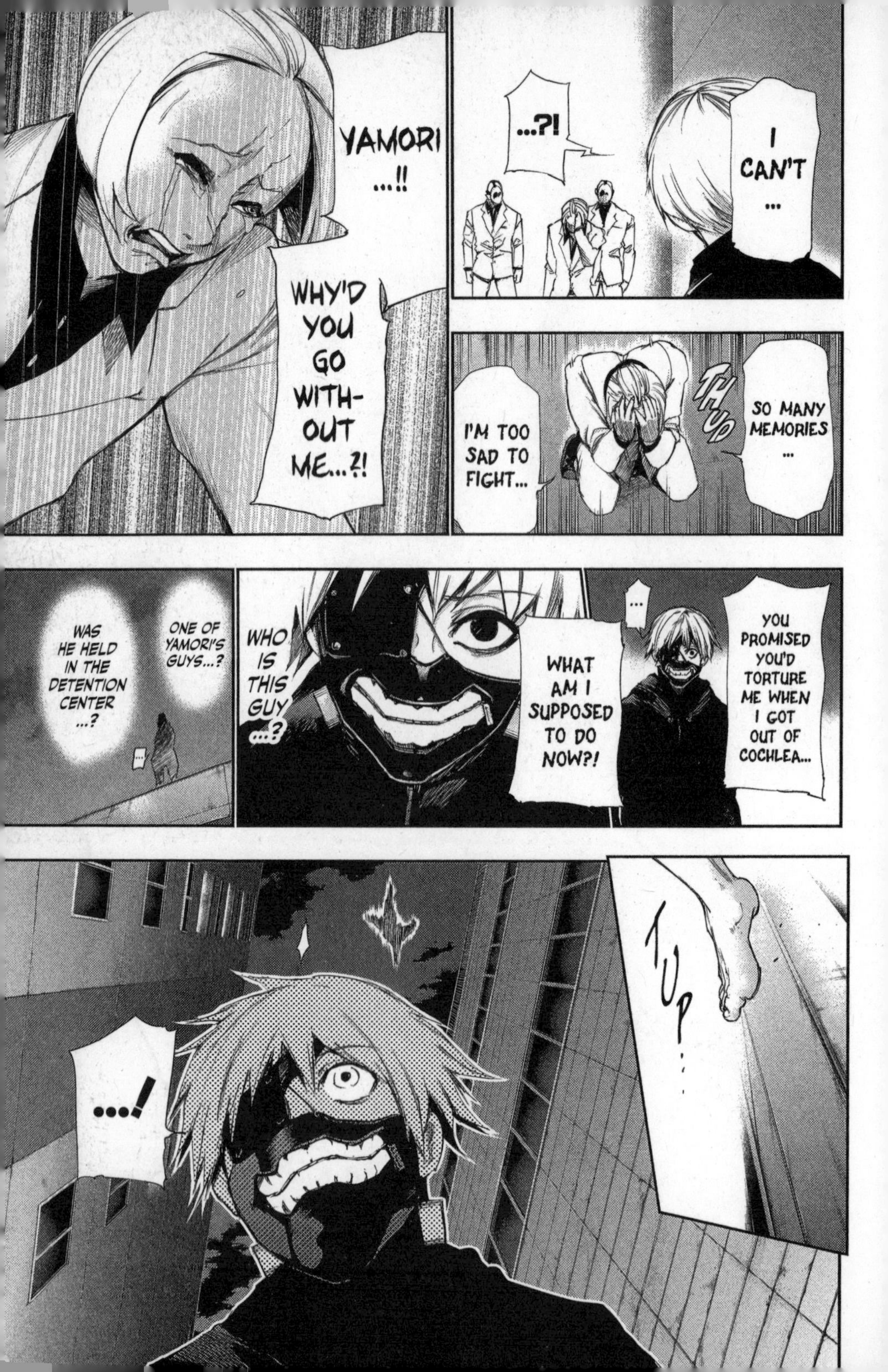
I CAN'T ...
...?!
SO MANY MEMORIES ...
THUD
I'M TOO SAD TO FIGHT...
YAMORI ...!!
WHY'D YOU GO WITH-OUT ME...?!
YOU PROMISED YOU'D TORTURE ME WHEN I GOT OUT OF COCHLEA...
...
WHAT AM I SUPPOSED TO DO NOW?!
WHO IS THIS GUY ...?
ONE OF YAMORI'S GUYS...?
WAS HE HELD IN THE DETENTION CENTER ...?
...
TUP...
...!

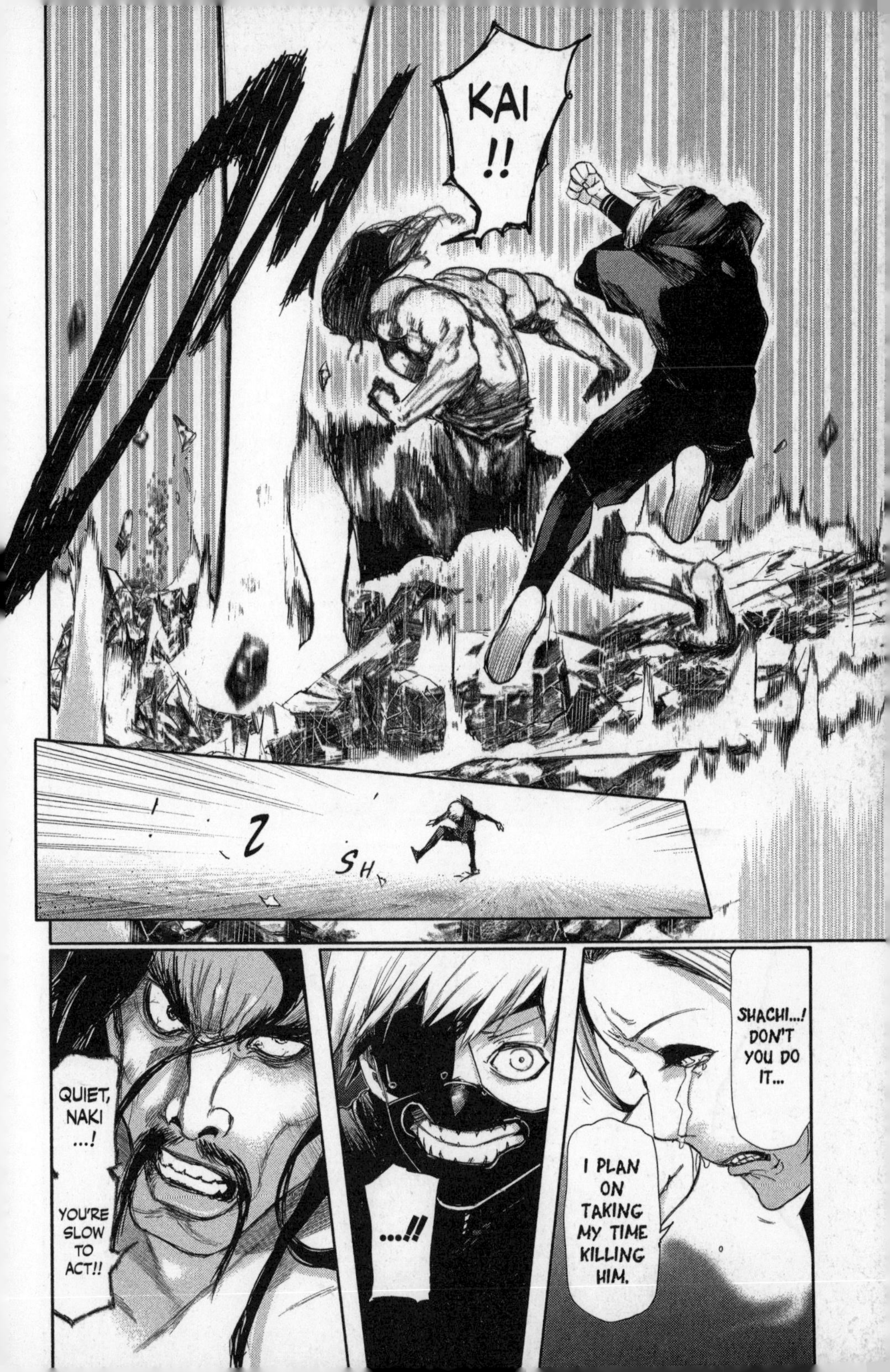
KAI !!
SH
SHACHI...! DON'T YOU DO IT...
I PLAN ON TAKING MY TIME KILLING HIM.
...!!
QUIET, NAKI ...!
YOU'RE SLOW TO ACT!!

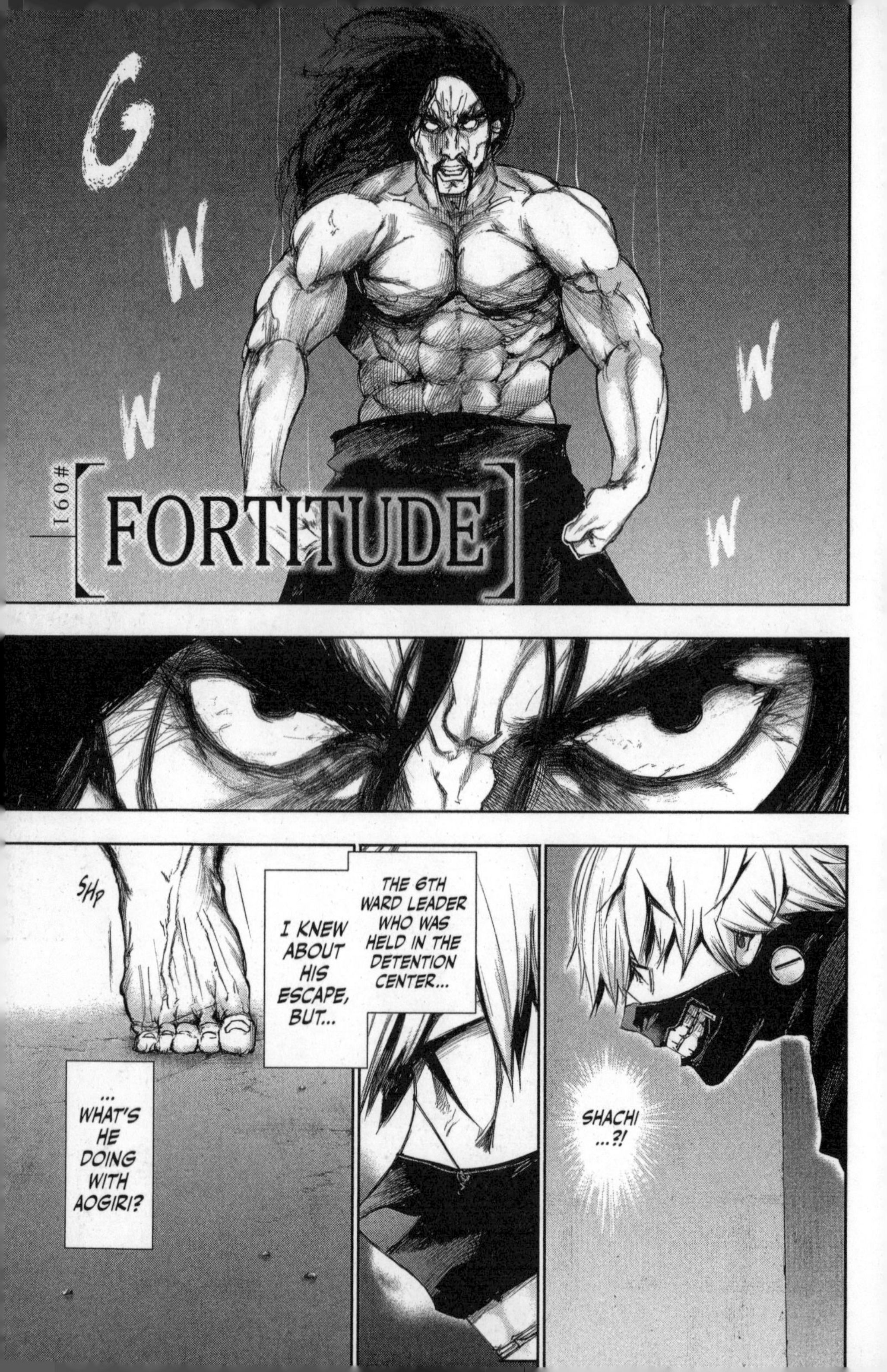
GWWWW
#091
[FORTITUDE]
SHACHI ...?!
THE 6TH WARD LEADER WHO WAS HELD IN THE DETENTION CENTER...
I KNEW ABOUT HIS ESCAPE, BUT...
SHP
... WHAT'S HE DOING WITH AOGIRI?

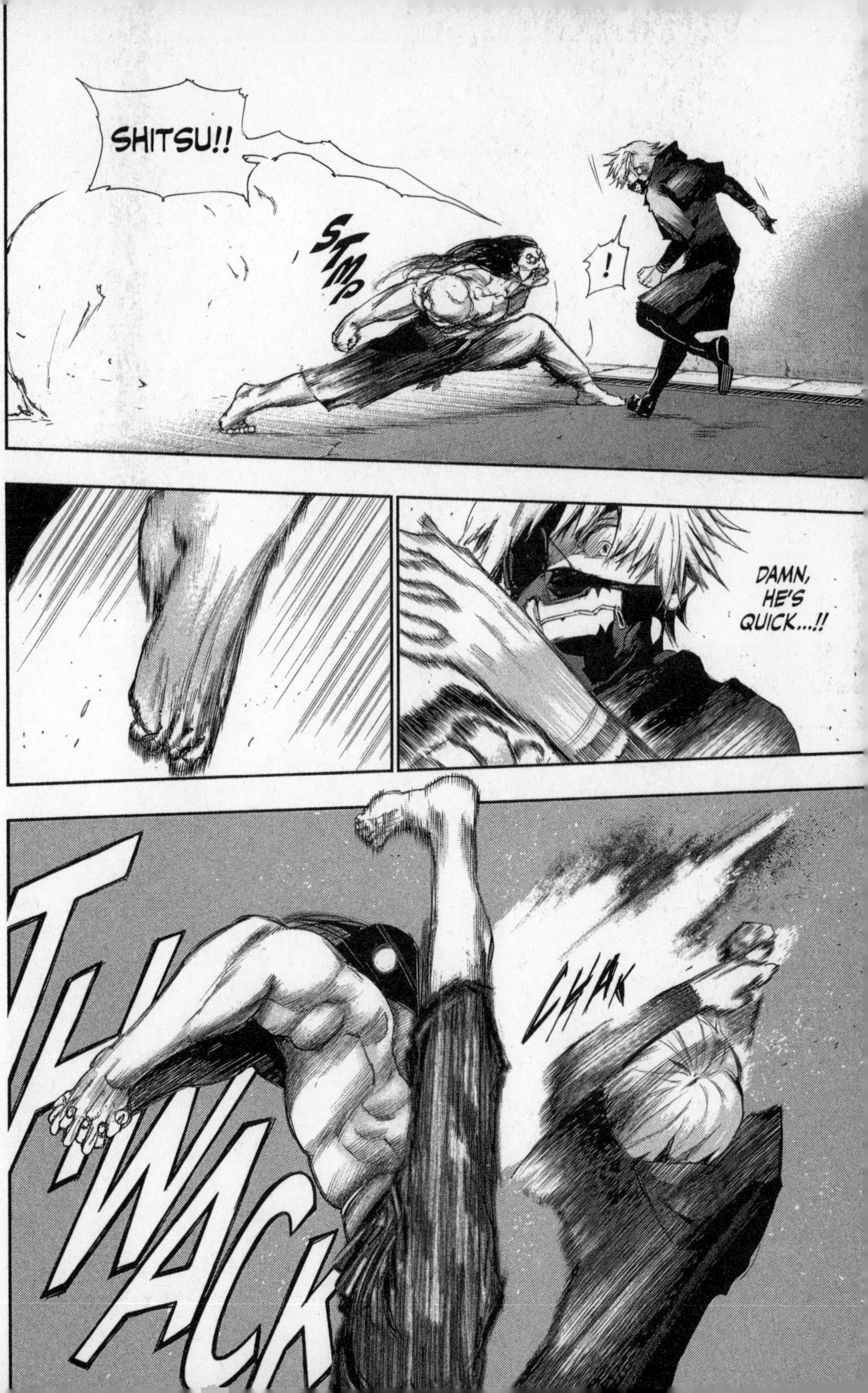
SHITSU!!
STMP
!
DAMN, HE'S QUICK...!!
CKAK
THWACK

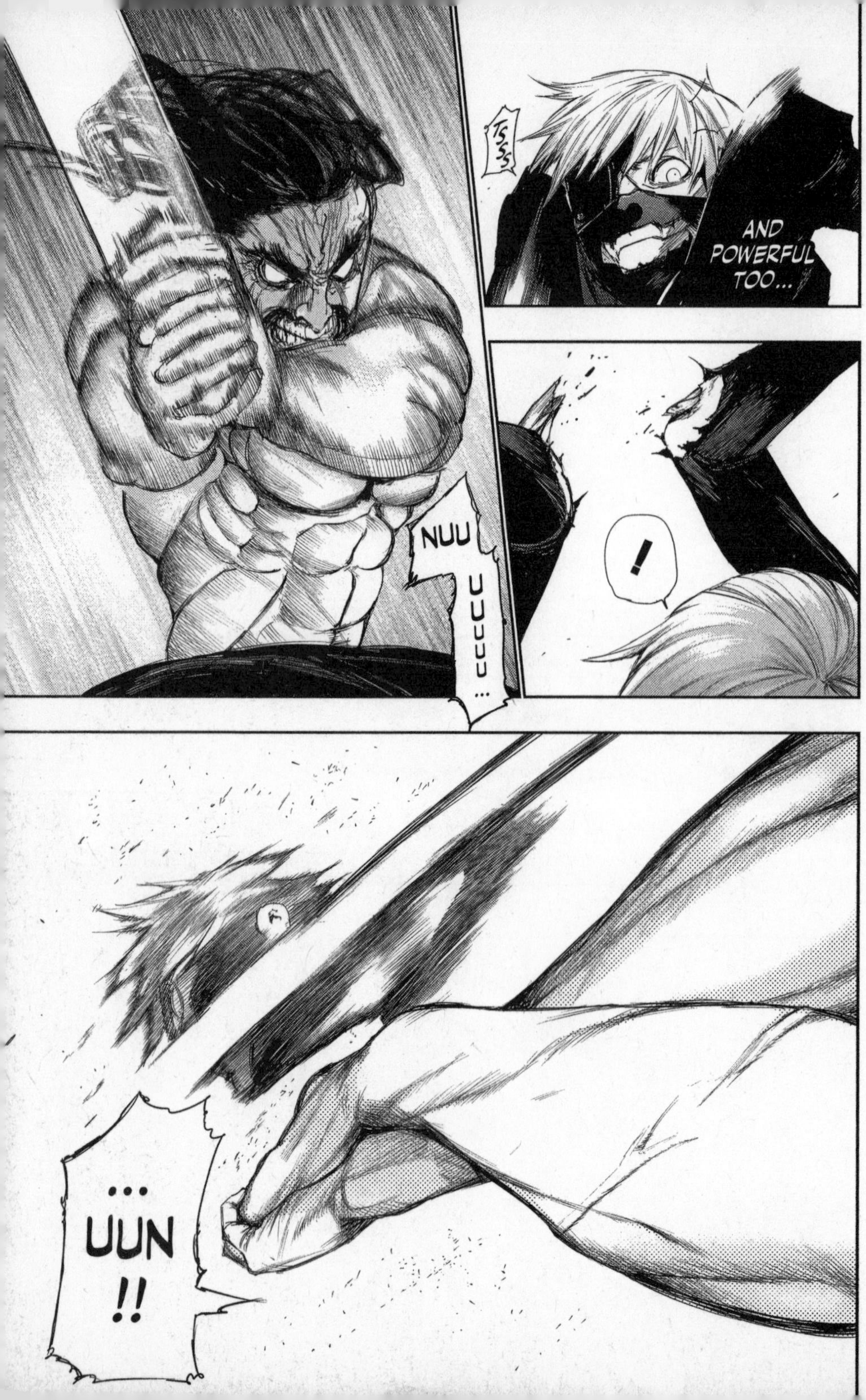
TSSS
AND POWERFUL TOO...
!
NUUUUUUU...
...UUN!!

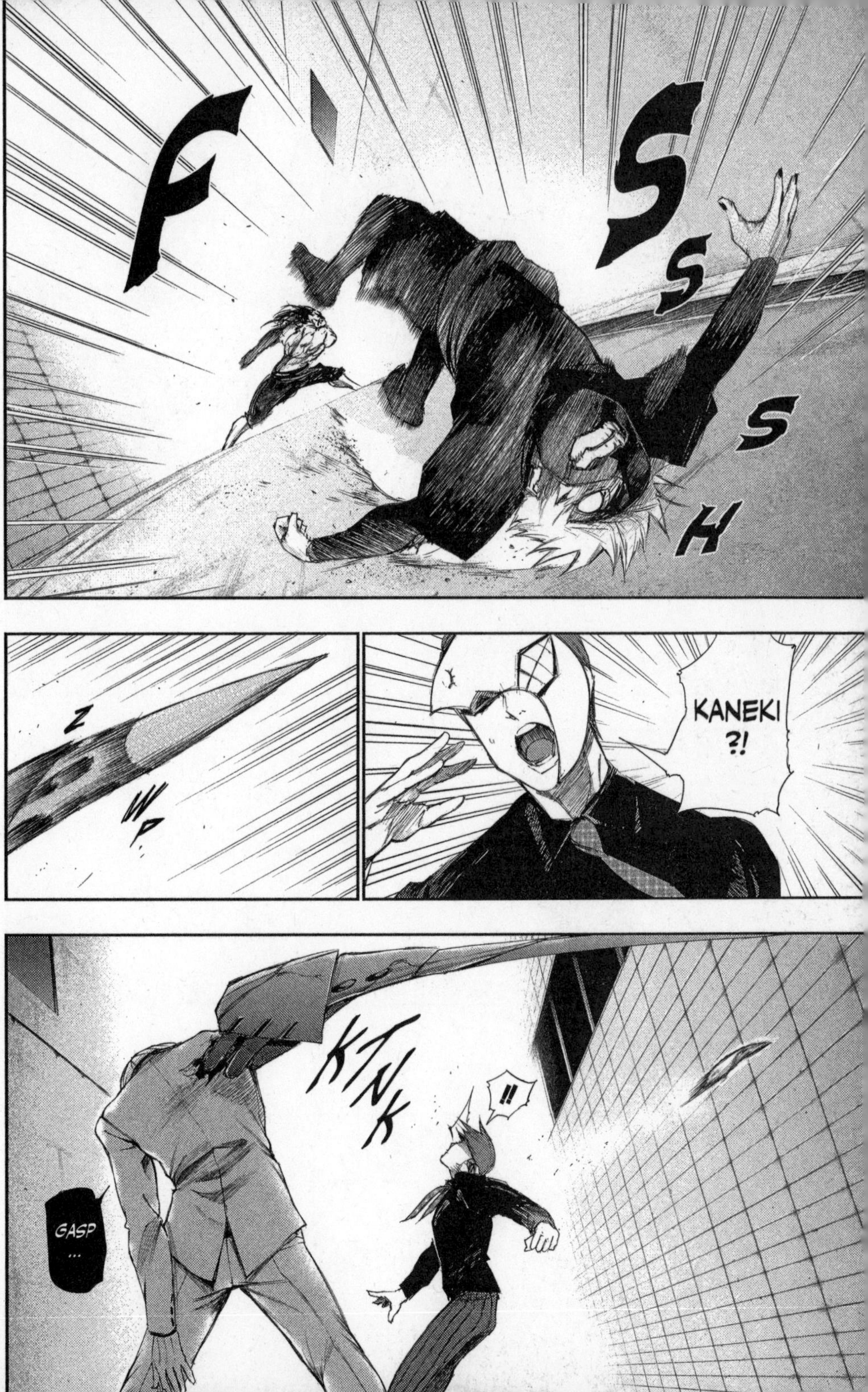
FSSSH
KANEKI ?!
ZWP
KINK
!!
GASP ...

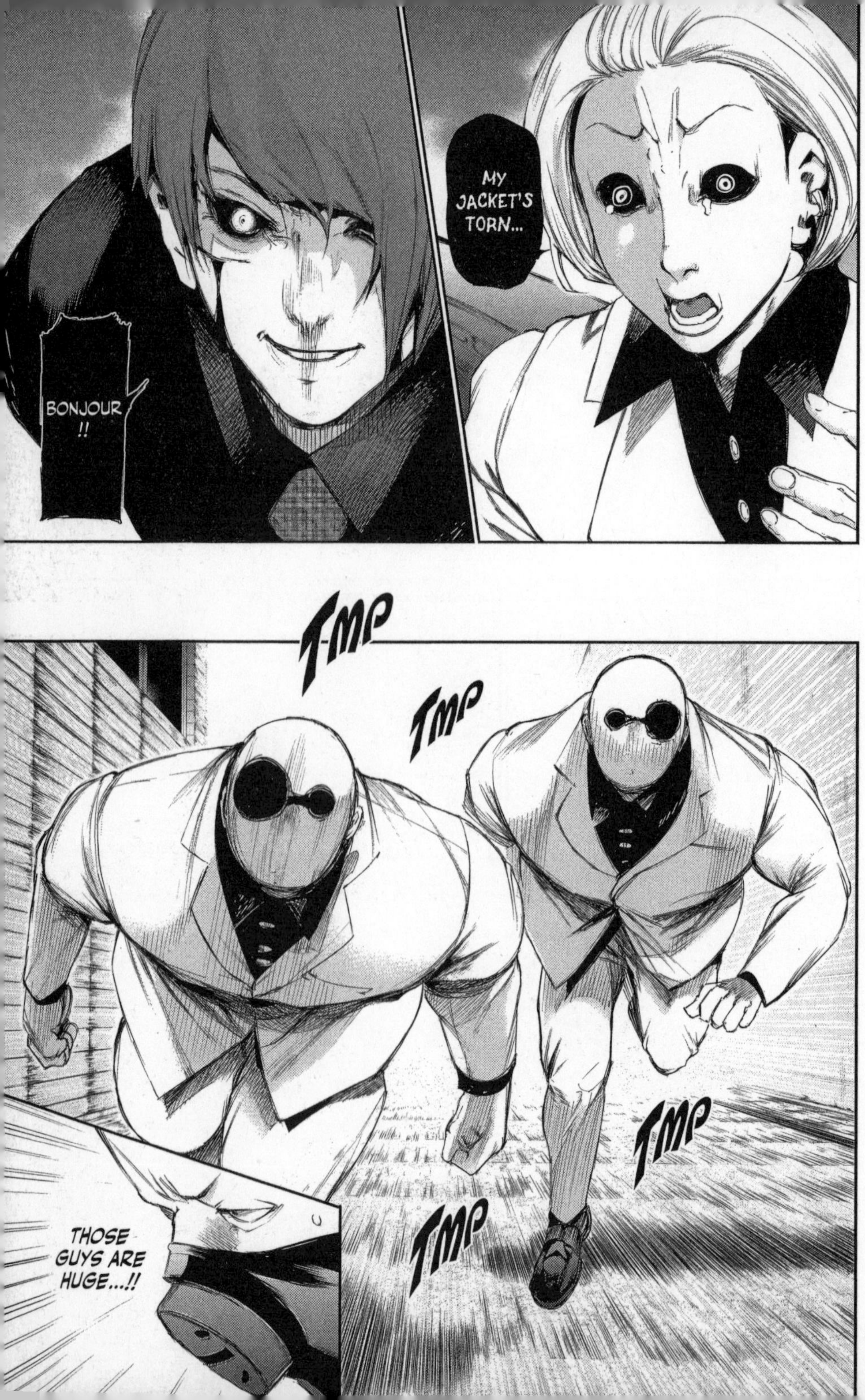
MY JACKET'S TORN...
BONJOUR!!
T-MP
TMP
TMP
TMP
THOSE GUYS ARE HUGE...!!

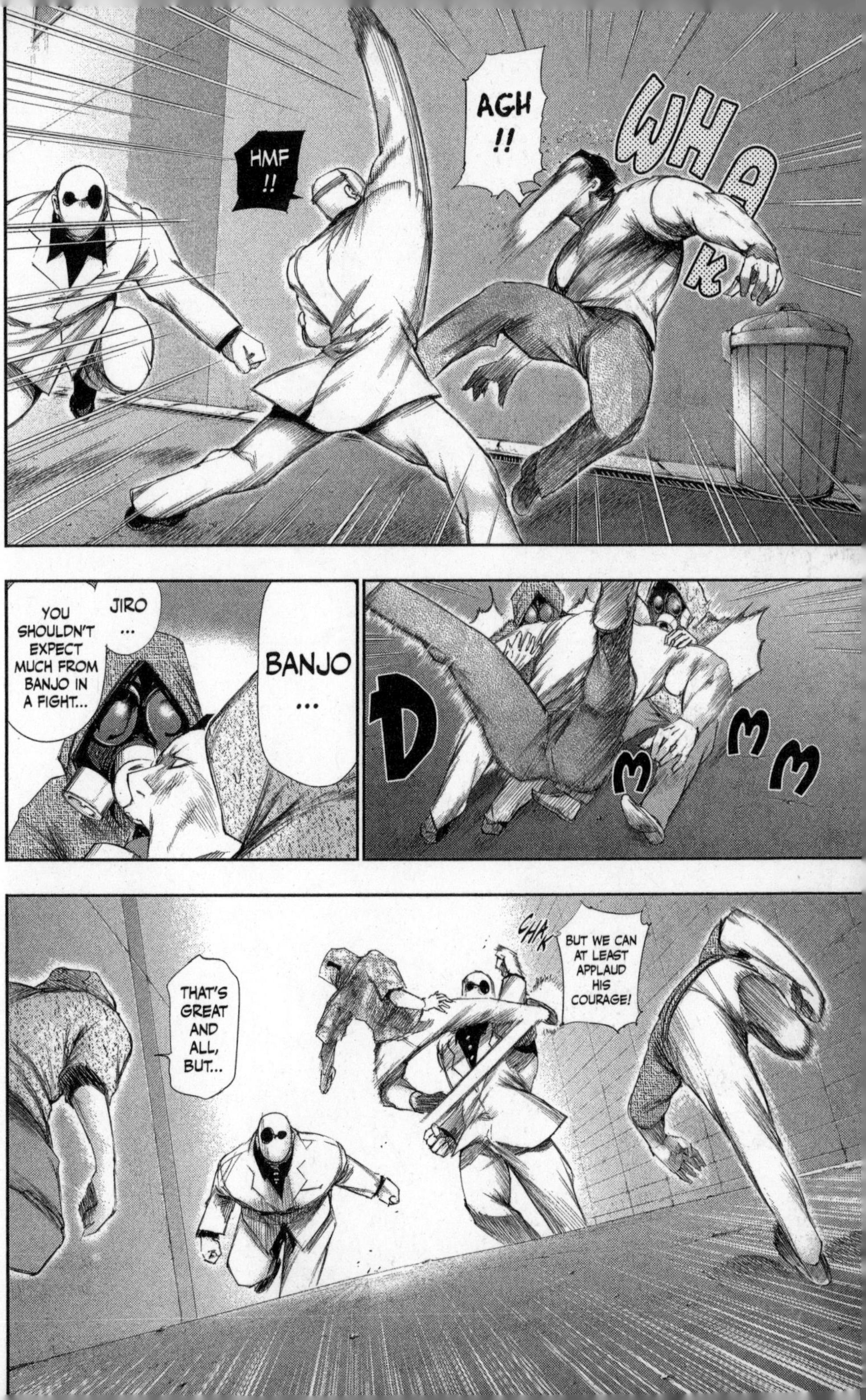
WHAK
AGH!!
HMF!!
BANJO...
JIRO...
YOU SHOULDN'T EXPECT MUCH FROM BANJO IN A FIGHT...
CHAK
BUT WE CAN AT LEAST APPLAUD HIS COURAGE!
THAT'S GREAT AND ALL, BUT...

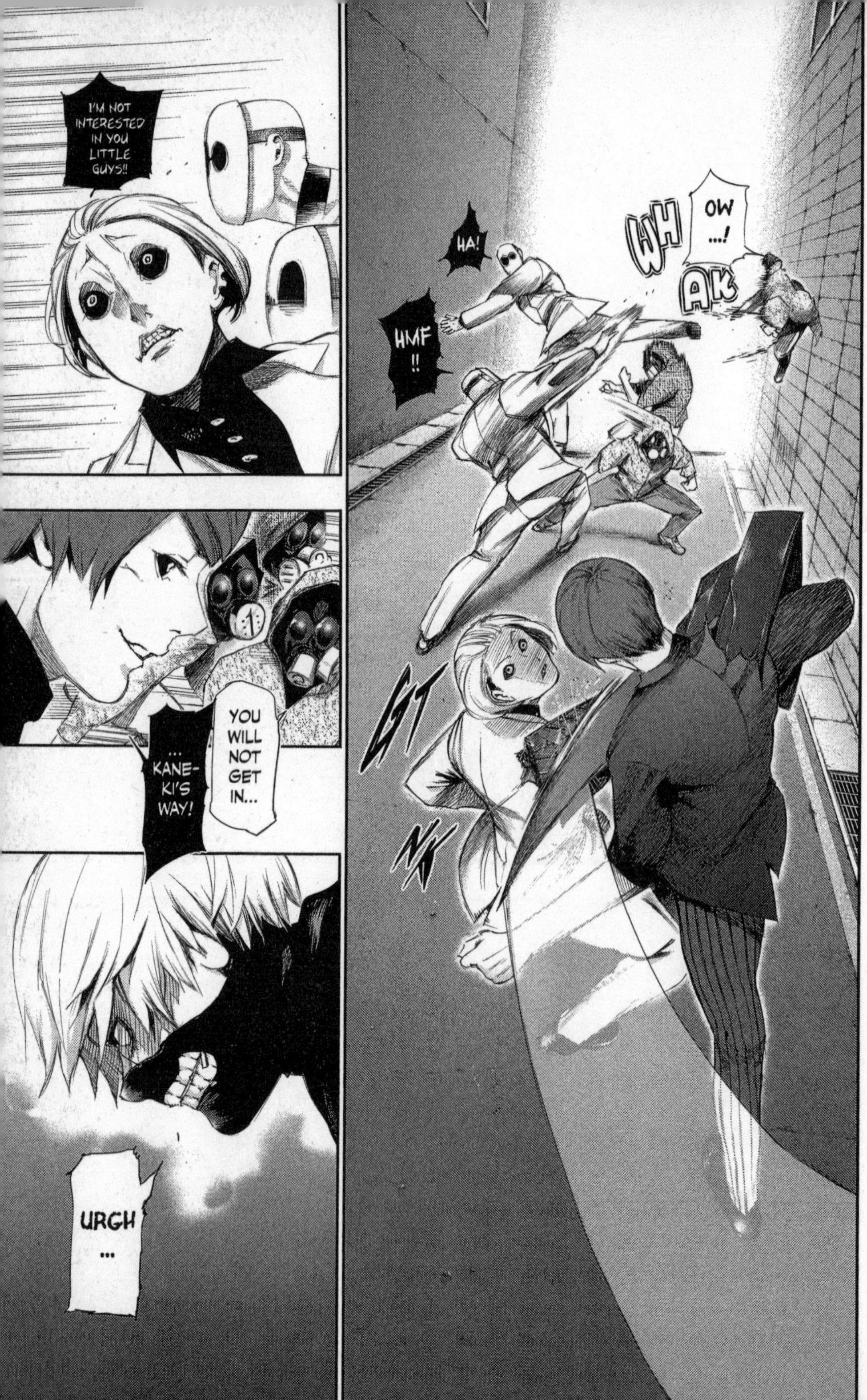

OW ...!
WHAK
HA!
HMF !!
I'M NOT INTERESTED IN YOU LITTLE GUYS!!
YOU WILL NOT GET IN...
...KANEKI'S WAY!
URGH ...

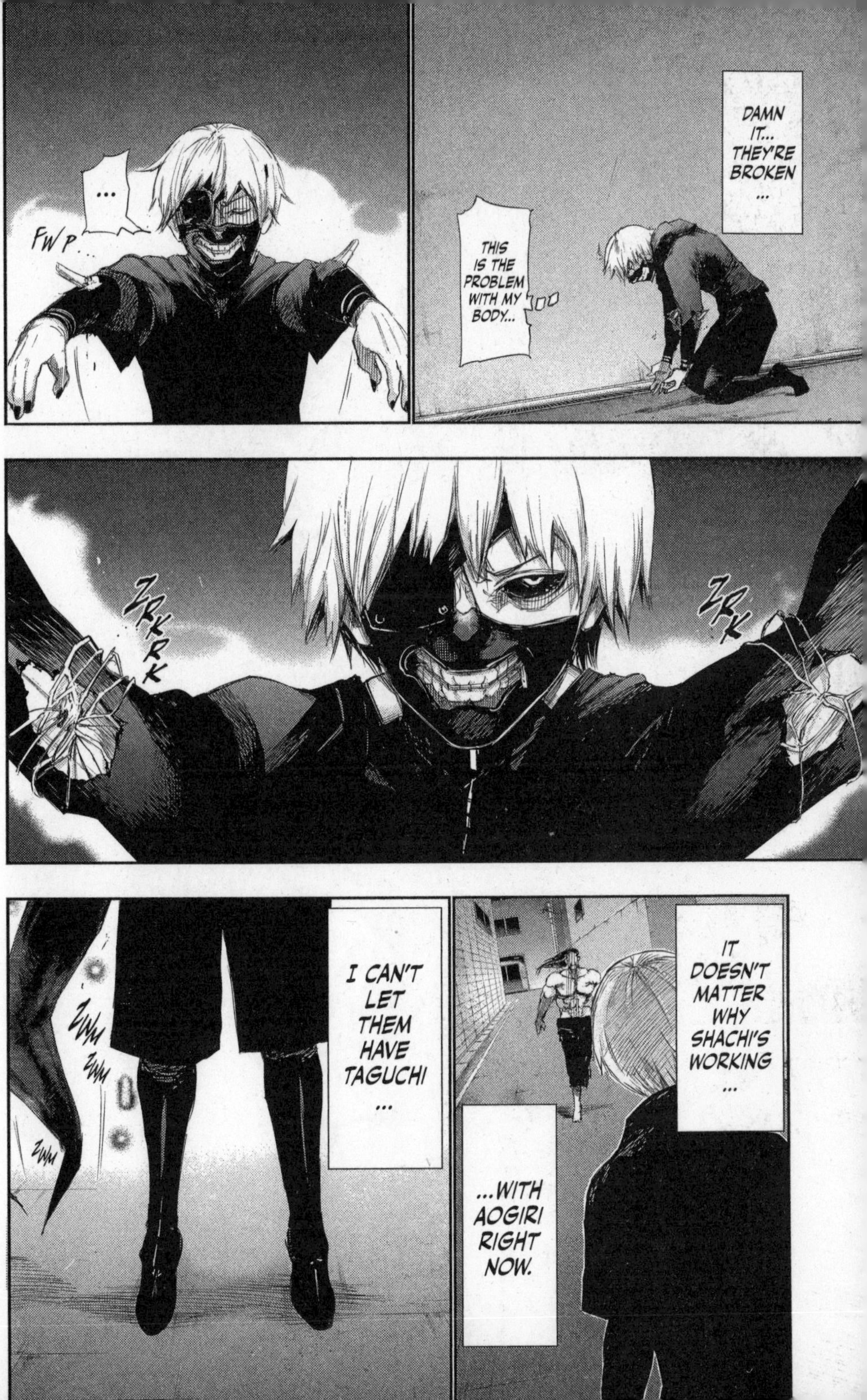
DAMN IT... THEY'RE BROKEN ...
THIS IS THE PROBLEM WITH MY BODY...
...
FWP...
ZRK
ZRKRK
IT DOESN'T MATTER WHY SHACHI'S WORKING ...
...WITH AOGIRI RIGHT NOW.
I CAN'T LET THEM HAVE TAGUCHI ...
ZWM
ZWM
ZWM

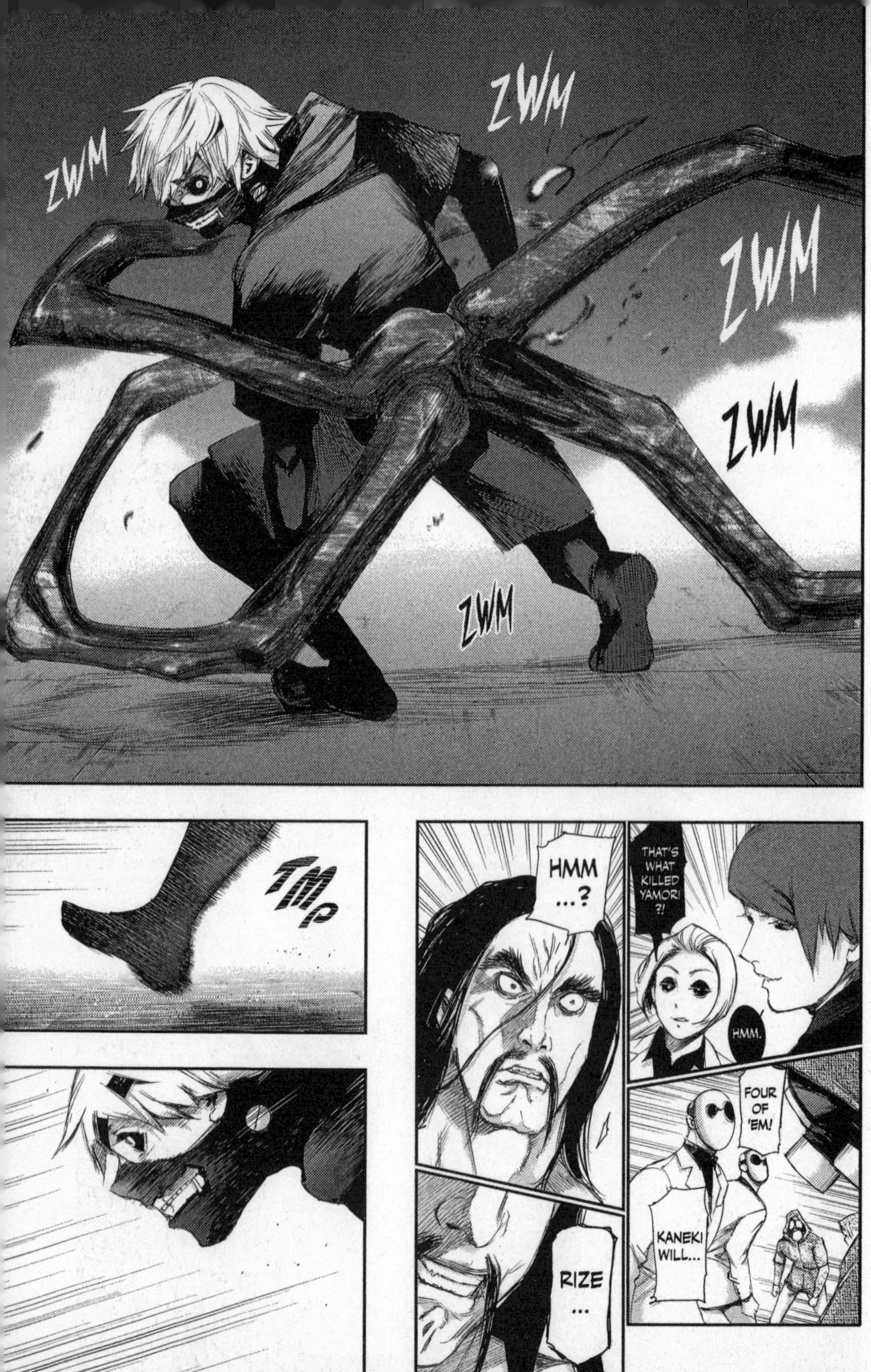
ZWM
ZWM
ZWM
ZWM
ZWM
THAT'S WHAT KILLED YAMORI?!
HMM.
HMM...?
FOUR OF 'EM!
KANEKI WILL...
RIZE...
TMP

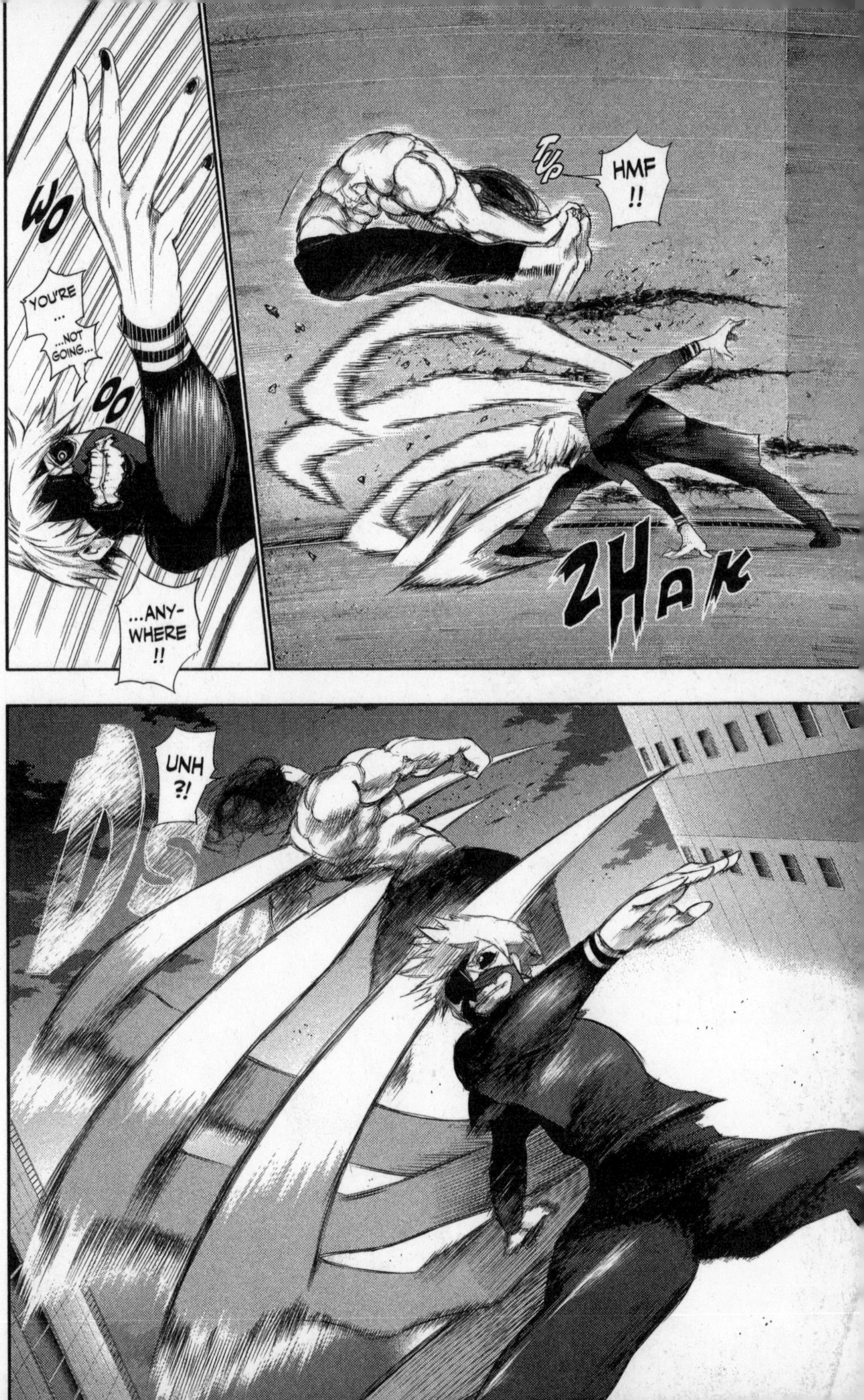
TUP
HMF !!
ZHAK
WO
YOU'RE ...
...NOT GOING...
OO
...ANY-WHERE !!
UNH ?!
DSH

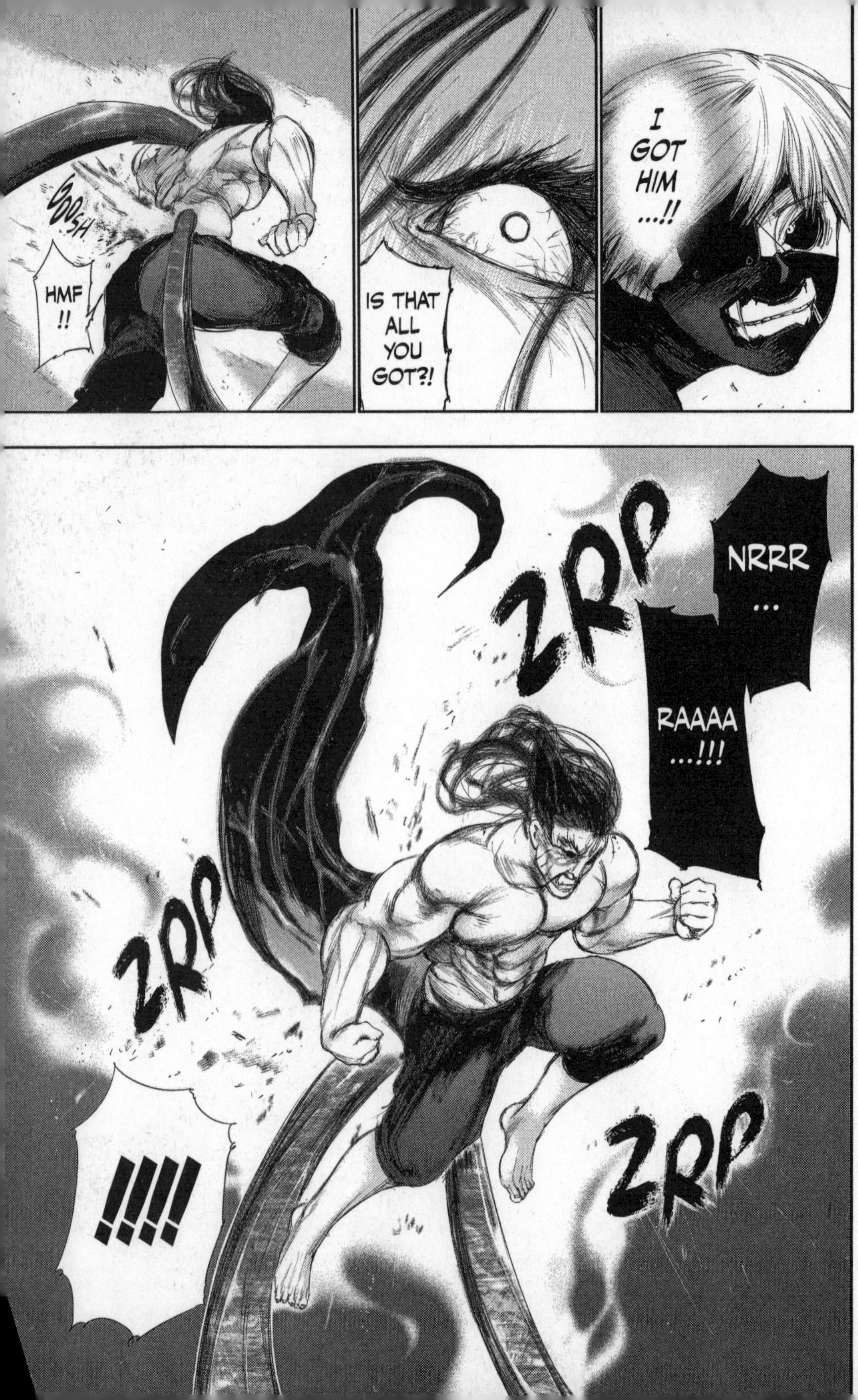

I GOT HIM ...!!
IS THAT ALL YOU GOT?!
WOOSH
HMF !!
NRRR ...
RAAAA ...!!!
ZRP
ZRP
ZRP
ZRP
!!!!!

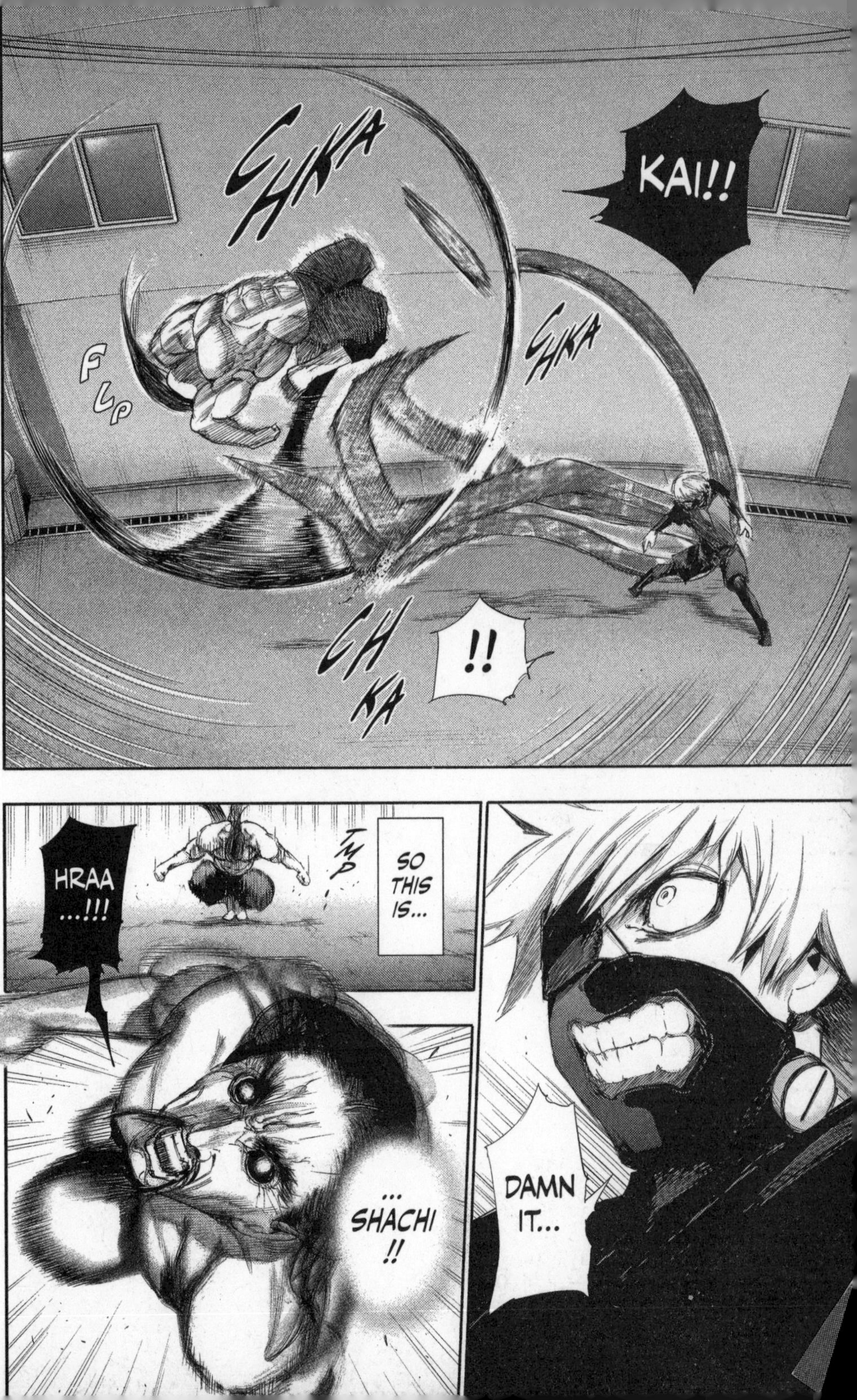
KAI!!
CHIKA
CHIKA
!!
CHIKA
FLIP
DAMN IT...
SO THIS IS...
TMP
HRAA ...!!!
...SHACHI!!

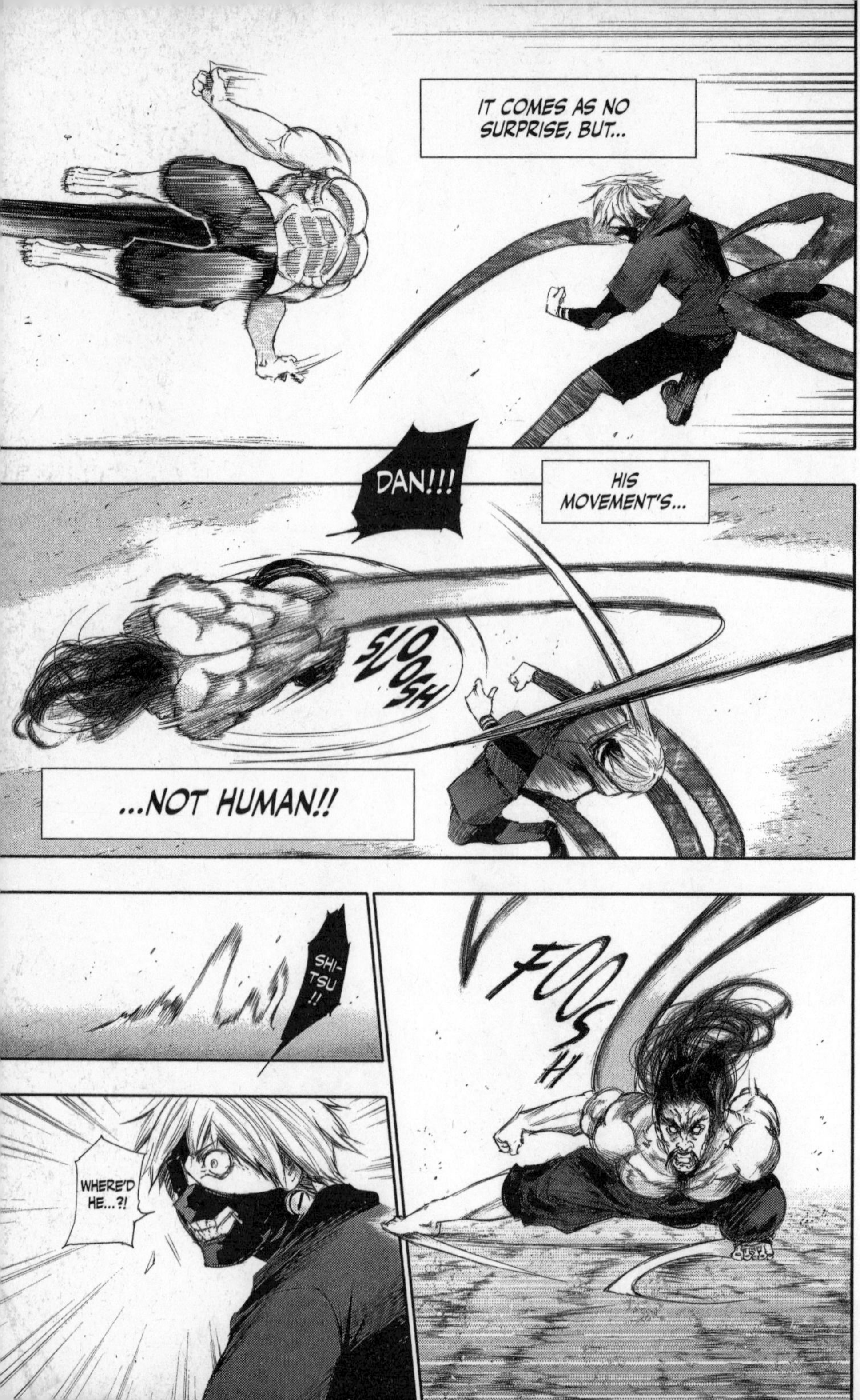
IT COMES AS NO SURPRISE, BUT...
HIS MOVEMENT'S...
DAN!!!
SLOOSH
...NOT HUMAN!!
FOOSH
SHI-TSU!!
WHERE'D HE...?!

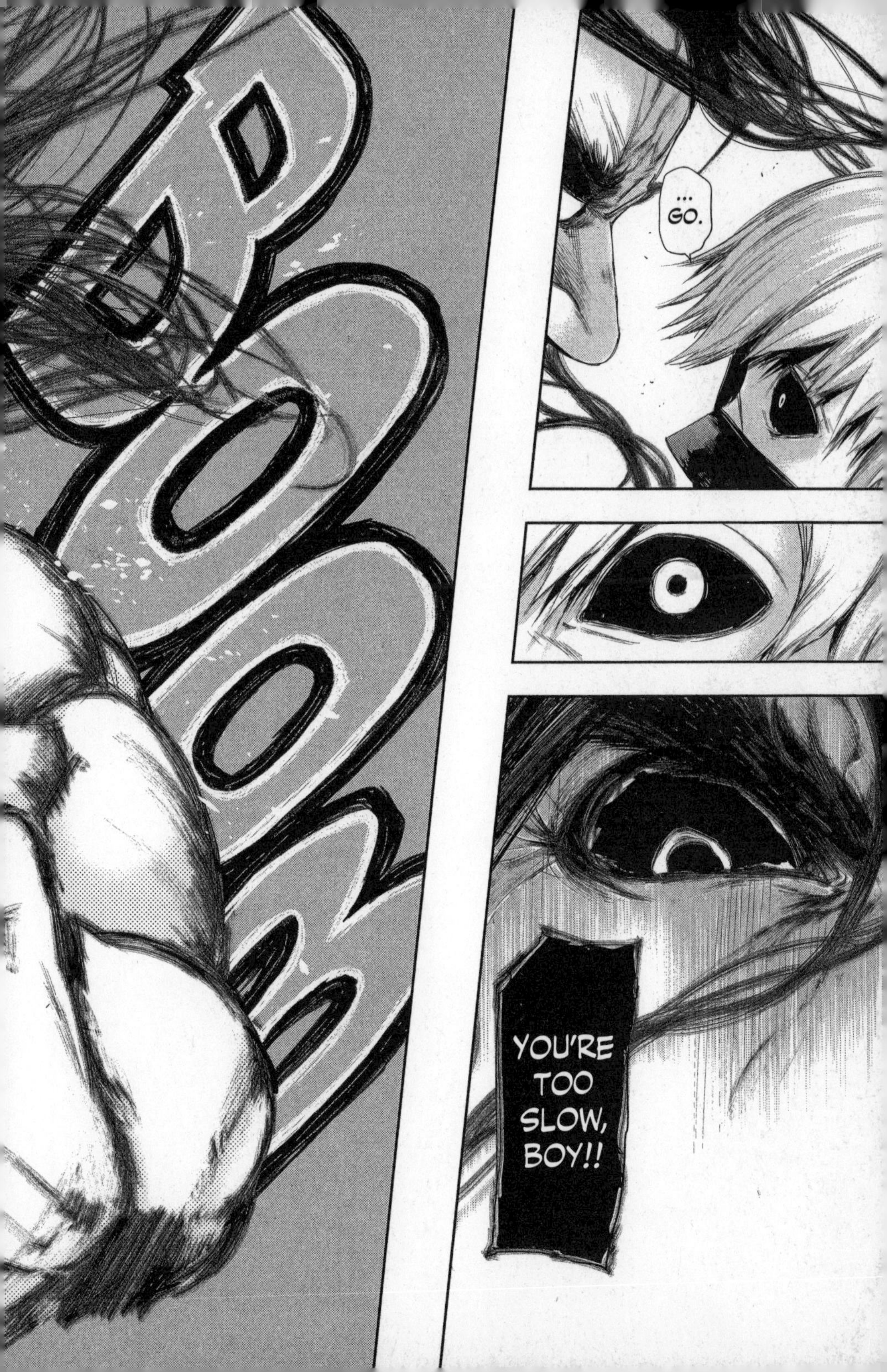
...GO.
YOU'RE TOO SLOW, BOY!!

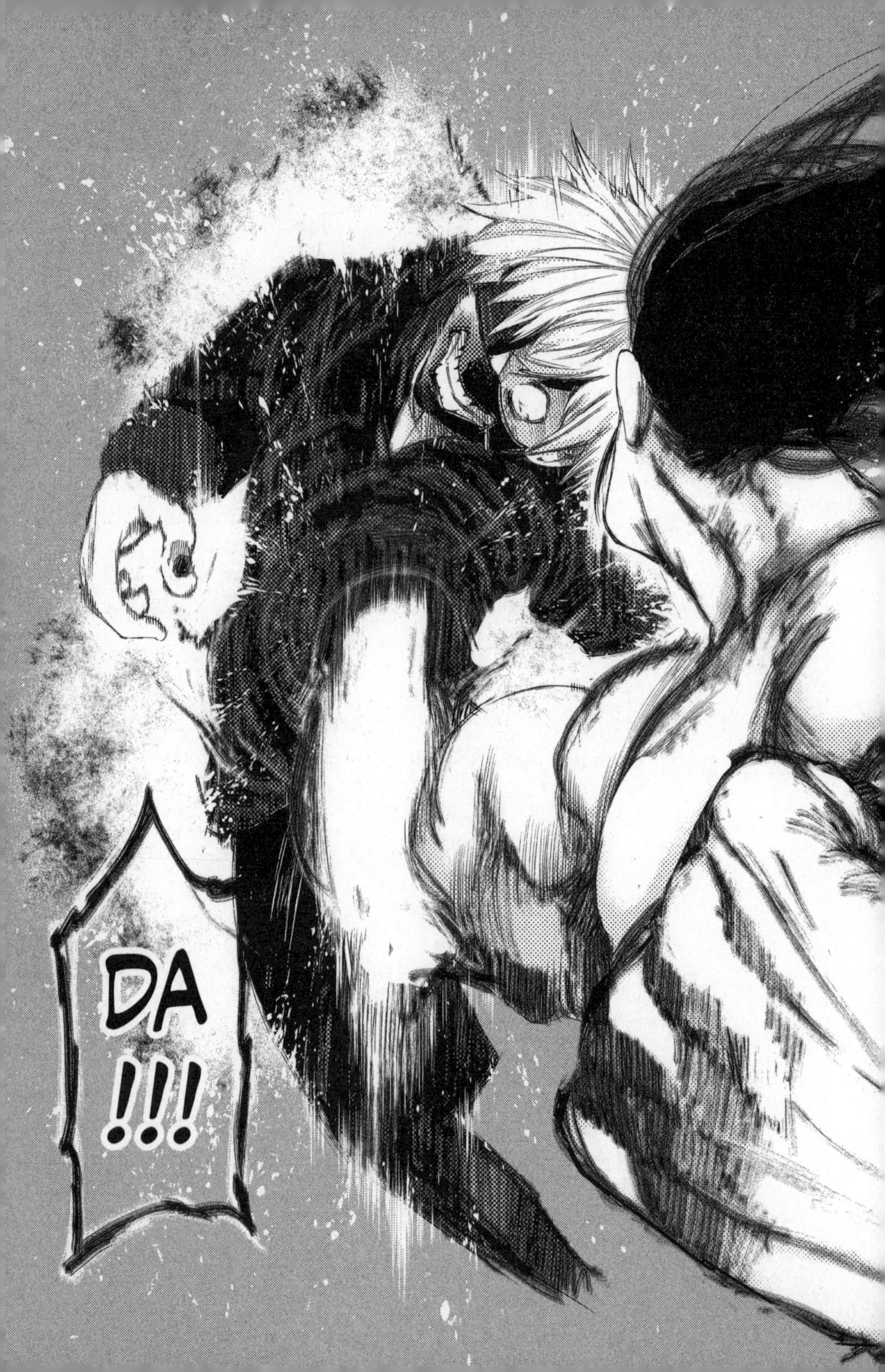
DA!!!

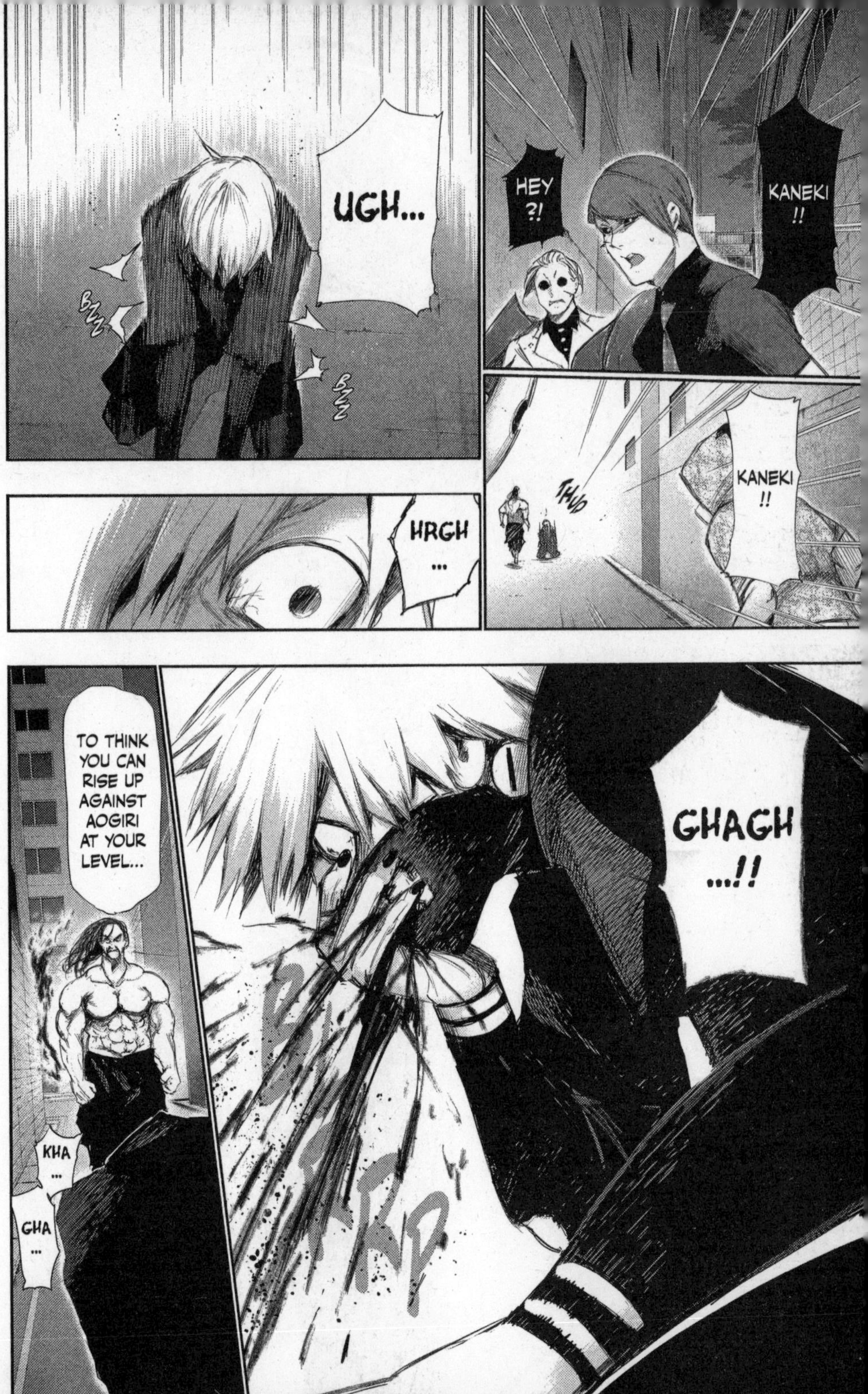
KANEKI !!
HEY ?!
UGH...
BZZ
BZZ
KANEKI !!
THUD
HRGH ...
GHAGH ...!!
TO THINK YOU CAN RISE UP AGAINST AOGIRI AT YOUR LEVEL...
KHA ...
GHA ...

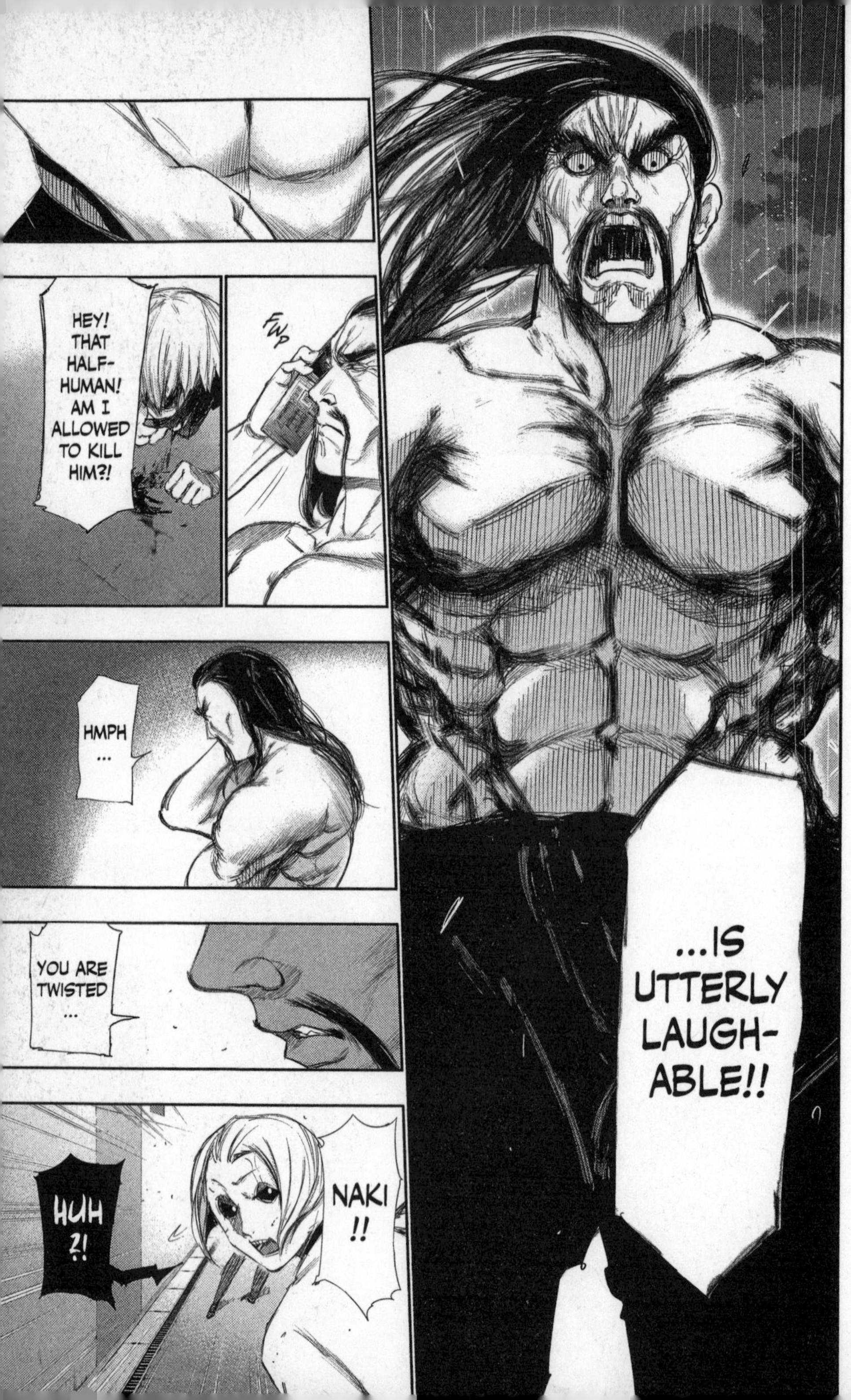
...IS UTTERLY LAUGHABLE!!
FWP
HEY! THAT HALF-HUMAN! AM I ALLOWED TO KILL HIM?!
HMPH ...
YOU ARE TWISTED ...
NAKI !!
HUH ?!

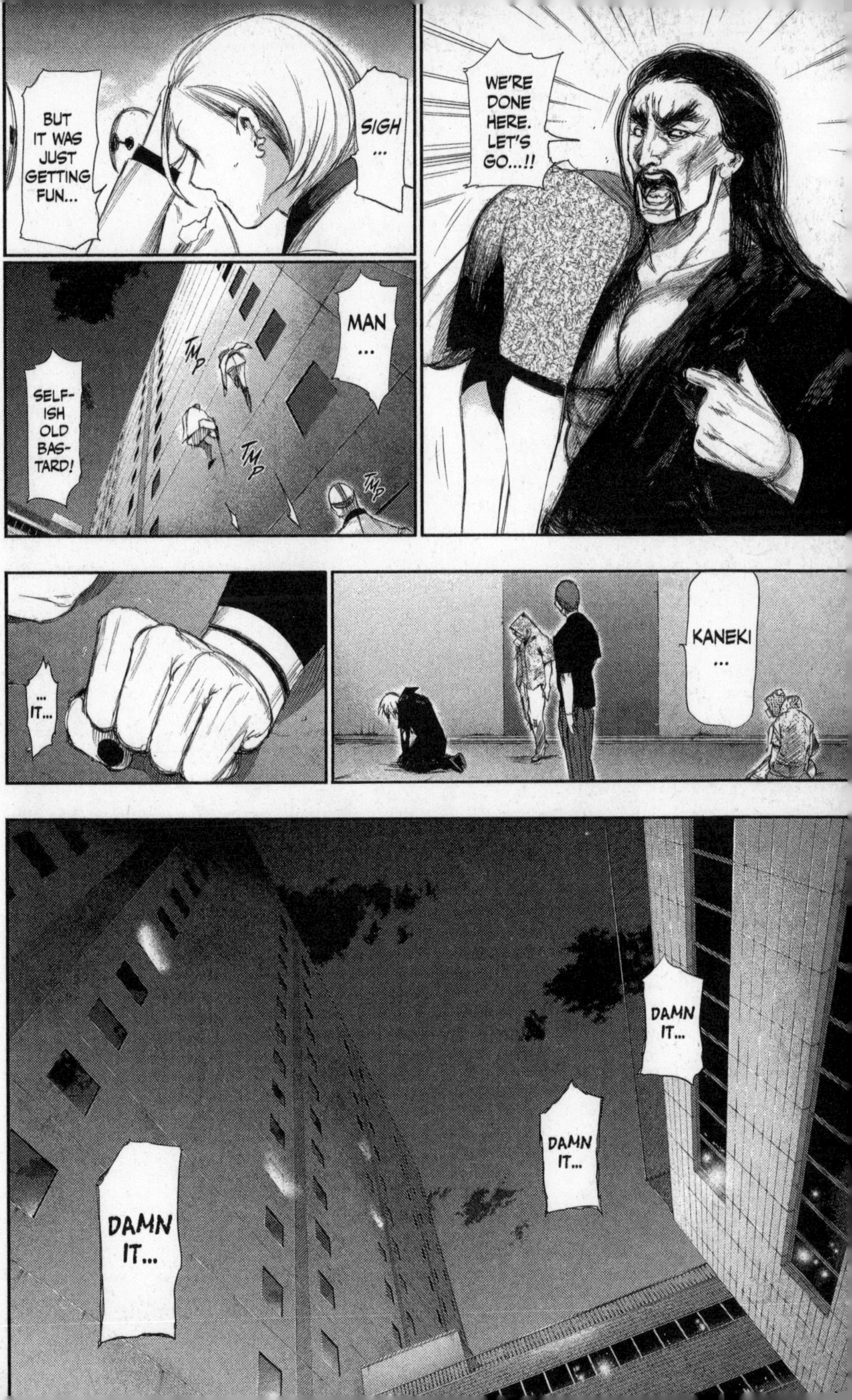
WE'RE DONE HERE. LET'S GO...!!
SIGH ...
BUT IT WAS JUST GETTING FUN...
MAN ...
TMP
TMP
SELF-ISH OLD BAS-TARD!
TMP
KANEKI ...
... IT...
DAMN IT...
DAMN IT...
DAMN IT...

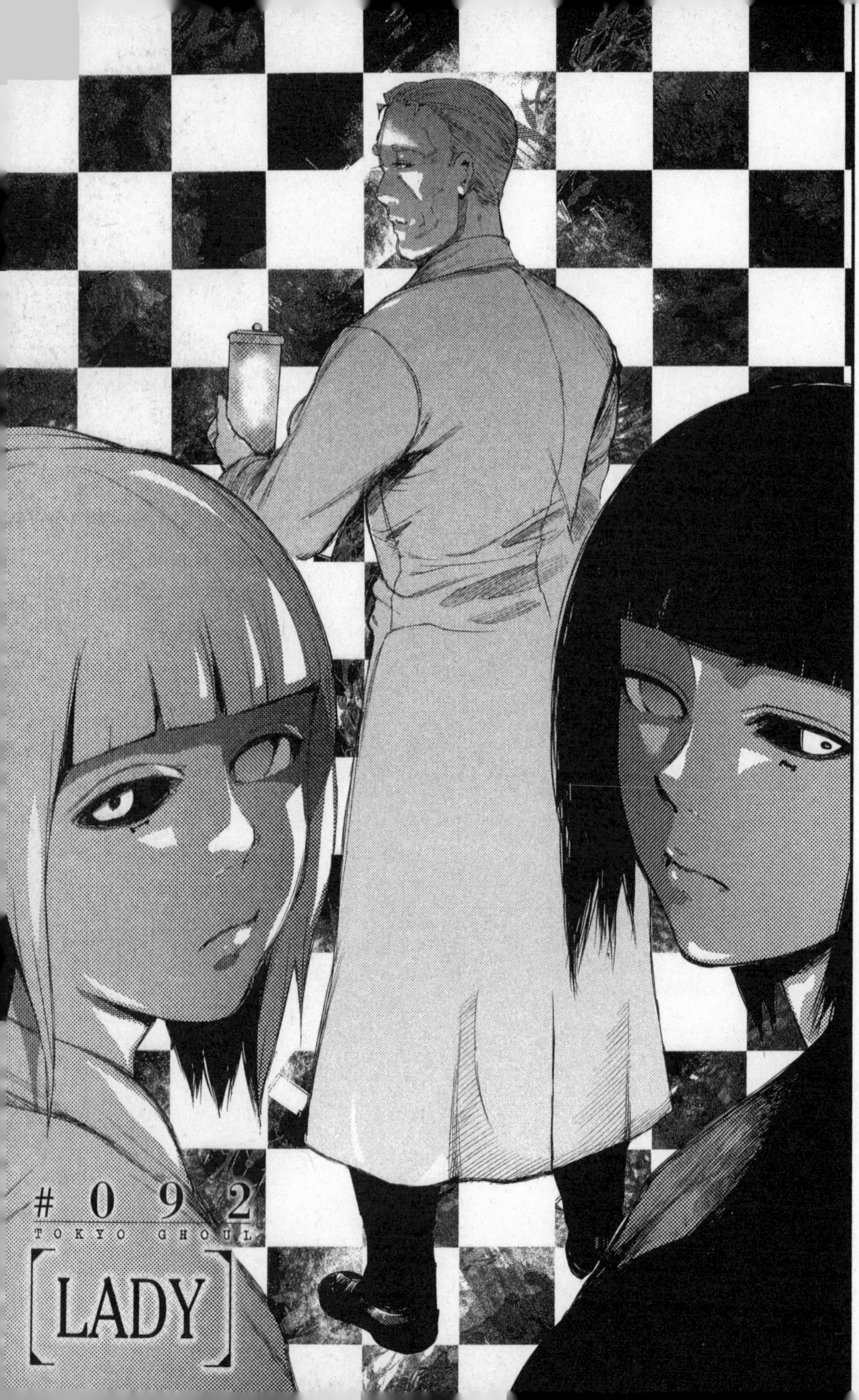
#092
TOKYO GHOUL
[LADY]

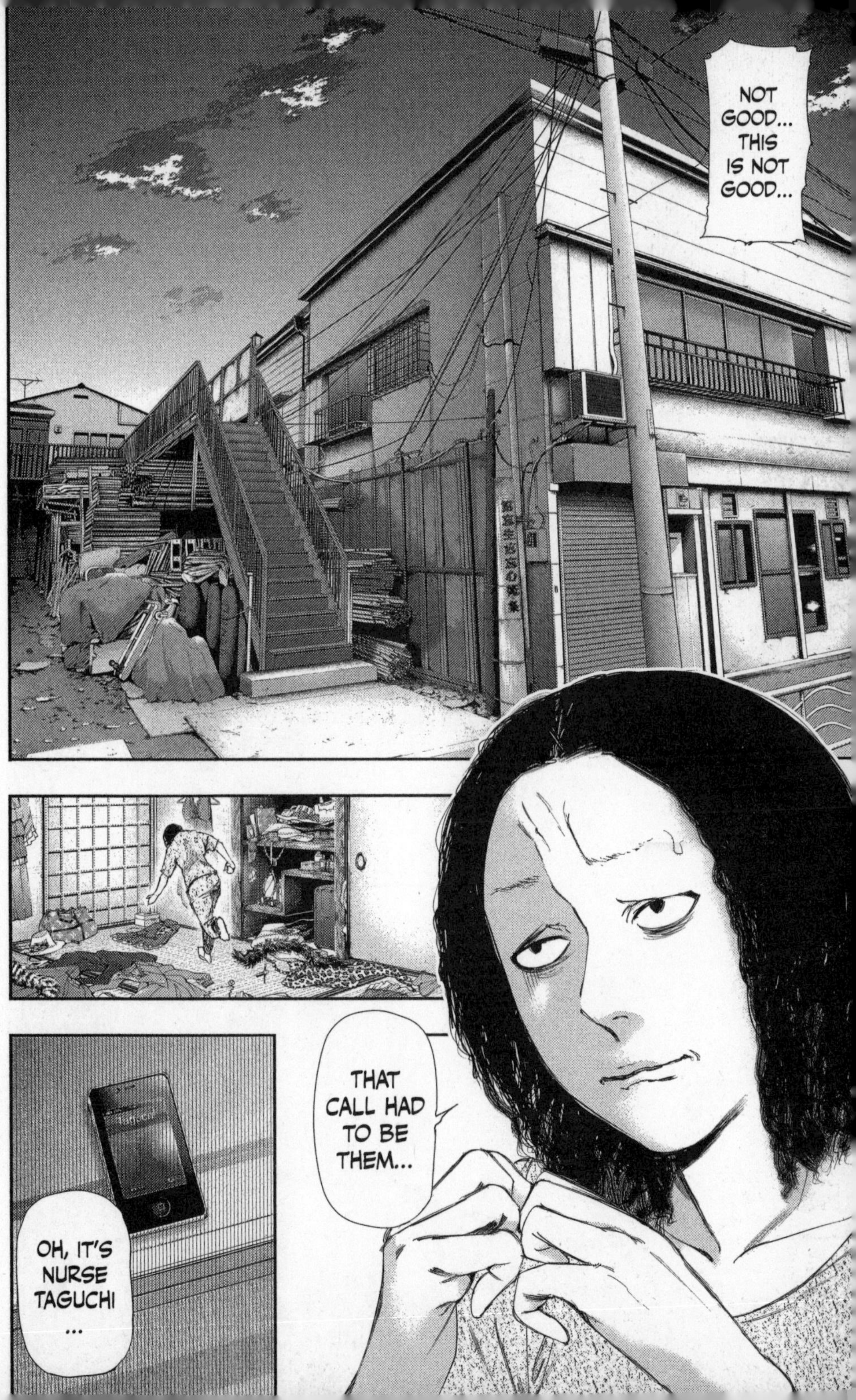
NOT GOOD... THIS IS NOT GOOD...
THAT CALL HAD TO BE THEM...
OH, IT'S NURSE TAGUCHI ...

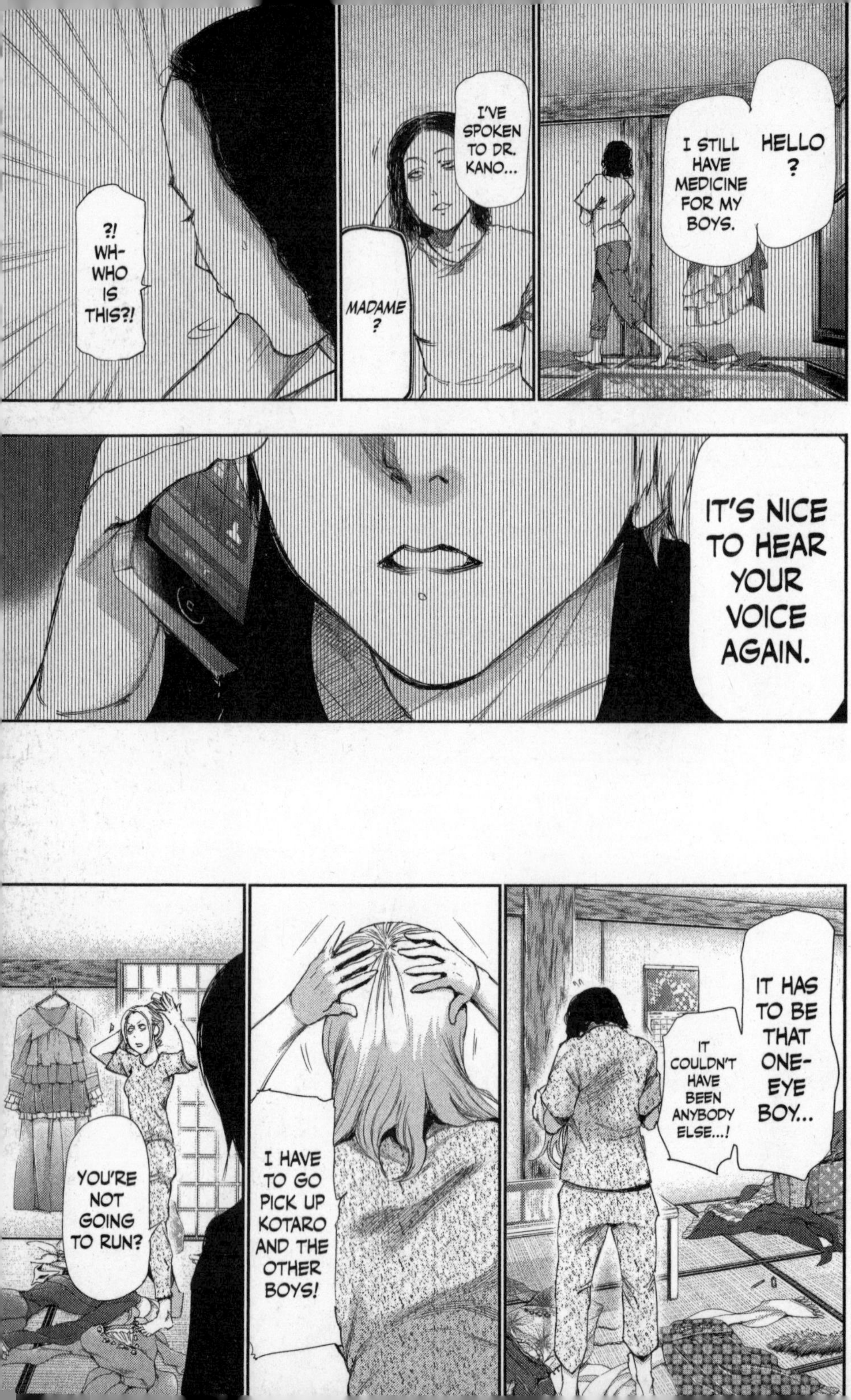
HELLO ?
I STILL HAVE MEDICINE FOR MY BOYS.
I'VE SPOKEN TO DR. KANO...
MADAME ?
?! WH-WHO IS THIS?!
IT'S NICE TO HEAR YOUR VOICE AGAIN.
IT HAS TO BE THAT ONE-EYE BOY...
IT COULDN'T HAVE BEEN ANYBODY ELSE...!
I HAVE TO GO PICK UP KOTARO AND THE OTHER BOYS!
YOU'RE NOT GOING TO RUN?

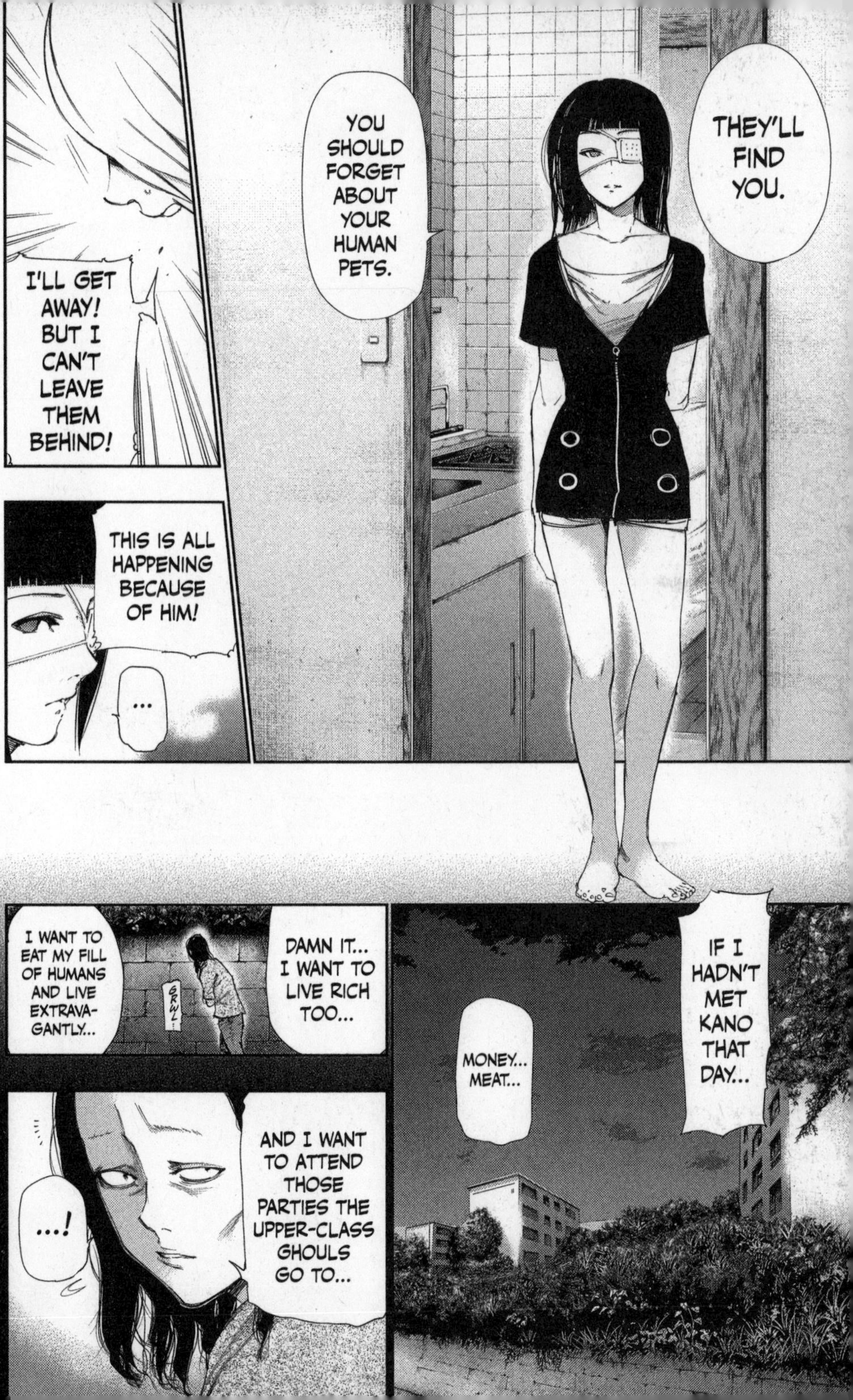
THEY'LL FIND YOU.
YOU SHOULD FORGET ABOUT YOUR HUMAN PETS.
I'LL GET AWAY! BUT I CAN'T LEAVE THEM BEHIND!
THIS IS ALL HAPPENING BECAUSE OF HIM!
...
IF I HADN'T MET KANO THAT DAY...
MONEY... MEAT...
DAMN IT... I WANT TO LIVE RICH TOO...
I WANT TO EAT MY FILL OF HUMANS AND LIVE EXTRAVA-GANTLY...
GRWL...
AND I WANT TO ATTEND THOSE PARTIES THE UPPER-CLASS GHOULS GO TO...
...!

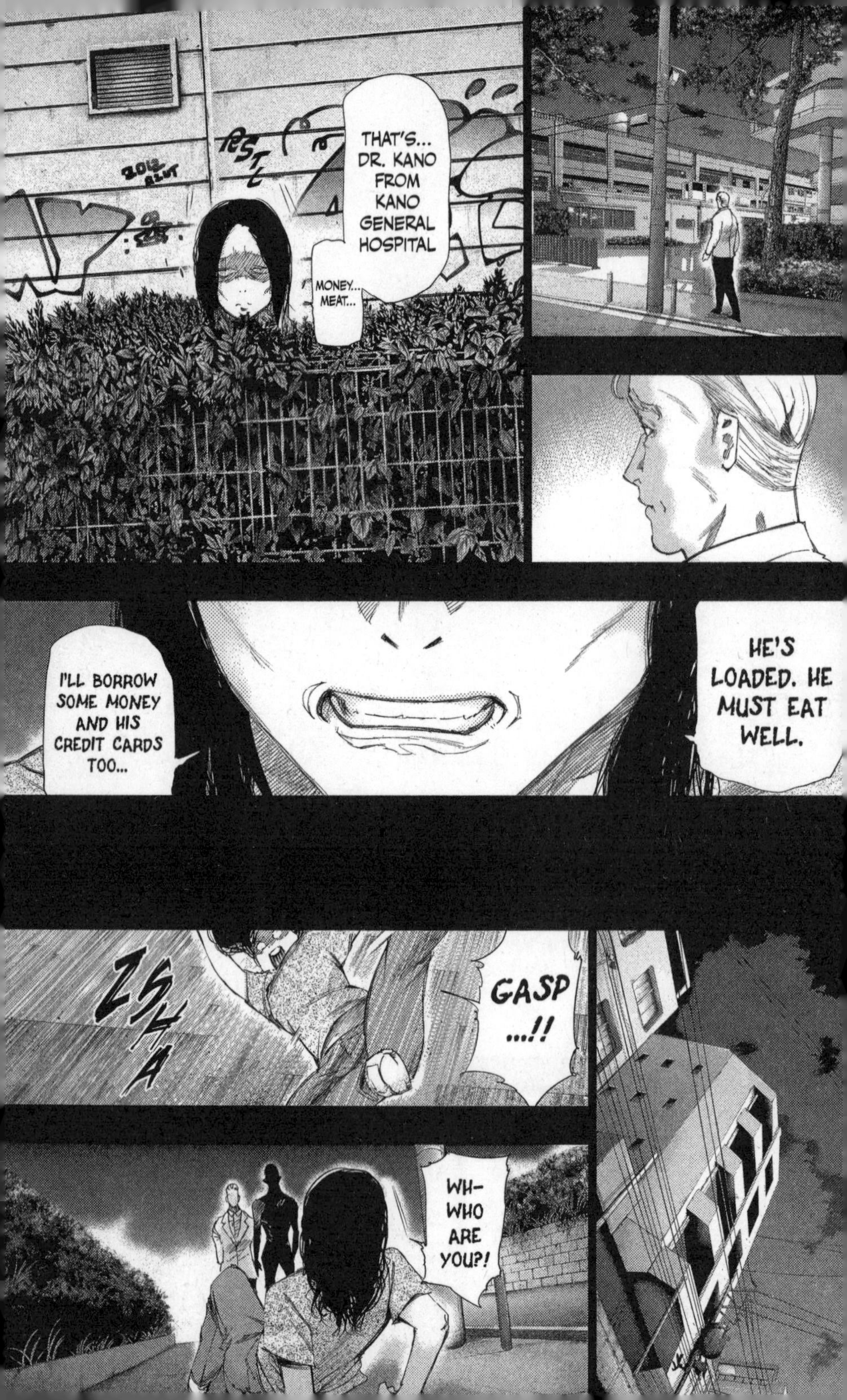
THAT'S... DR. KANO FROM KANO GENERAL HOSPITAL
MONEY... MEAT...
HE'S LOADED. HE MUST EAT WELL.
I'LL BORROW SOME MONEY AND HIS CREDIT CARDS TOO...
GASP ...!!
ZSHA
WH-WHO ARE YOU?!

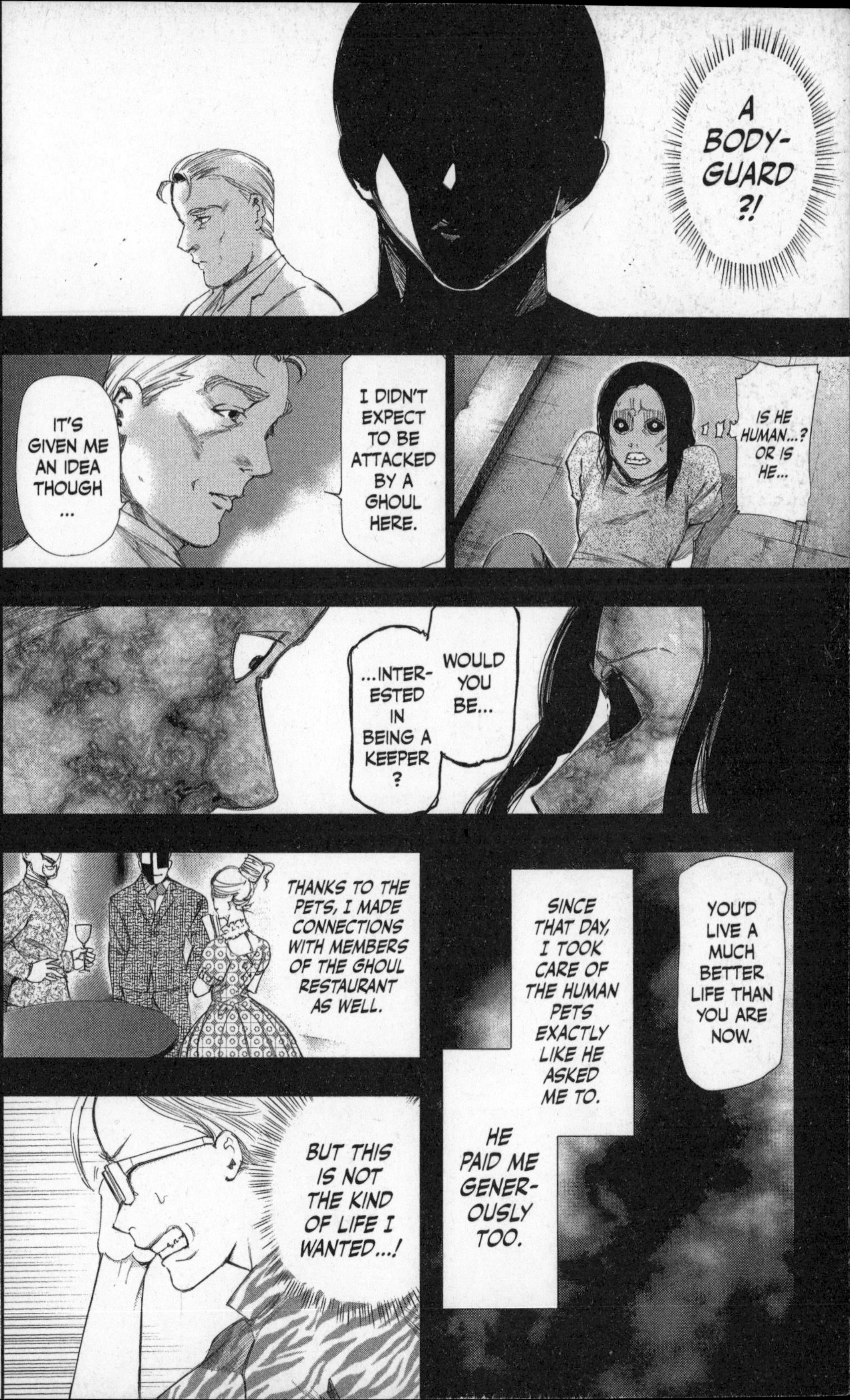
A BODY-GUARD ?!
IS HE HUMAN...? OR IS HE...
I DIDN'T EXPECT TO BE ATTACKED BY A GHOUL HERE.
IT'S GIVEN ME AN IDEA THOUGH...
WOULD YOU BE...
...INTER-ESTED IN BEING A KEEPER?
YOU'D LIVE A MUCH BETTER LIFE THAN YOU ARE NOW.
SINCE THAT DAY, I TOOK CARE OF THE HUMAN PETS EXACTLY LIKE HE ASKED ME TO.
HE PAID ME GENER-OUSLY TOO.
THANKS TO THE PETS, I MADE CONNECTIONS WITH MEMBERS OF THE GHOUL RESTAURANT AS WELL.
BUT THIS IS NOT THE KIND OF LIFE I WANTED...!

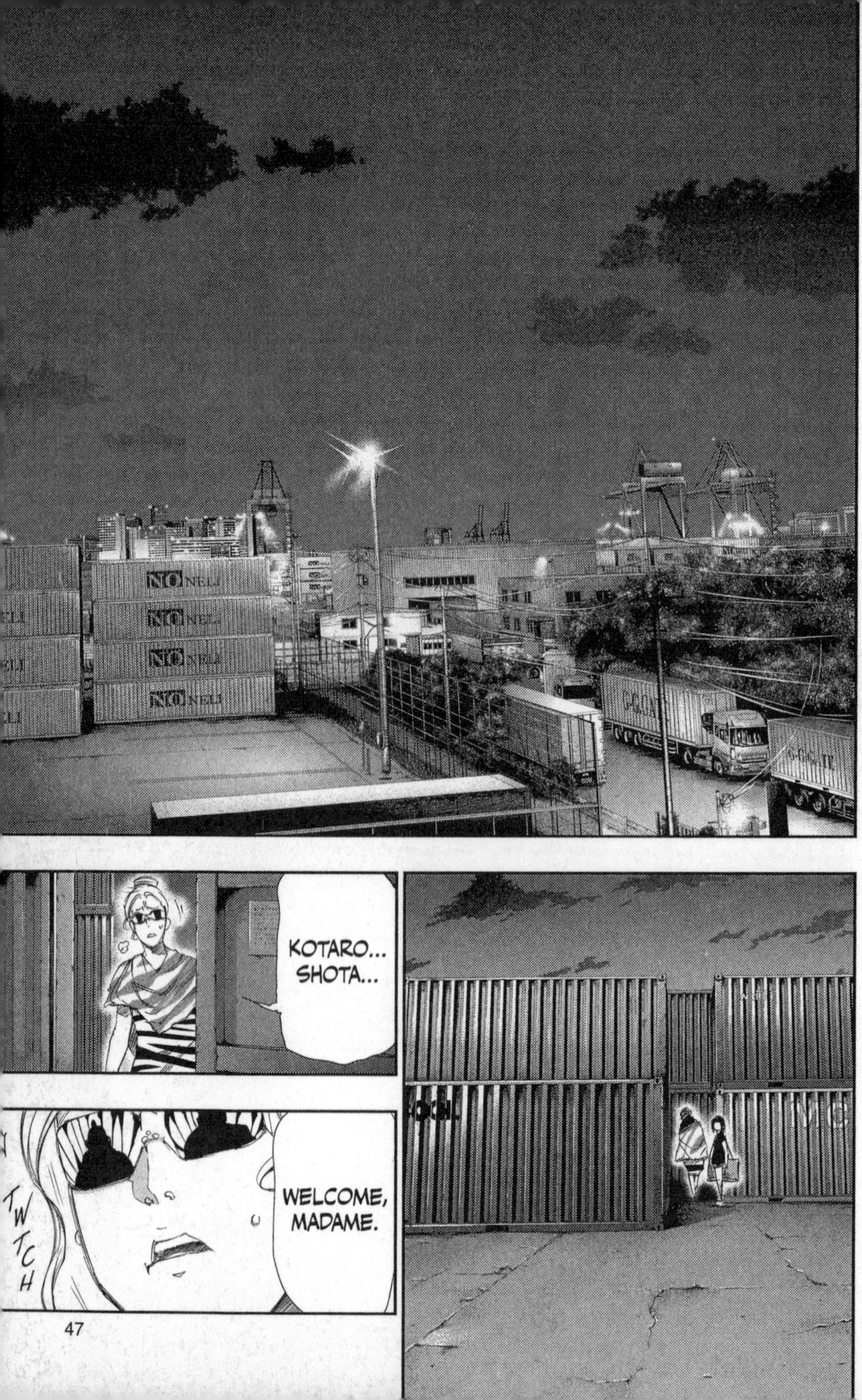
KOTARO... SHOTA...
WELCOME, MADAME.
TWITCH

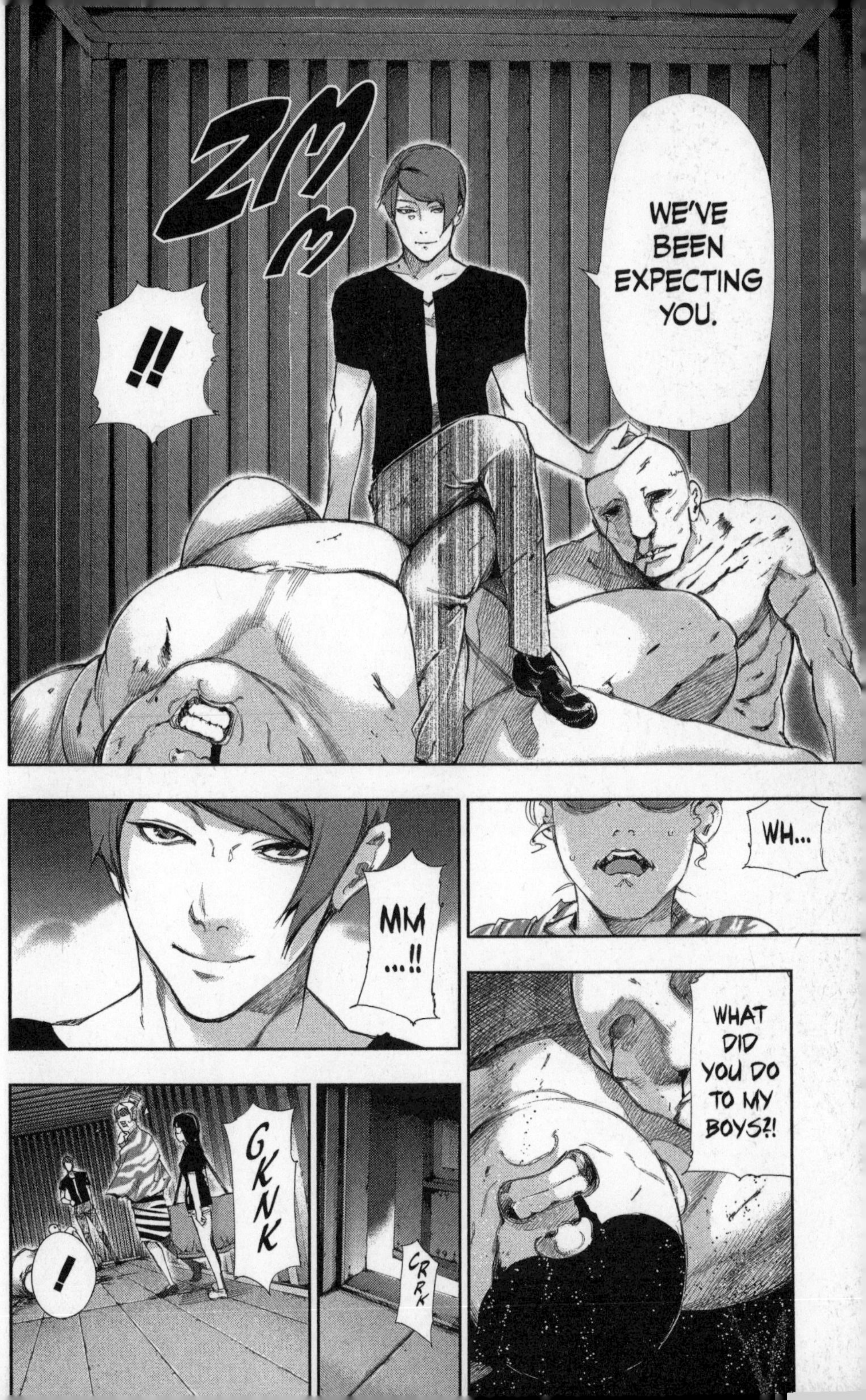
WE'VE BEEN EXPECTING YOU.
ZMMM
!!
WH...
MM ...!!
WHAT DID YOU DO TO MY BOYS?!
CRRK
GKNK
!

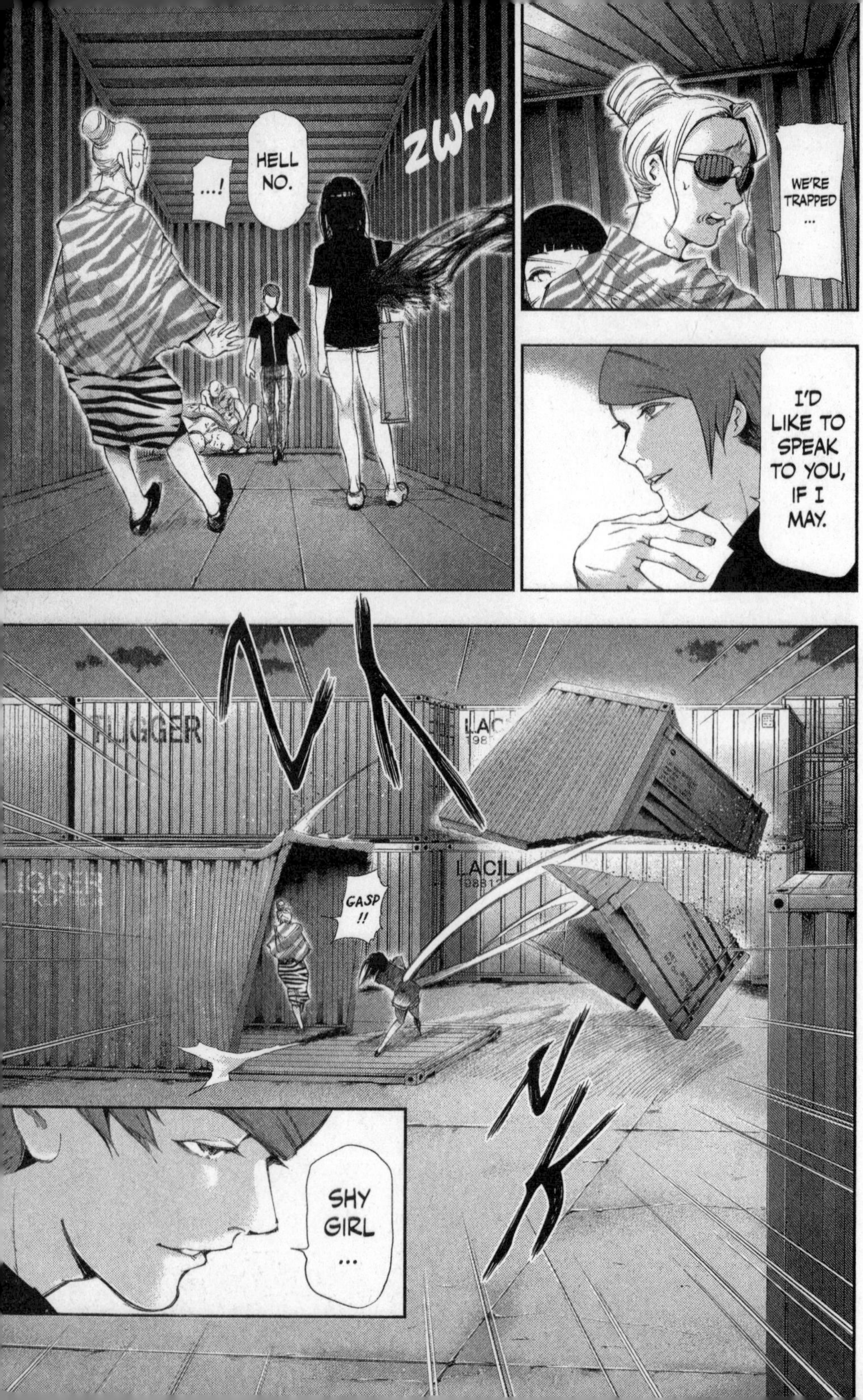
WE'RE TRAPPED ...
I'D LIKE TO SPEAK TO YOU, IF I MAY.
ZWM
HELL NO.
...!
GASP !!
SHY GIRL ...

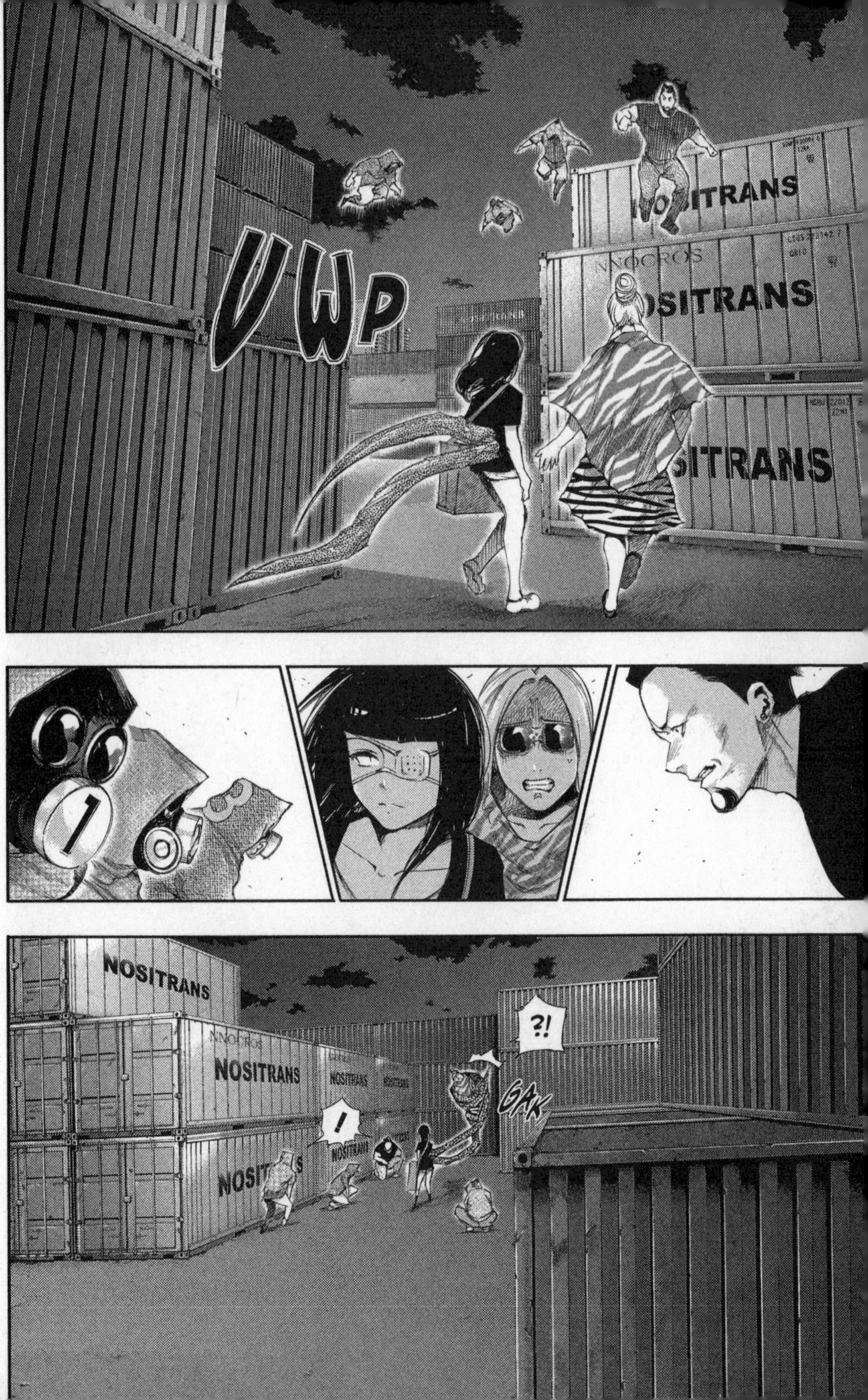
NOSITRANS
NNOCROS
NOSITRANS
NOSITRANS
VWP
?!
GAK
!
NOSITRANS
NNOCROS
NOSITRANS
NOSITRANS
NOSITRANS

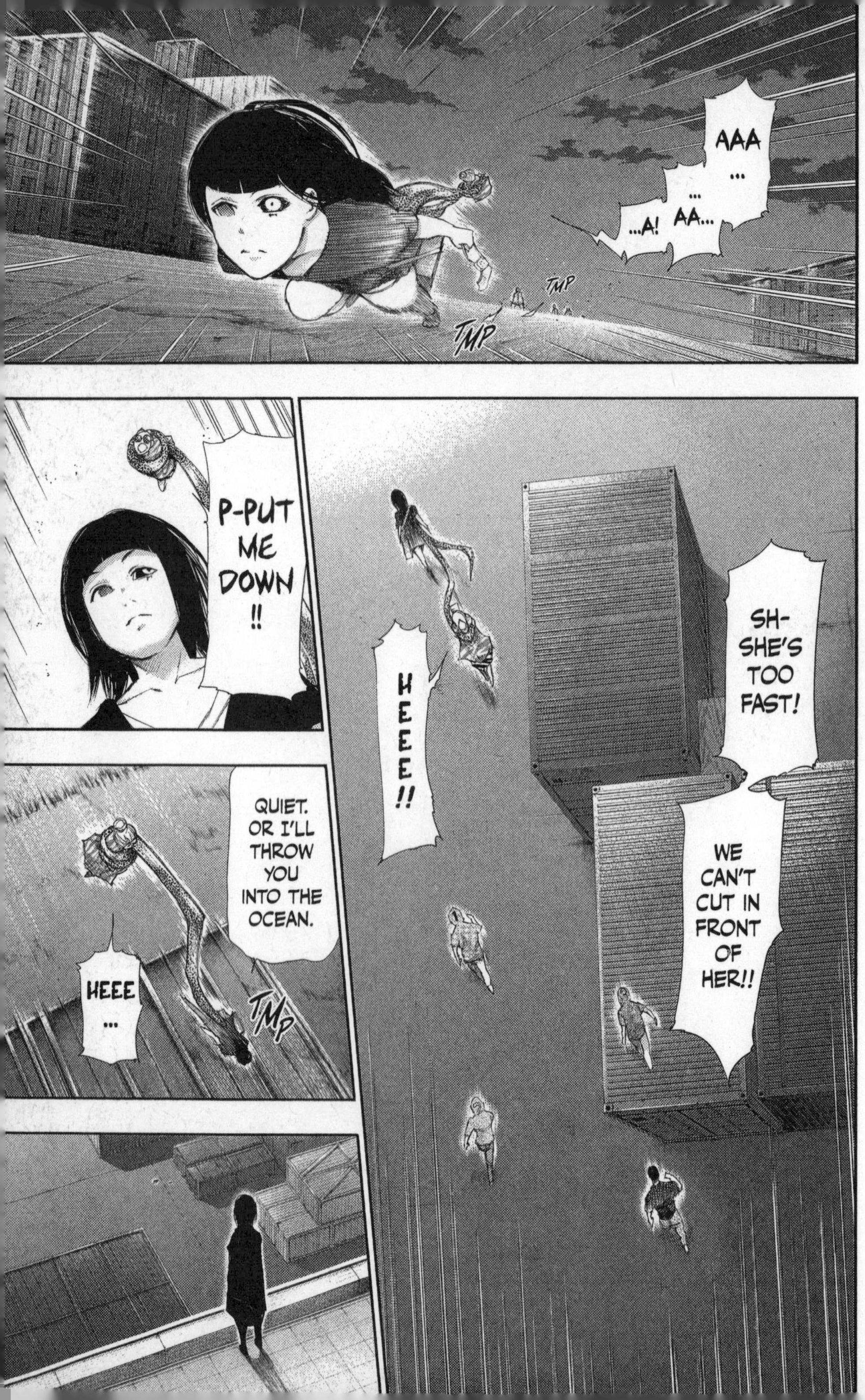
AAA ... ... AA... ...A!
TMP
TMP
SH- SHE'S TOO FAST!
WE CAN'T CUT IN FRONT OF HER!!
HEEEE!!
P-PUT ME DOWN!!
QUIET. OR I'LL THROW YOU INTO THE OCEAN.
HEEE...
TMP

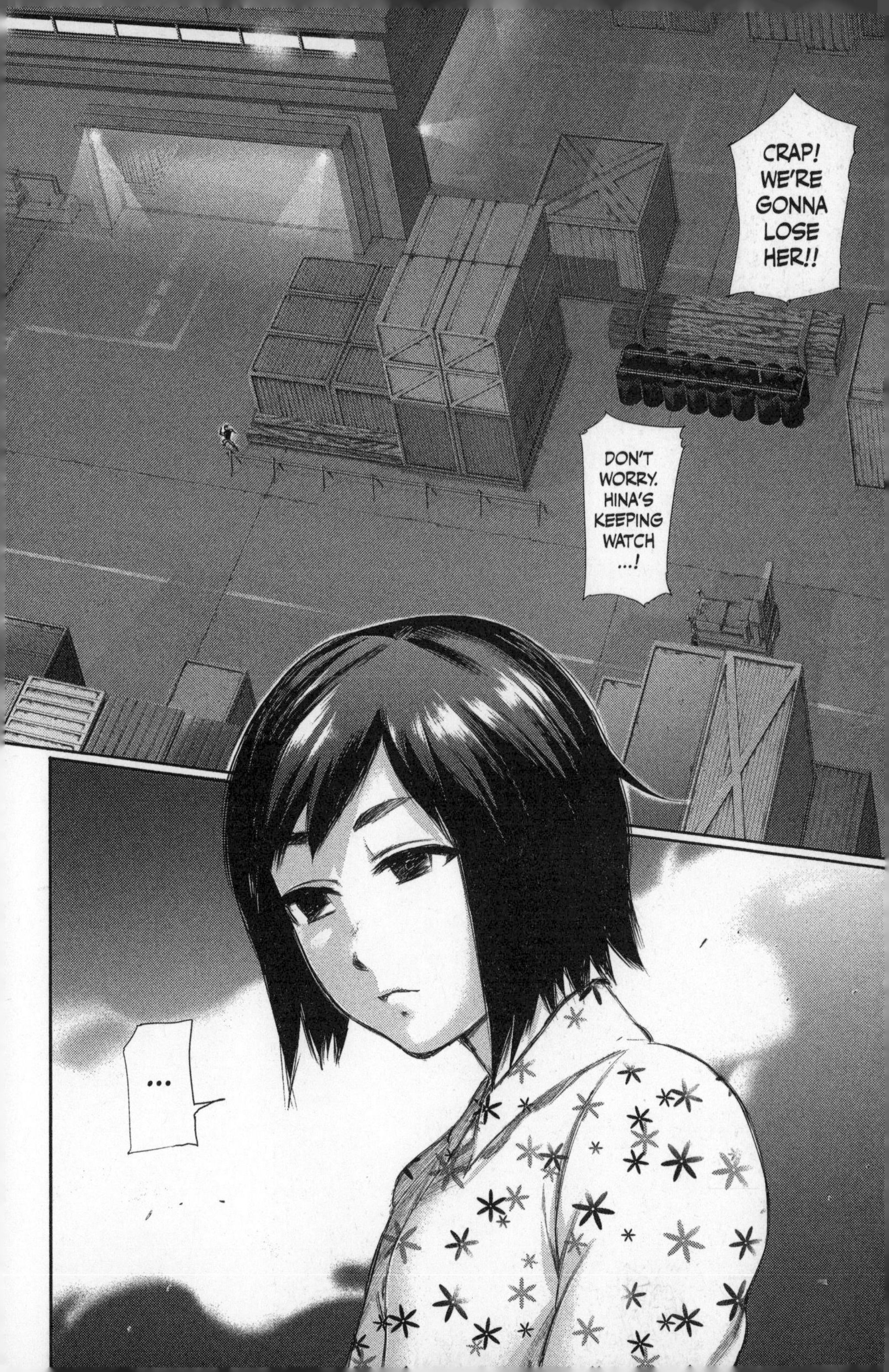
CRAP! WE'RE GONNA LOSE HER!!
DON'T WORRY. HINA'S KEEPING WATCH ...!
...

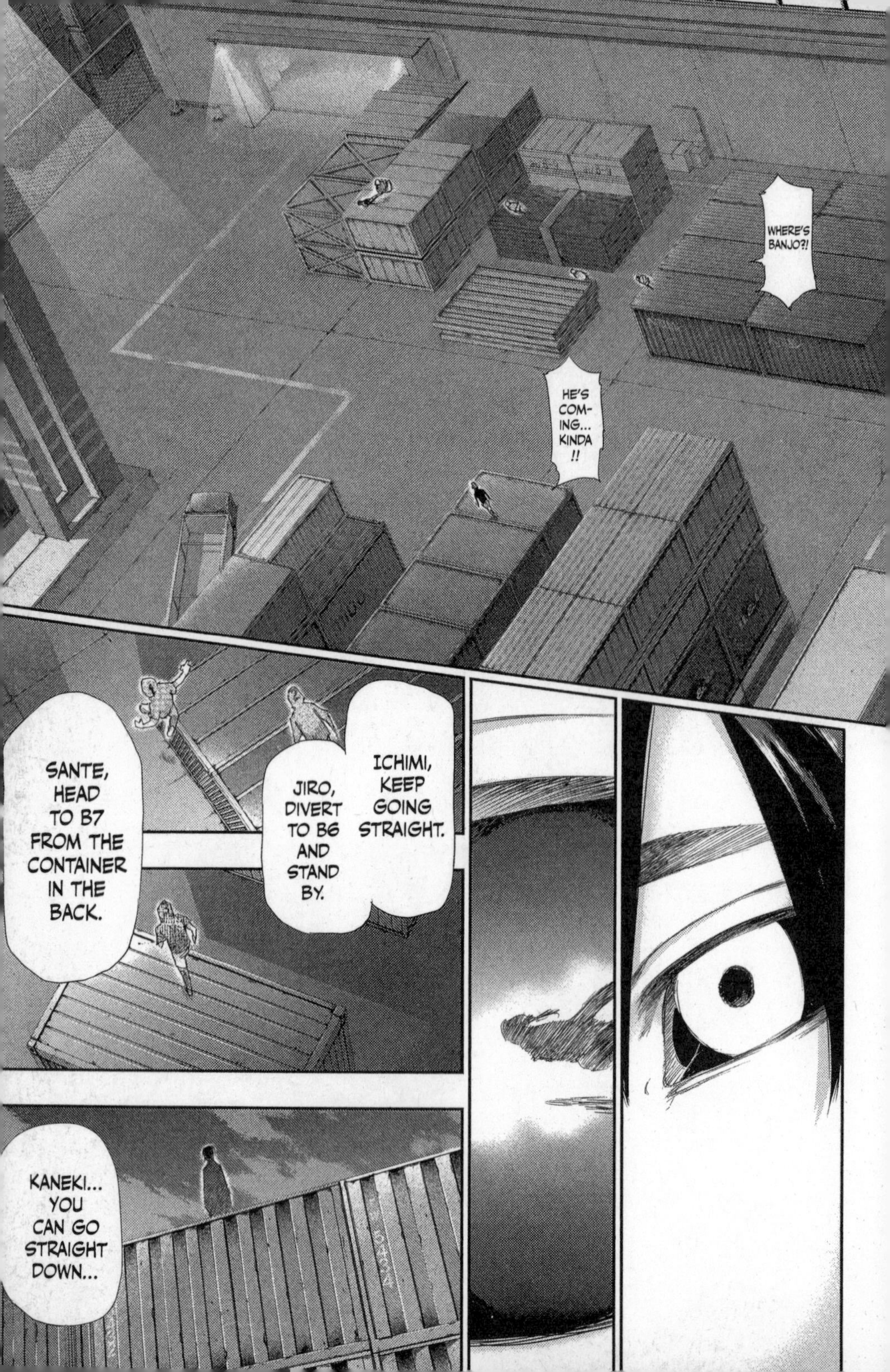
WHERE'S BANJO?!
HE'S COMING... KINDA!!
ICHIMI, KEEP GOING STRAIGHT.
JIRO, DIVERT TO B6 AND STAND BY.
SANTE, HEAD TO B7 FROM THE CONTAINER IN THE BACK.
KANEKI... YOU CAN GO STRAIGHT DOWN...

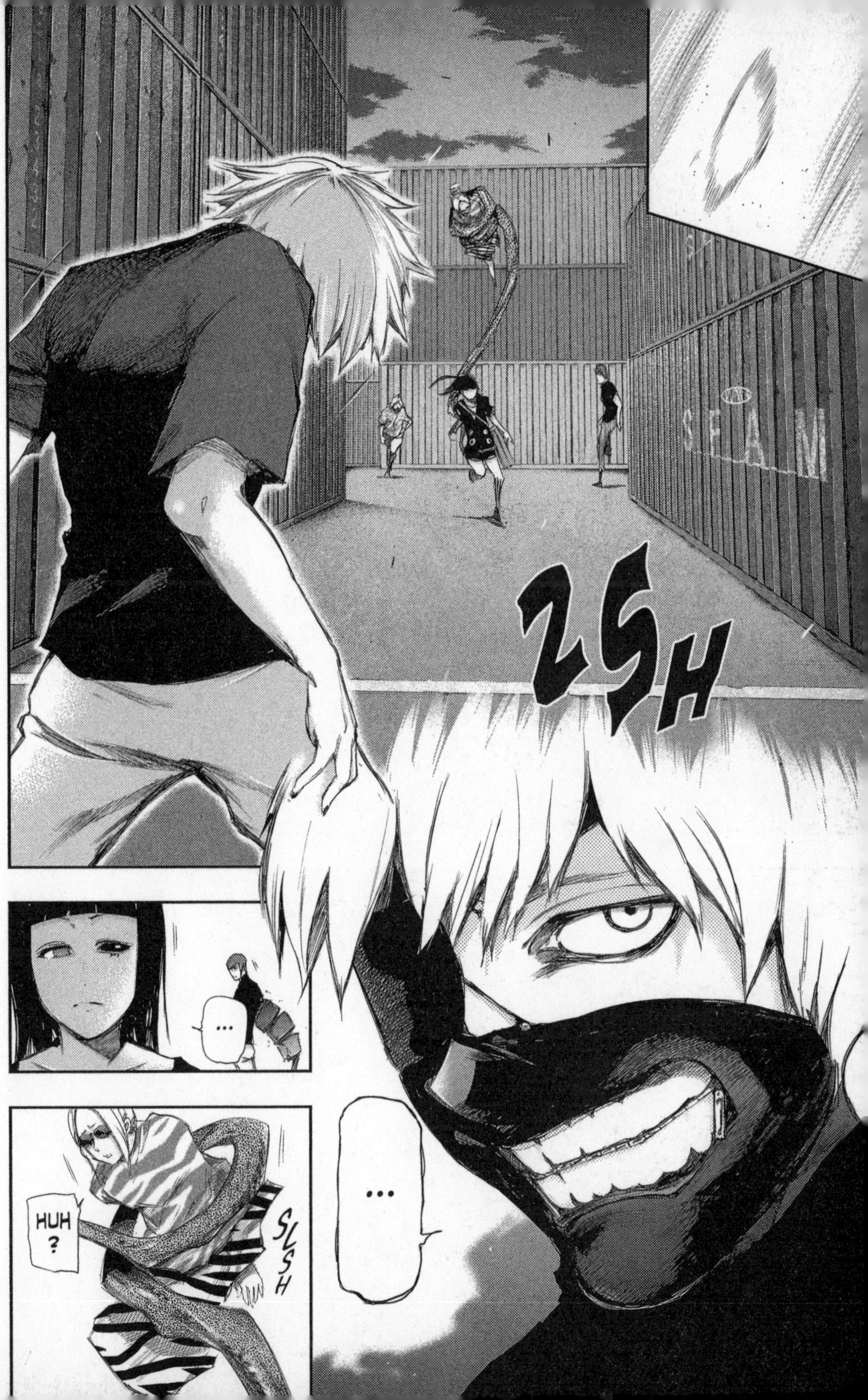
...
ZSH
...
...
HUH ?
SLSH

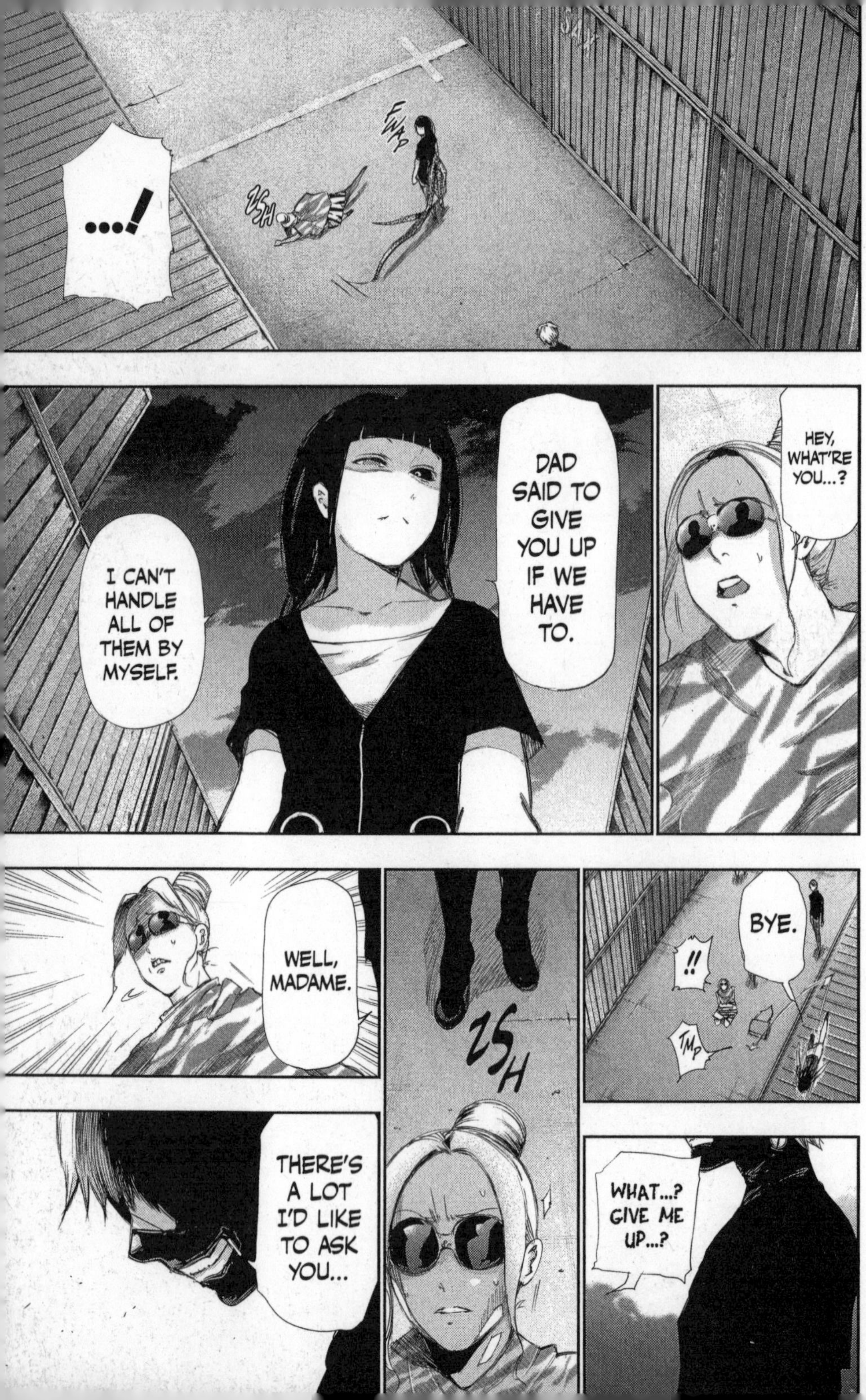
FWAP
ZSH
...!
HEY, WHAT'RE YOU...?
DAD SAID TO GIVE YOU UP IF WE HAVE TO.
I CAN'T HANDLE ALL OF THEM BY MYSELF.
BYE.
!!
TMP
WHAT...? GIVE ME UP...?
ZSH
WELL, MADAME.
THERE'S A LOT I'D LIKE TO ASK YOU...

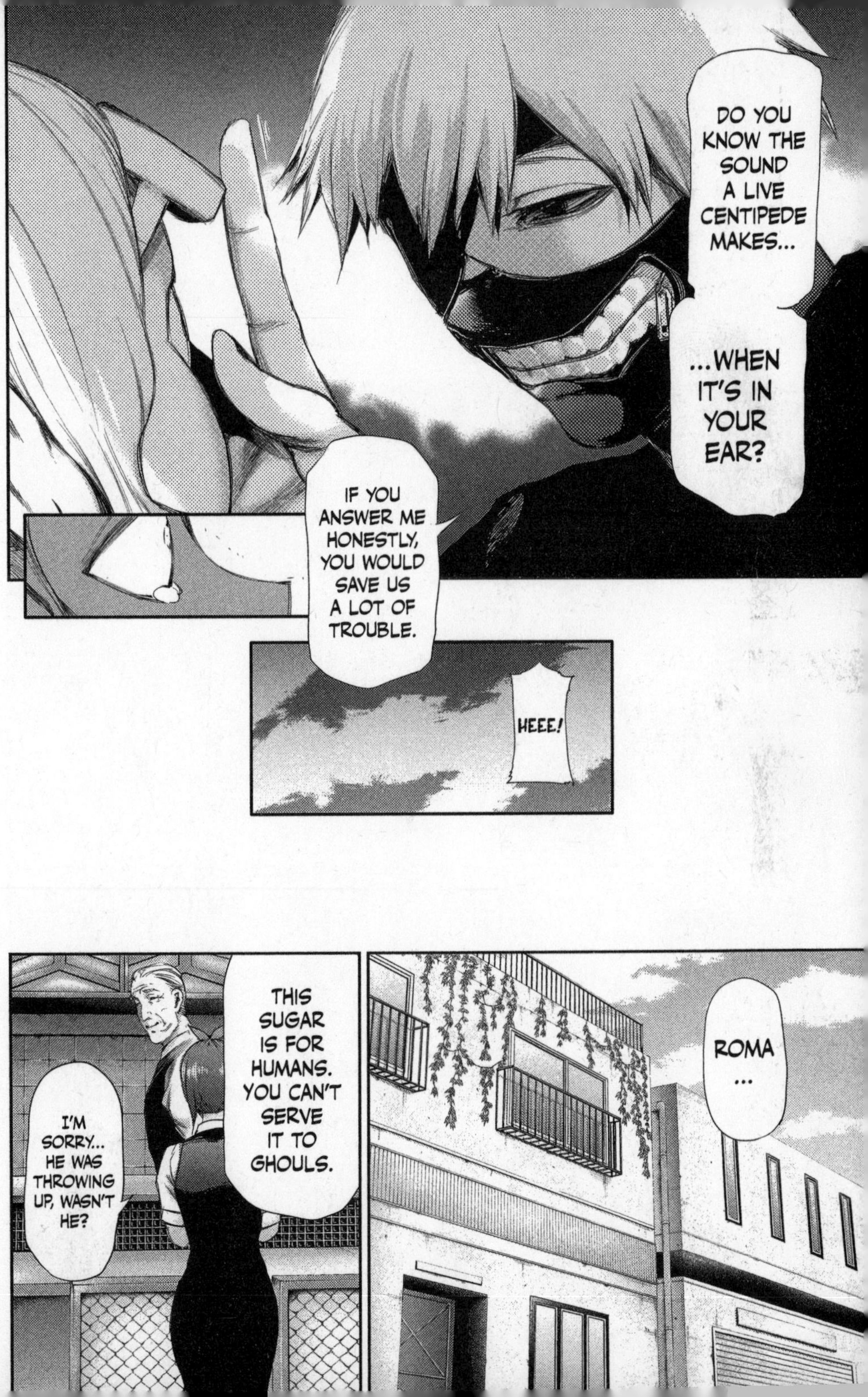
DO YOU KNOW THE SOUND A LIVE CENTIPEDE MAKES...
...WHEN IT'S IN YOUR EAR?
IF YOU ANSWER ME HONESTLY, YOU WOULD SAVE US A LOT OF TROUBLE.
HEEE!
ROMA ...
THIS SUGAR IS FOR HUMANS. YOU CAN'T SERVE IT TO GHOULS.
I'M SORRY... HE WAS THROWING UP, WASN'T HE?

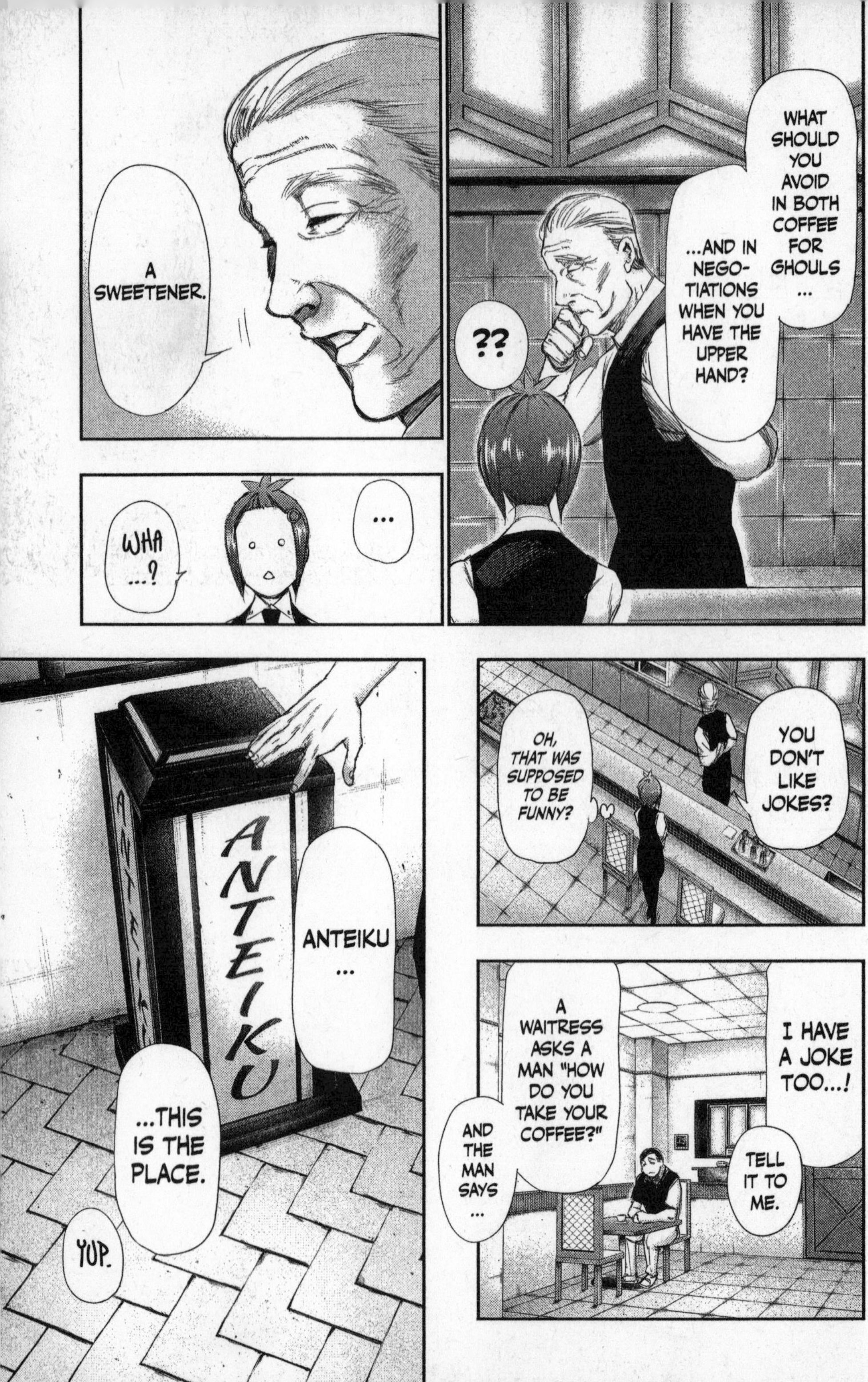
WHAT SHOULD YOU AVOID IN BOTH COFFEE FOR GHOULS ...
...AND IN NEGOTIATIONS WHEN YOU HAVE THE UPPER HAND?
??
A SWEETENER.
...
WHA ...?
YOU DON'T LIKE JOKES?
OH, THAT WAS SUPPOSED TO BE FUNNY?
I HAVE A JOKE TOO...!
TELL IT TO ME.
A WAITRESS ASKS A MAN "HOW DO YOU TAKE YOUR COFFEE?"
AND THE MAN SAYS ...
ANTEIKU
ANTEIKU ...
...THIS IS THE PLACE.
YUP.

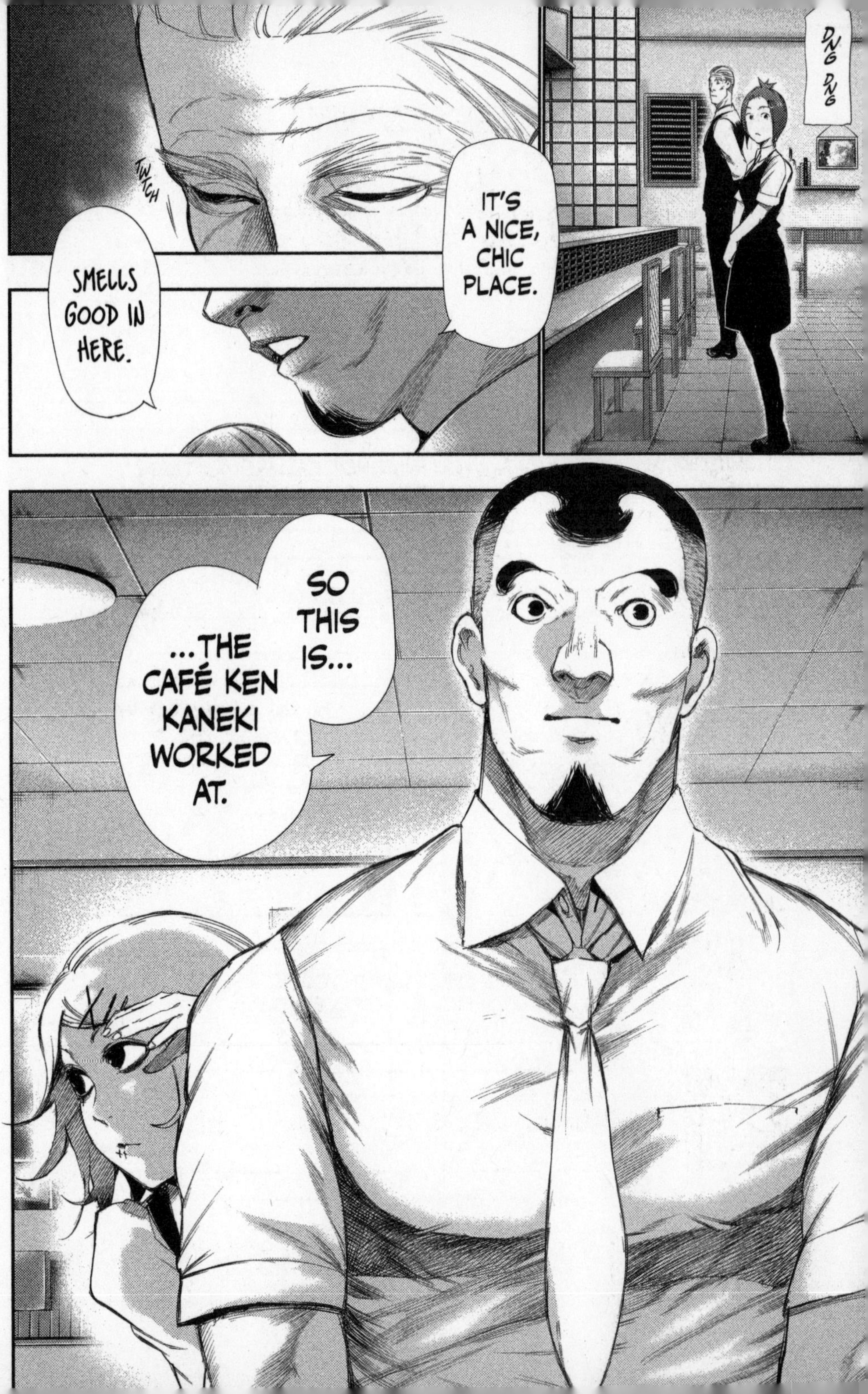
DNG DNG
TWITCH
IT'S A NICE, CHIC PLACE.
SMELLS GOOD IN HERE.
SO THIS IS...
...THE CAFÉ KEN KANEKI WORKED AT.

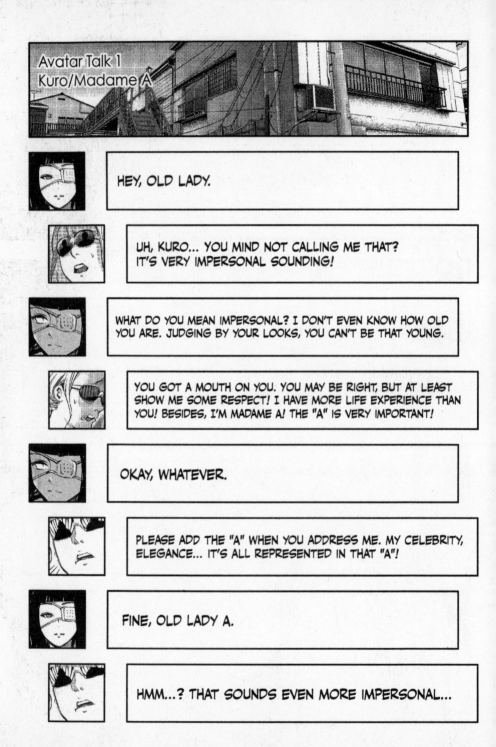

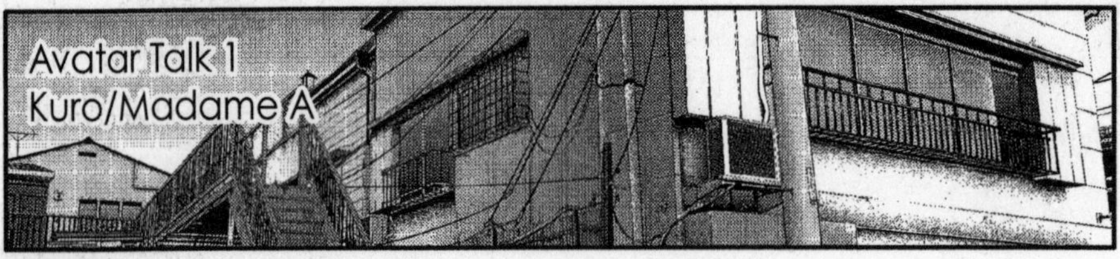
Avatar Talk 1
Kuro/Madame A

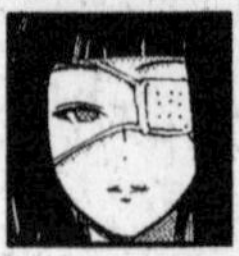

HEY, OLD LADY.

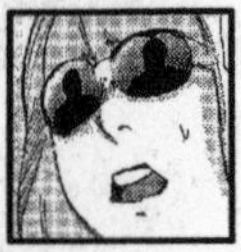

UH, KURO... YOU MIND NOT CALLING ME THAT?
IT'S VERY IMPERSONAL SOUNDING!

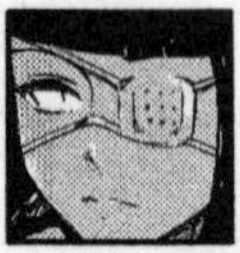

WHAT DO YOU MEAN IMPERSONAL? I DON'T EVEN KNOW HOW OLD YOU ARE. JUDGING BY YOUR LOOKS, YOU CAN'T BE THAT YOUNG.

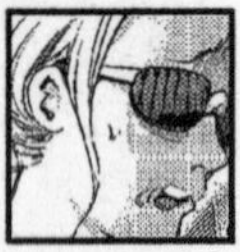

YOU GOT A MOUTH ON YOU. YOU MAY BE RIGHT, BUT AT LEAST SHOW ME SOME RESPECT! I HAVE MORE LIFE EXPERIENCE THAN YOU! BESIDES, I'M MADAME A! THE "A" IS VERY IMPORTANT!

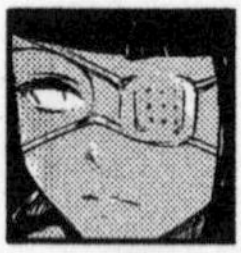

OKAY, WHATEVER.

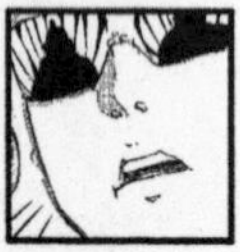

PLEASE ADD THE "A" WHEN YOU ADDRESS ME. MY CELEBRITY, ELEGANCE... IT'S ALL REPRESENTED IN THAT "A"!

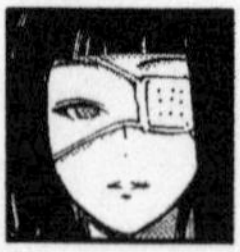

FINE, OLD LADY A.

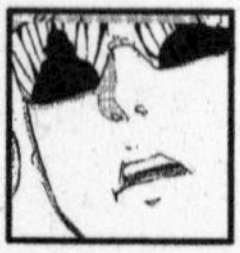

HMM...? THAT SOUNDS EVEN MORE IMPERSONAL...

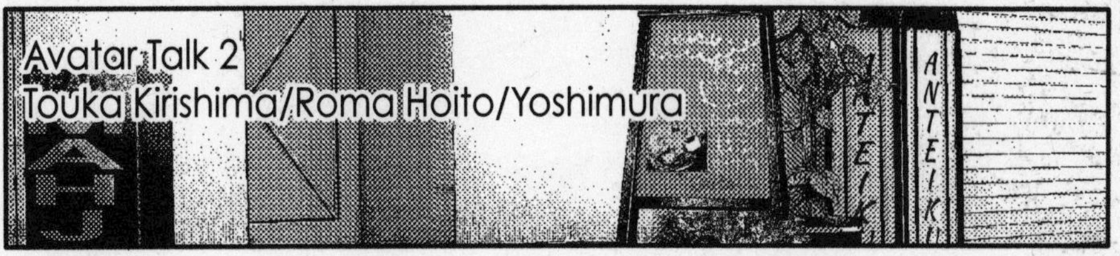
ANTEIKU

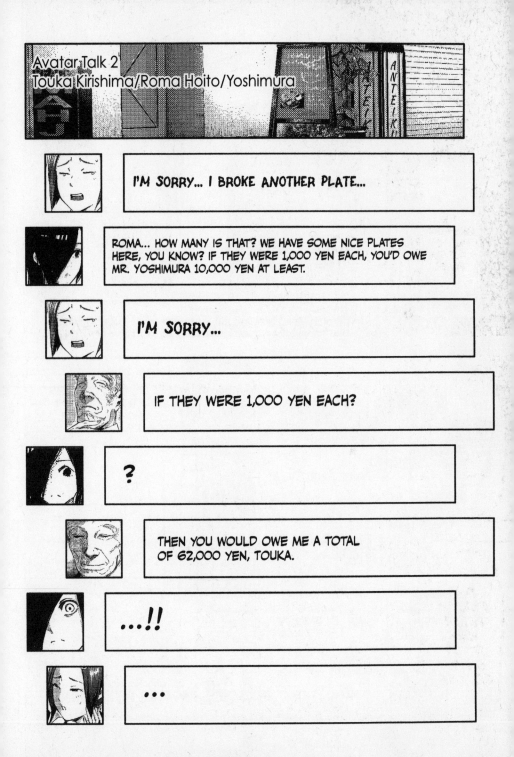

Avatar Talk 2
Touka Kirishima/Roma Hoito/Yoshimura

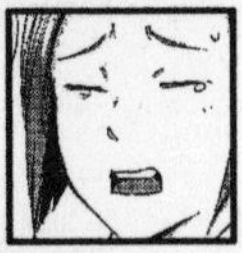

I'M SORRY... I BROKE ANOTHER PLATE...

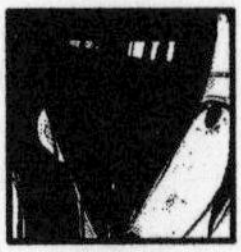

ROMA... HOW MANY IS THAT? WE HAVE SOME NICE PLATES HERE, YOU KNOW? IF THEY WERE 1,000 YEN EACH, YOU'D OWE MR. YOSHIMURA 10,000 YEN AT LEAST.

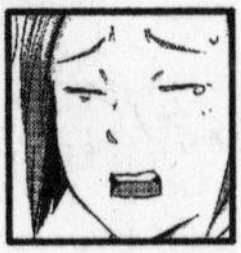

I'M SORRY...

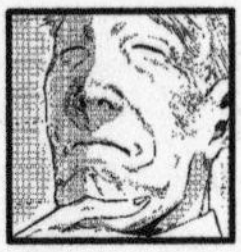

IF THEY WERE 1,000 YEN EACH?

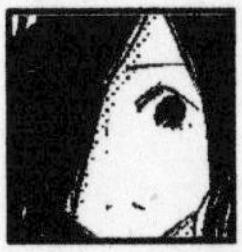

?

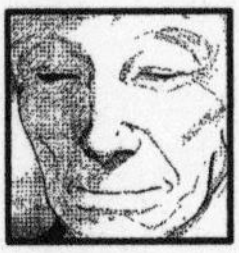

THEN YOU WOULD OWE ME A TOTAL OF 62,000 YEN, TOUKA.

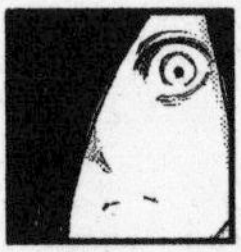

...!!

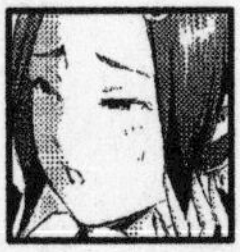

...

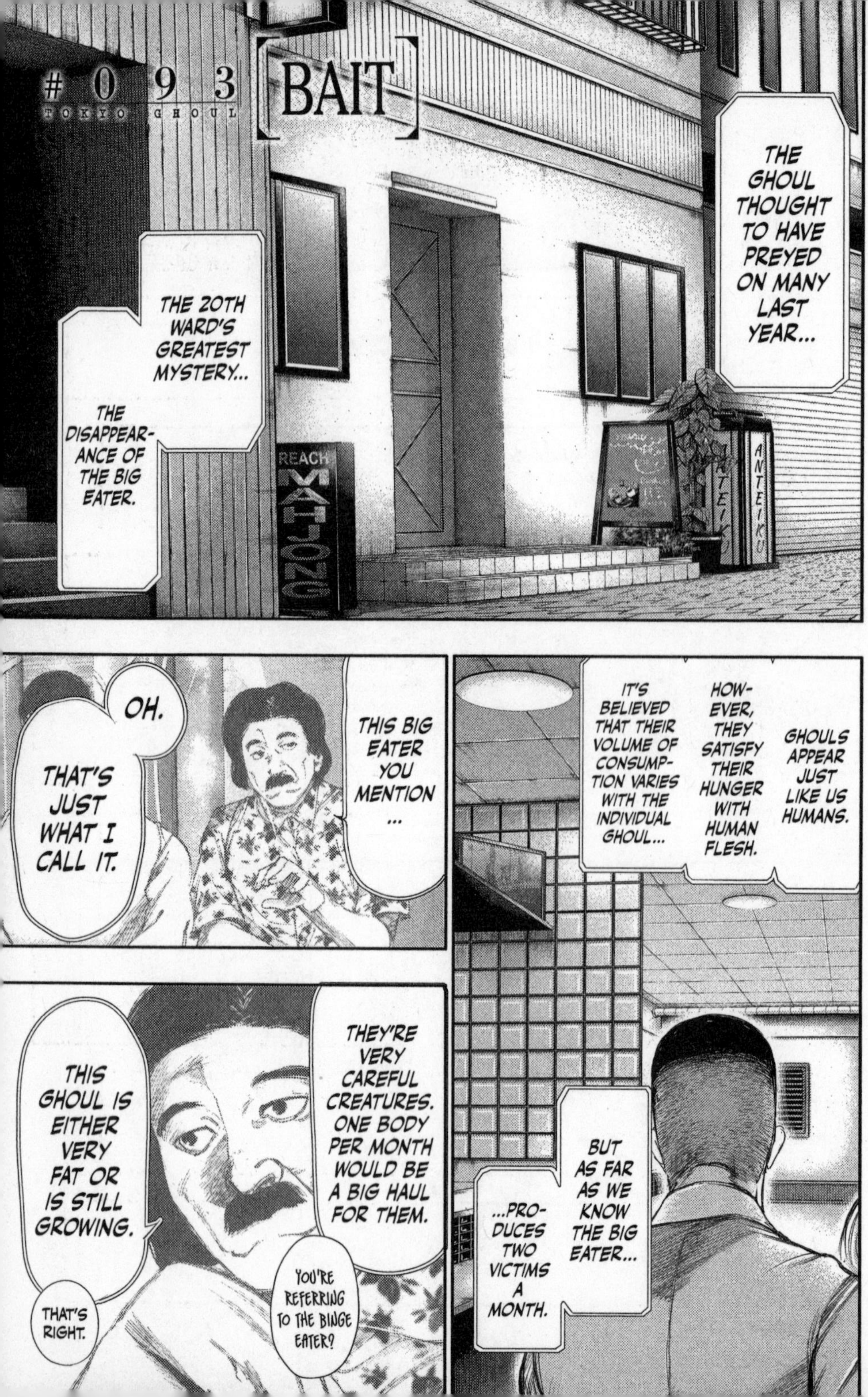

#093 [BAIT]
TOKYO GHOUL
THE GHOUL THOUGHT TO HAVE PREYED ON MANY LAST YEAR...
THE 20TH WARD'S GREATEST MYSTERY...
THE DISAPPEARANCE OF THE BIG EATER.
REACH MAHJONG
ANTEIKU
GHOULS APPEAR JUST LIKE US HUMANS.
HOWEVER, THEY SATISFY THEIR HUNGER WITH HUMAN FLESH.
IT'S BELIEVED THAT THEIR VOLUME OF CONSUMPTION VARIES WITH THE INDIVIDUAL GHOUL...
BUT AS FAR AS WE KNOW THE BIG EATER...
...PRODUCES TWO VICTIMS A MONTH.
THIS BIG EATER YOU MENTION...
OH.
THAT'S JUST WHAT I CALL IT.
THEY'RE VERY CAREFUL CREATURES. ONE BODY PER MONTH WOULD BE A BIG HAUL FOR THEM.
THIS GHOUL IS EITHER VERY FAT OR IS STILL GROWING.
YOU'RE REFERRING TO THE BINGE EATER?
THAT'S RIGHT.

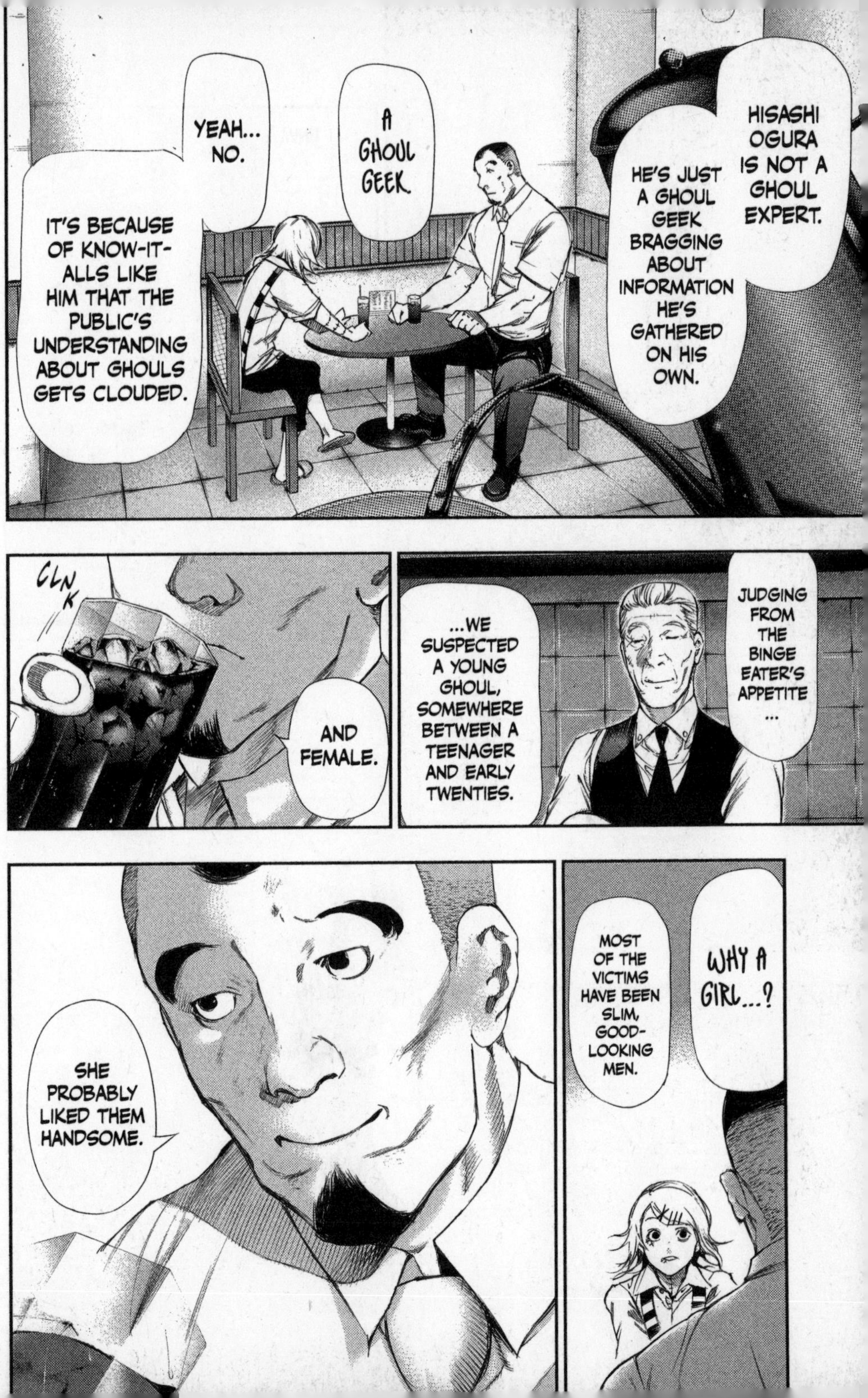
HISASHI OGURA IS NOT A GHOUL EXPERT.
HE'S JUST A GHOUL GEEK BRAGGING ABOUT INFORMATION HE'S GATHERED ON HIS OWN.
A GHOUL GEEK.
YEAH... NO.
IT'S BECAUSE OF KNOW-IT-ALLS LIKE HIM THAT THE PUBLIC'S UNDERSTANDING ABOUT GHOULS GETS CLOUDED.
JUDGING FROM THE BINGE EATER'S APPETITE ...
...WE SUSPECTED A YOUNG GHOUL, SOMEWHERE BETWEEN A TEENAGER AND EARLY TWENTIES.
AND FEMALE.
CLNK
WHY A GIRL...?
MOST OF THE VICTIMS HAVE BEEN SLIM, GOOD-LOOKING MEN.
SHE PROBABLY LIKED THEM HANDSOME.

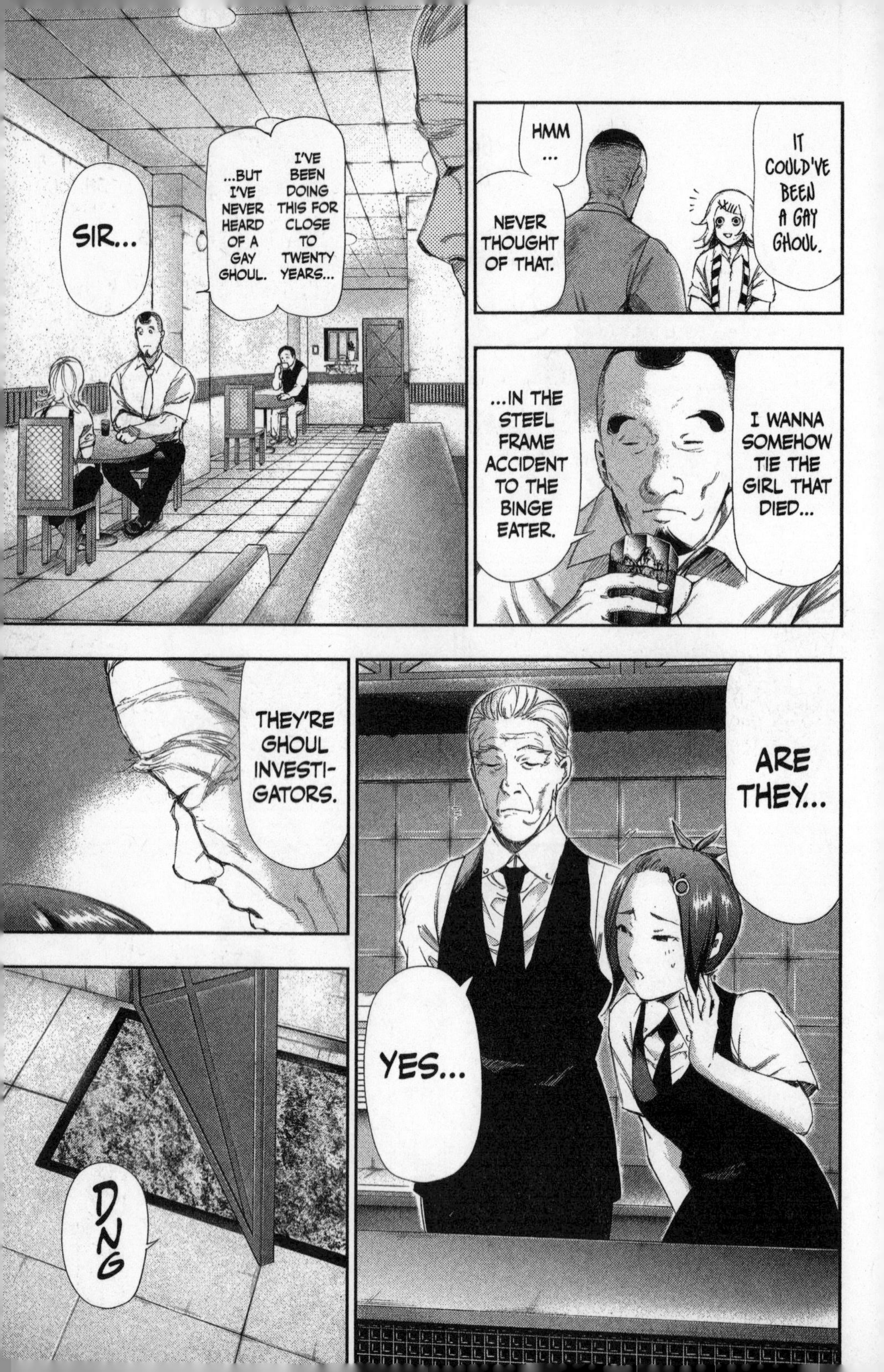
IT COULD'VE BEEN A GAY GHOUL.
HMM...
NEVER THOUGHT OF THAT.
I WANNA SOMEHOW TIE THE GIRL THAT DIED...
...IN THE STEEL FRAME ACCIDENT TO THE BINGE EATER.
I'VE BEEN DOING THIS FOR CLOSE TO TWENTY YEARS...
...BUT I'VE NEVER HEARD OF A GAY GHOUL.
SIR...
ARE THEY...
YES...
THEY'RE GHOUL INVESTI-GATORS.
DNG

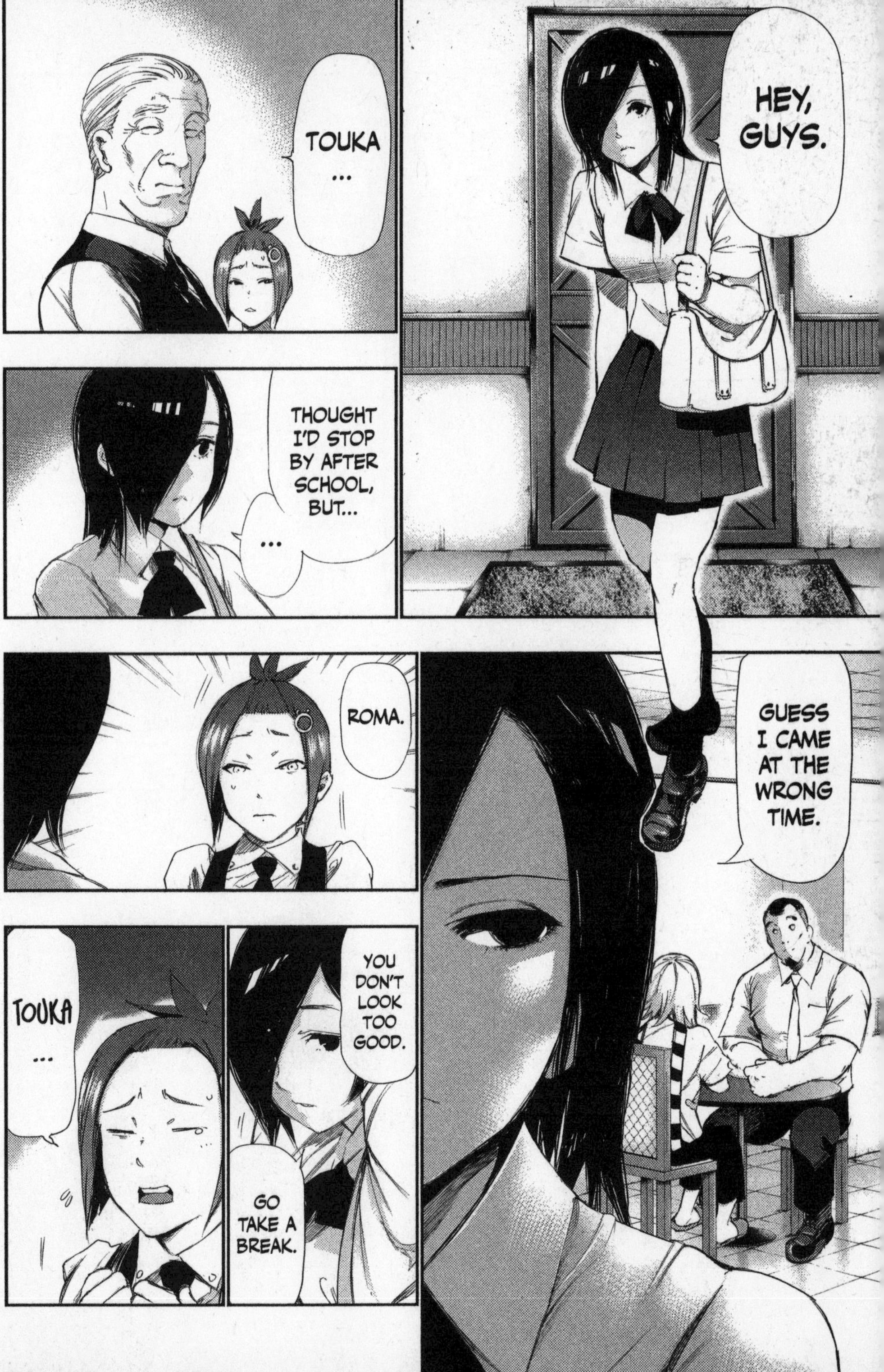
HEY, GUYS.
TOUKA ...
THOUGHT I'D STOP BY AFTER SCHOOL, BUT...
...
GUESS I CAME AT THE WRONG TIME.
ROMA.
YOU DON'T LOOK TOO GOOD.
GO TAKE A BREAK.
TOUKA ...

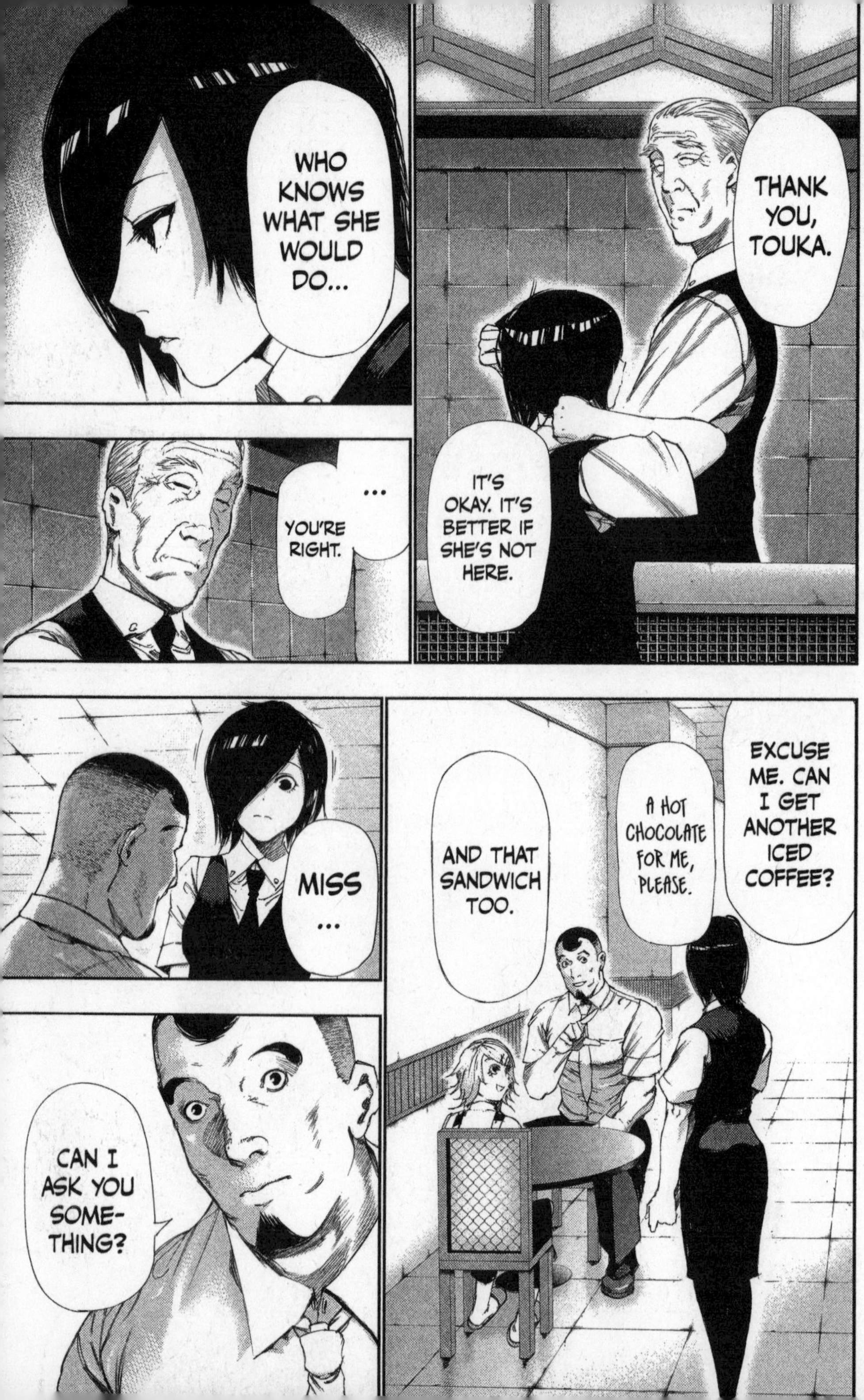
THANK YOU, TOUKA.
IT'S OKAY. IT'S BETTER IF SHE'S NOT HERE.
WHO KNOWS WHAT SHE WOULD DO...
...
YOU'RE RIGHT.
EXCUSE ME. CAN I GET ANOTHER ICED COFFEE?
A HOT CHOCOLATE FOR ME, PLEASE.
AND THAT SANDWICH TOO.
MISS ...
CAN I ASK YOU SOME-THING?

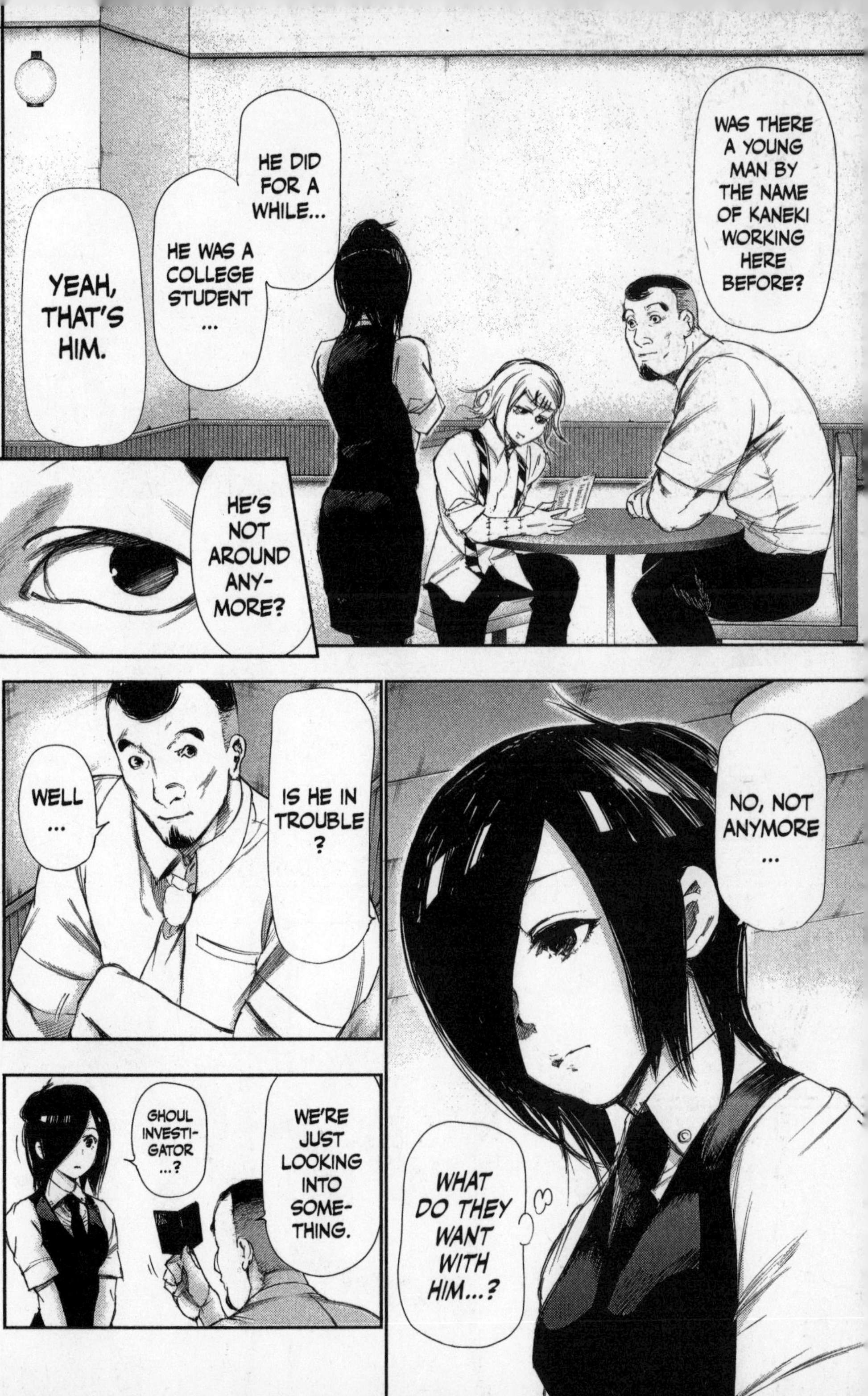
WAS THERE A YOUNG MAN BY THE NAME OF KANEKI WORKING HERE BEFORE?
HE DID FOR A WHILE...
HE WAS A COLLEGE STUDENT ...
YEAH, THAT'S HIM.
HE'S NOT AROUND ANY-MORE?
NO, NOT ANYMORE ...
WHAT DO THEY WANT WITH HIM...?
IS HE IN TROUBLE ?
WELL ...
WE'RE JUST LOOKING INTO SOME-THING.
GHOUL INVESTI-GATOR ...?

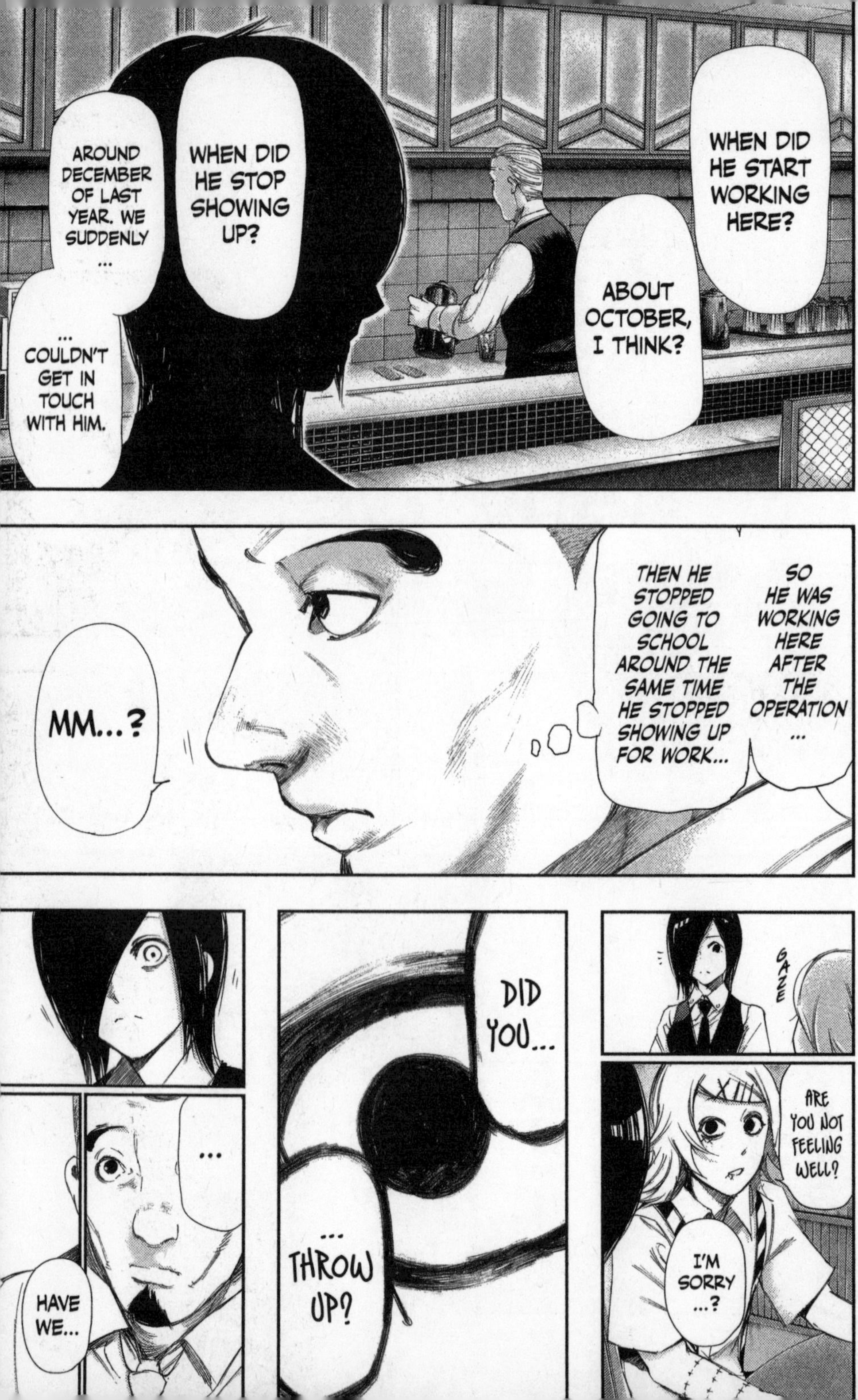
WHEN DID HE START WORKING HERE?
ABOUT OCTOBER, I THINK?
WHEN DID HE STOP SHOWING UP?
AROUND DECEMBER OF LAST YEAR. WE SUDDENLY ...
... COULDN'T GET IN TOUCH WITH HIM.
SO HE WAS WORKING HERE AFTER THE OPERATION ...
THEN HE STOPPED GOING TO SCHOOL AROUND THE SAME TIME HE STOPPED SHOWING UP FOR WORK...
MM...?
GAZE
ARE YOU NOT FEELING WELL?
I'M SORRY ...?
DID YOU...
... THROW UP?
...
HAVE WE...

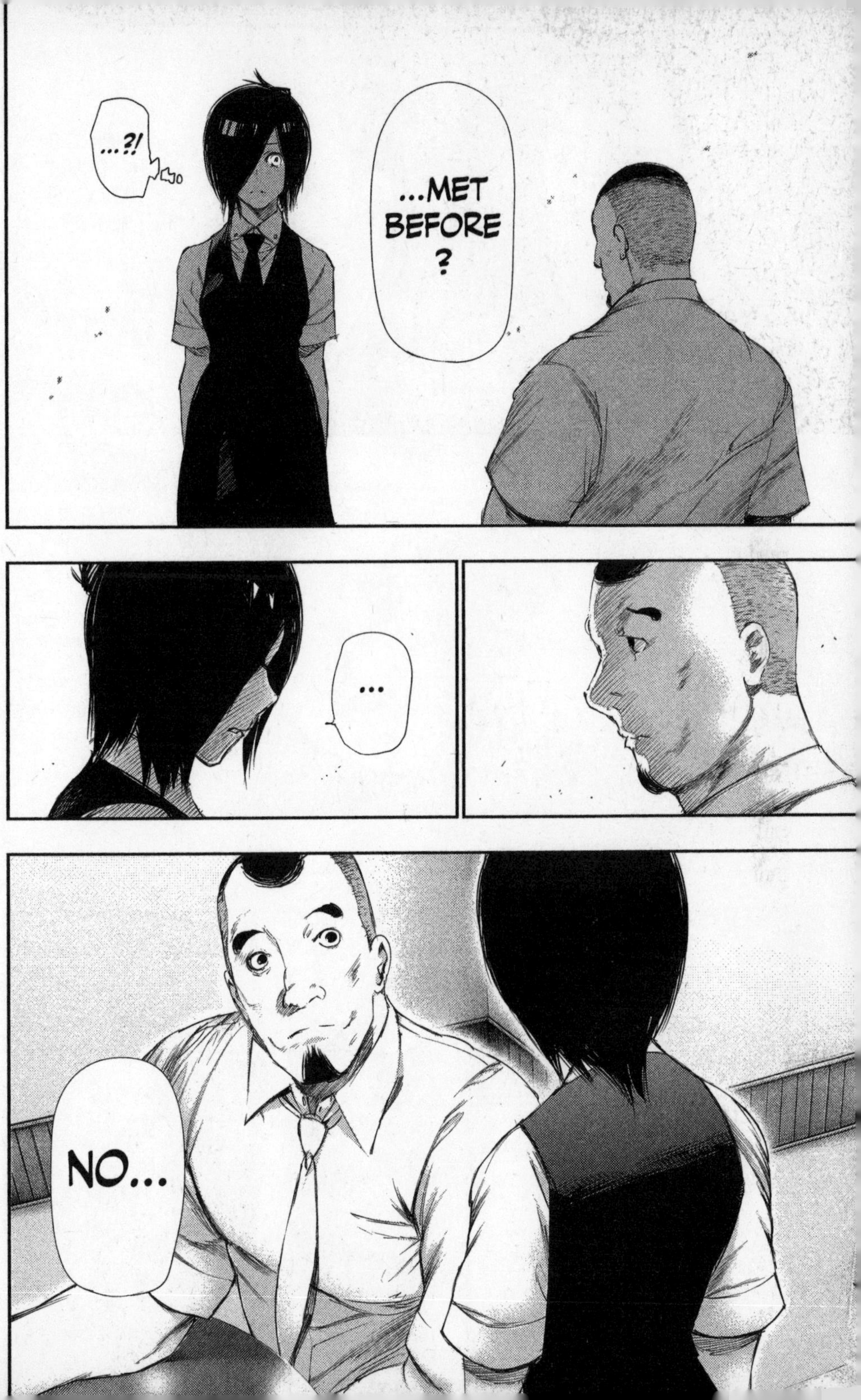
...MET BEFORE?
...?!
...
NO...

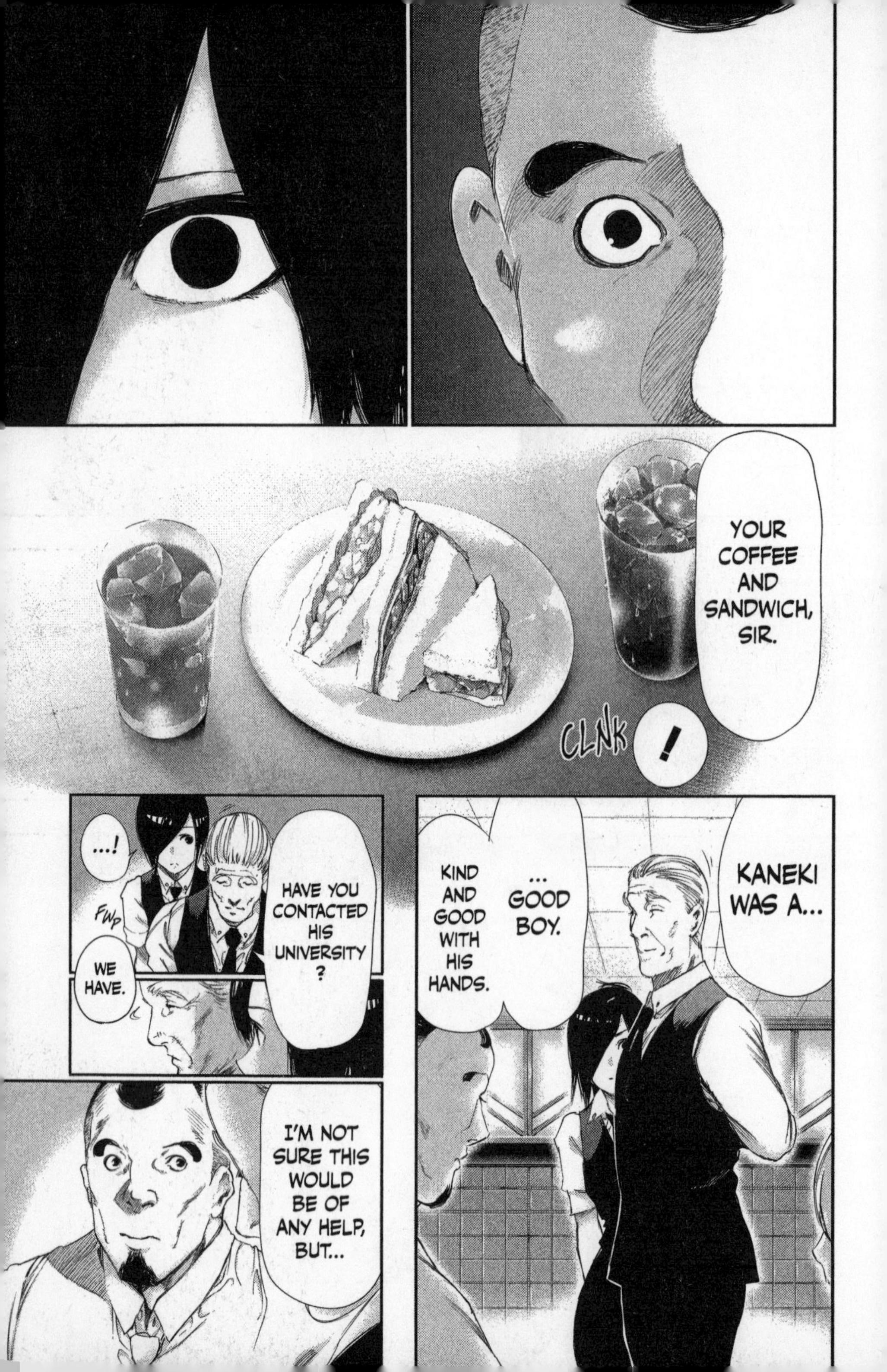
YOUR COFFEE AND SANDWICH, SIR.
!
CLNK
KANEKI WAS A...
... GOOD BOY.
KIND AND GOOD WITH HIS HANDS.
HAVE YOU CONTACTED HIS UNIVERSITY?
...!
FWP
WE HAVE.
I'M NOT SURE THIS WOULD BE OF ANY HELP, BUT...

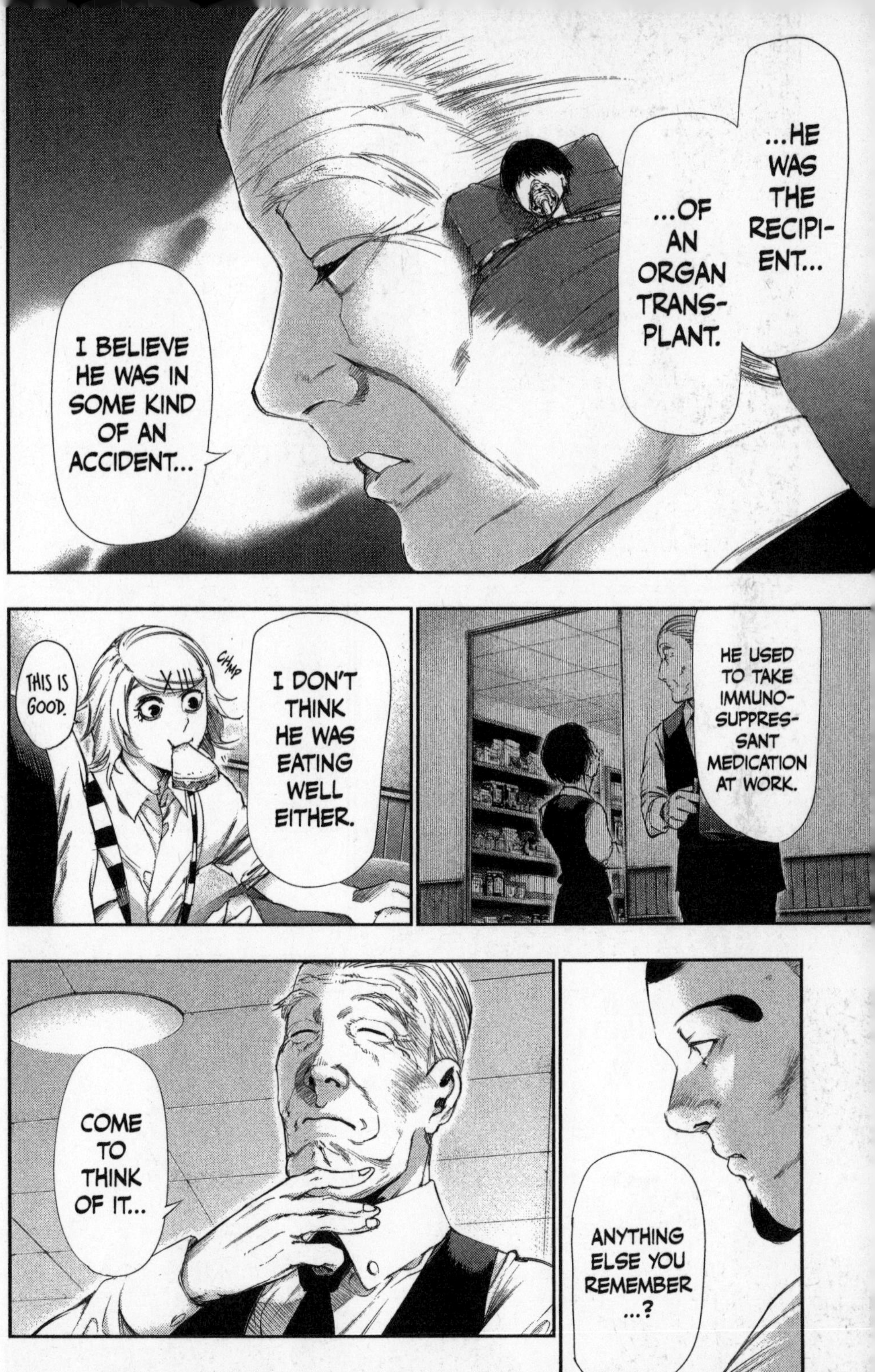
...HE WAS THE RECIPI- ENT...
...OF AN ORGAN TRANS- PLANT.
I BELIEVE HE WAS IN SOME KIND OF AN ACCIDENT...
HE USED TO TAKE IMMUNO- SUPPRES- SANT MEDICATION AT WORK.
I DON'T THINK HE WAS EATING WELL EITHER.
CHMP
THIS IS GOOD.
ANYTHING ELSE YOU REMEMBER ...?
COME TO THINK OF IT...

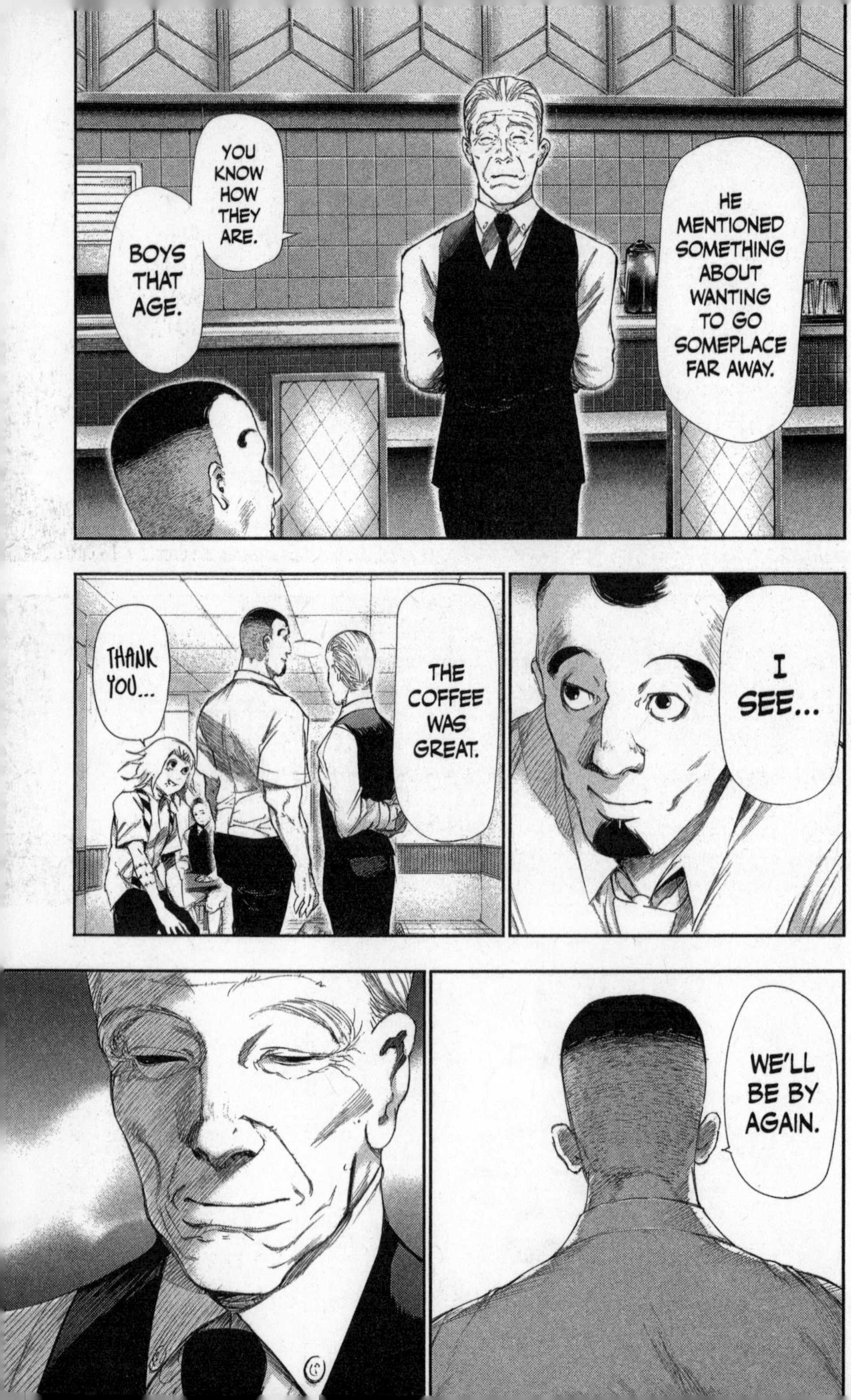
HE MENTIONED SOMETHING ABOUT WANTING TO GO SOMEPLACE FAR AWAY.
YOU KNOW HOW THEY ARE.
BOYS THAT AGE.
I SEE...
THE COFFEE WAS GREAT.
THANK YOU...
WE'LL BE BY AGAIN.

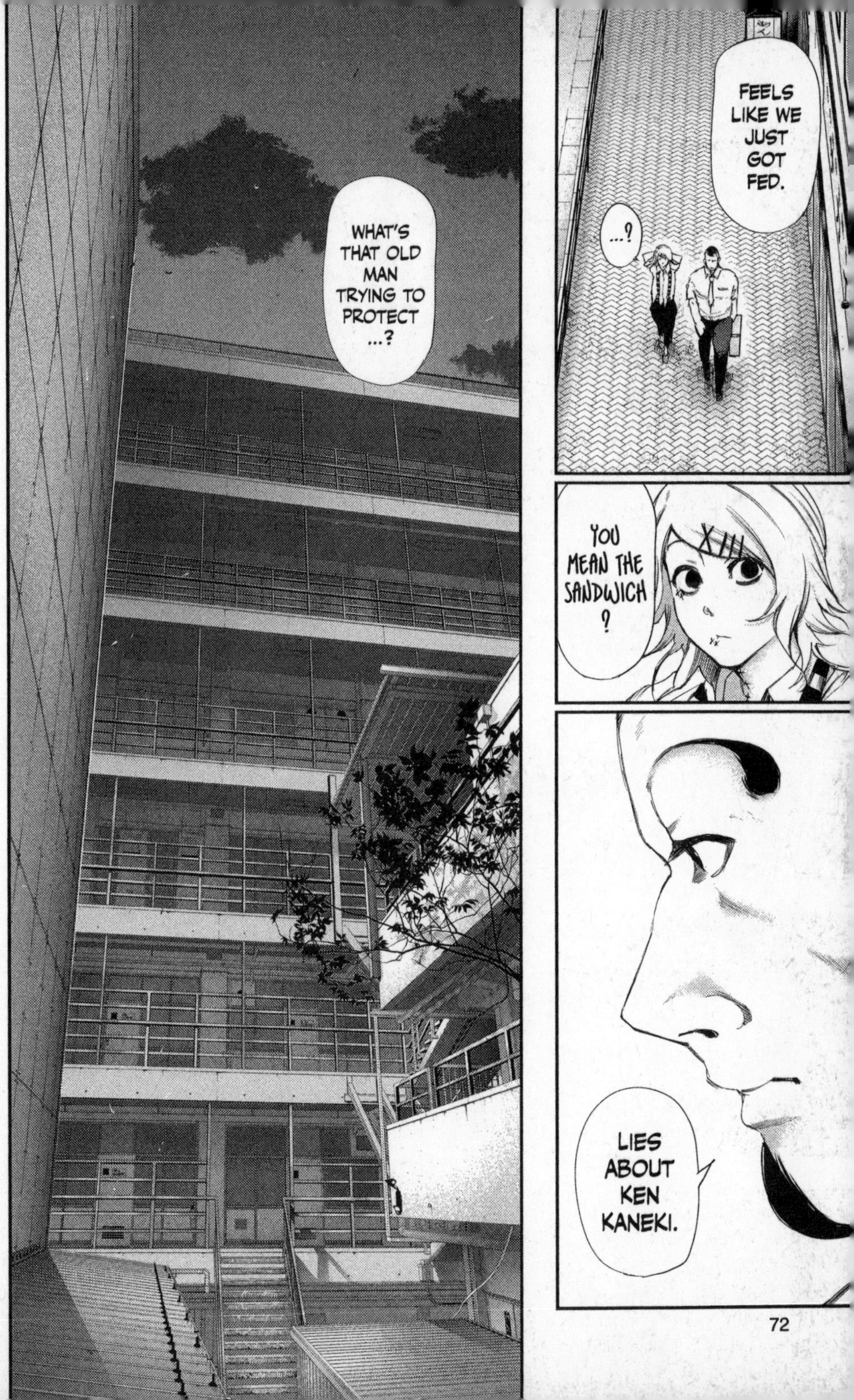
FEELS LIKE WE JUST GOT FED.
...?
YOU MEAN THE SANDWICH?
LIES ABOUT KEN KANEKI.
WHAT'S THAT OLD MAN TRYING TO PROTECT ...?

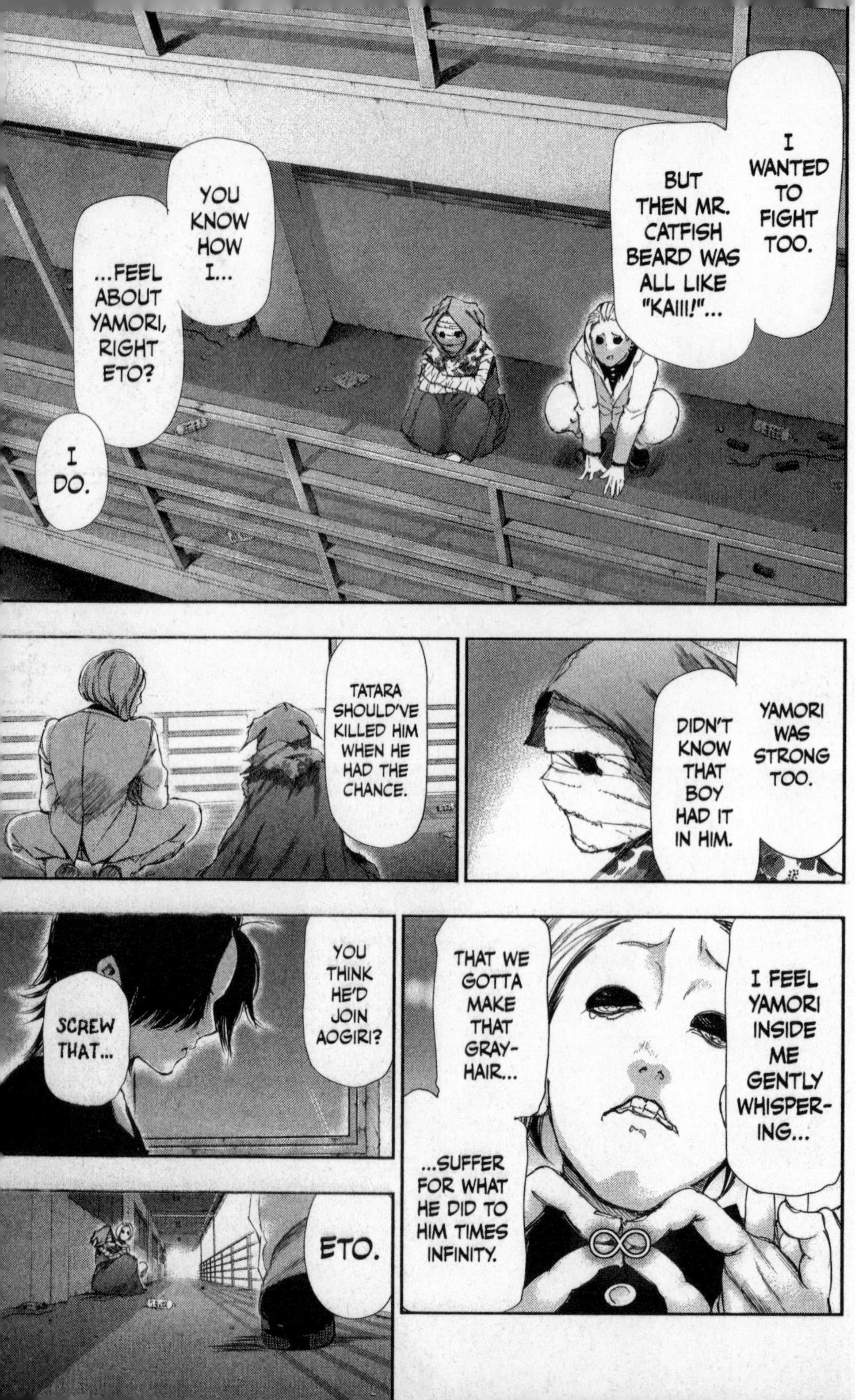
I WANTED TO FIGHT TOO.
BUT THEN MR. CATFISH BEARD WAS ALL LIKE "KAIII!"...
YOU KNOW HOW I...
...FEEL ABOUT YAMORI, RIGHT ETO?
I DO.
YAMORI WAS STRONG TOO.
DIDN'T KNOW THAT BOY HAD IT IN HIM.
TATARA SHOULD'VE KILLED HIM WHEN HE HAD THE CHANCE.
I FEEL YAMORI INSIDE ME GENTLY WHISPER-ING...
THAT WE GOTTA MAKE THAT GRAY-HAIR...
...SUFFER FOR WHAT HE DID TO HIM TIMES INFINITY.
YOU THINK HE'D JOIN AOGIRI?
SCREW THAT...
ETO.

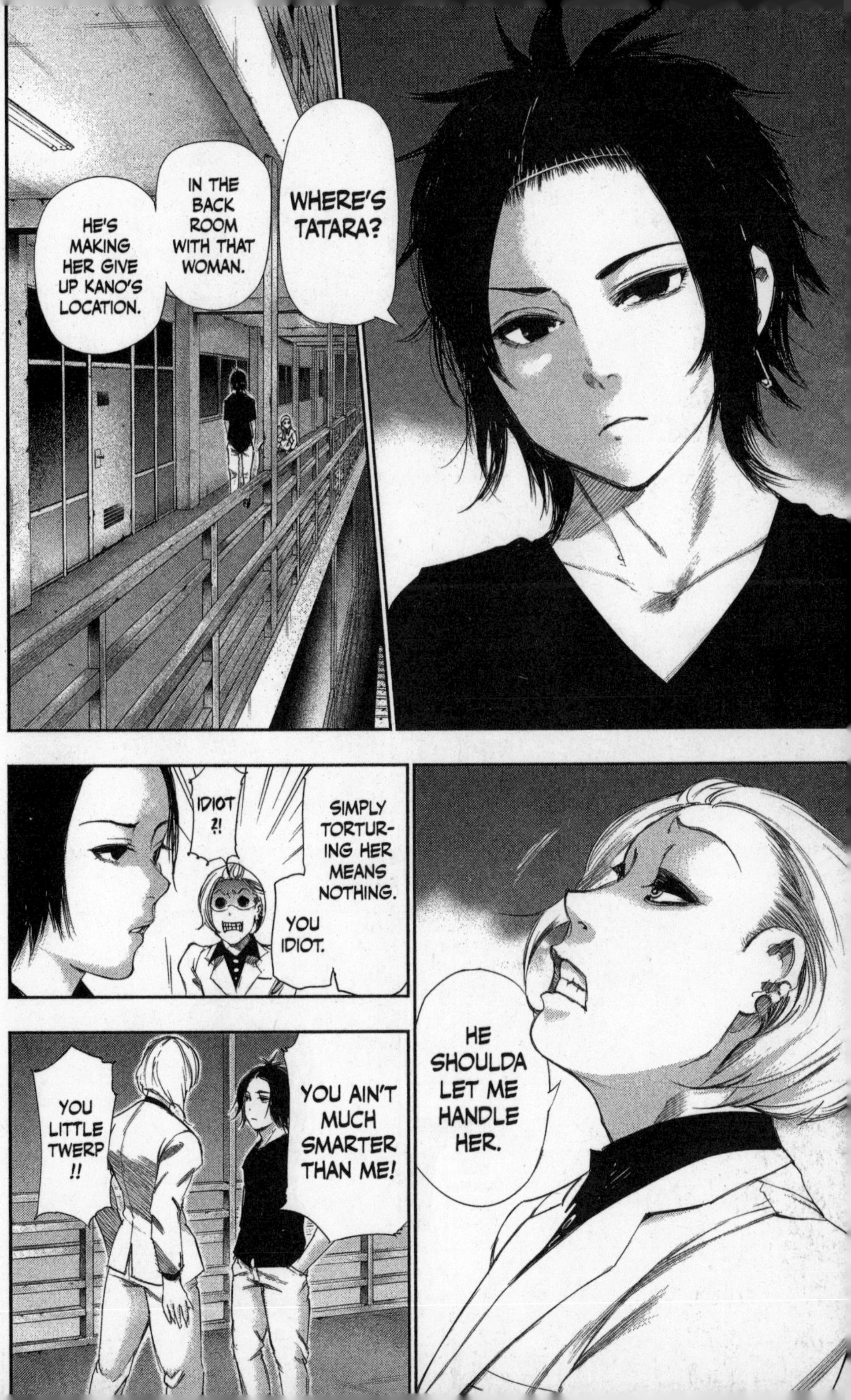
WHERE'S TATARA?
IN THE BACK ROOM WITH THAT WOMAN.
HE'S MAKING HER GIVE UP KANO'S LOCATION.
HE SHOULDA LET ME HANDLE HER.
SIMPLY TORTURING HER MEANS NOTHING.
YOU IDIOT.
IDIOT ?!
YOU AIN'T MUCH SMARTER THAN ME!
YOU LITTLE TWERP !!

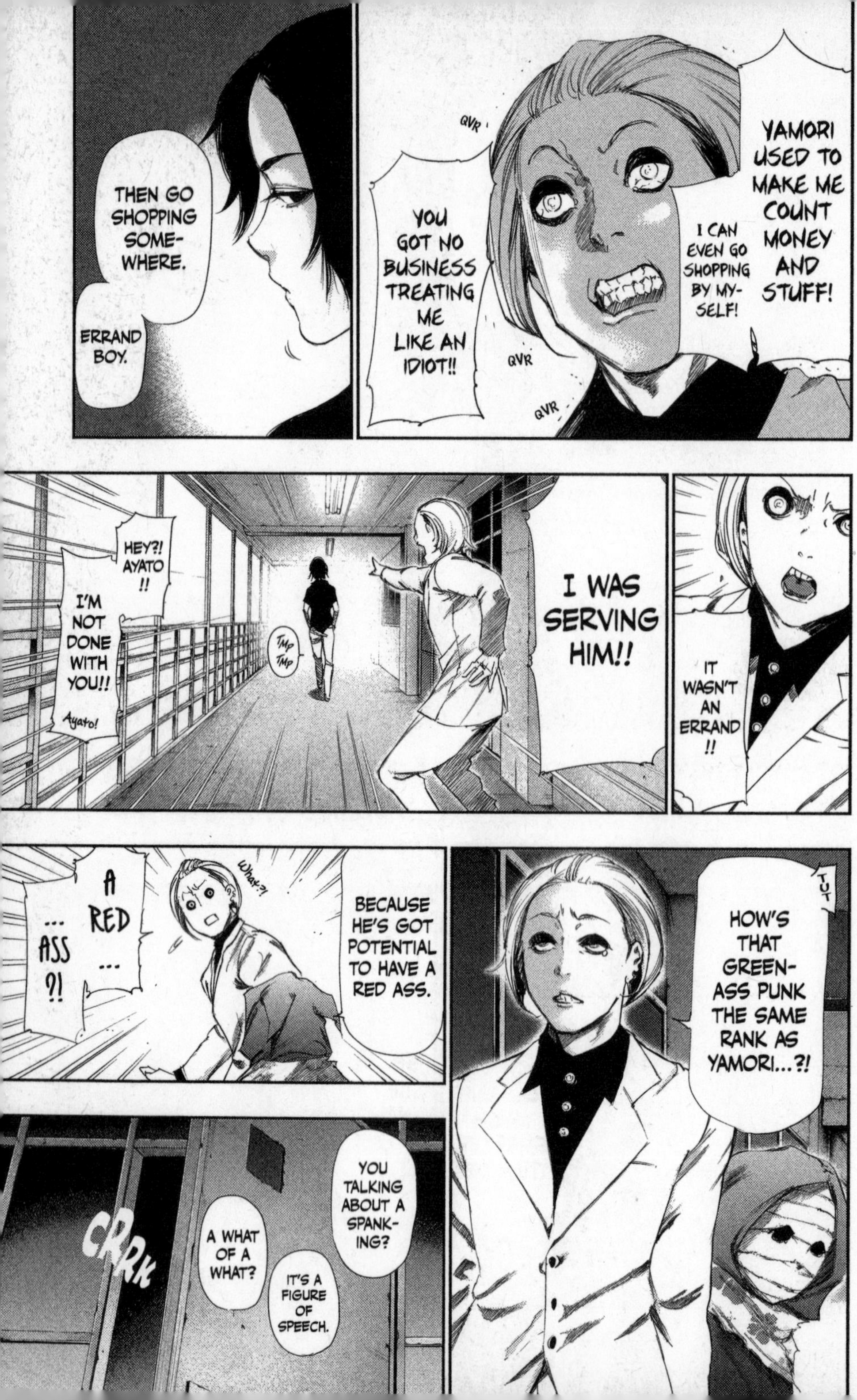
QVR
YAMORI USED TO MAKE ME COUNT MONEY AND STUFF!
I CAN EVEN GO SHOPPING BY MY-SELF!
YOU GOT NO BUSINESS TREATING ME LIKE AN IDIOT!!
QVR
QVR
THEN GO SHOPPING SOME-WHERE.
ERRAND BOY.
IT WASN'T AN ERRAND!!
I WAS SERVING HIM!!
HEY?! AYATO!!
I'M NOT DONE WITH YOU!!
Ayato!
TMP TMP
TUT
HOW'S THAT GREEN-ASS PUNK THE SAME RANK AS YAMORI...?!
BECAUSE HE'S GOT POTENTIAL TO HAVE A RED ASS.
What?!
A RED...
...ASS?!
YOU TALKING ABOUT A SPANK-ING?
A WHAT OF A WHAT?
IT'S A FIGURE OF SPEECH.
CRRK

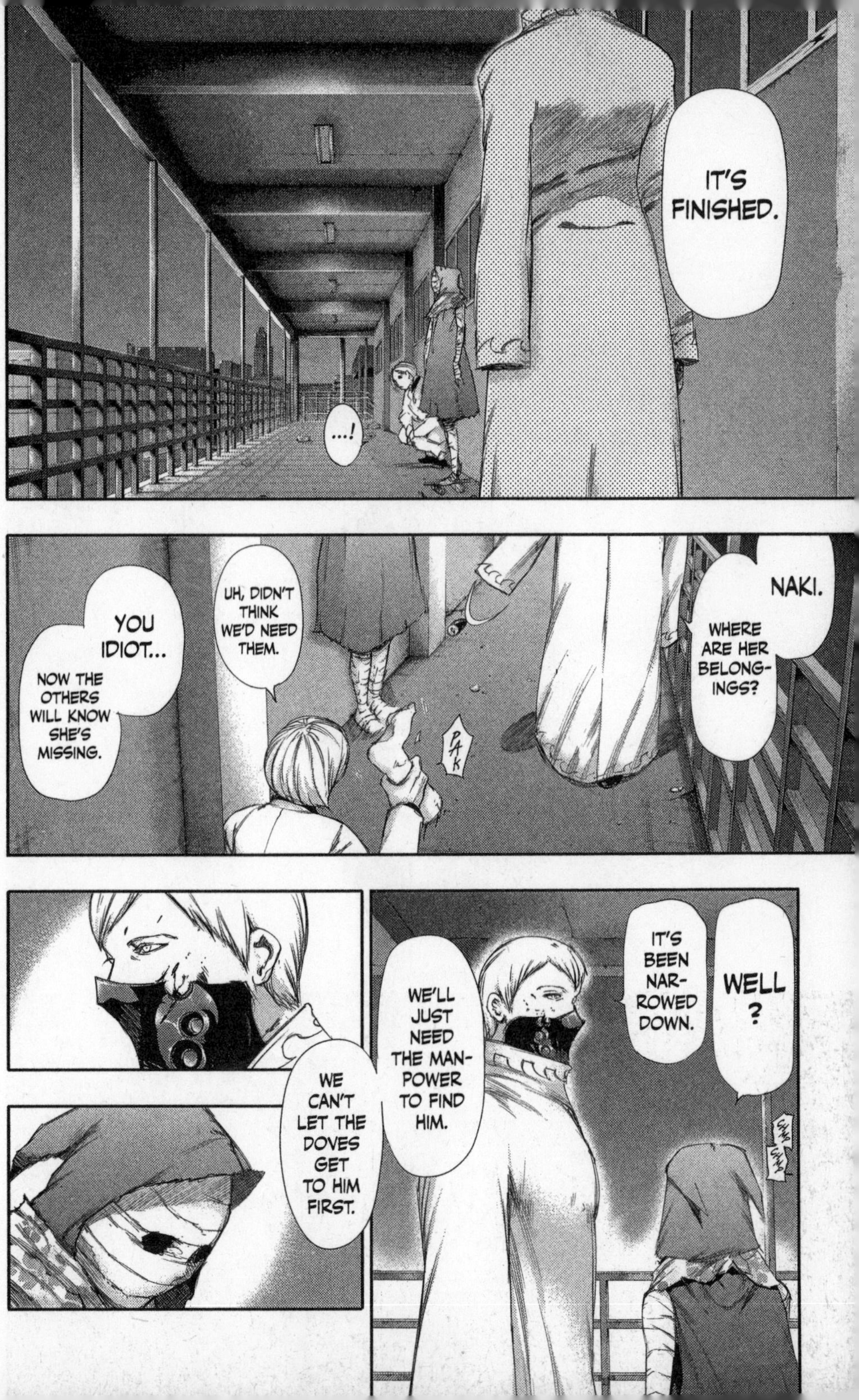
IT'S FINISHED.
...!
NAKI.
WHERE ARE HER BELONG-INGS?
PAK
UH, DIDN'T THINK WE'D NEED THEM.
YOU IDIOT...
NOW THE OTHERS WILL KNOW SHE'S MISSING.
WELL?
IT'S BEEN NAR-ROWED DOWN.
WE'LL JUST NEED THE MAN-POWER TO FIND HIM.
WE CAN'T LET THE DOVES GET TO HIM FIRST.

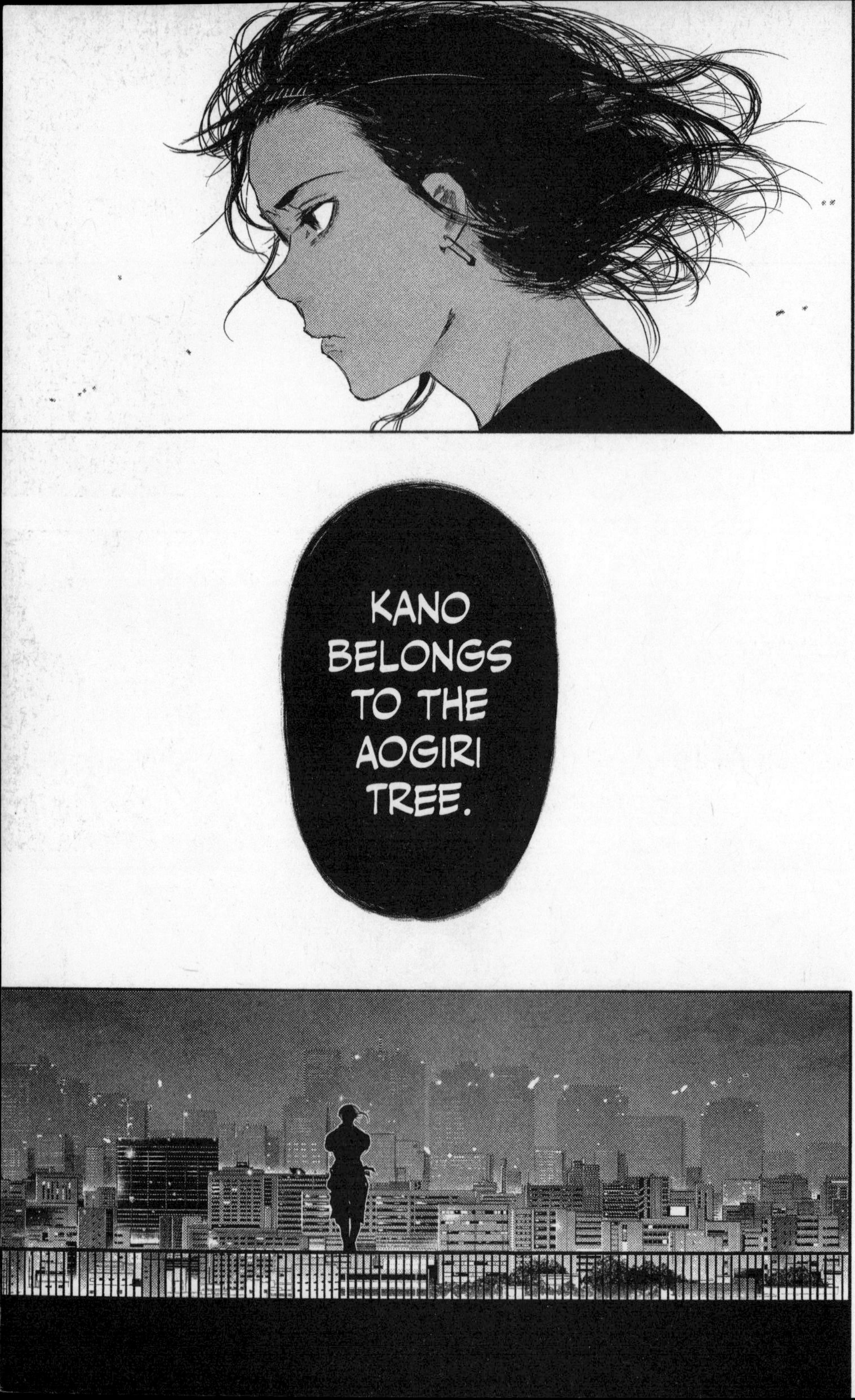
KANO BELONGS TO THE AOGIRI TREE.

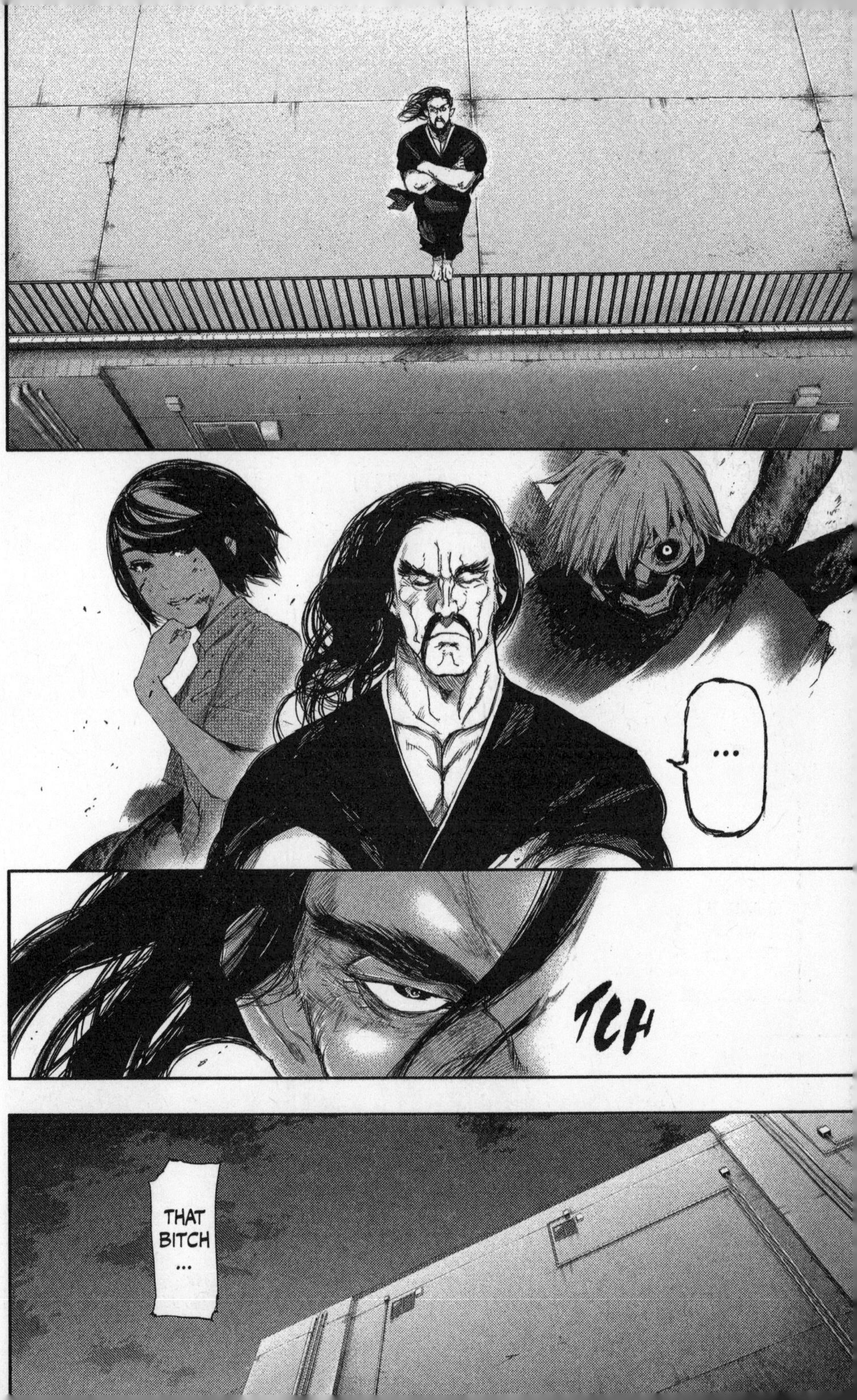
...
TCH
THAT BITCH ...

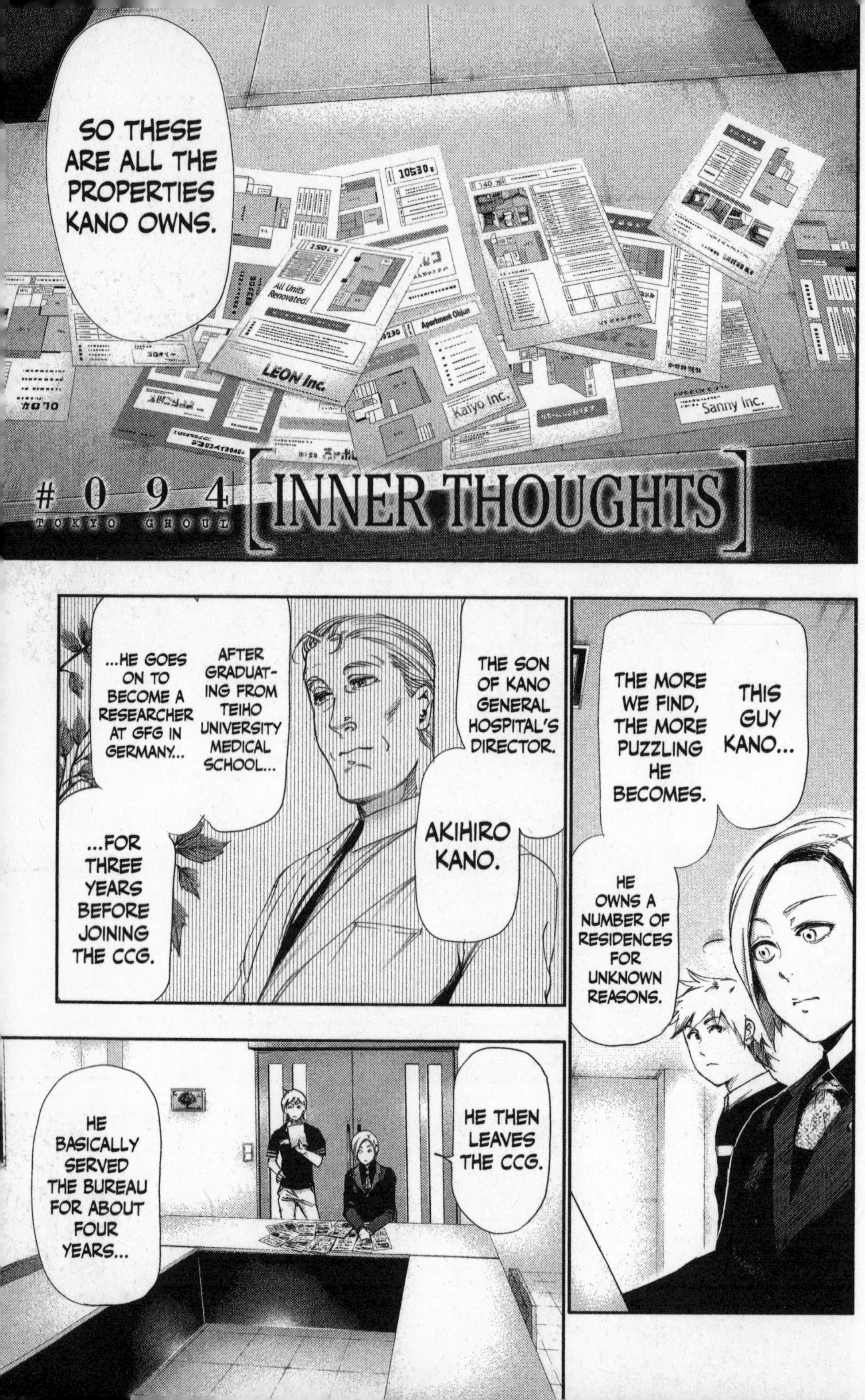
SO THESE ARE ALL THE PROPERTIES KANO OWNS.
All Units Renovated!
LEON Inc.
Kaiyo Inc.
Sanny Inc.
#094 INNER THOUGHTS
TOKYO GHOUL
THIS GUY KANO...
THE MORE WE FIND, THE MORE PUZZLING HE BECOMES.
HE OWNS A NUMBER OF RESIDENCES FOR UNKNOWN REASONS.
THE SON OF KANO GENERAL HOSPITAL'S DIRECTOR.
AKIHIRO KANO.
AFTER GRADUATING FROM TEIHO UNIVERSITY MEDICAL SCHOOL...
...HE GOES ON TO BECOME A RESEARCHER AT GFG IN GERMANY...
...FOR THREE YEARS BEFORE JOINING THE CCG.
HE THEN LEAVES THE CCG.
HE BASICALLY SERVED THE BUREAU FOR ABOUT FOUR YEARS...

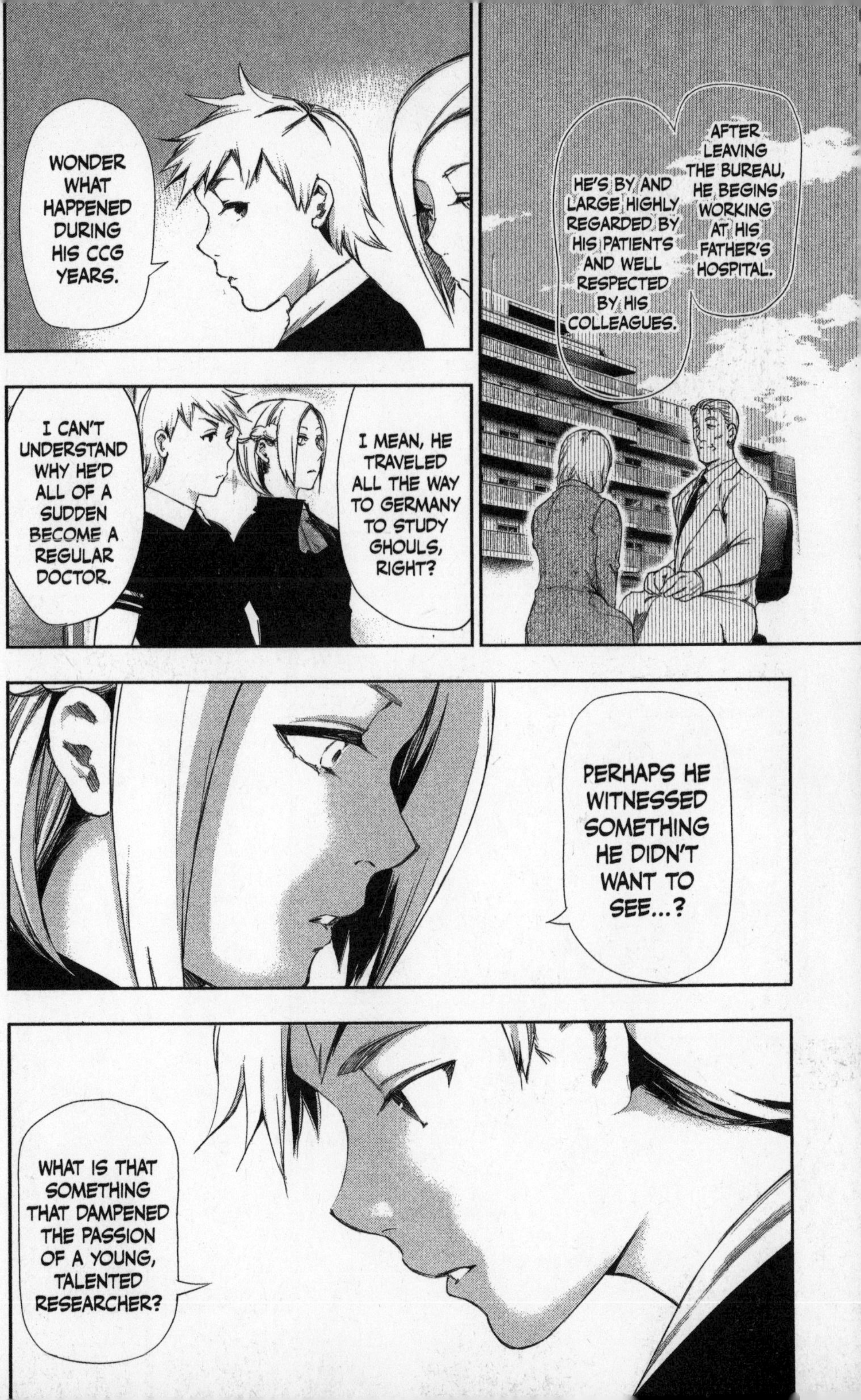
AFTER LEAVING THE BUREAU, HE BEGINS WORKING AT HIS FATHER'S HOSPITAL.
HE'S BY AND LARGE HIGHLY REGARDED BY HIS PATIENTS AND WELL RESPECTED BY HIS COLLEAGUES.
WONDER WHAT HAPPENED DURING HIS CCG YEARS.
I MEAN, HE TRAVELED ALL THE WAY TO GERMANY TO STUDY GHOULS, RIGHT?
I CAN'T UNDERSTAND WHY HE'D ALL OF A SUDDEN BECOME A REGULAR DOCTOR.
PERHAPS HE WITNESSED SOMETHING HE DIDN'T WANT TO SEE...?
WHAT IS THAT SOMETHING THAT DAMPENED THE PASSION OF A YOUNG, TALENTED RESEARCHER?

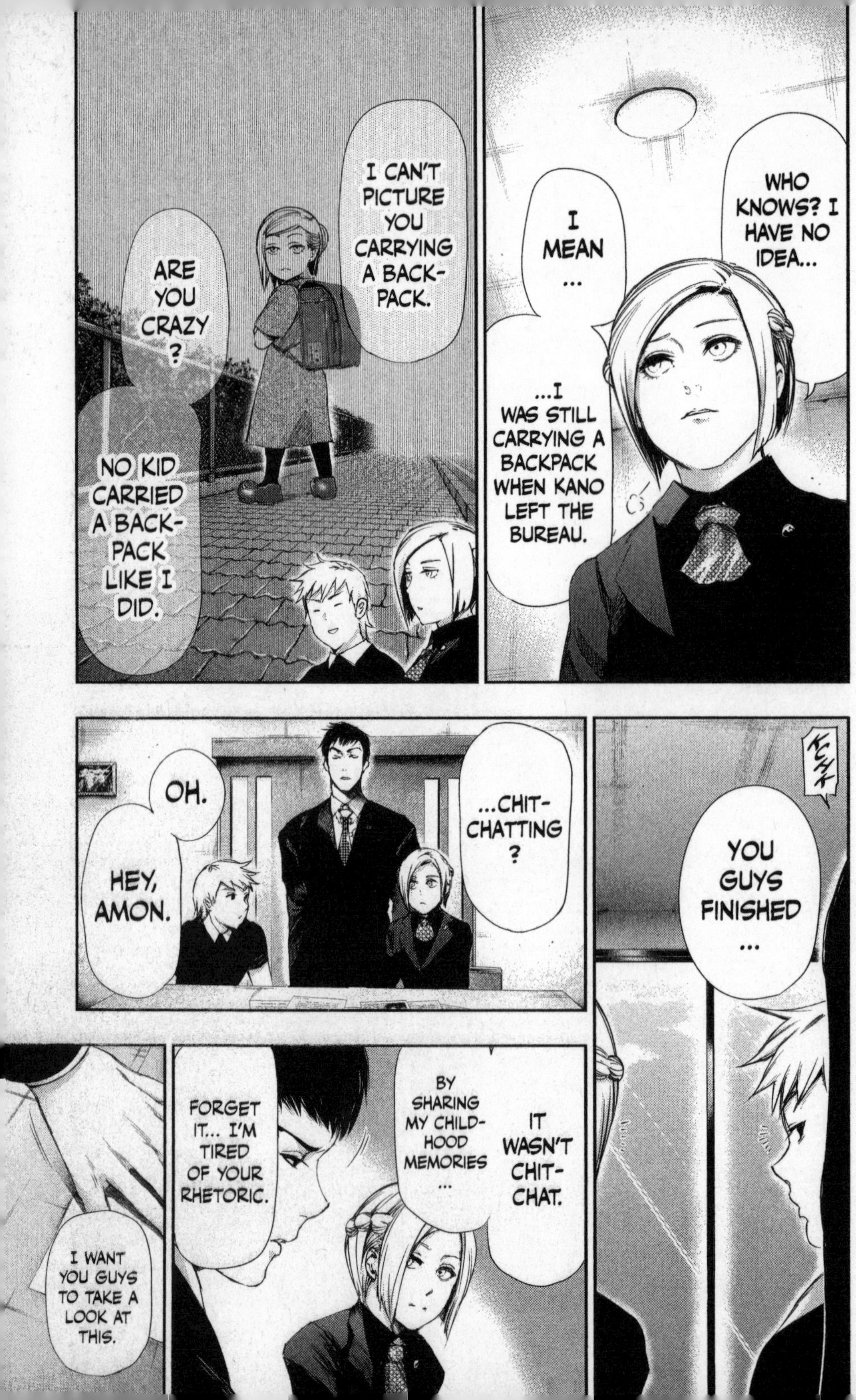
WHO KNOWS? I HAVE NO IDEA...
I MEAN...
...I WAS STILL CARRYING A BACKPACK WHEN KANO LEFT THE BUREAU.
I CAN'T PICTURE YOU CARRYING A BACK-PACK.
ARE YOU CRAZY?
NO KID CARRIED A BACK-PACK LIKE I DID.
KCHK
YOU GUYS FINISHED...
...CHIT-CHATTING?
OH.
HEY, AMON.
IT WASN'T CHIT-CHAT.
BY SHARING MY CHILD-HOOD MEMORIES...
FORGET IT... I'M TIRED OF YOUR RHETORIC.
I WANT YOU GUYS TO TAKE A LOOK AT THIS.

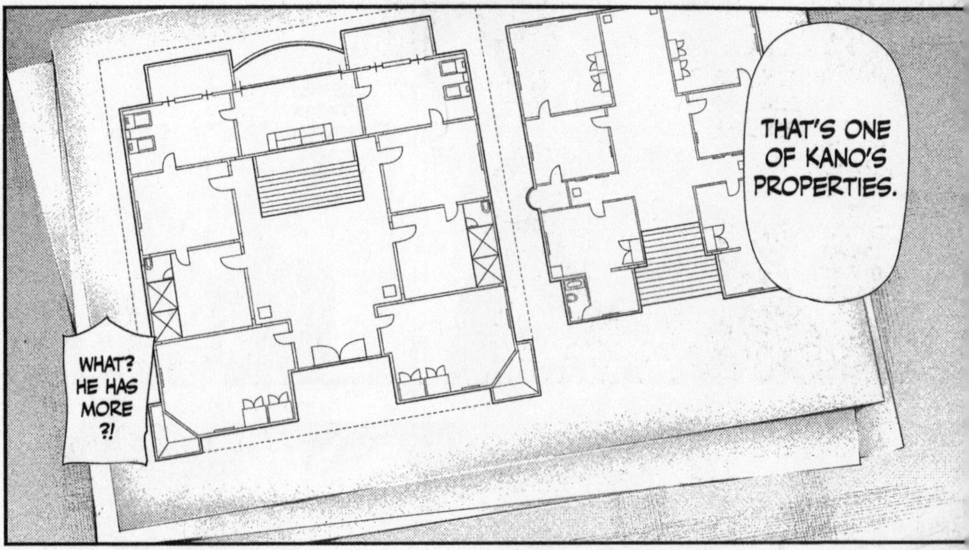
THAT'S ONE OF KANO'S PROPERTIES.
WHAT? HE HAS MORE ?!
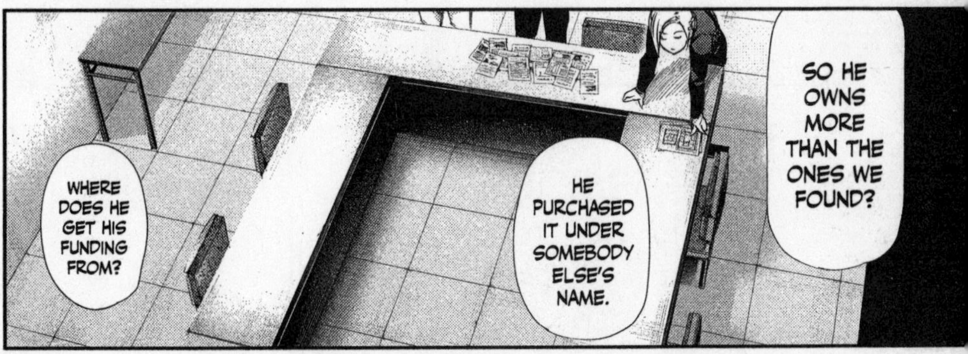
SO HE OWNS MORE THAN THE ONES WE FOUND?
HE PURCHASED IT UNDER SOMEBODY ELSE'S NAME.
WHERE DOES HE GET HIS FUNDING FROM?
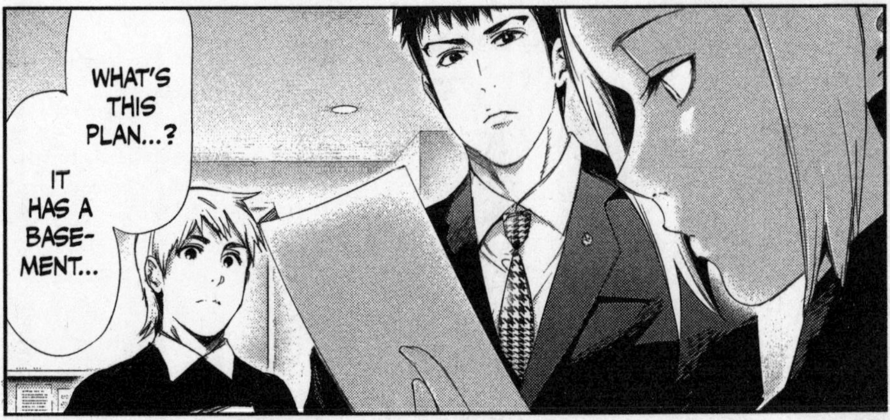
WHAT'S THIS PLAN...?
IT HAS A BASEMENT...

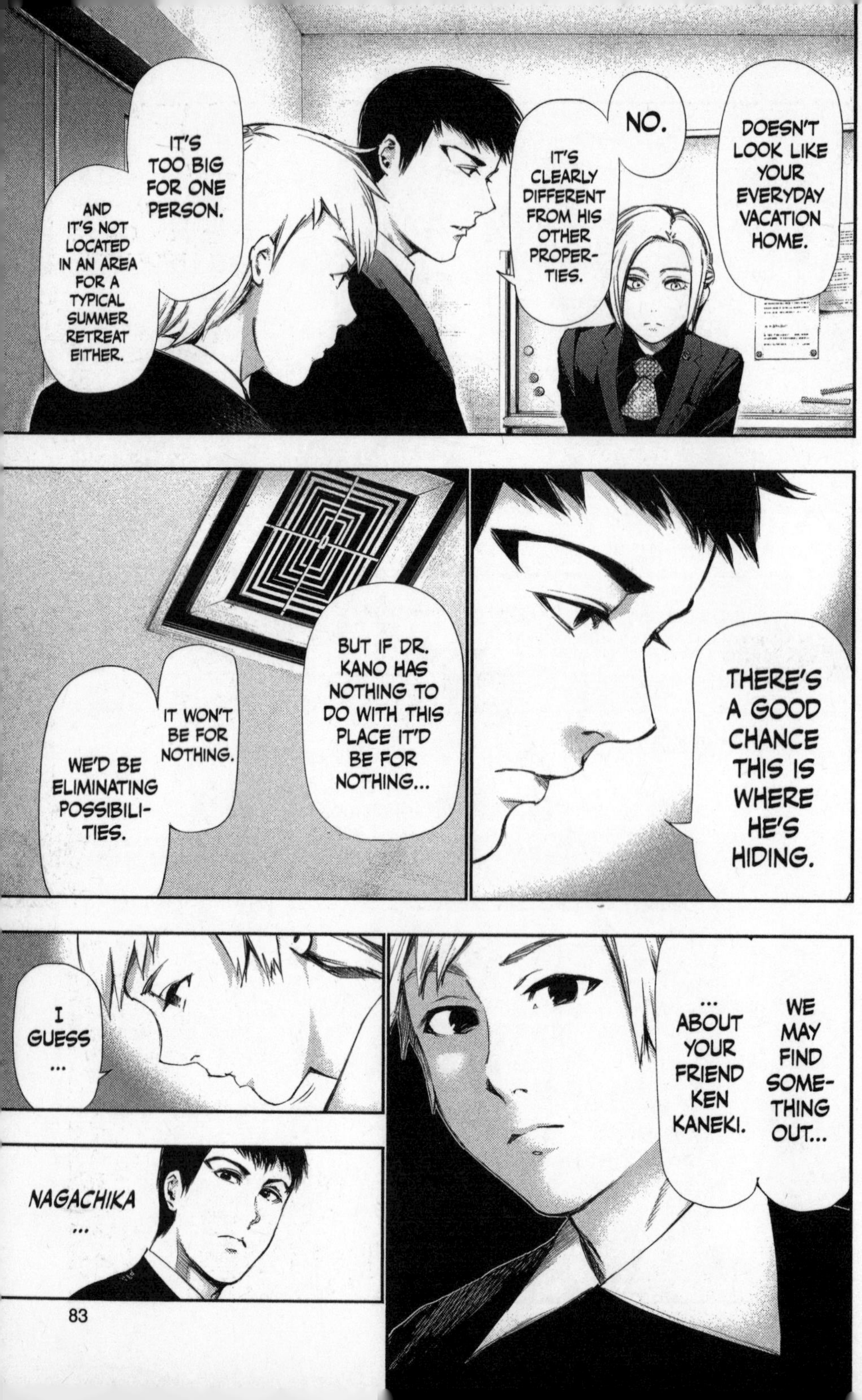
DOESN'T LOOK LIKE YOUR EVERYDAY VACATION HOME.
NO.
IT'S CLEARLY DIFFERENT FROM HIS OTHER PROPER-TIES.
IT'S TOO BIG FOR ONE PERSON.
AND IT'S NOT LOCATED IN AN AREA FOR A TYPICAL SUMMER RETREAT EITHER.
THERE'S A GOOD CHANCE THIS IS WHERE HE'S HIDING.
BUT IF DR. KANO HAS NOTHING TO DO WITH THIS PLACE IT'D BE FOR NOTHING...
IT WON'T BE FOR NOTHING.
WE'D BE ELIMINATING POSSIBILI-TIES.
WE MAY FIND SOME-THING OUT...
...ABOUT YOUR FRIEND KEN KANEKI.
I GUESS...
NAGACHIKA...

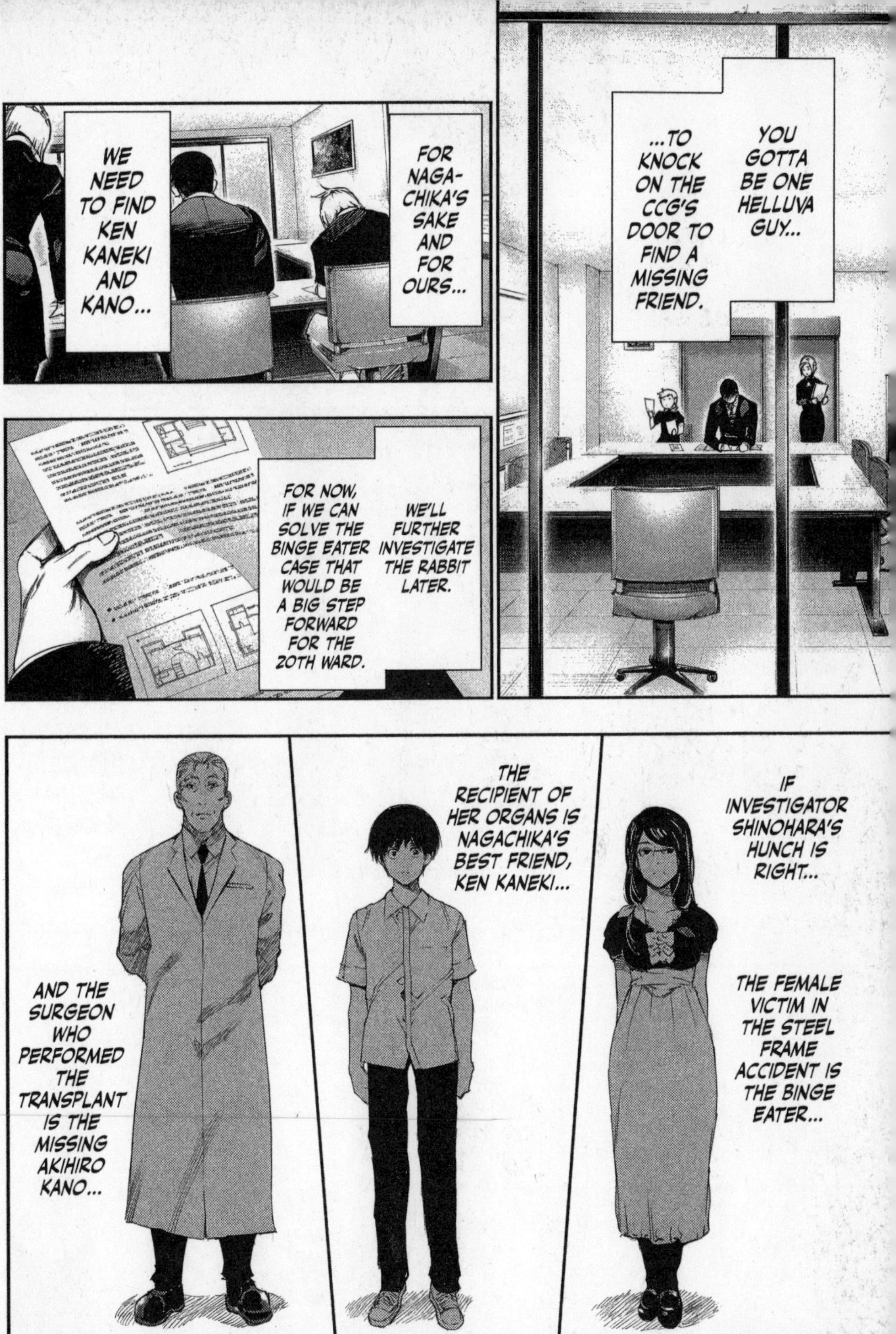
YOU GOTTA BE ONE HELLUVA GUY...
...TO KNOCK ON THE CCG'S DOOR TO FIND A MISSING FRIEND.
FOR NAGACHIKA'S SAKE AND FOR OURS...
WE NEED TO FIND KEN KANEKI AND KANO...
WE'LL FURTHER INVESTIGATE THE RABBIT LATER.
FOR NOW, IF WE CAN SOLVE THE BINGE EATER CASE THAT WOULD BE A BIG STEP FORWARD FOR THE 20TH WARD.
IF INVESTIGATOR SHINOHARA'S HUNCH IS RIGHT...
THE FEMALE VICTIM IN THE STEEL FRAME ACCIDENT IS THE BINGE EATER...
THE RECIPIENT OF HER ORGANS IS NAGACHIKA'S BEST FRIEND, KEN KANEKI...
AND THE SURGEON WHO PERFORMED THE TRANSPLANT IS THE MISSING AKIHIRO KANO...

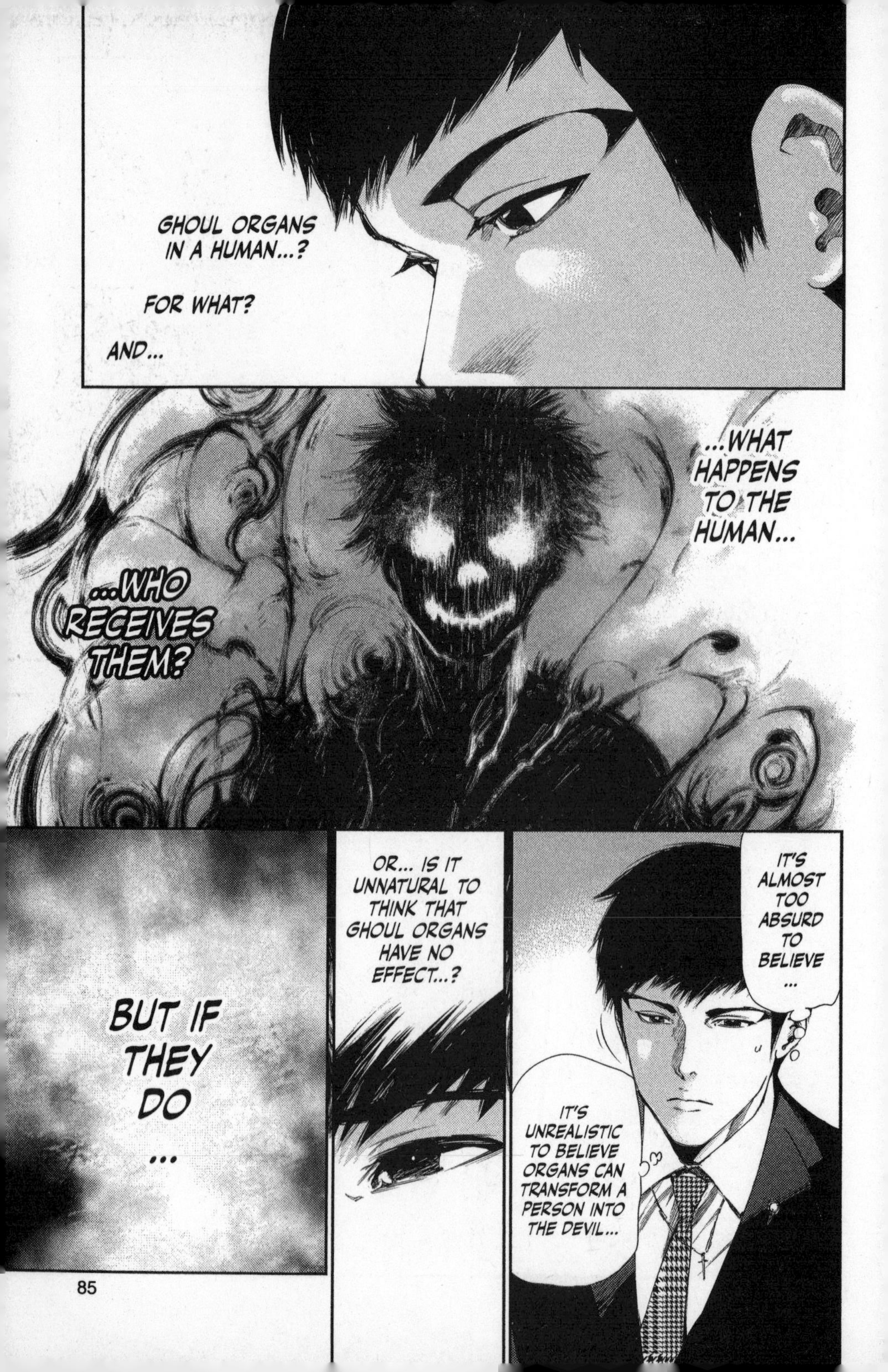
GHOUL ORGANS IN A HUMAN...?
FOR WHAT?
AND...
...WHAT HAPPENS TO THE HUMAN...
...WHO RECEIVES THEM?
IT'S ALMOST TOO ABSURD TO BELIEVE...
IT'S UNREALISTIC TO BELIEVE ORGANS CAN TRANSFORM A PERSON INTO THE DEVIL...
OR... IS IT UNNATURAL TO THINK THAT GHOUL ORGANS HAVE NO EFFECT...?
BUT IF THEY DO...

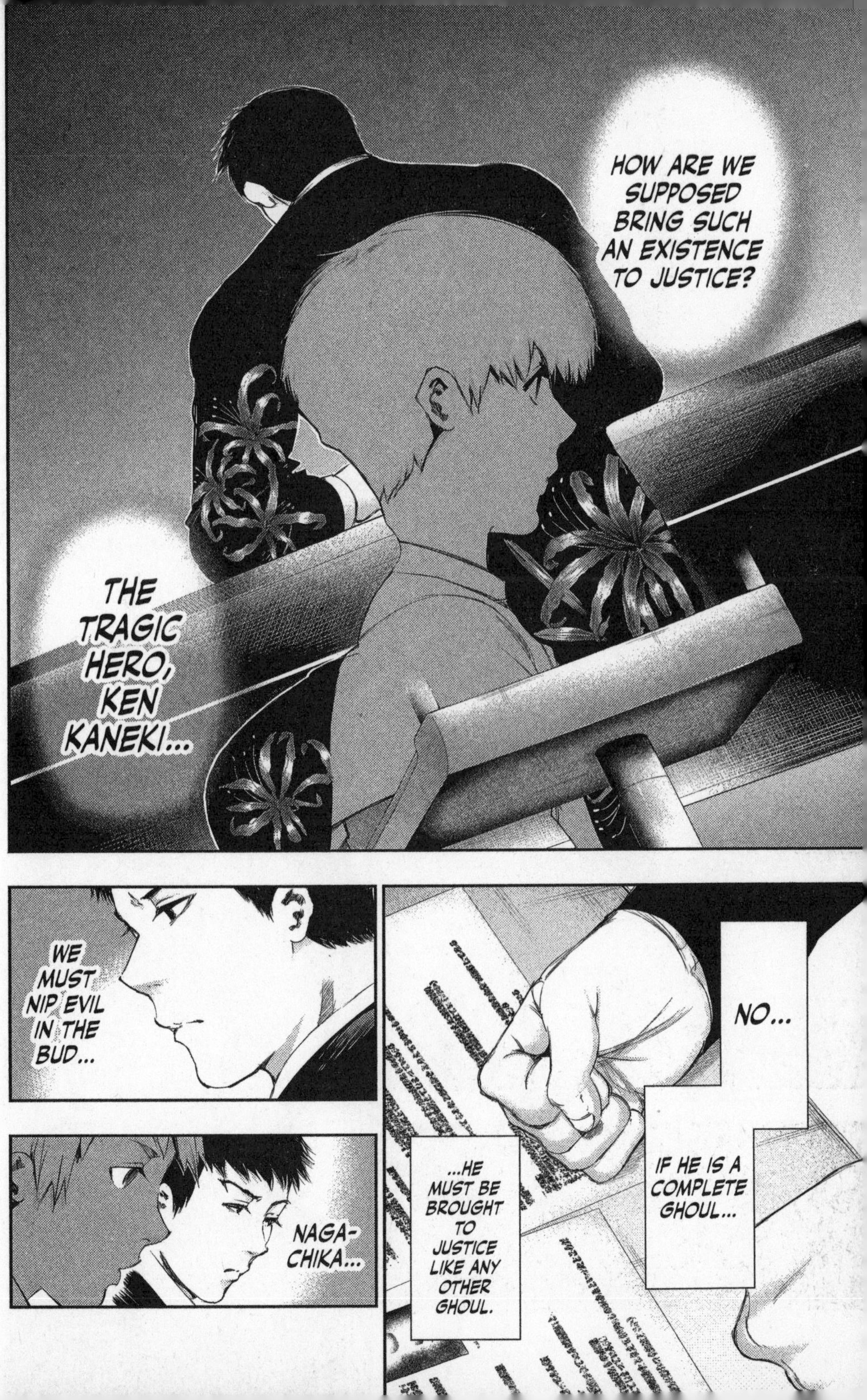
HOW ARE WE SUPPOSED BRING SUCH AN EXISTENCE TO JUSTICE?
THE TRAGIC HERO, KEN KANEKI...
NO...
IF HE IS A COMPLETE GHOUL...
...HE MUST BE BROUGHT TO JUSTICE LIKE ANY OTHER GHOUL.
WE MUST NIP EVIL IN THE BUD...
NAGA-CHIKA...

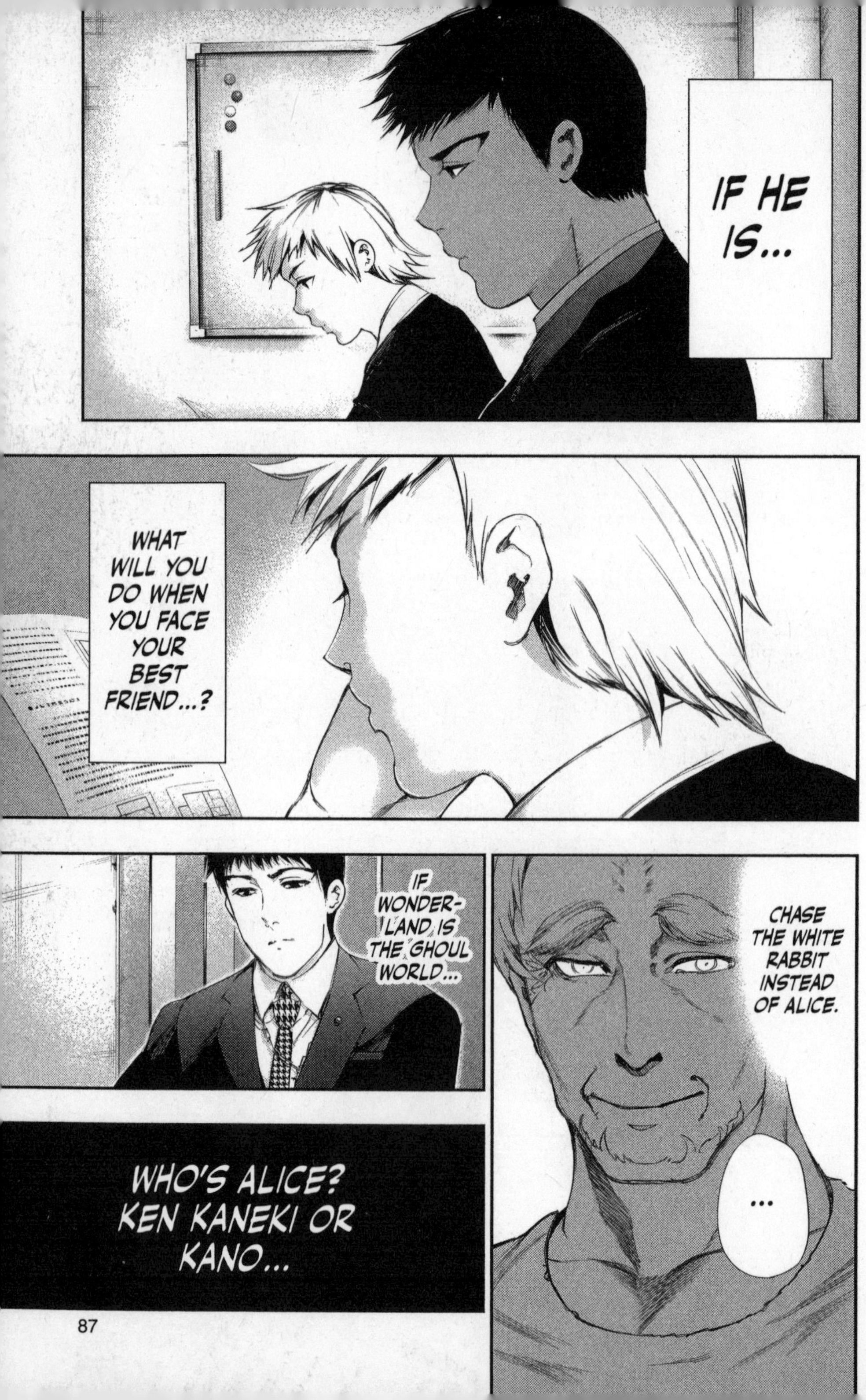
IF HE IS...
WHAT WILL YOU DO WHEN YOU FACE YOUR BEST FRIEND...?
CHASE THE WHITE RABBIT INSTEAD OF ALICE.
...
IF WONDERLAND IS THE GHOUL WORLD...
WHO'S ALICE? KEN KANEKI OR KANO...

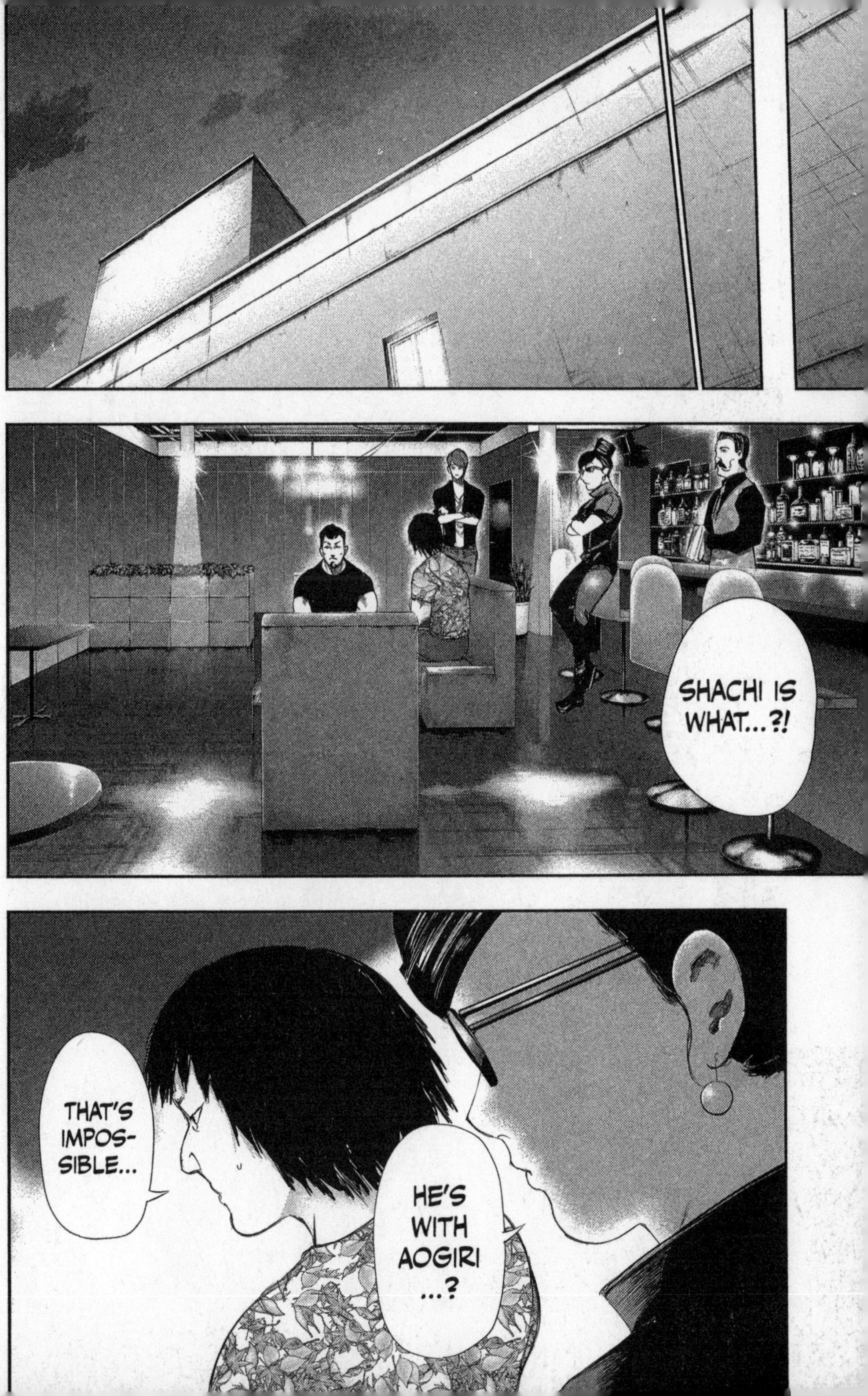
SHACHI IS WHAT...?!
HE'S WITH AOGIRI ...?
THAT'S IMPOS-SIBLE...

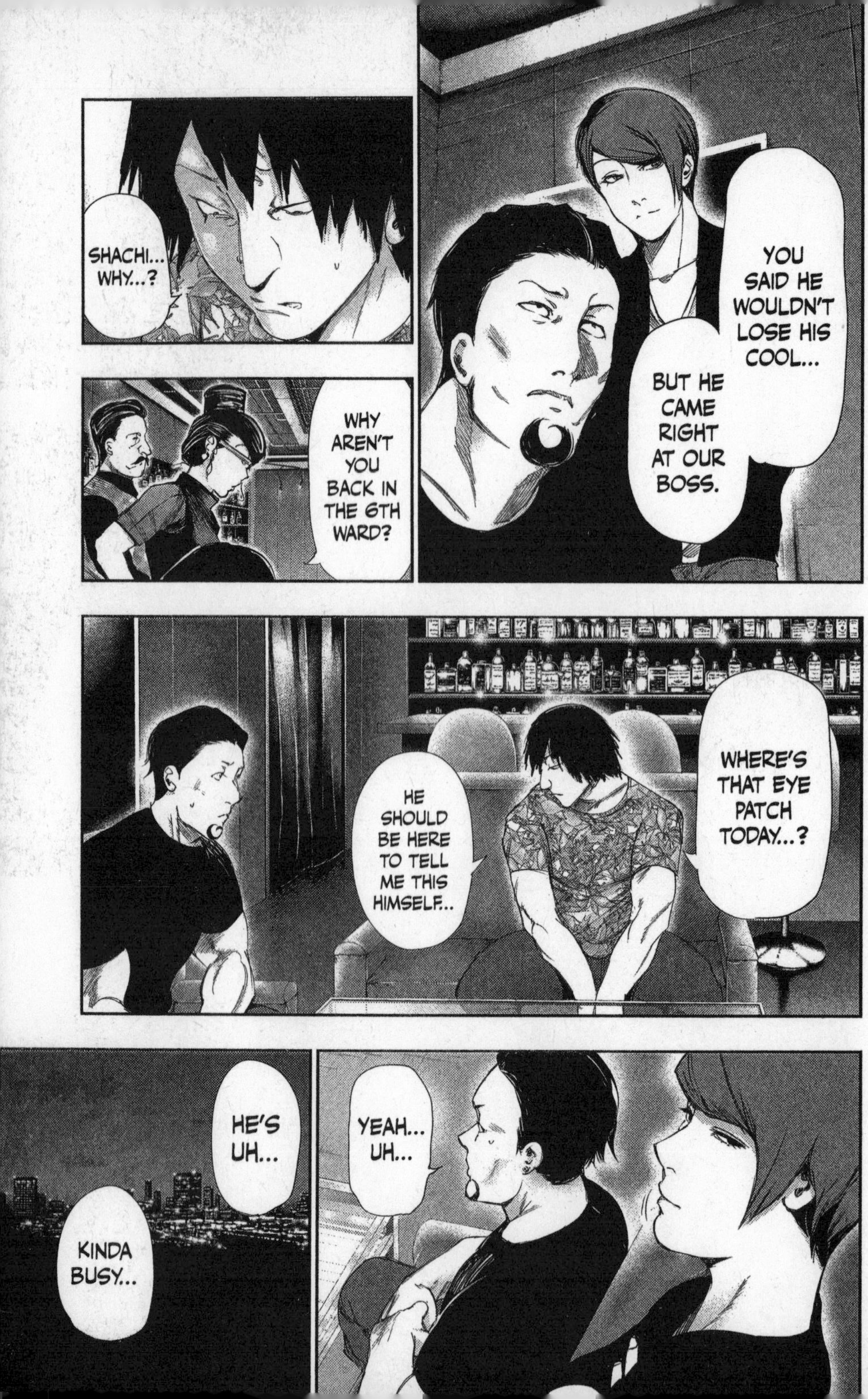
YOU SAID HE WOULDN'T LOSE HIS COOL...
BUT HE CAME RIGHT AT OUR BOSS.
SHACHI... WHY...?
WHY AREN'T YOU BACK IN THE 6TH WARD?
WHERE'S THAT EYE PATCH TODAY...?
HE SHOULD BE HERE TO TELL ME THIS HIMSELF...
YEAH... UH...
HE'S UH...
KINDA BUSY...

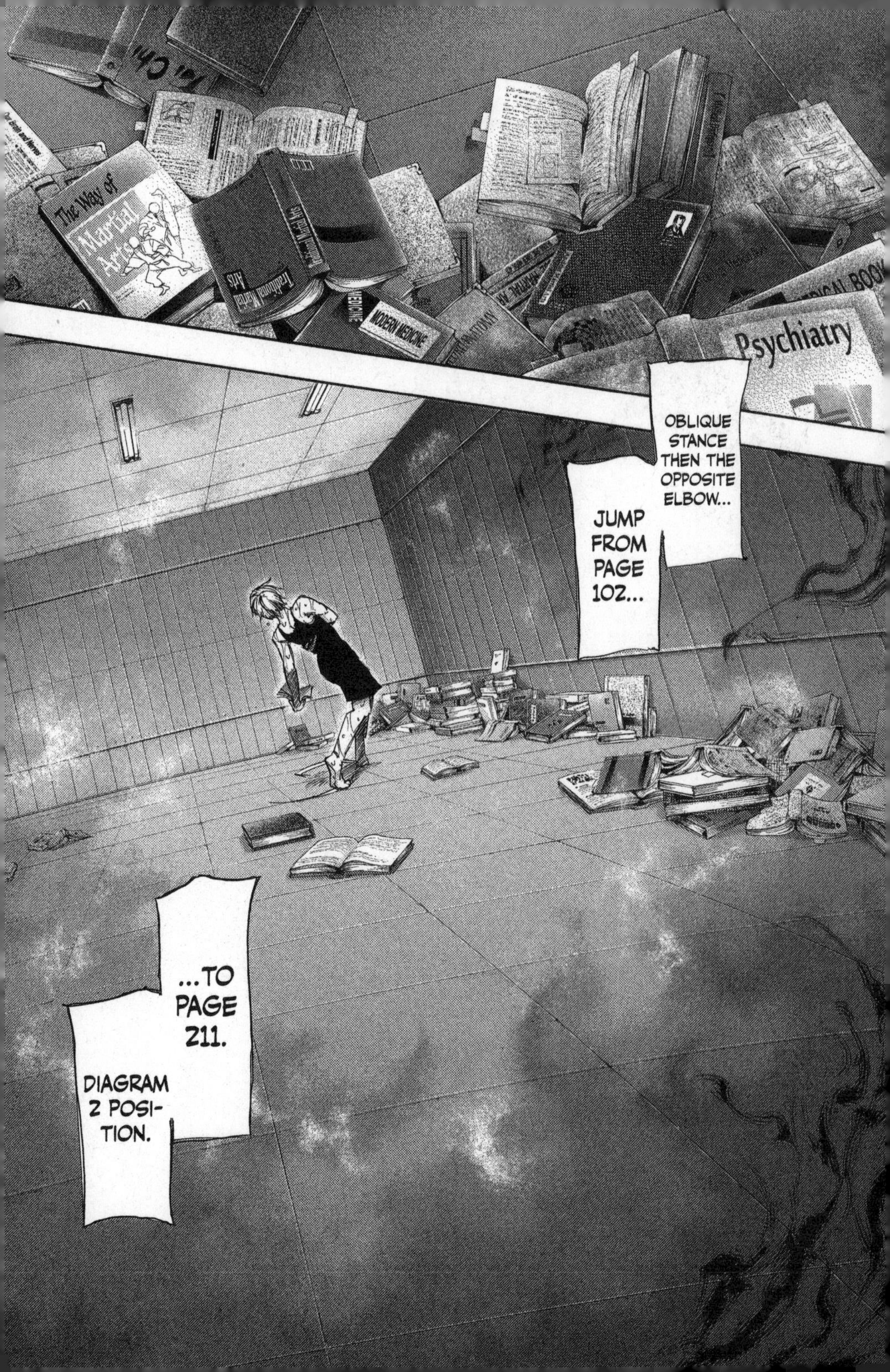
Psychiatry
MODERN MEDICINE
MEDICINE
Traditional Martial Arts
The Way of Martial Arts
OBLIQUE STANCE THEN THE OPPOSITE ELBOW...
JUMP FROM PAGE 102...
...TO PAGE 211.
DIAGRAM 2 POSITION.

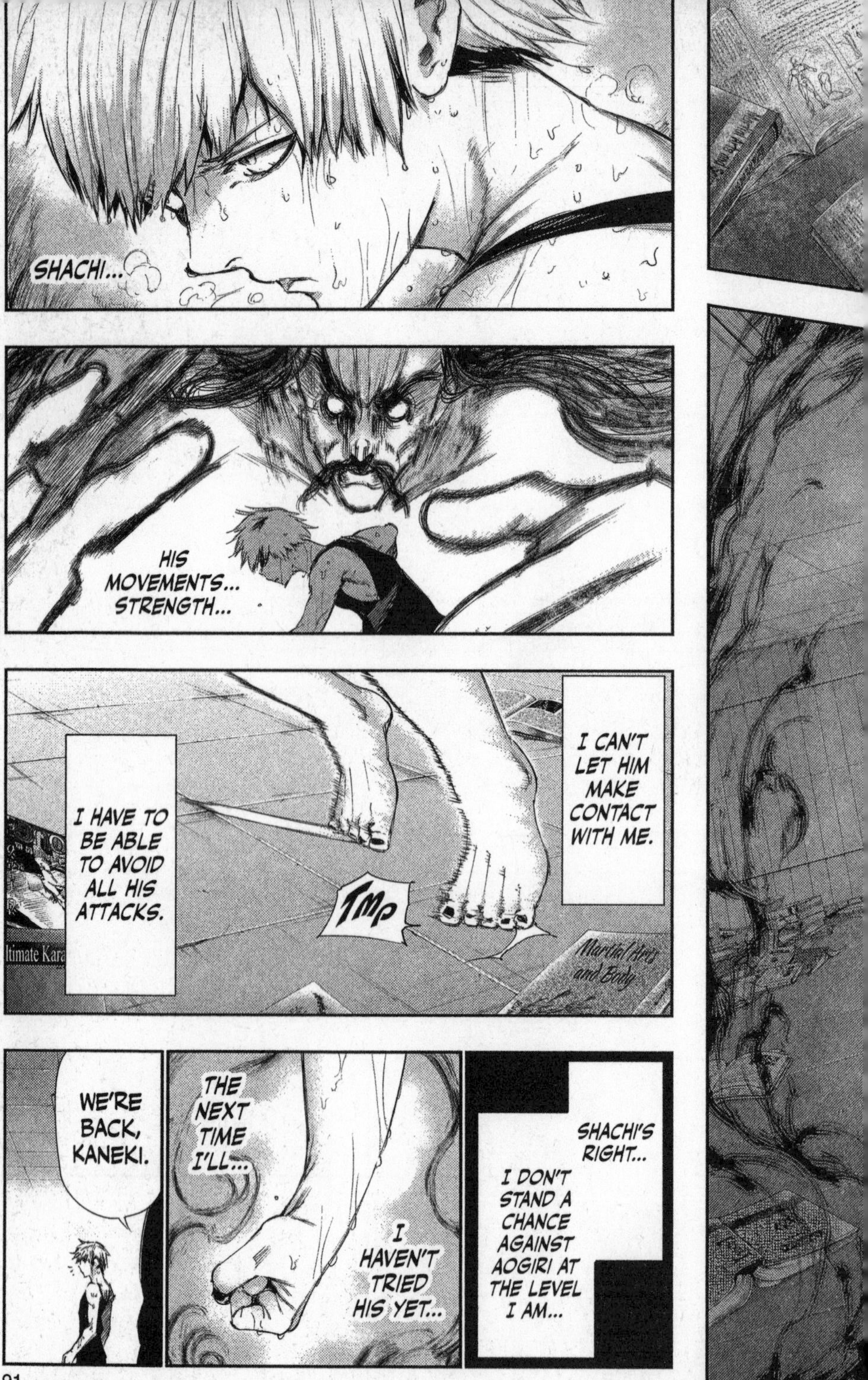
SHACHI...
HIS MOVEMENTS... STRENGTH...
I CAN'T LET HIM MAKE CONTACT WITH ME.
TMP
Martial Arts and Body
I HAVE TO BE ABLE TO AVOID ALL HIS ATTACKS.
ltimate Kara
SHACHI'S RIGHT...
I DON'T STAND A CHANCE AGAINST AOGIRI AT THE LEVEL I AM...
THE NEXT TIME I'LL...
I HAVEN'T TRIED HIS YET...
WE'RE BACK, KANEKI.

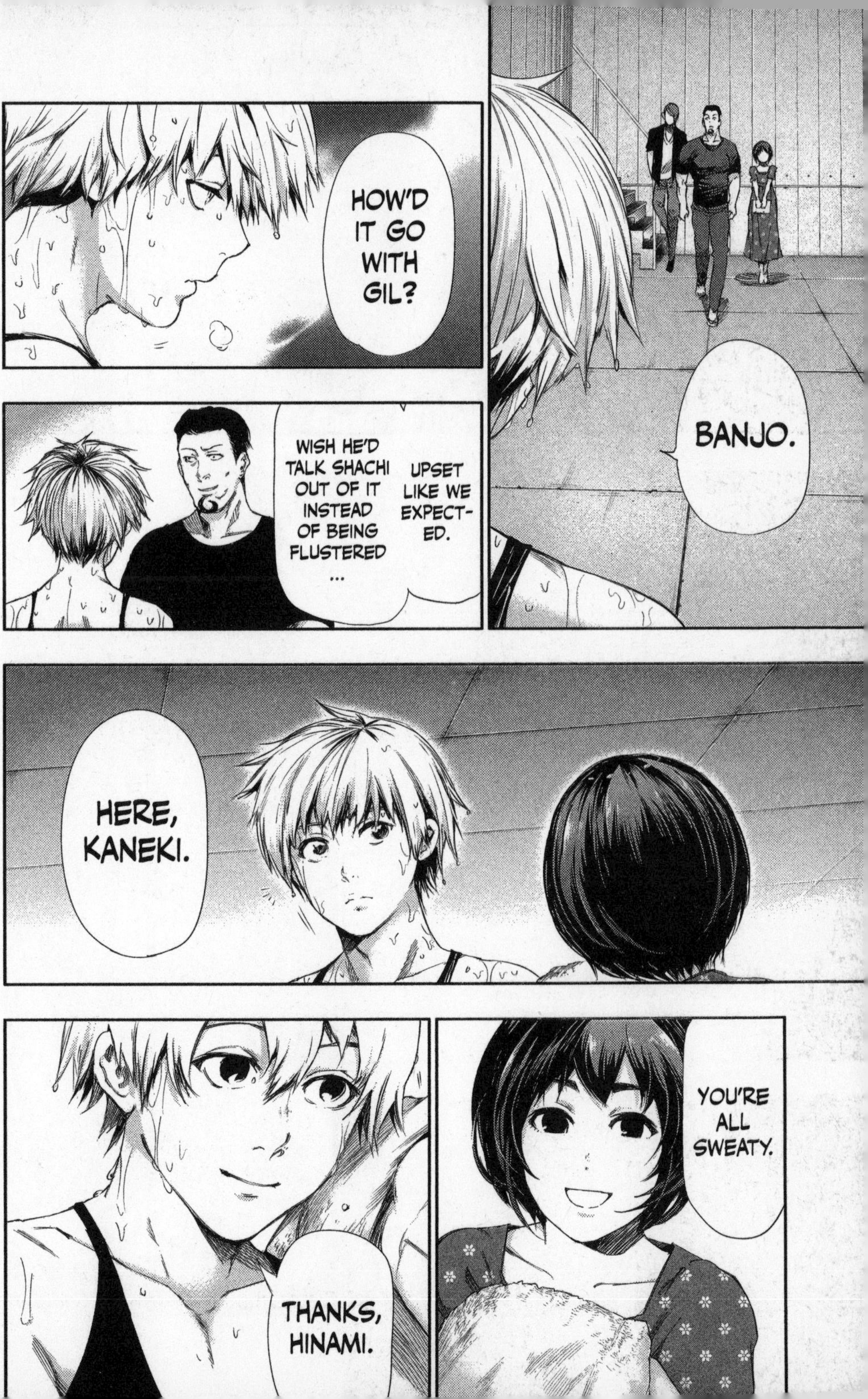
BANJO.
HOW'D IT GO WITH GIL?
UPSET LIKE WE EXPECT-ED.
WISH HE'D TALK SHACHI OUT OF IT INSTEAD OF BEING FLUSTERED...
HERE, KANEKI.
YOU'RE ALL SWEATY.
THANKS, HINAMI.

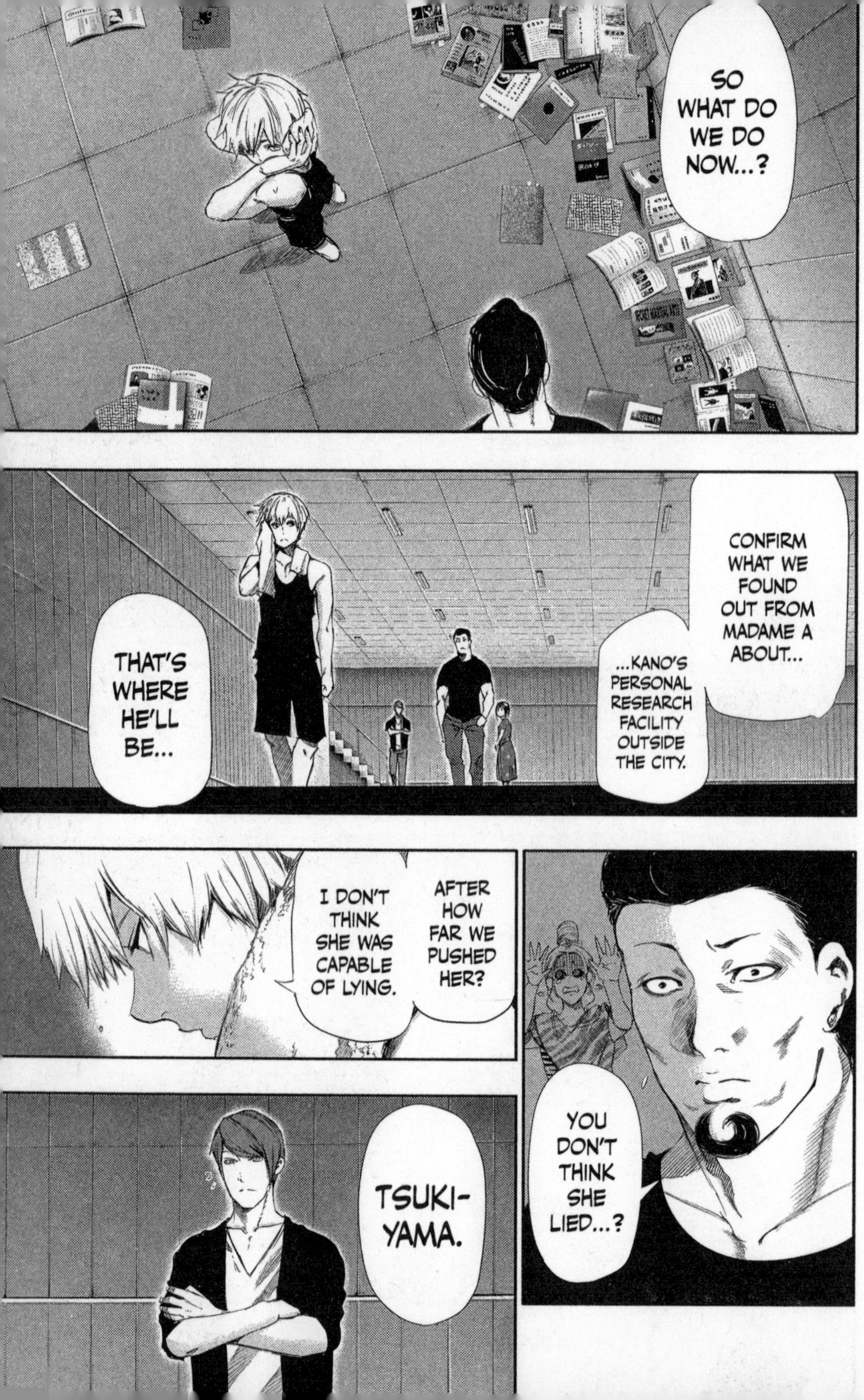
SO WHAT DO WE DO NOW...?
CONFIRM WHAT WE FOUND OUT FROM MADAME A ABOUT...
...KANO'S PERSONAL RESEARCH FACILITY OUTSIDE THE CITY.
THAT'S WHERE HE'LL BE...
YOU DON'T THINK SHE LIED...?
AFTER HOW FAR WE PUSHED HER?
I DON'T THINK SHE WAS CAPABLE OF LYING.
TSUKI-YAMA.

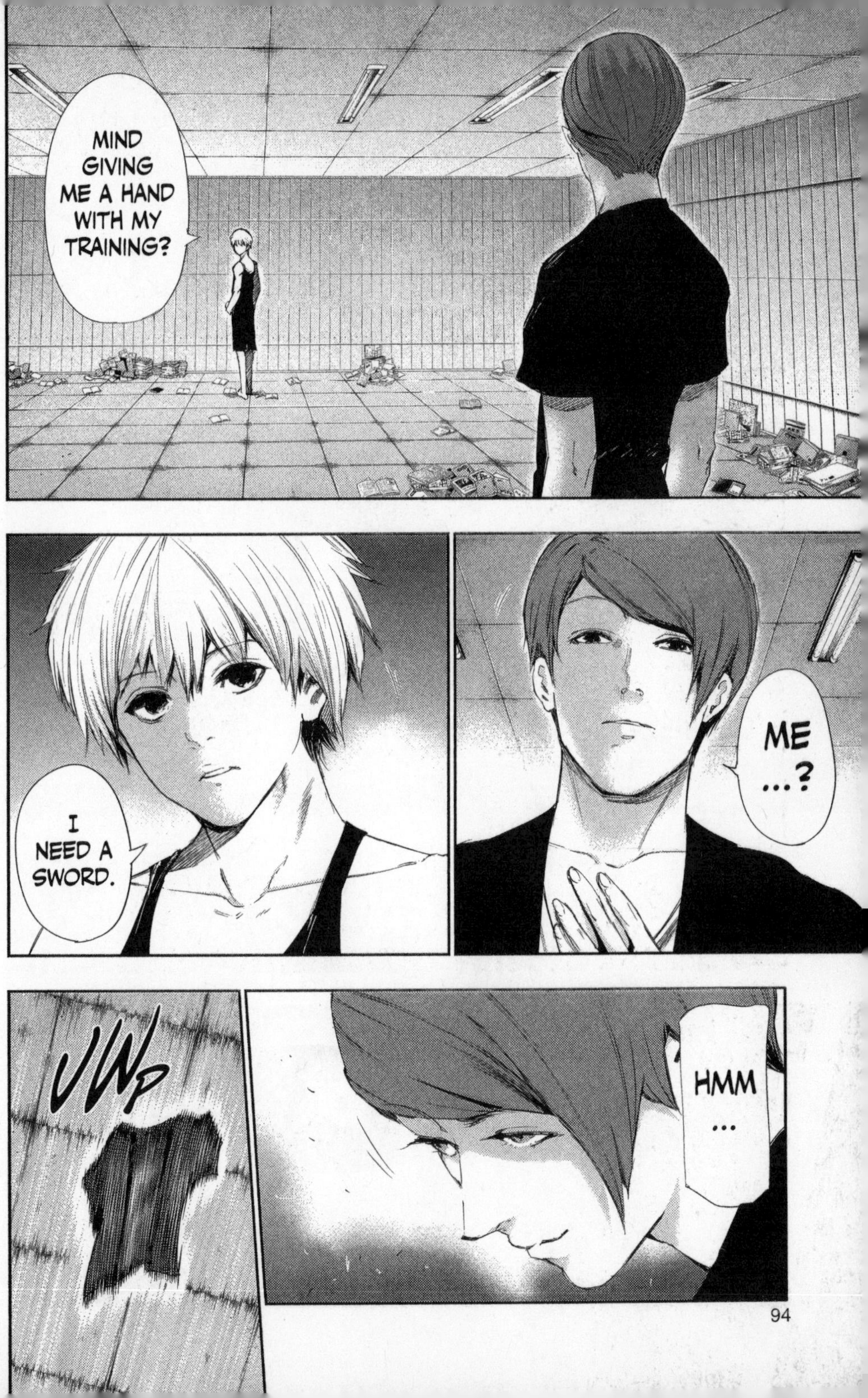
MIND GIVING ME A HAND WITH MY TRAINING?
ME ...?
I NEED A SWORD.
HMM ...
VWP

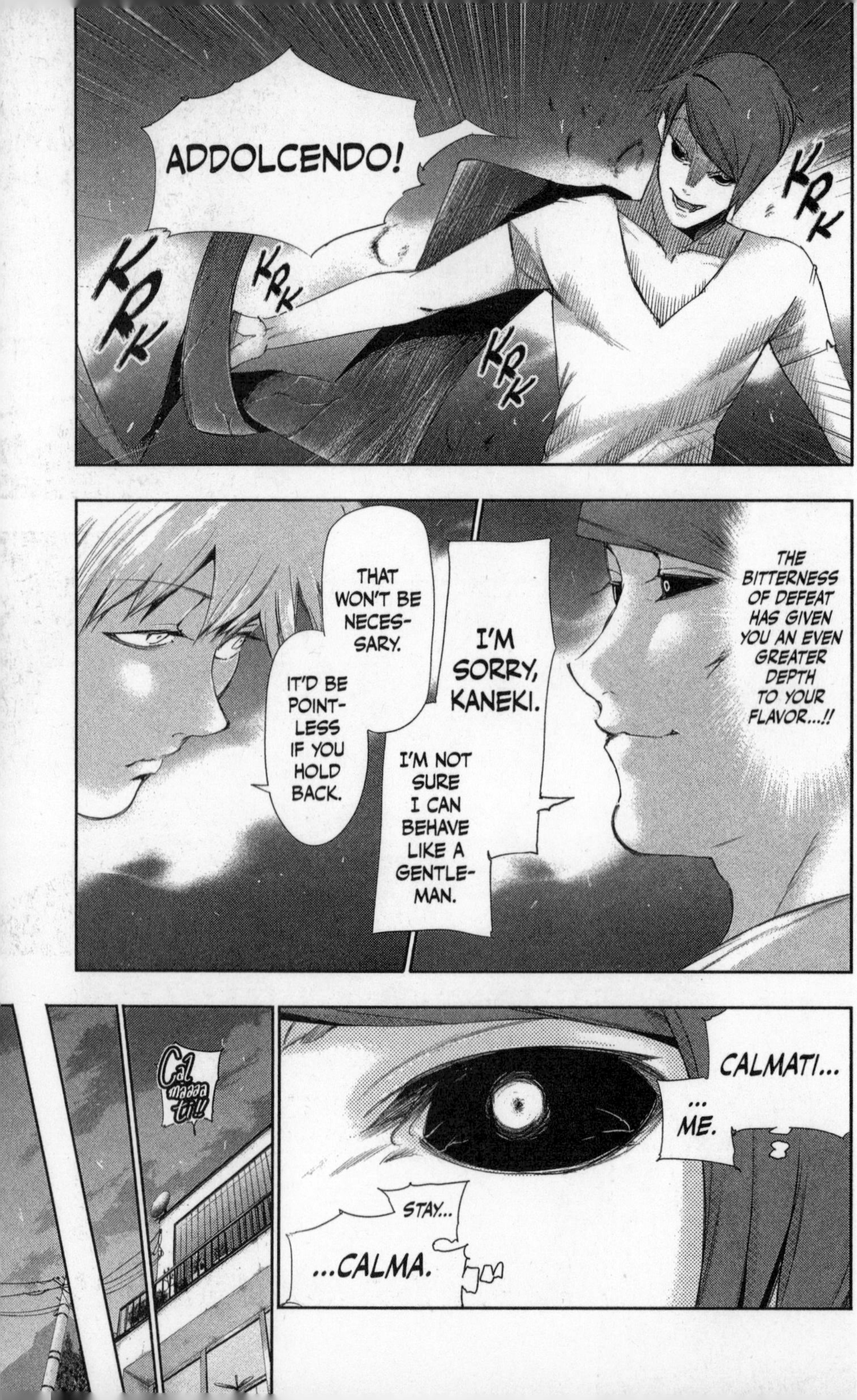
KRK
ADDOLCENDO!
KRK
KRK
KRK
THE BITTERNESS OF DEFEAT HAS GIVEN YOU AN EVEN GREATER DEPTH TO YOUR FLAVOR...!!
I'M SORRY, KANEKI.
I'M NOT SURE I CAN BEHAVE LIKE A GENTLE-MAN.
THAT WON'T BE NECES-SARY.
IT'D BE POINT-LESS IF YOU HOLD BACK.
CALMATI...
... ME.
STAY...
...CALMA.
Cal maaaa ti!!

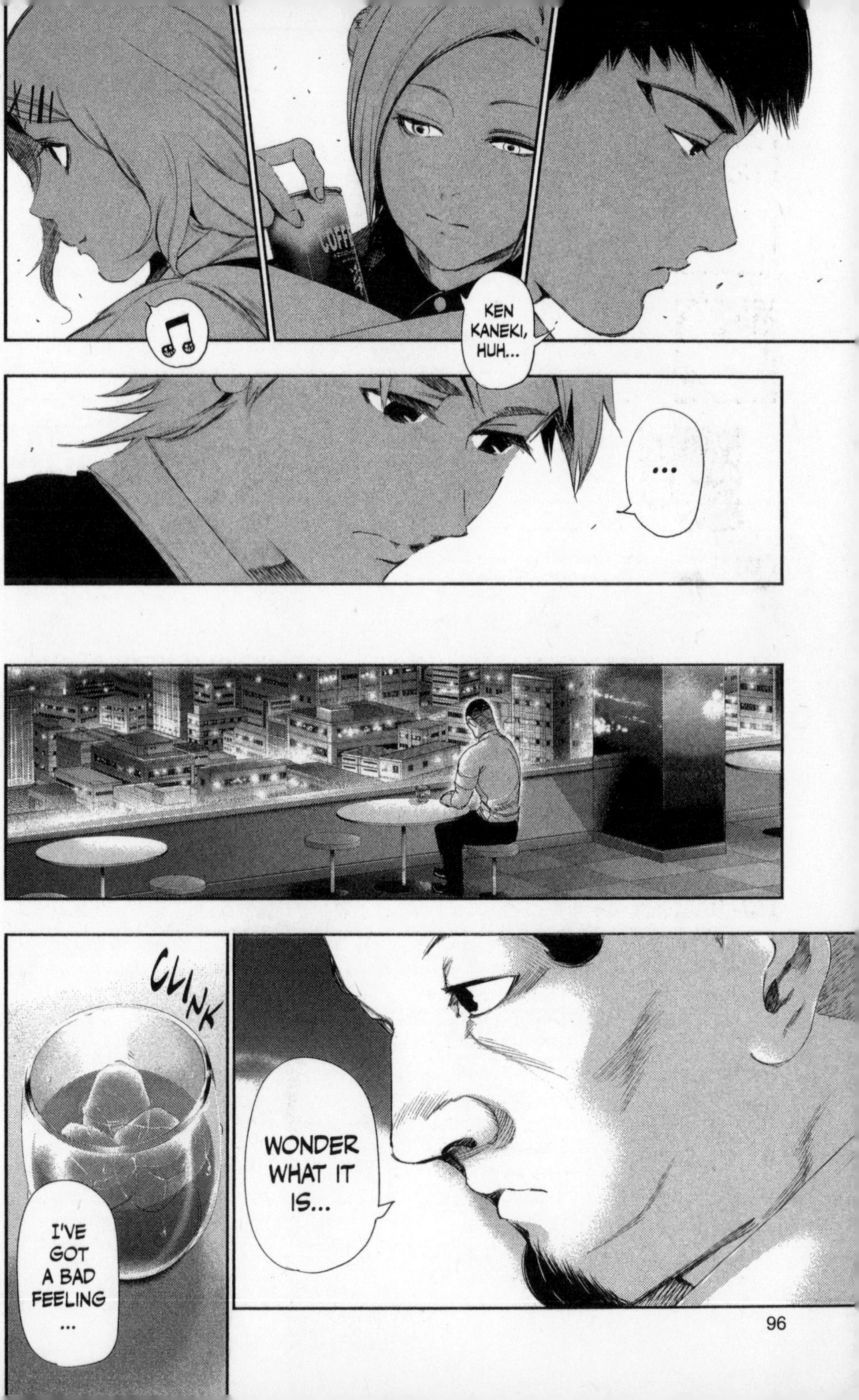
KEN KANEKI, HUH...
...
WONDER WHAT IT IS...
CLINK
I'VE GOT A BAD FEELING ...

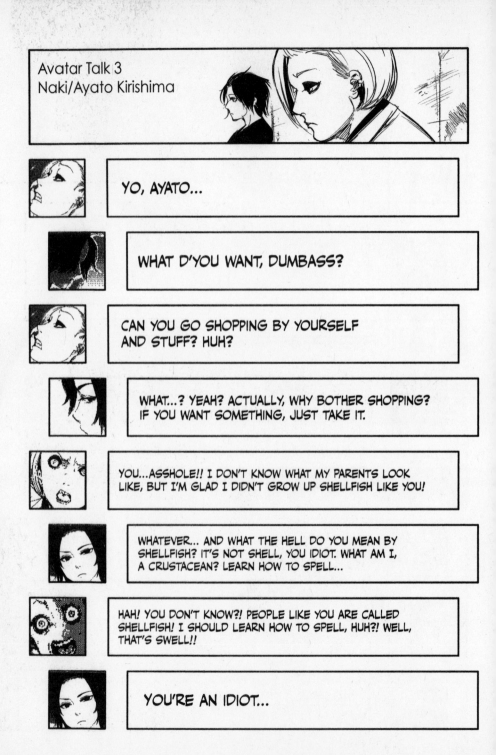

Avatar Talk 3
Naki/Ayato Kirishima

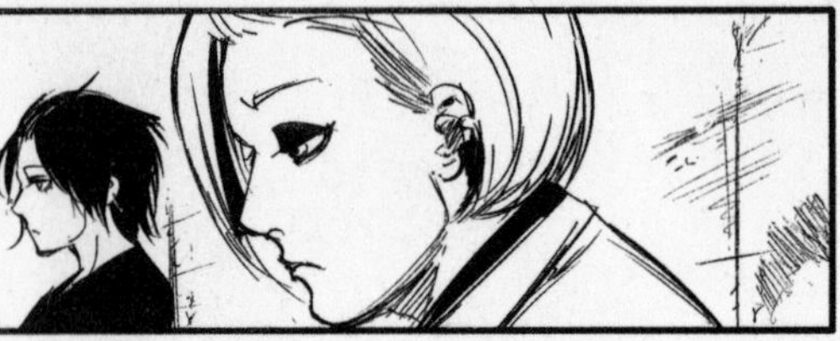

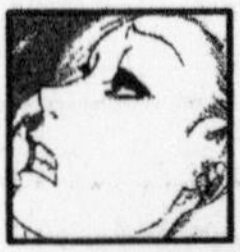

YO, AYATO...

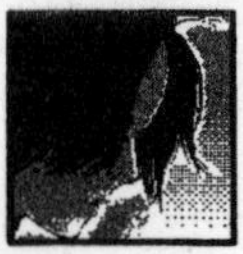

WHAT D'YOU WANT, DUMBASS?

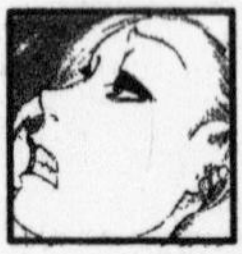

CAN YOU GO SHOPPING BY YOURSELF AND STUFF? HUH?

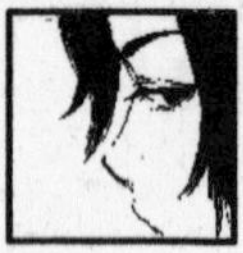

WHAT...? YEAH? ACTUALLY, WHY BOTHER SHOPPING? IF YOU WANT SOMETHING, JUST TAKE IT.

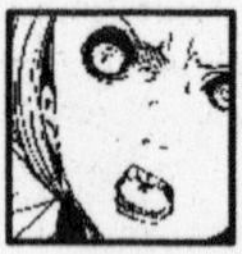

YOU...ASSHOLE!! I DON'T KNOW WHAT MY PARENTS LOOK LIKE, BUT I'M GLAD I DIDN'T GROW UP SHELLFISH LIKE YOU!

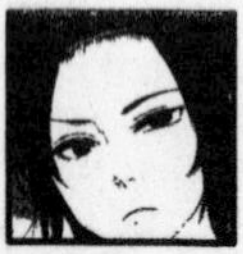

WHATEVER... AND WHAT THE HELL DO YOU MEAN BY SHELLFISH? IT'S NOT SHELL, YOU IDIOT. WHAT AM I, A CRUSTACEAN? LEARN HOW TO SPELL...

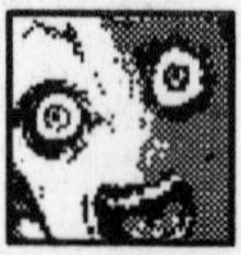

HAH! YOU DON'T KNOW?! PEOPLE LIKE YOU ARE CALLED SHELLFISH! I SHOULD LEARN HOW TO SPELL, HUH?! WELL, THAT'S SWELL!!

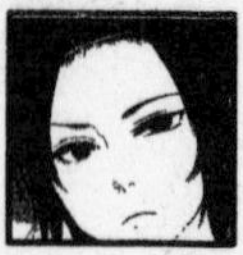

YOU'RE AN IDIOT...

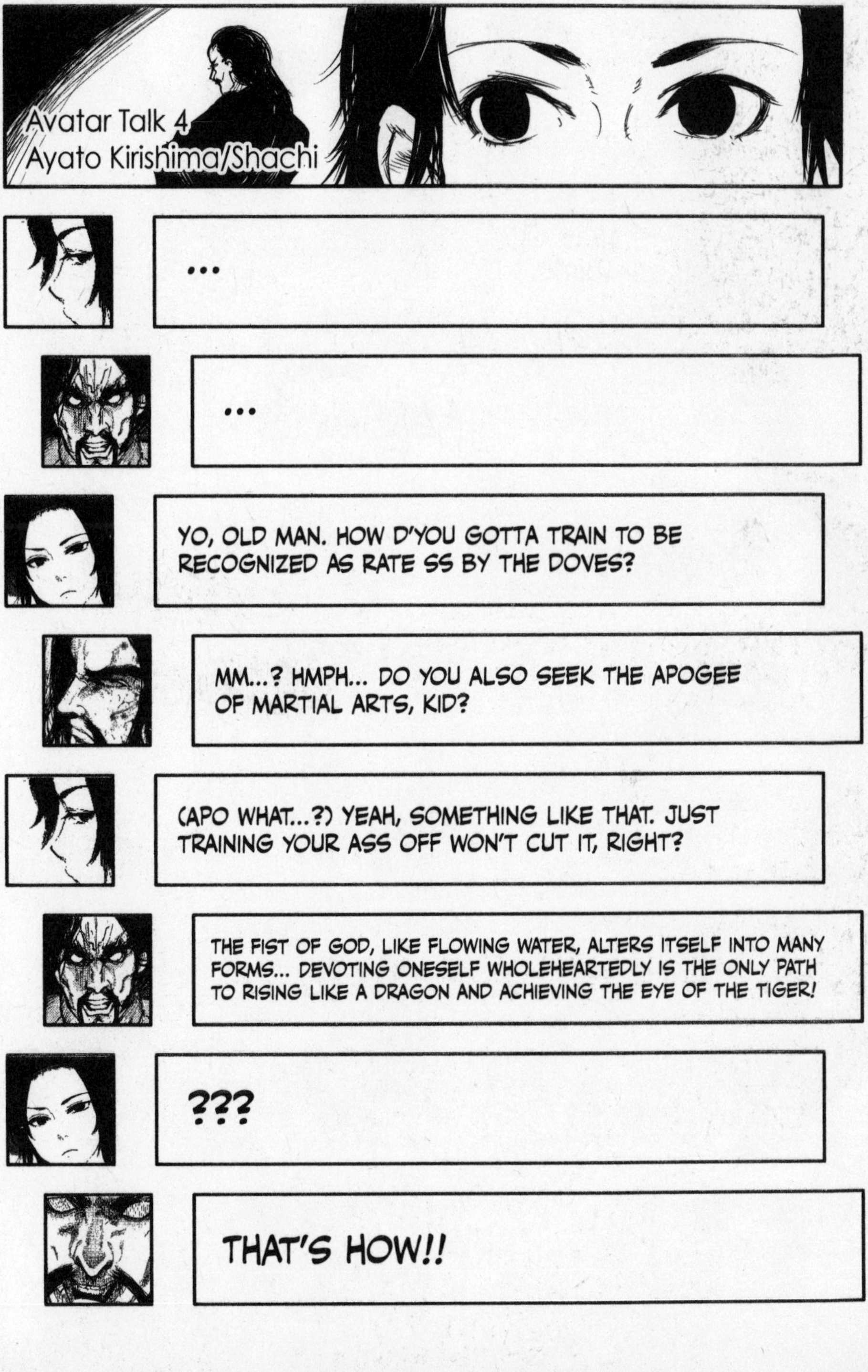
Avatar Talk 4
Ayato Kirishima/Shachi
...
...
YO, OLD MAN. HOW D'YOU GOTTA TRAIN TO BE RECOGNIZED AS RATE SS BY THE DOVES?
MM...? HMPH... DO YOU ALSO SEEK THE APOGEE OF MARTIAL ARTS, KID?
(APO WHAT...?) YEAH, SOMETHING LIKE THAT. JUST TRAINING YOUR ASS OFF WON'T CUT IT, RIGHT?
THE FIST OF GOD, LIKE FLOWING WATER, ALTERS ITSELF INTO MANY FORMS... DEVOTING ONESELF WHOLEHEARTEDLY IS THE ONLY PATH TO RISING LIKE A DRAGON AND ACHIEVING THE EYE OF THE TIGER!
???
THAT'S HOW!!

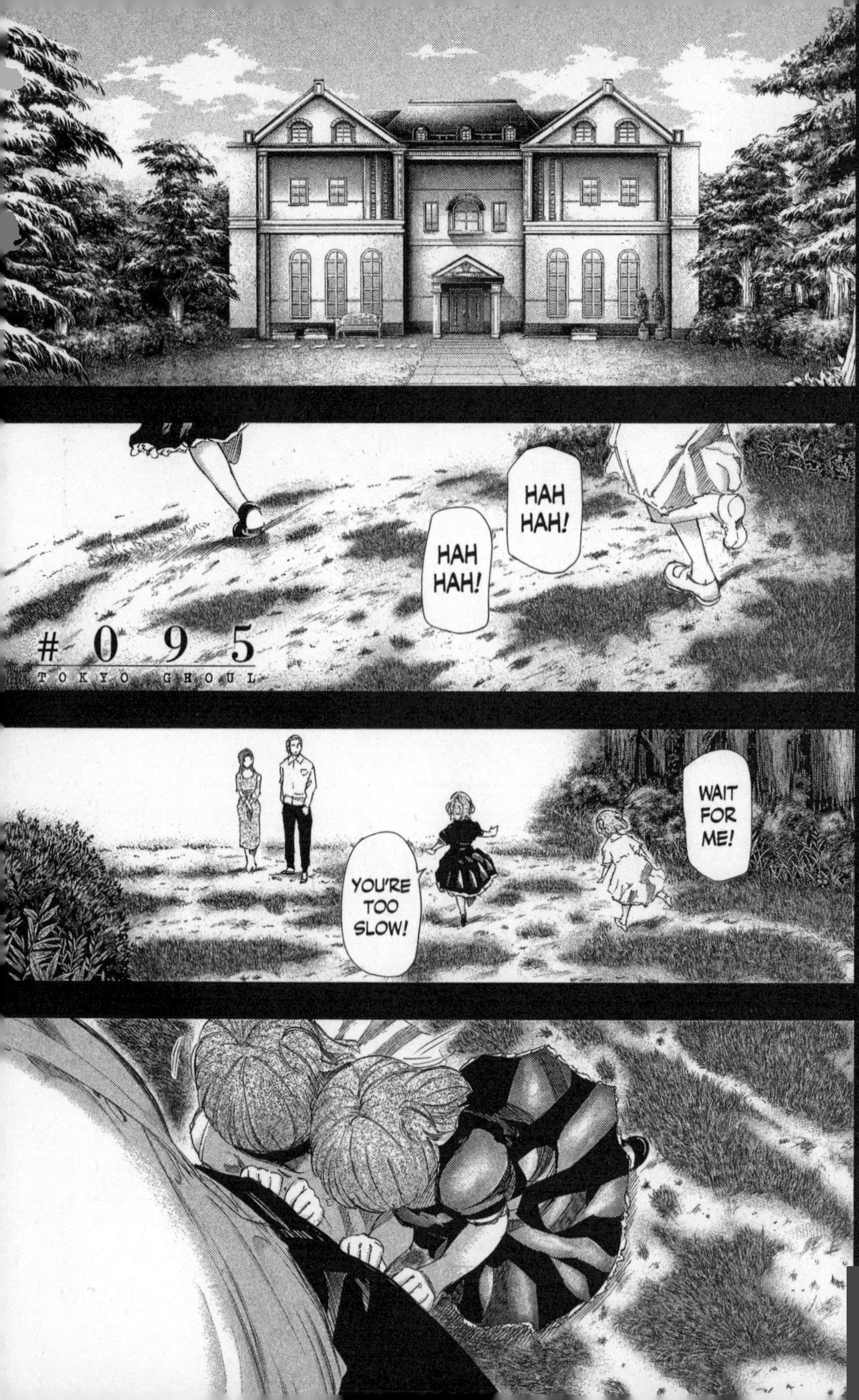
HAH HAH!
HAH HAH!
#095
TOKYO GHOUL
WAIT FOR ME!
YOU'RE TOO SLOW!

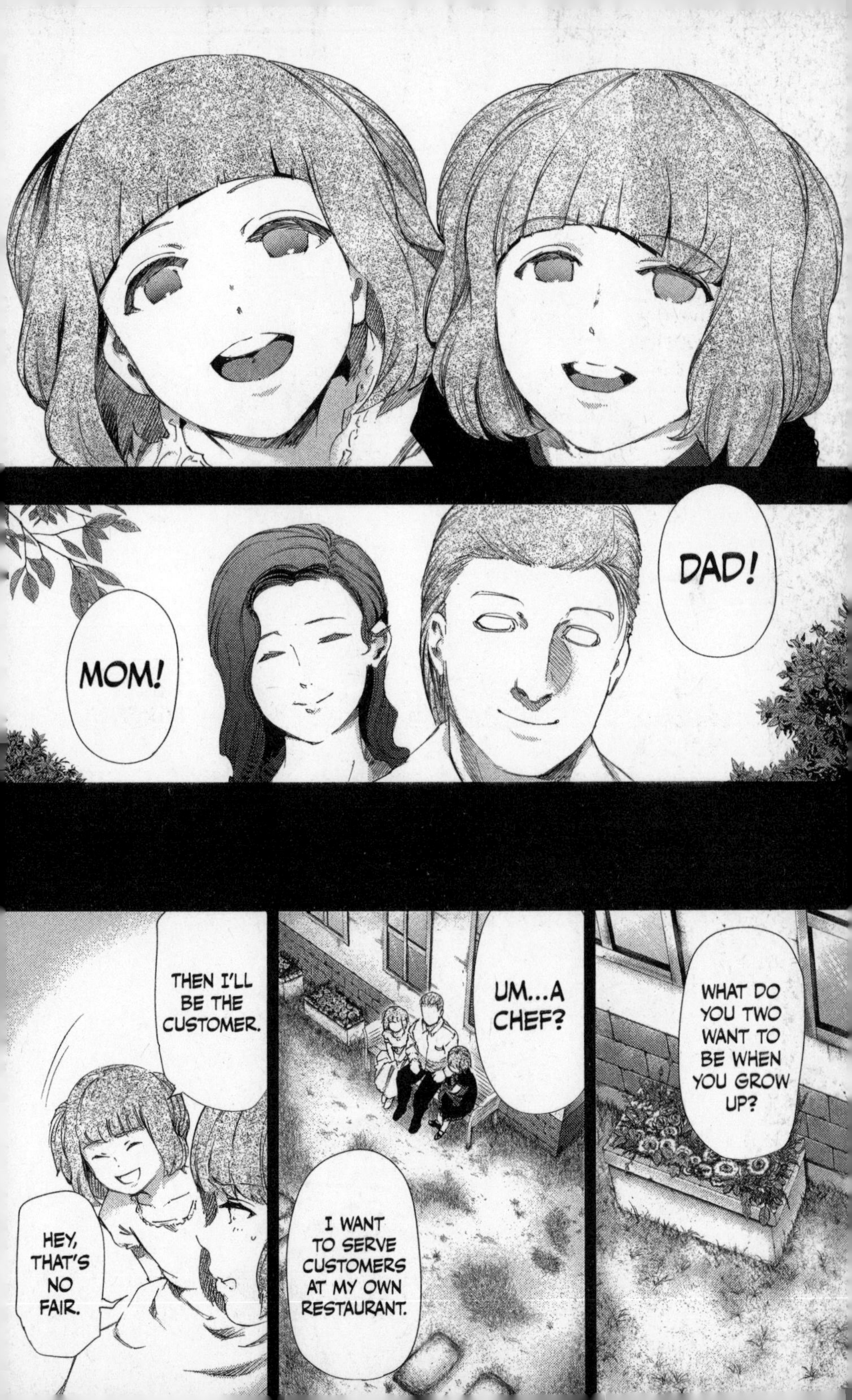
DAD!
MOM!
WHAT DO YOU TWO WANT TO BE WHEN YOU GROW UP?
UM...A CHEF?
I WANT TO SERVE CUSTOMERS AT MY OWN RESTAURANT.
THEN I'LL BE THE CUSTOMER.
HEY, THAT'S NO FAIR.

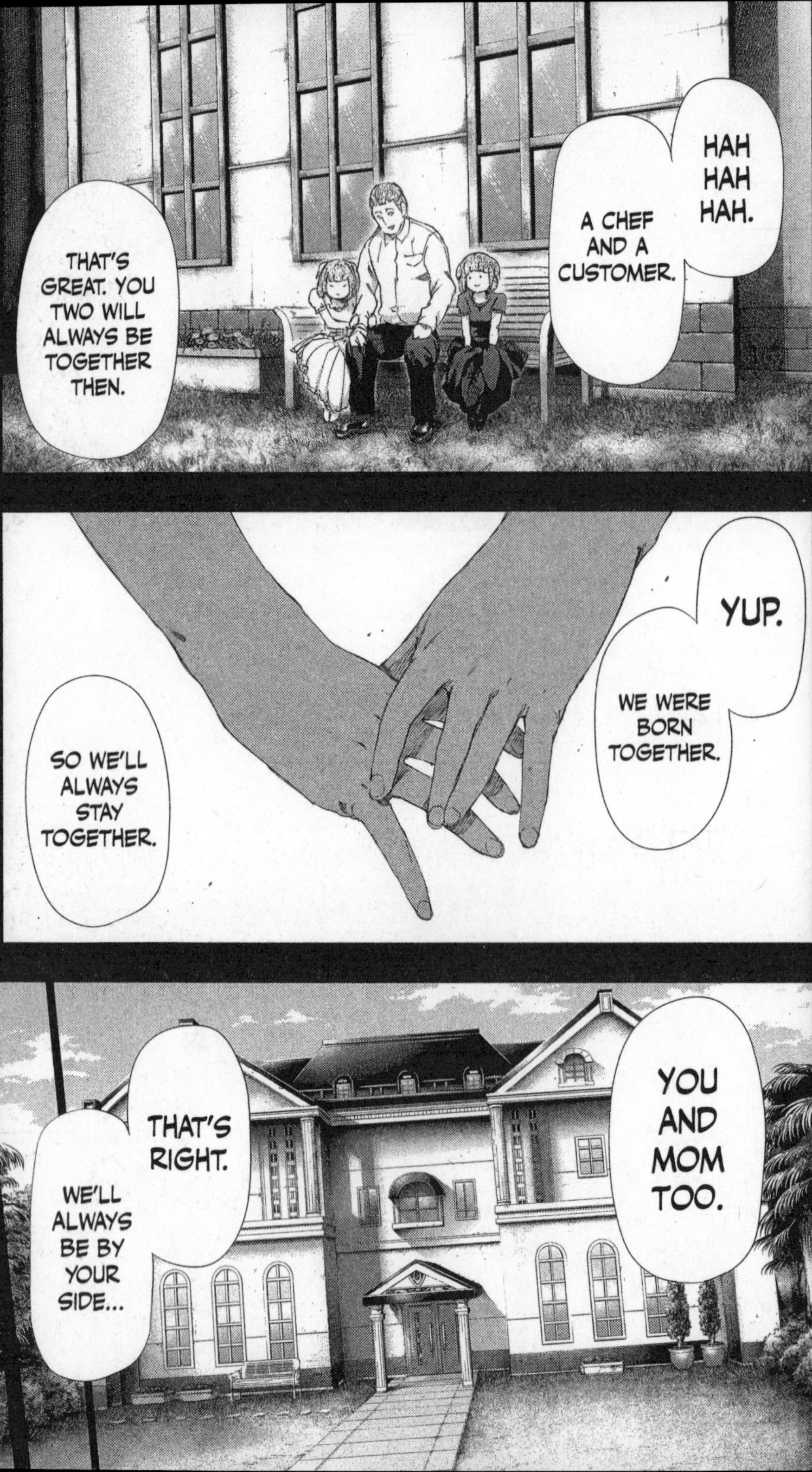
HAH HAH HAH.
A CHEF AND A CUSTOMER.
THAT'S GREAT. YOU TWO WILL ALWAYS BE TOGETHER THEN.
YUP.
WE WERE BORN TOGETHER.
SO WE'LL ALWAYS STAY TOGETHER.
YOU AND MOM TOO.
THAT'S RIGHT.
WE'LL ALWAYS BE BY YOUR SIDE...

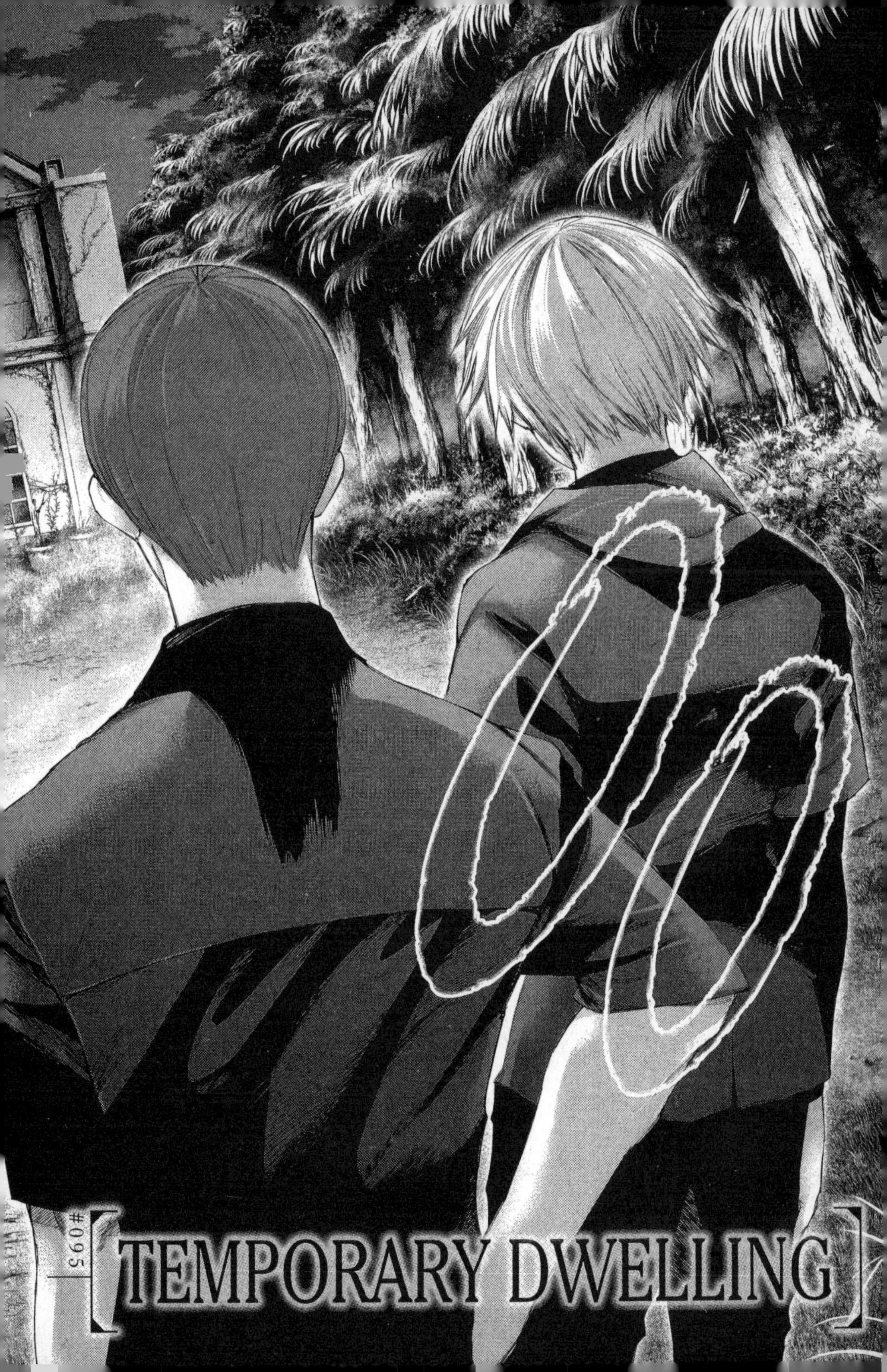

#095
TEMPORARY DWELLING

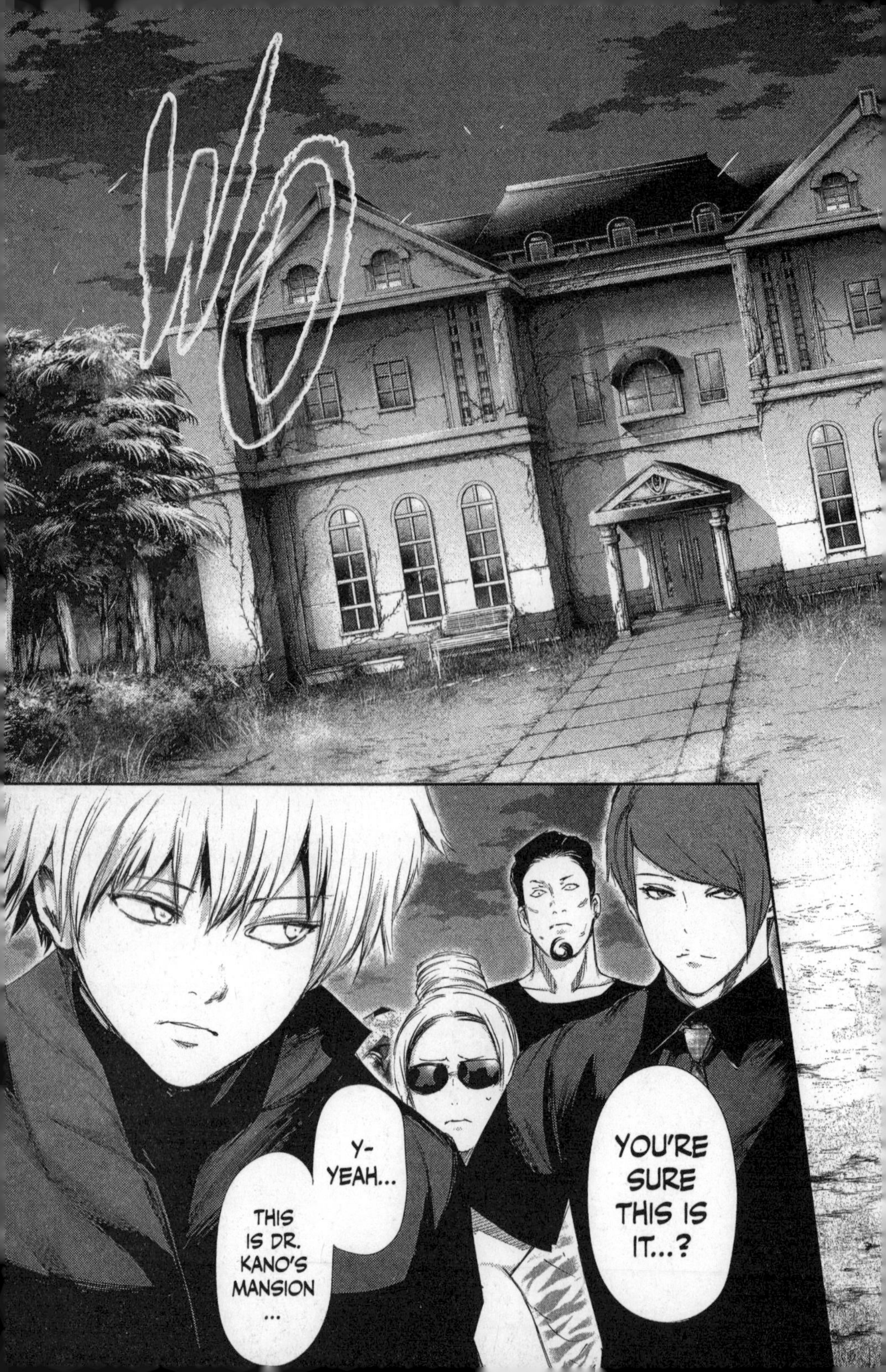
YOU'RE SURE THIS IS IT...?
Y- YEAH...
THIS IS DR. KANO'S MANSION ...

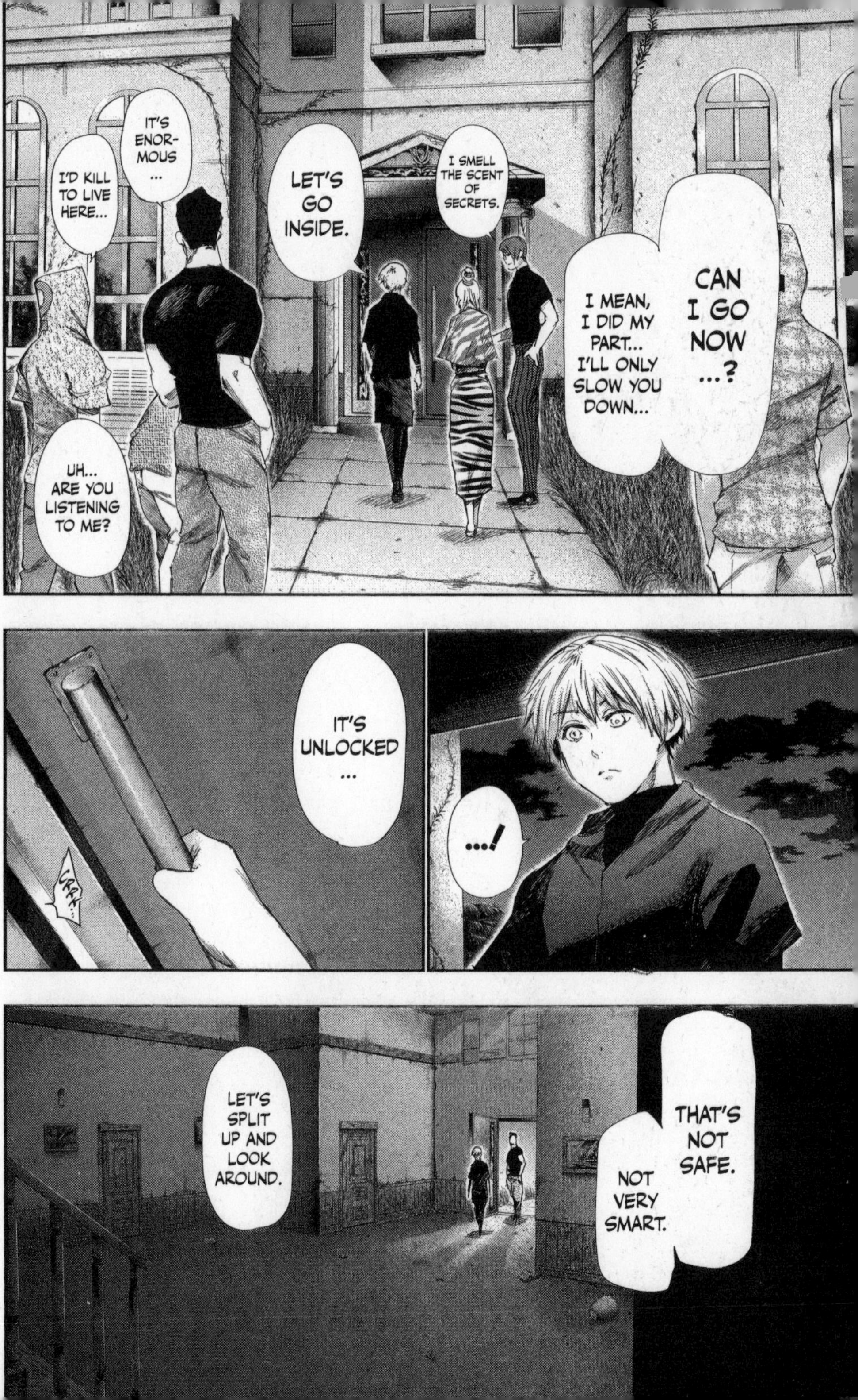

CAN I GO NOW ...?
I MEAN, I DID MY PART... I'LL ONLY SLOW YOU DOWN...
I SMELL THE SCENT OF SECRETS.
LET'S GO INSIDE.
IT'S ENORMOUS ...
I'D KILL TO LIVE HERE...
UH... ARE YOU LISTENING TO ME?
...!
IT'S UNLOCKED ...
CRRK...
THAT'S NOT SAFE.
NOT VERY SMART.
LET'S SPLIT UP AND LOOK AROUND.

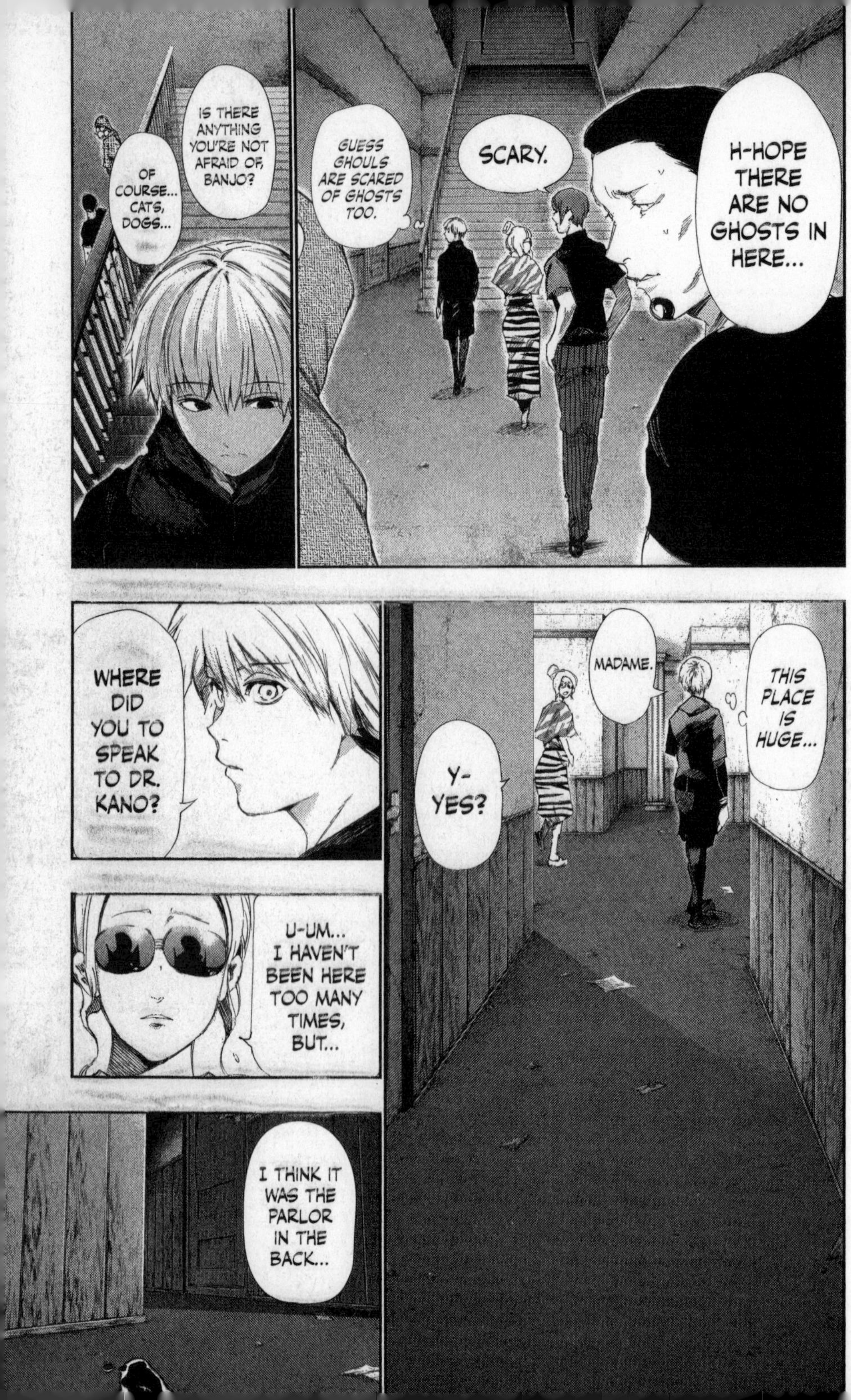
H-HOPE THERE ARE NO GHOSTS IN HERE...
SCARY.
GUESS GHOULS ARE SCARED OF GHOSTS TOO.
IS THERE ANYTHING YOU'RE NOT AFRAID OF, BANJO?
OF COURSE... CATS, DOGS...
THIS PLACE IS HUGE...
MADAME.
Y-YES?
WHERE DID YOU TO SPEAK TO DR. KANO?
U-UM... I HAVEN'T BEEN HERE TOO MANY TIMES, BUT...
I THINK IT WAS THE PARLOR IN THE BACK...

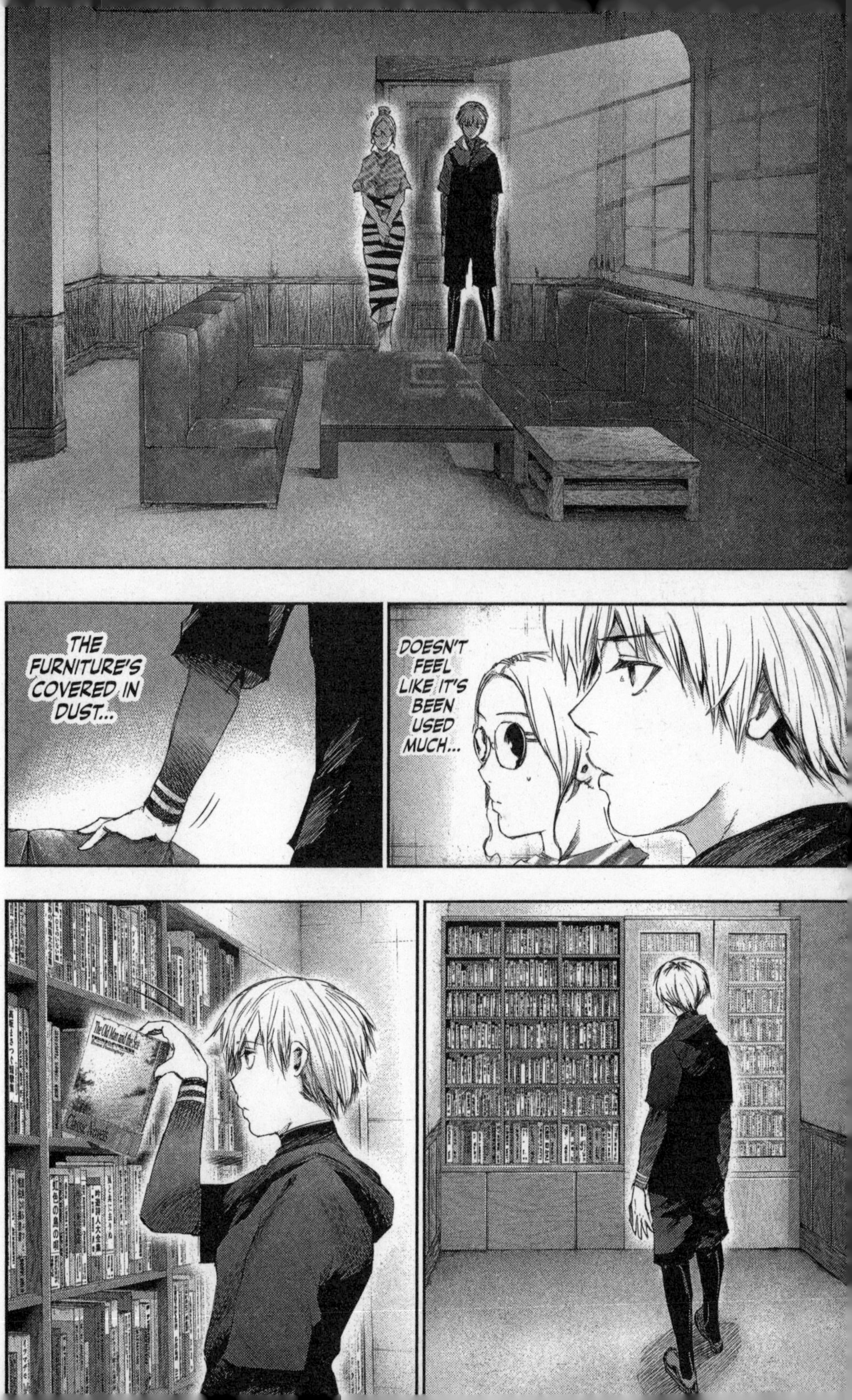
DOESN'T FEEL LIKE IT'S BEEN USED MUCH...
THE FURNITURE'S COVERED IN DUST...

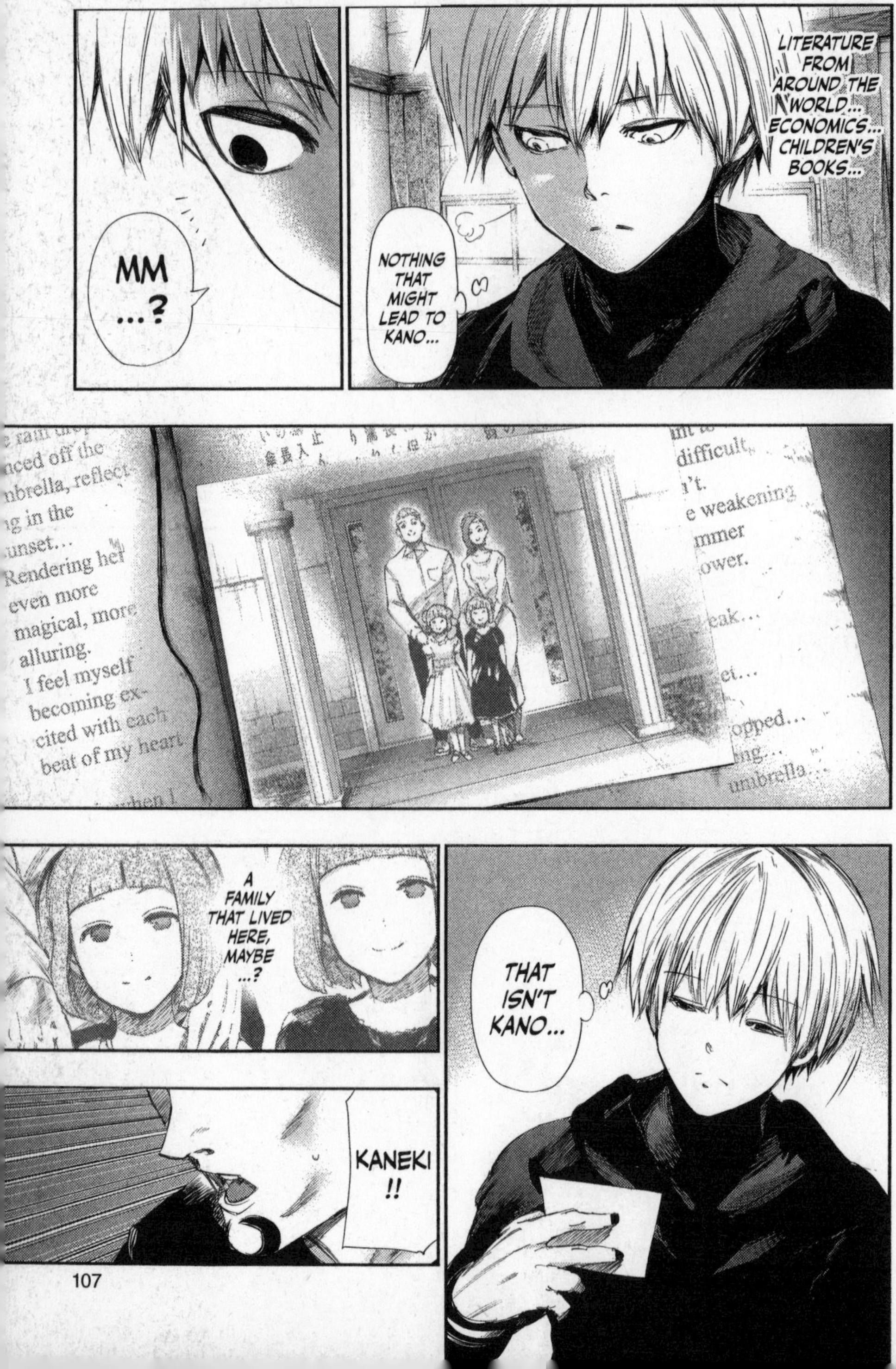
LITERATURE FROM AROUND THE WORLD... ECONOMICS... CHILDREN'S BOOKS...
NOTHING THAT MIGHT LEAD TO KANO...
MM ...?
aced off the umbrella, reflect
g in the sunset...
Rendering her even more magical, more alluring.
I feel myself becoming ex- cited with each beat of my heart
difficult,
e weakening
umbrella...
THAT ISN'T KANO...
A FAMILY THAT LIVED HERE, MAYBE ...?
KANEKI !!

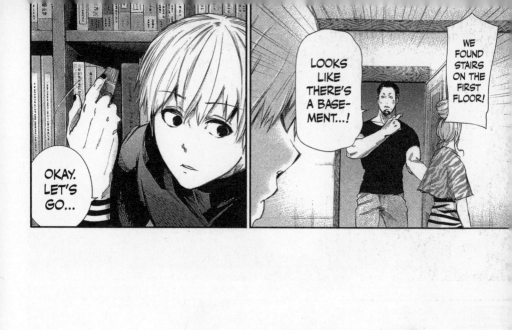

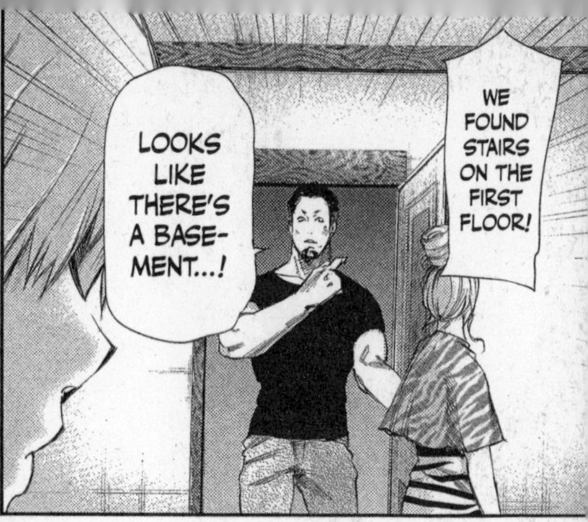
WE FOUND STAIRS ON THE FIRST FLOOR!
LOOKS LIKE THERE'S A BASE- MENT...!
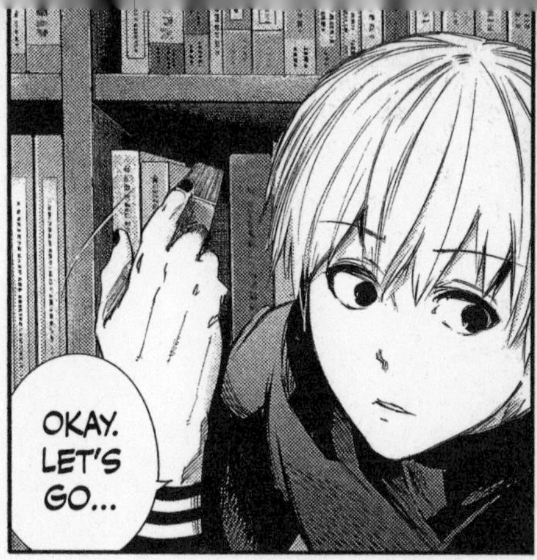
OKAY. LET'S GO...
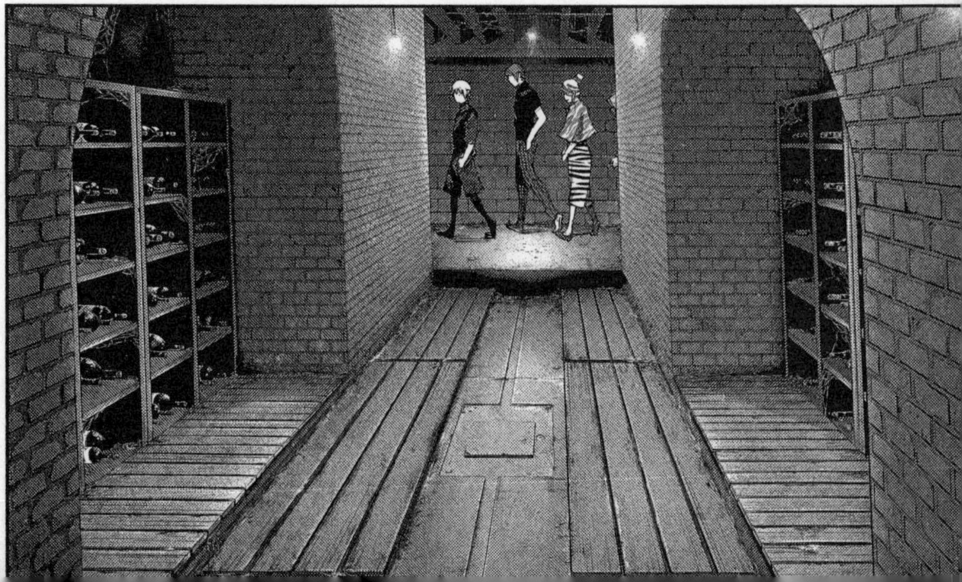

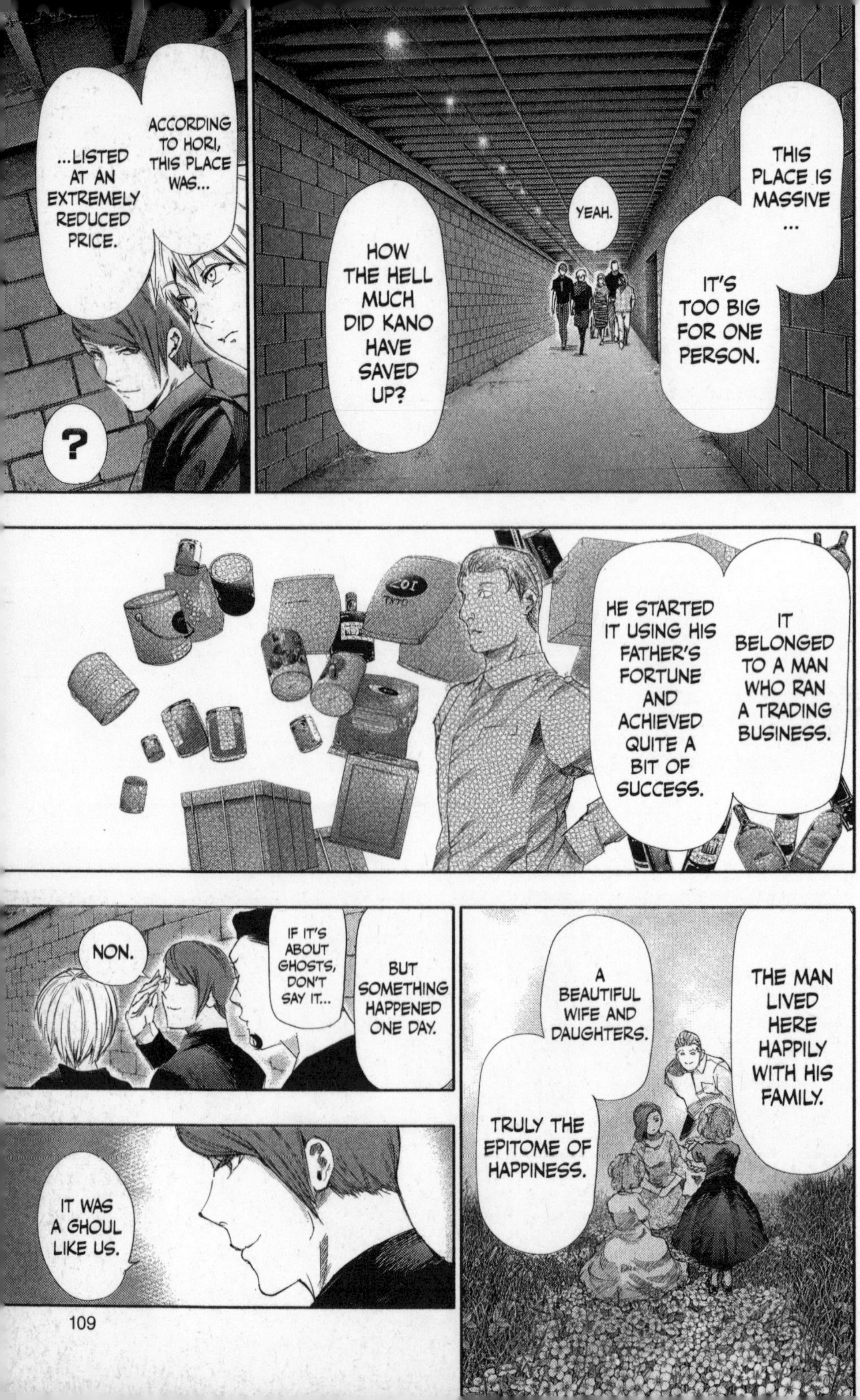
THIS PLACE IS MASSIVE...
IT'S TOO BIG FOR ONE PERSON.
YEAH.
HOW THE HELL MUCH DID KANO HAVE SAVED UP?
ACCORDING TO HORI, THIS PLACE WAS...
...LISTED AT AN EXTREMELY REDUCED PRICE.
?
IT BELONGED TO A MAN WHO RAN A TRADING BUSINESS.
HE STARTED IT USING HIS FATHER'S FORTUNE AND ACHIEVED QUITE A BIT OF SUCCESS.
THE MAN LIVED HERE HAPPILY WITH HIS FAMILY.
A BEAUTIFUL WIFE AND DAUGHTERS.
TRULY THE EPITOME OF HAPPINESS.
BUT SOMETHING HAPPENED ONE DAY.
IF IT'S ABOUT GHOSTS, DON'T SAY IT...
NON.
IT WAS A GHOUL LIKE US.

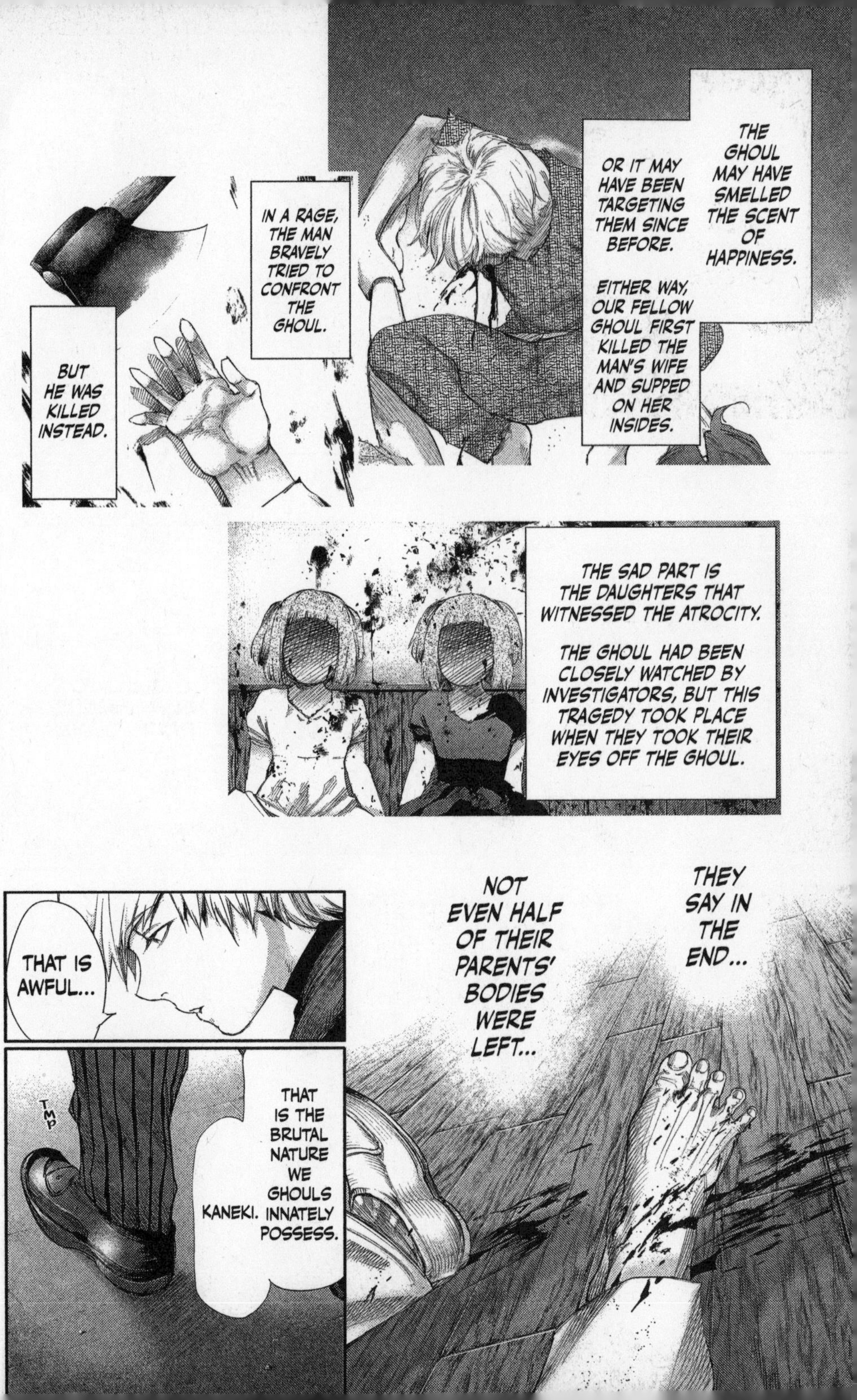
THE GHOUL MAY HAVE SMELLED THE SCENT OF HAPPINESS.
OR IT MAY HAVE BEEN TARGETING THEM SINCE BEFORE.
EITHER WAY, OUR FELLOW GHOUL FIRST KILLED THE MAN'S WIFE AND SUPPED ON HER INSIDES.
IN A RAGE, THE MAN BRAVELY TRIED TO CONFRONT THE GHOUL.
BUT HE WAS KILLED INSTEAD.
THE SAD PART IS THE DAUGHTERS THAT WITNESSED THE ATROCITY.
THE GHOUL HAD BEEN CLOSELY WATCHED BY INVESTIGATORS, BUT THIS TRAGEDY TOOK PLACE WHEN THEY TOOK THEIR EYES OFF THE GHOUL.
THEY SAY IN THE END...
NOT EVEN HALF OF THEIR PARENTS' BODIES WERE LEFT...
THAT IS AWFUL...
TMP
THAT IS THE BRUTAL NATURE WE GHOULS INNATELY POSSESS.
KANEKI.

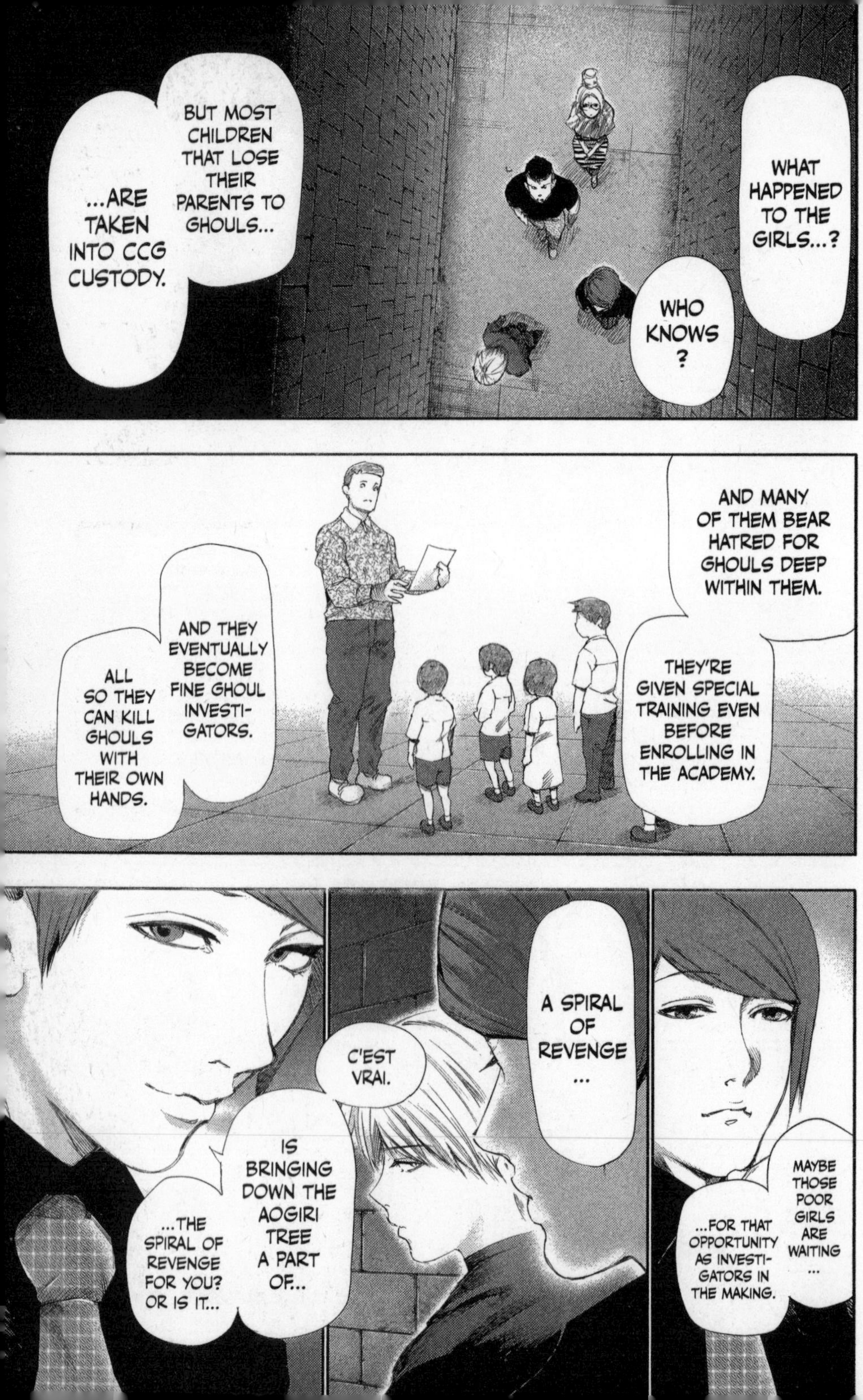
WHAT HAPPENED TO THE GIRLS...?
WHO KNOWS?
BUT MOST CHILDREN THAT LOSE THEIR PARENTS TO GHOULS...
...ARE TAKEN INTO CCG CUSTODY.
AND MANY OF THEM BEAR HATRED FOR GHOULS DEEP WITHIN THEM.
THEY'RE GIVEN SPECIAL TRAINING EVEN BEFORE ENROLLING IN THE ACADEMY.
AND THEY EVENTUALLY BECOME FINE GHOUL INVESTIGATORS.
ALL SO THEY CAN KILL GHOULS WITH THEIR OWN HANDS.
MAYBE THOSE POOR GIRLS ARE WAITING...
...FOR THAT OPPORTUNITY AS INVESTIGATORS IN THE MAKING.
A SPIRAL OF REVENGE...
C'EST VRAI.
IS BRINGING DOWN THE AOGIRI TREE A PART OF...
...THE SPIRAL OF REVENGE FOR YOU? OR IS IT...

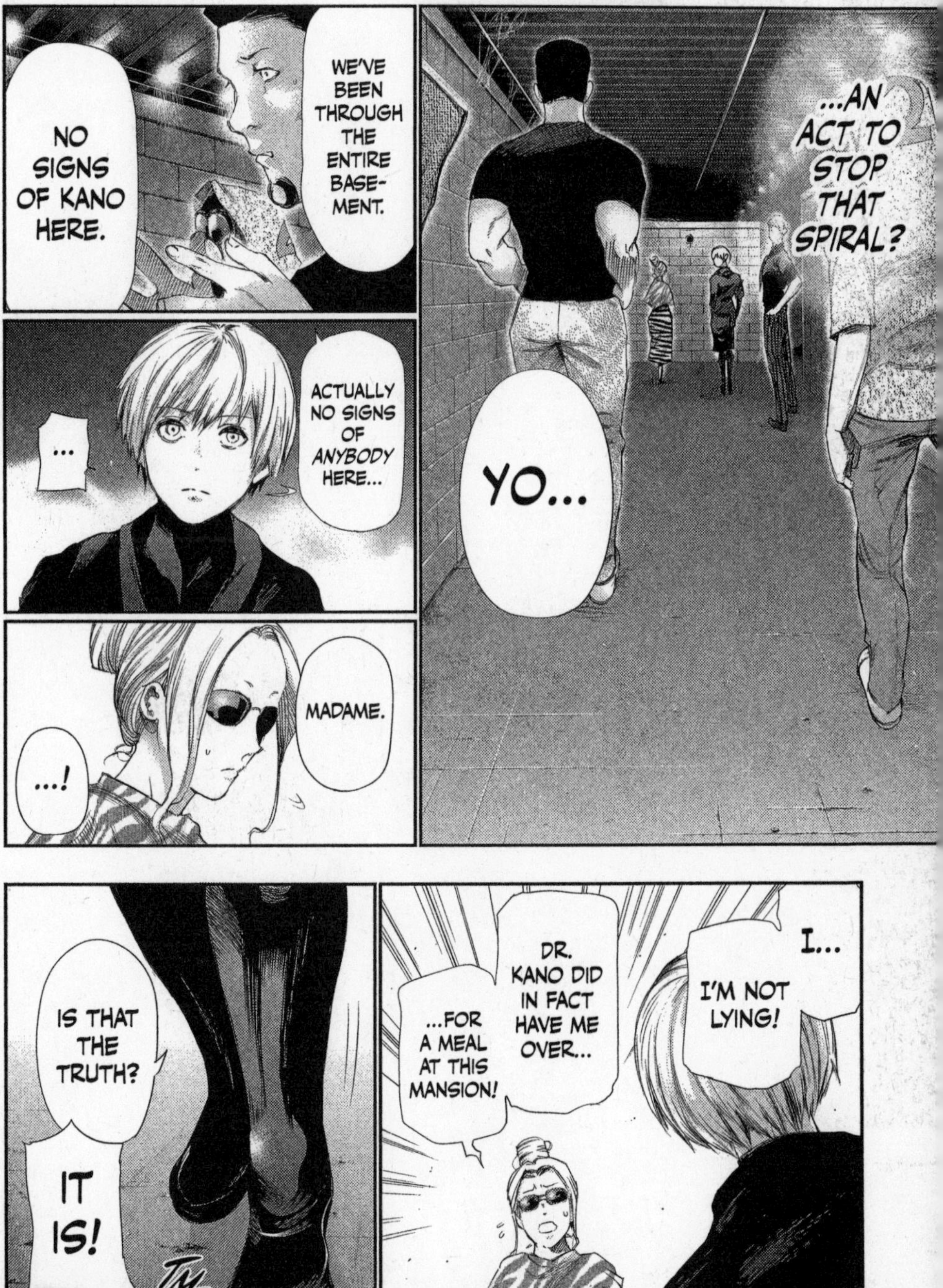
...AN ACT TO STOP THAT SPIRAL?
YO...
WE'VE BEEN THROUGH THE ENTIRE BASEMENT.
NO SIGNS OF KANO HERE.
ACTUALLY NO SIGNS OF *ANYBODY* HERE...
...
MADAME.
...!
I...
I'M NOT LYING!
DR. KANO DID IN FACT HAVE ME OVER...
...FOR A MEAL AT THIS MANSION!
IS THAT THE TRUTH?
IT IS!
TMP

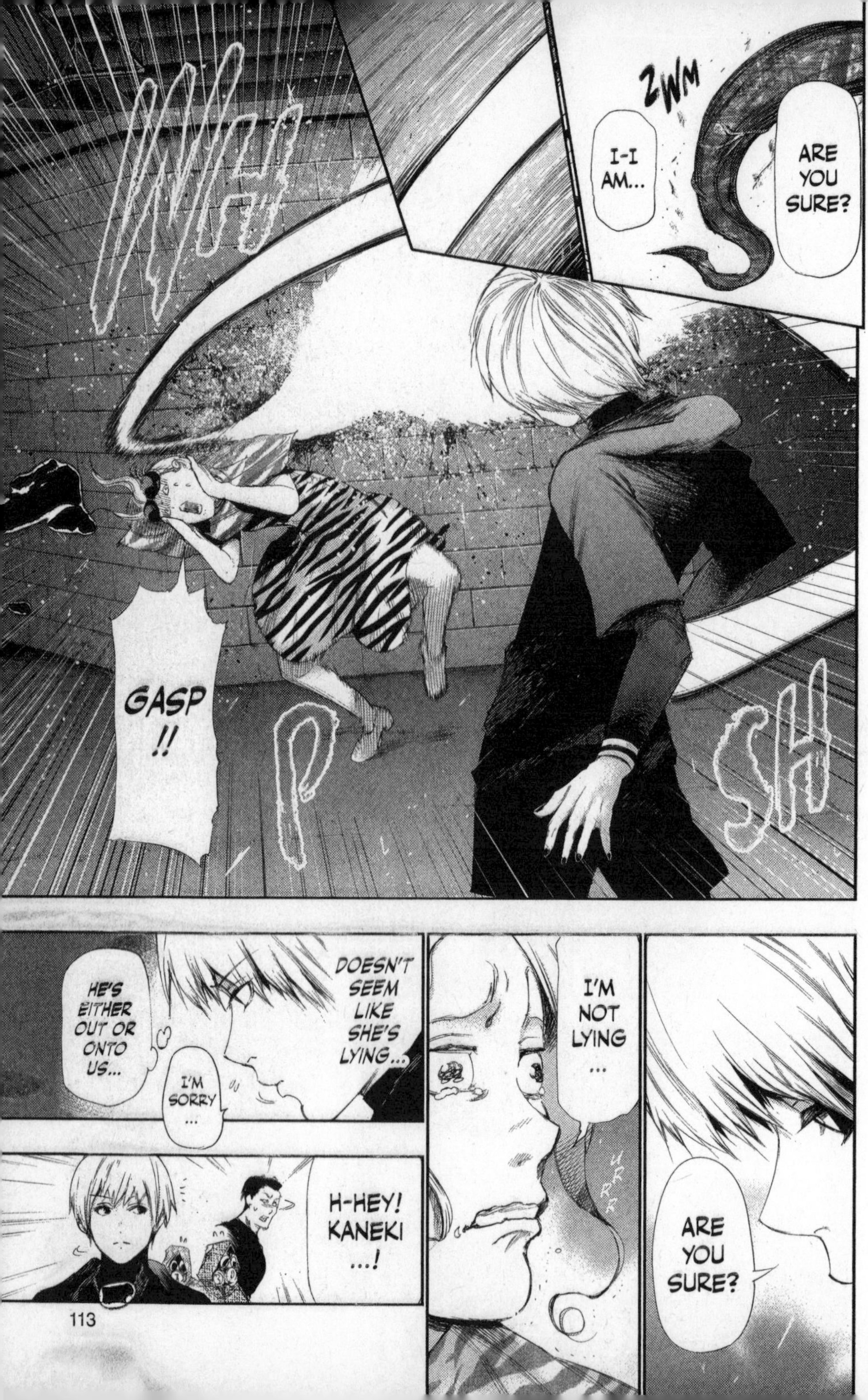
ZWM
ARE YOU SURE?
I-I AM...
WH
SH
P
GASP !!
ARE YOU SURE?
I'M NOT LYING ...
DOESN'T SEEM LIKE SHE'S LYING...
HE'S EITHER OUT OR ONTO US...
I'M SORRY ...
H-HEY! KANEKI ...!

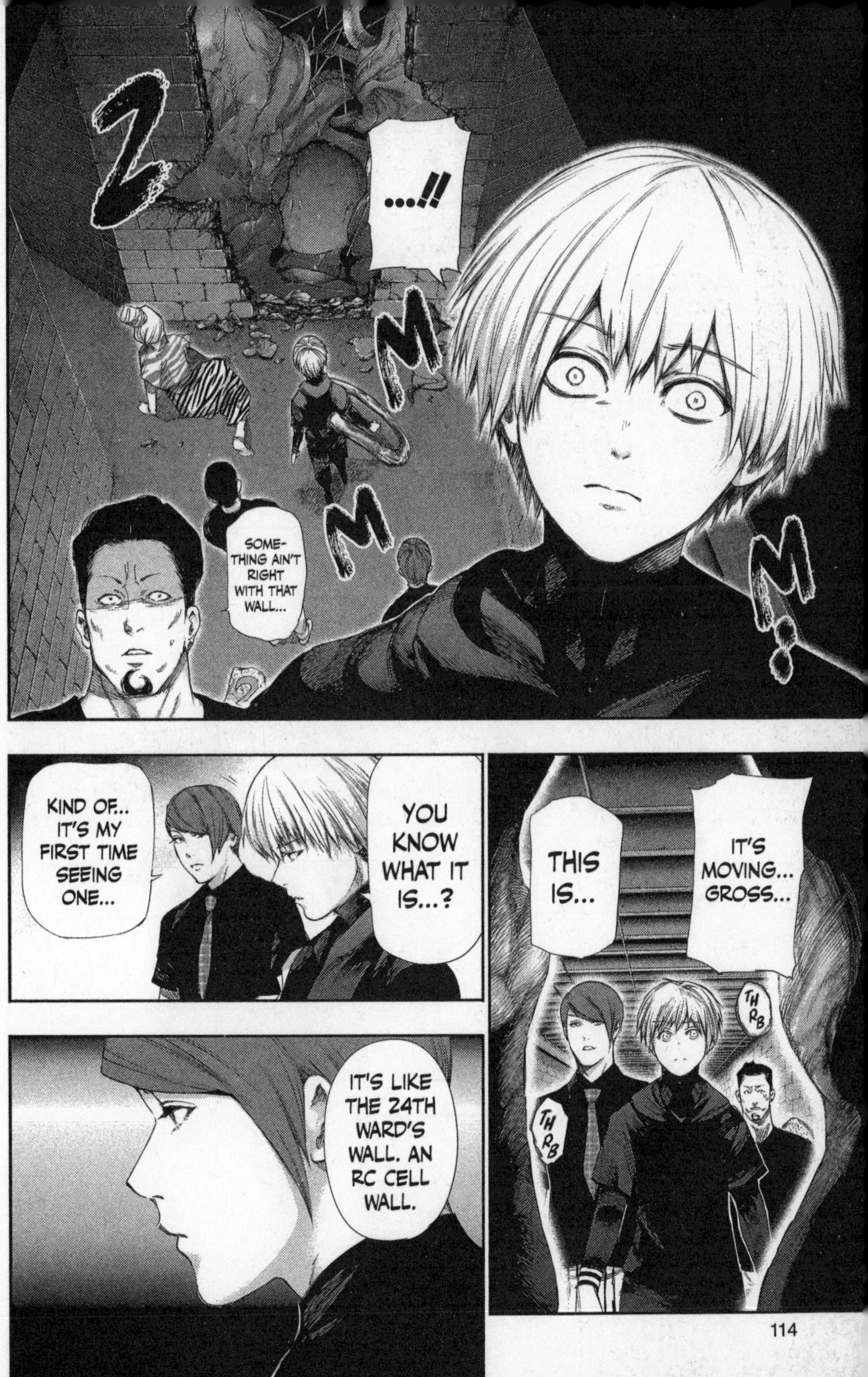
...!!
ZMMMM...
SOMETHING AIN'T RIGHT WITH THAT WALL...
IT'S MOVING... GROSS...
THIS IS...
THRB
THRB
YOU KNOW WHAT IT IS...?
KIND OF... IT'S MY FIRST TIME SEEING ONE...
IT'S LIKE THE 24TH WARD'S WALL. AN RC CELL WALL.

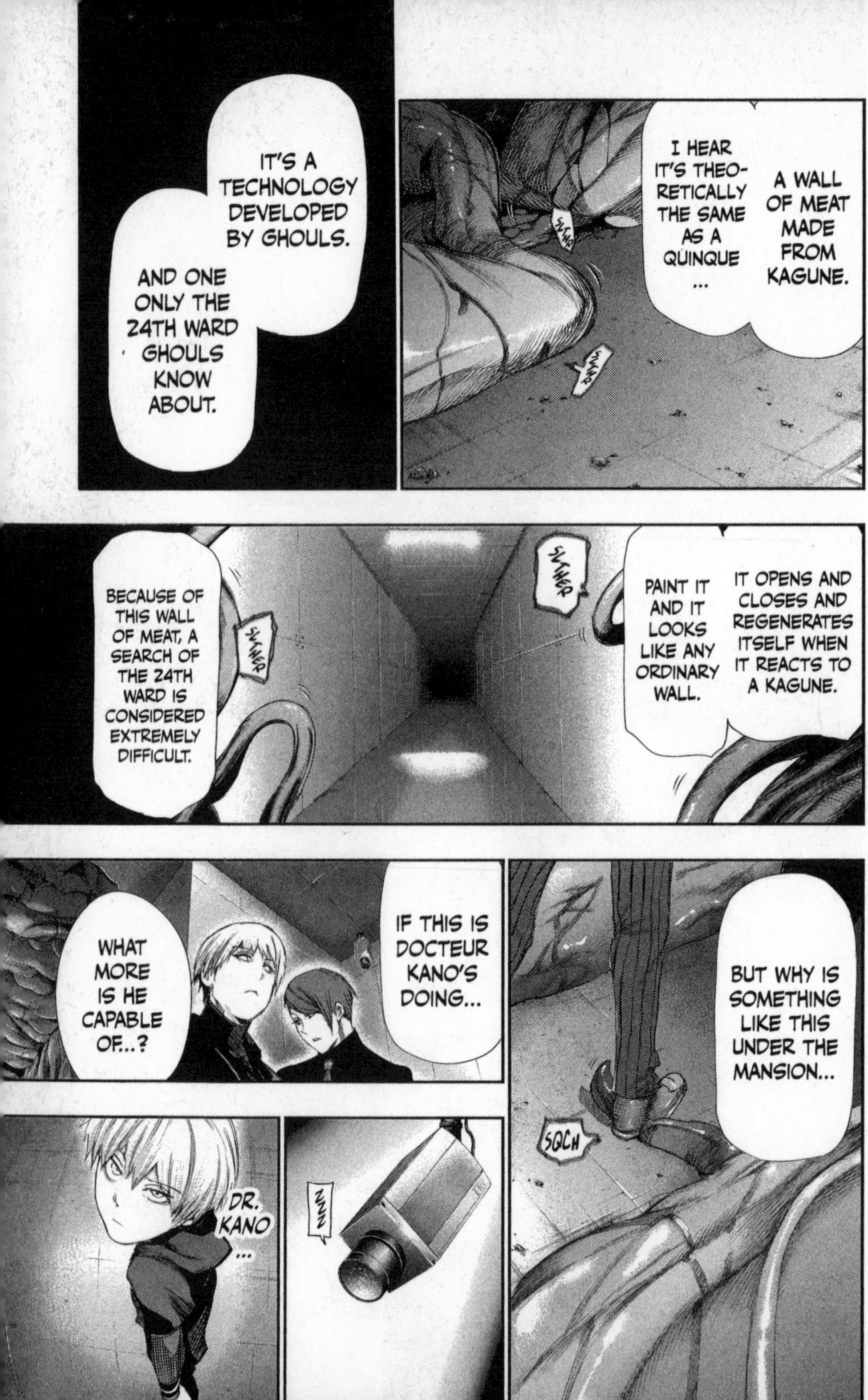
A WALL OF MEAT MADE FROM KAGUNE.
I HEAR IT'S THEO-RETICALLY THE SAME AS A QUINQUE ...
IT'S A TECHNOLOGY DEVELOPED BY GHOULS.
AND ONE ONLY THE 24TH WARD GHOULS KNOW ABOUT.
IT OPENS AND CLOSES AND REGENERATES ITSELF WHEN IT REACTS TO A KAGUNE.
PAINT IT AND IT LOOKS LIKE ANY ORDINARY WALL.
BECAUSE OF THIS WALL OF MEAT, A SEARCH OF THE 24TH WARD IS CONSIDERED EXTREMELY DIFFICULT.
BUT WHY IS SOMETHING LIKE THIS UNDER THE MANSION...
SQCH
IF THIS IS DOCTEUR KANO'S DOING...
WHAT MORE IS HE CAPABLE OF...?
DR. KANO ...

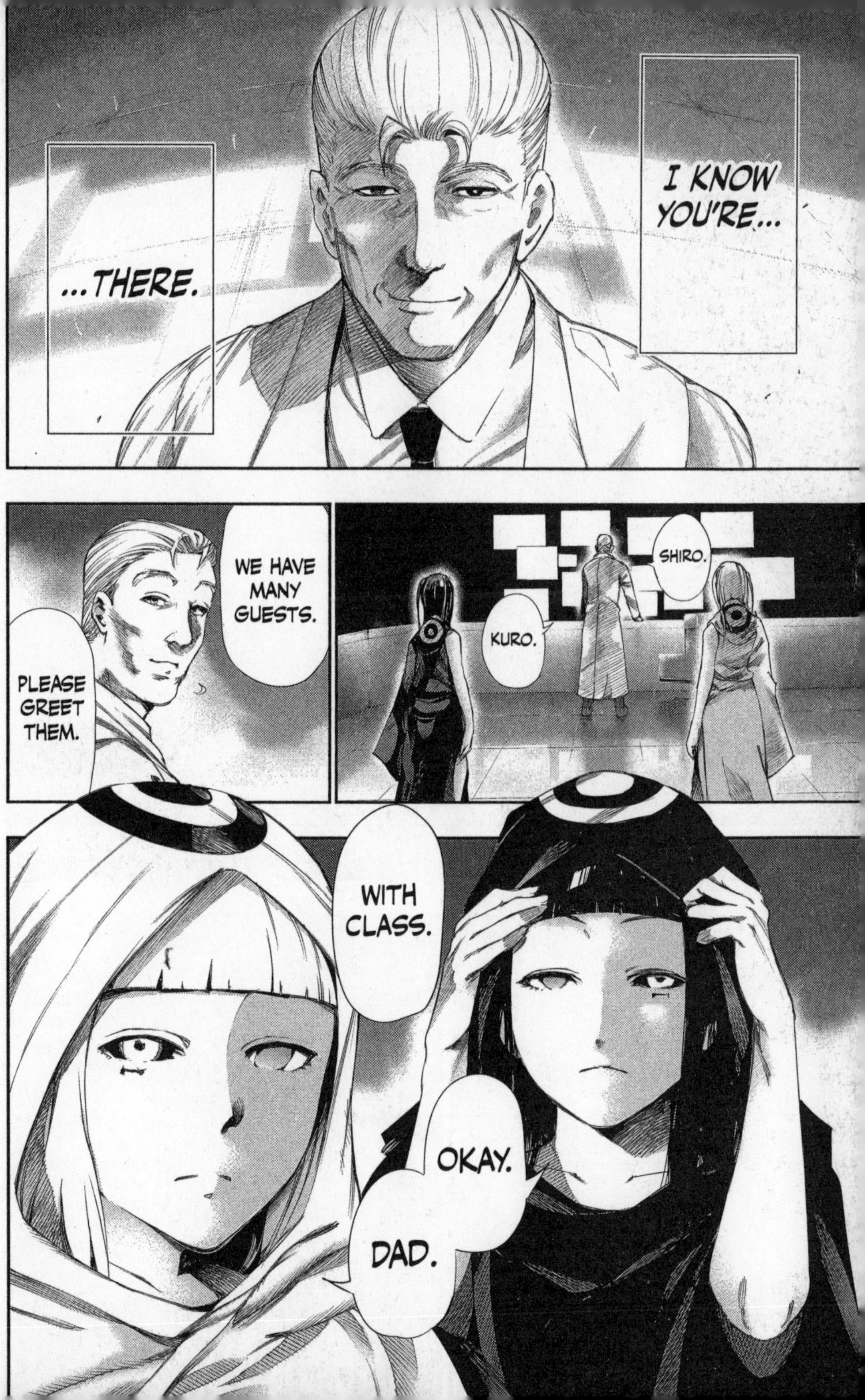
I KNOW YOU'RE...
...THERE.
SHIRO.
KURO.
WE HAVE MANY GUESTS.
PLEASE GREET THEM.
WITH CLASS.
OKAY.
DAD.

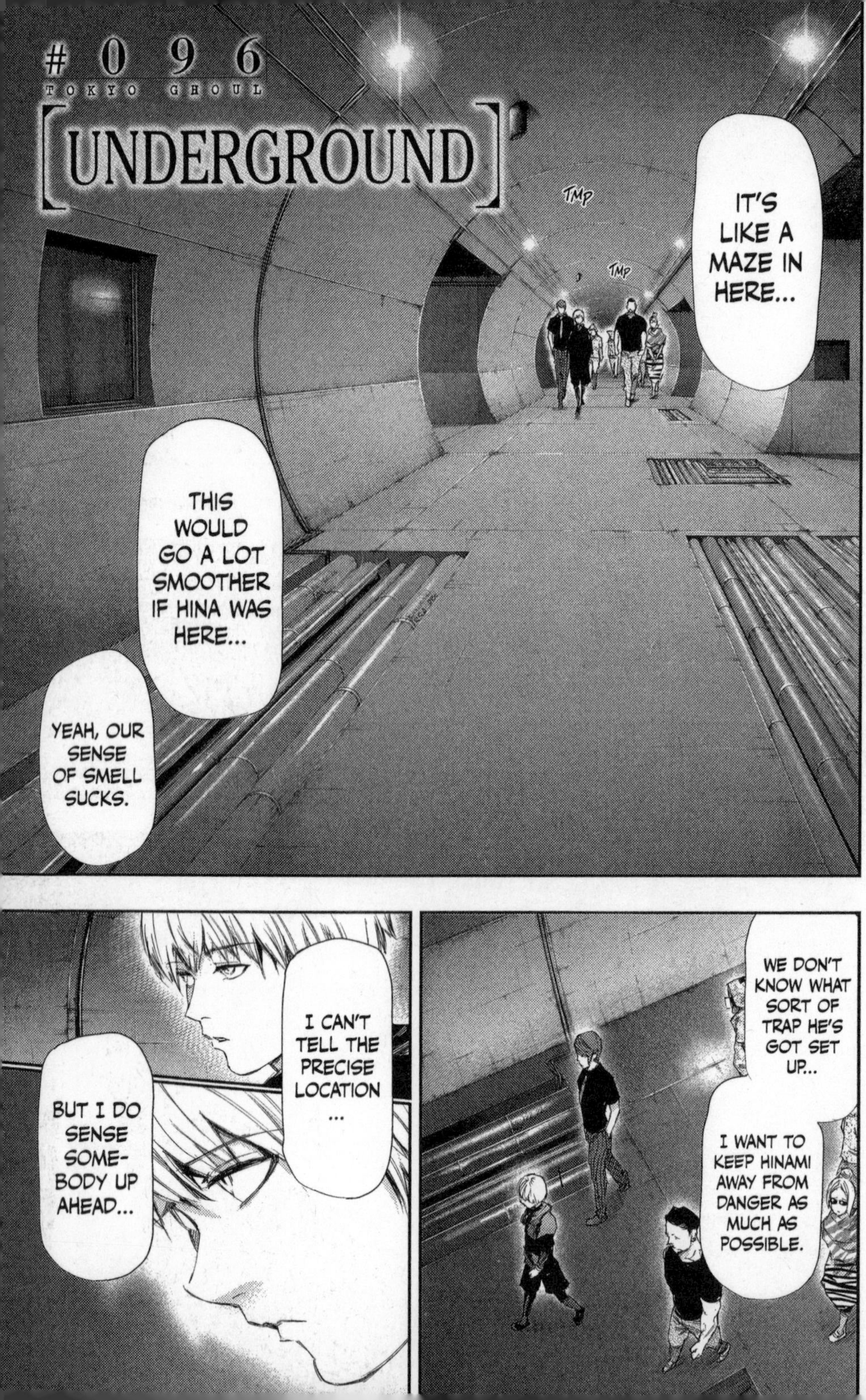
#096
TOKYO GHOUL
[UNDERGROUND]
IT'S LIKE A MAZE IN HERE...
TMP
TMP
THIS WOULD GO A LOT SMOOTHER IF HINA WAS HERE...
YEAH, OUR SENSE OF SMELL SUCKS.
WE DON'T KNOW WHAT SORT OF TRAP HE'S GOT SET UP...
I WANT TO KEEP HINAMI AWAY FROM DANGER AS MUCH AS POSSIBLE.
I CAN'T TELL THE PRECISE LOCATION...
BUT I DO SENSE SOME-BODY UP AHEAD...

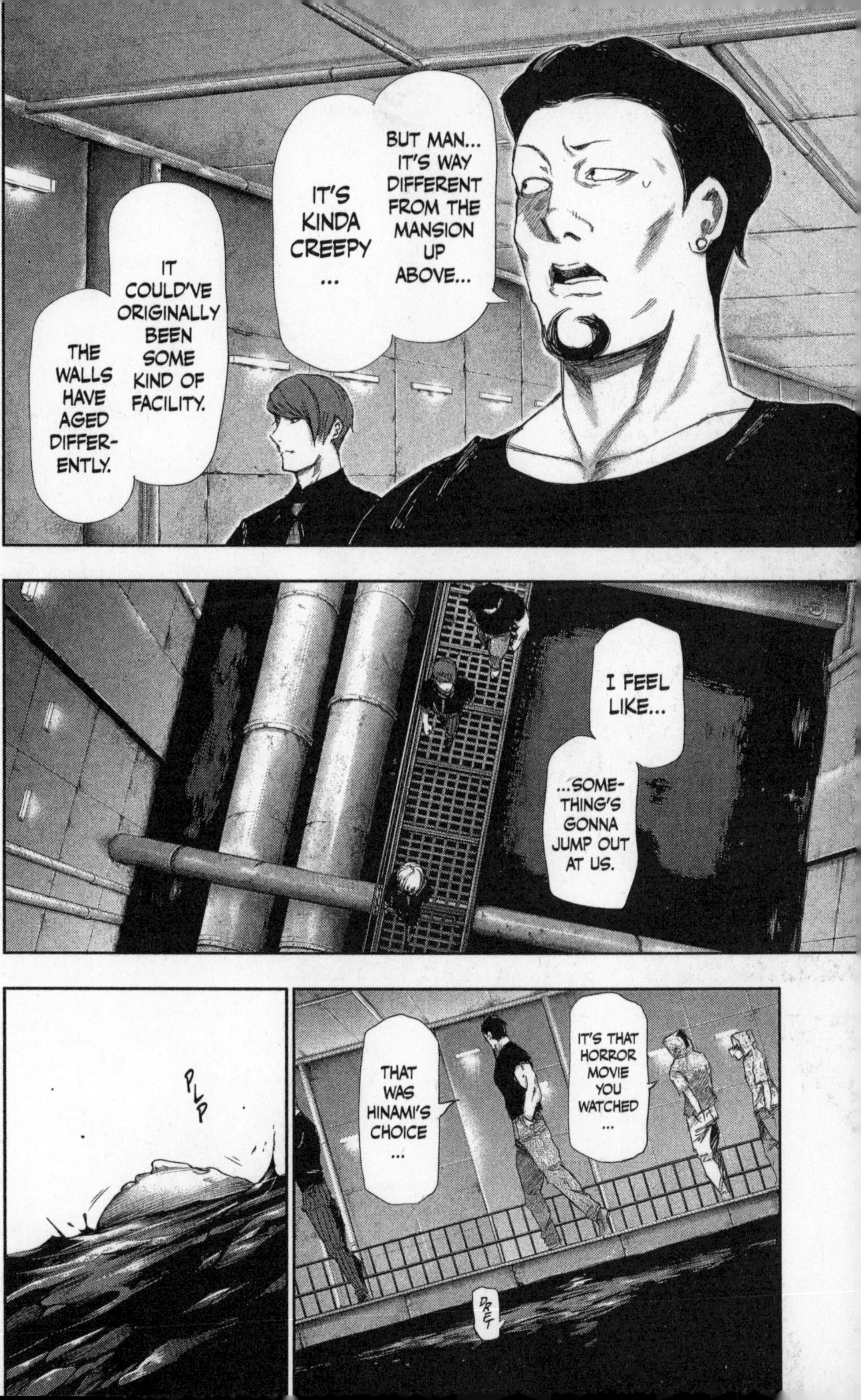
BUT MAN... IT'S WAY DIFFERENT FROM THE MANSION UP ABOVE...
IT'S KINDA CREEPY...
IT COULD'VE ORIGINALLY BEEN SOME KIND OF FACILITY.
THE WALLS HAVE AGED DIFFER-ENTLY.
I FEEL LIKE...
...SOME-THING'S GONNA JUMP OUT AT US.
IT'S THAT HORROR MOVIE YOU WATCHED...
THAT WAS HINAMI'S CHOICE...
DRET
PLP

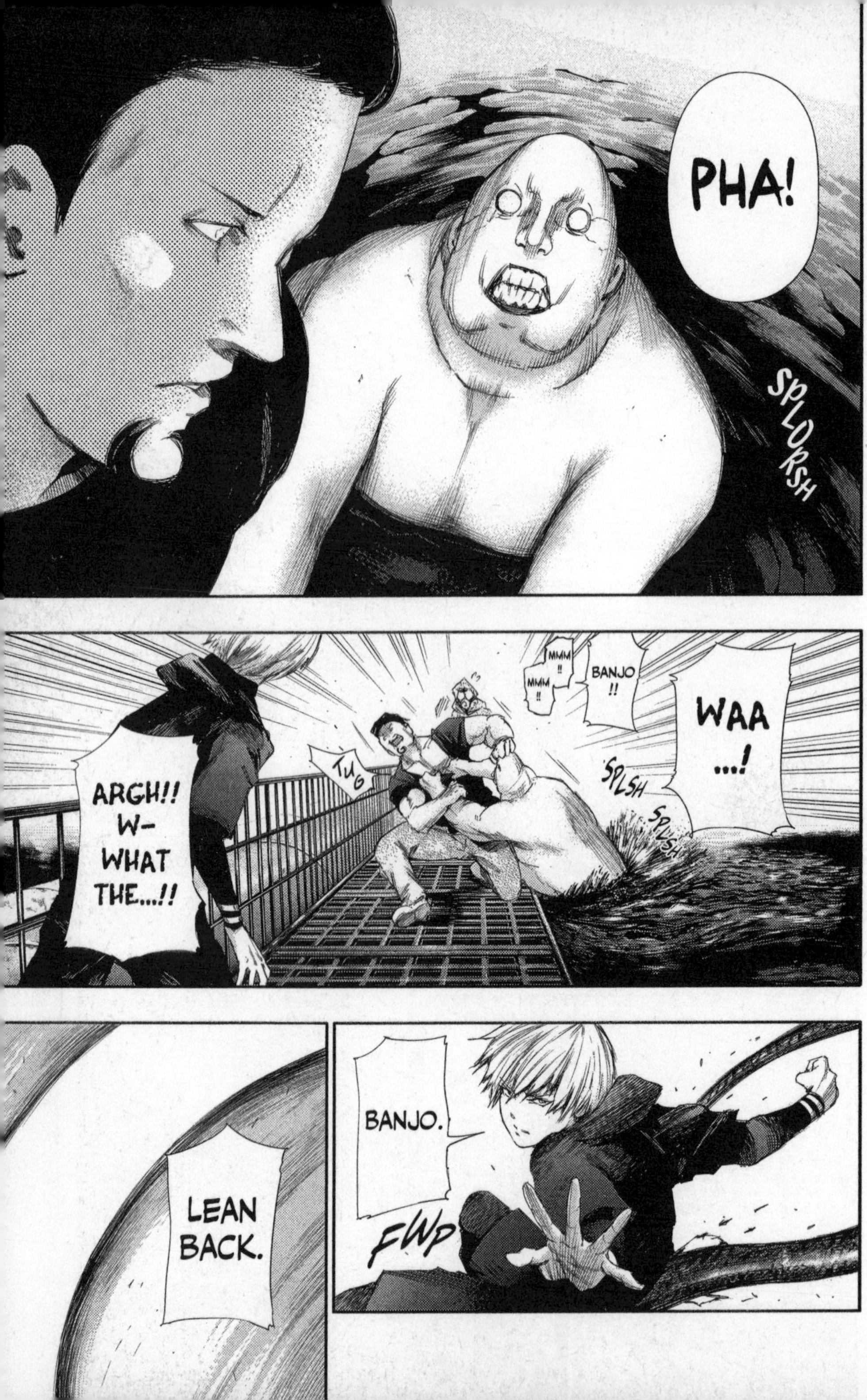
PHA!
SPLORSH
WAA ...!
BANJO !!
MMM !!
MMM !!
SPLSH
SPLSH
TUG
ARGH!! W- WHAT THE...!!
BANJO.
FWP
LEAN BACK.

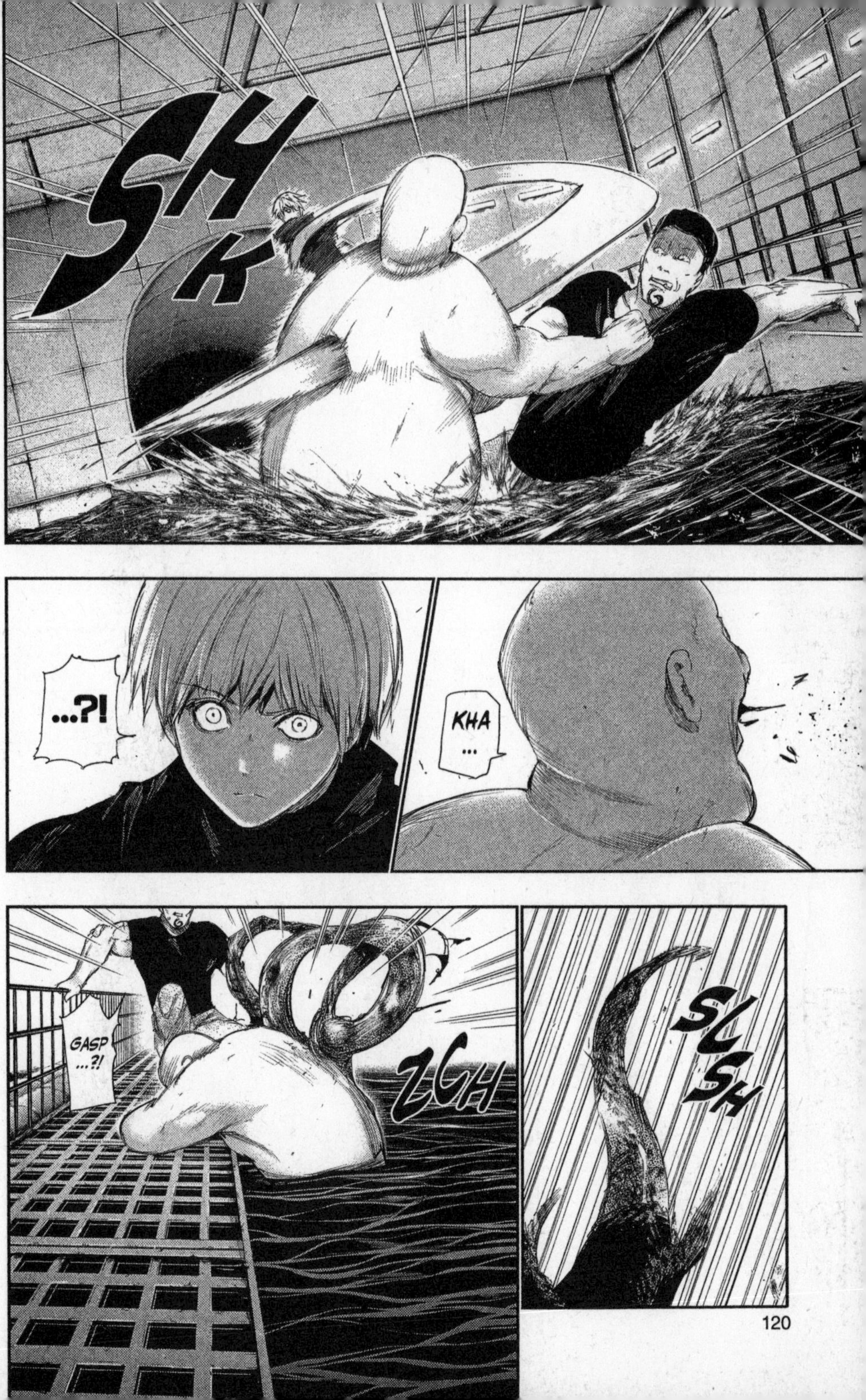
SHK
KHA ...
...?!
SLSH
GASP ...?!
ZCH

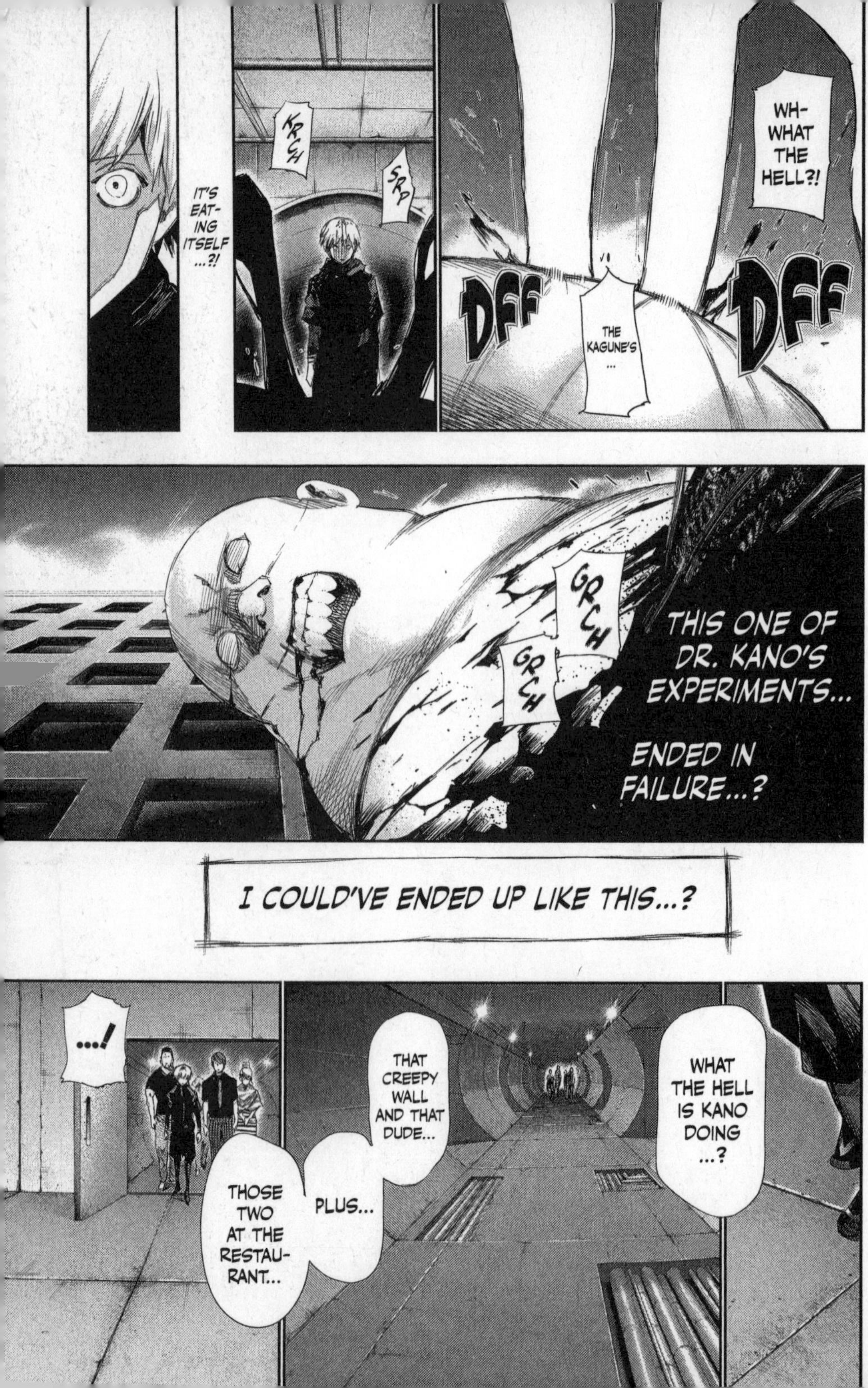
WH-WHAT THE HELL?!
DFF
THE KAGUNE'S...
DFF
KRCH
SRP
IT'S EATING ITSELF...?!
GRCH
GRCH
THIS ONE OF DR. KANO'S EXPERIMENTS...
ENDED IN FAILURE...?
I COULD'VE ENDED UP LIKE THIS...?
WHAT THE HELL IS KANO DOING...?
THAT CREEPY WALL AND THAT DUDE...
PLUS...
THOSE TWO AT THE RESTAURANT...
...!

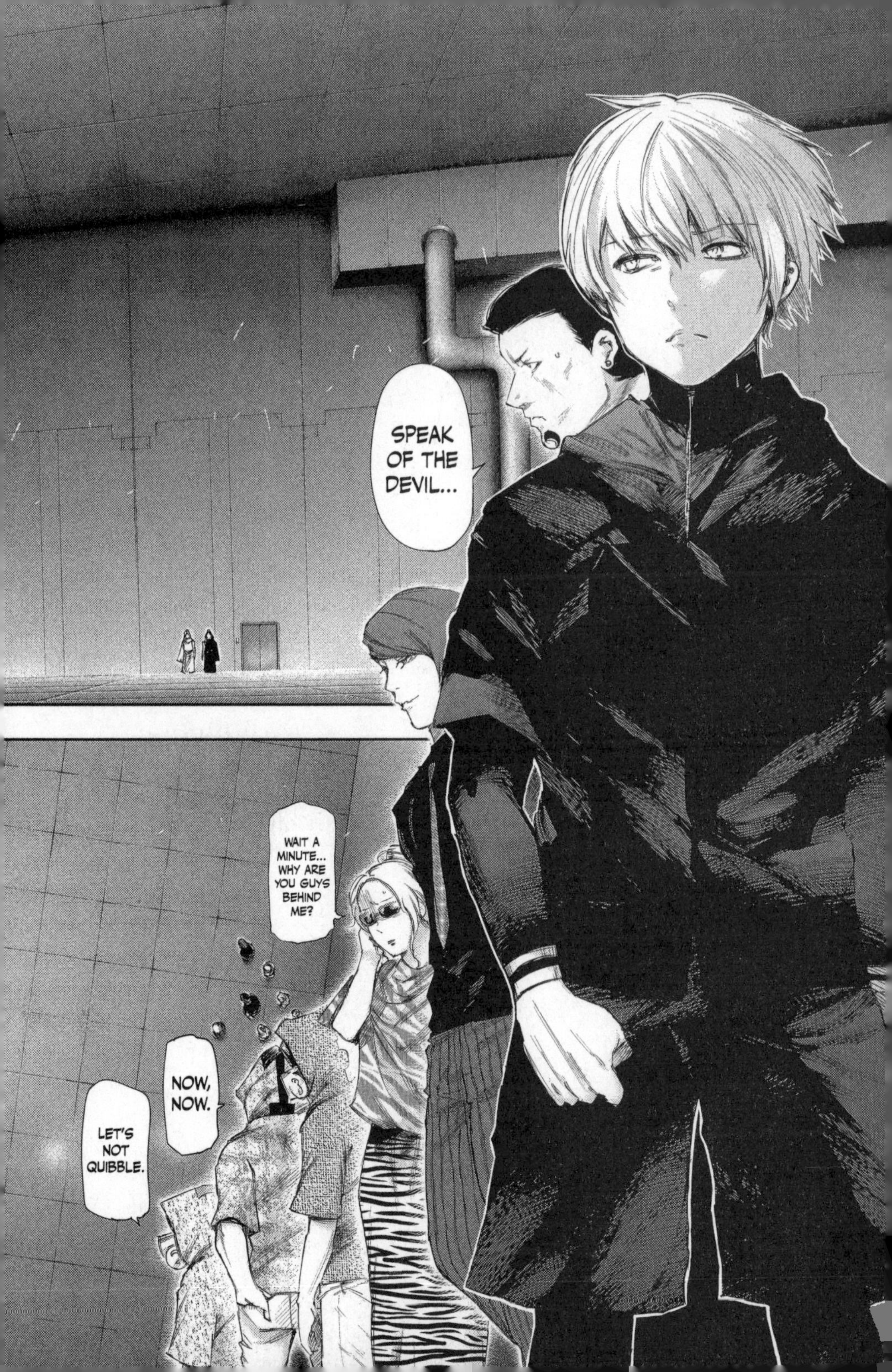
SPEAK OF THE DEVIL...
WAIT A MINUTE... WHY ARE YOU GUYS BEHIND ME?
NOW, NOW.
LET'S NOT QUIBBLE.

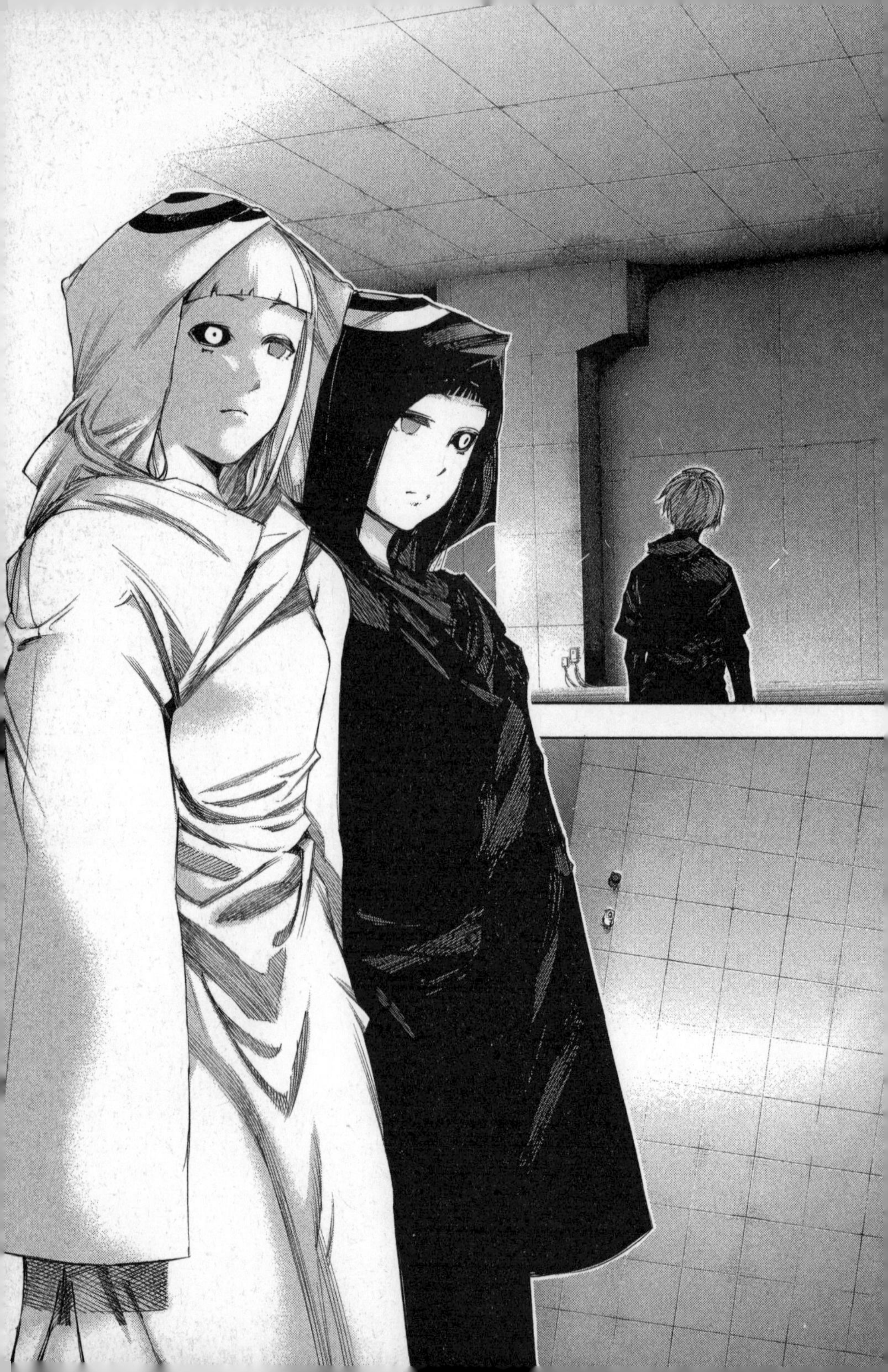

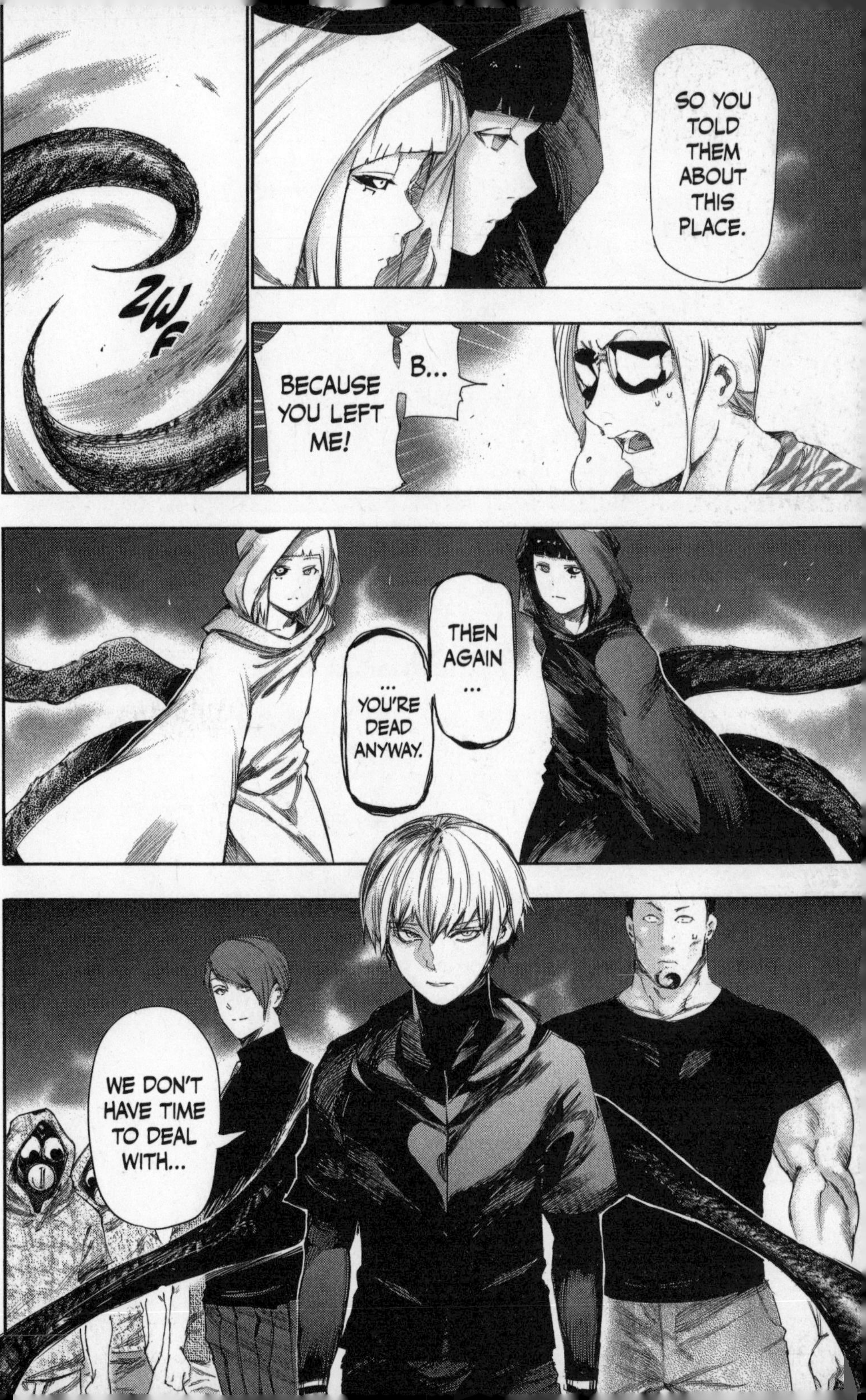
SO YOU TOLD THEM ABOUT THIS PLACE.
B...
BECAUSE YOU LEFT ME!
ZWF
THEN AGAIN...
...YOU'RE DEAD ANYWAY.
WE DON'T HAVE TIME TO DEAL WITH...

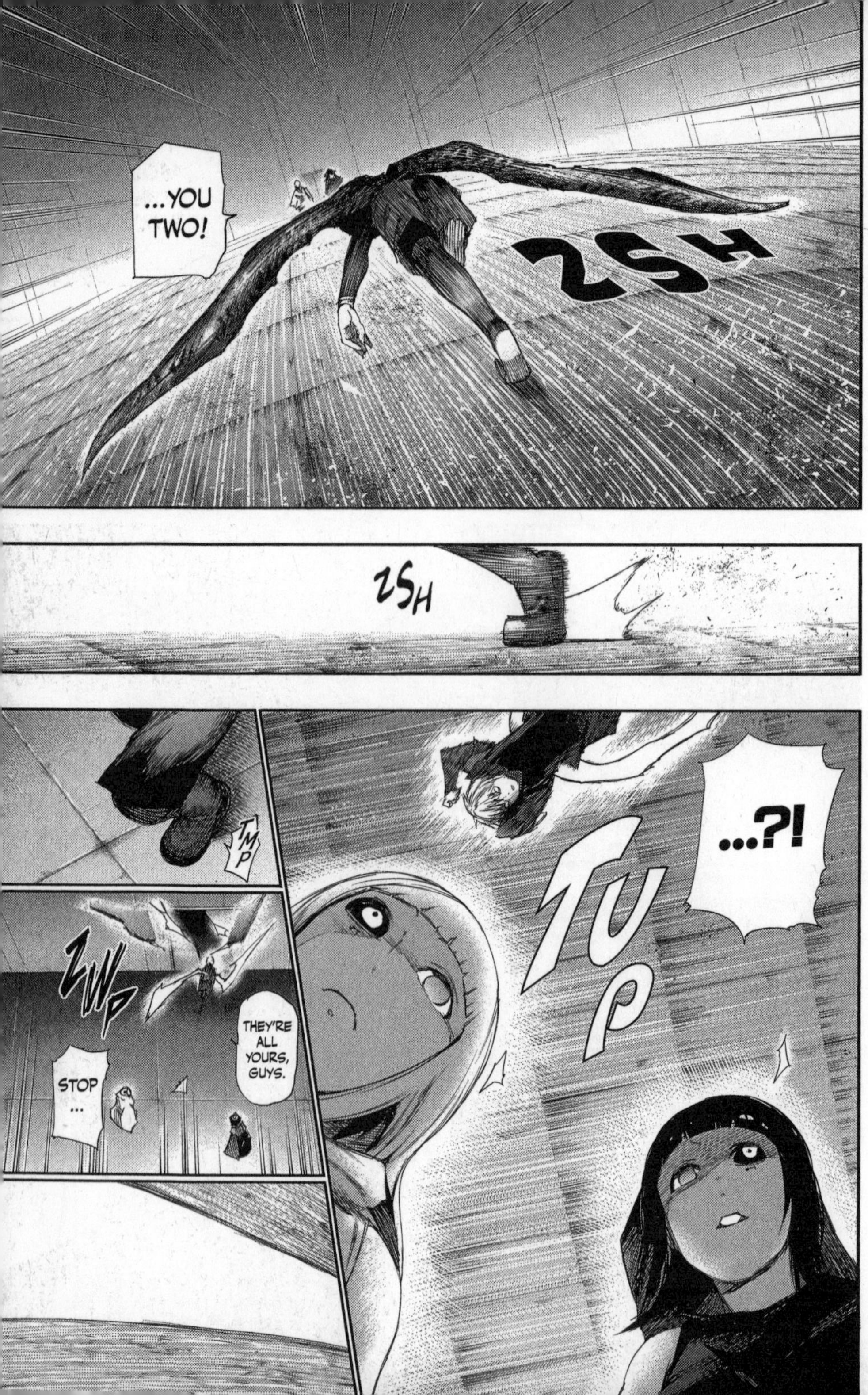
...YOU TWO!
ZSH
ZSH
...?!
TUP
TMP
ZWP
THEY'RE ALL YOURS, GUYS.
STOP ...

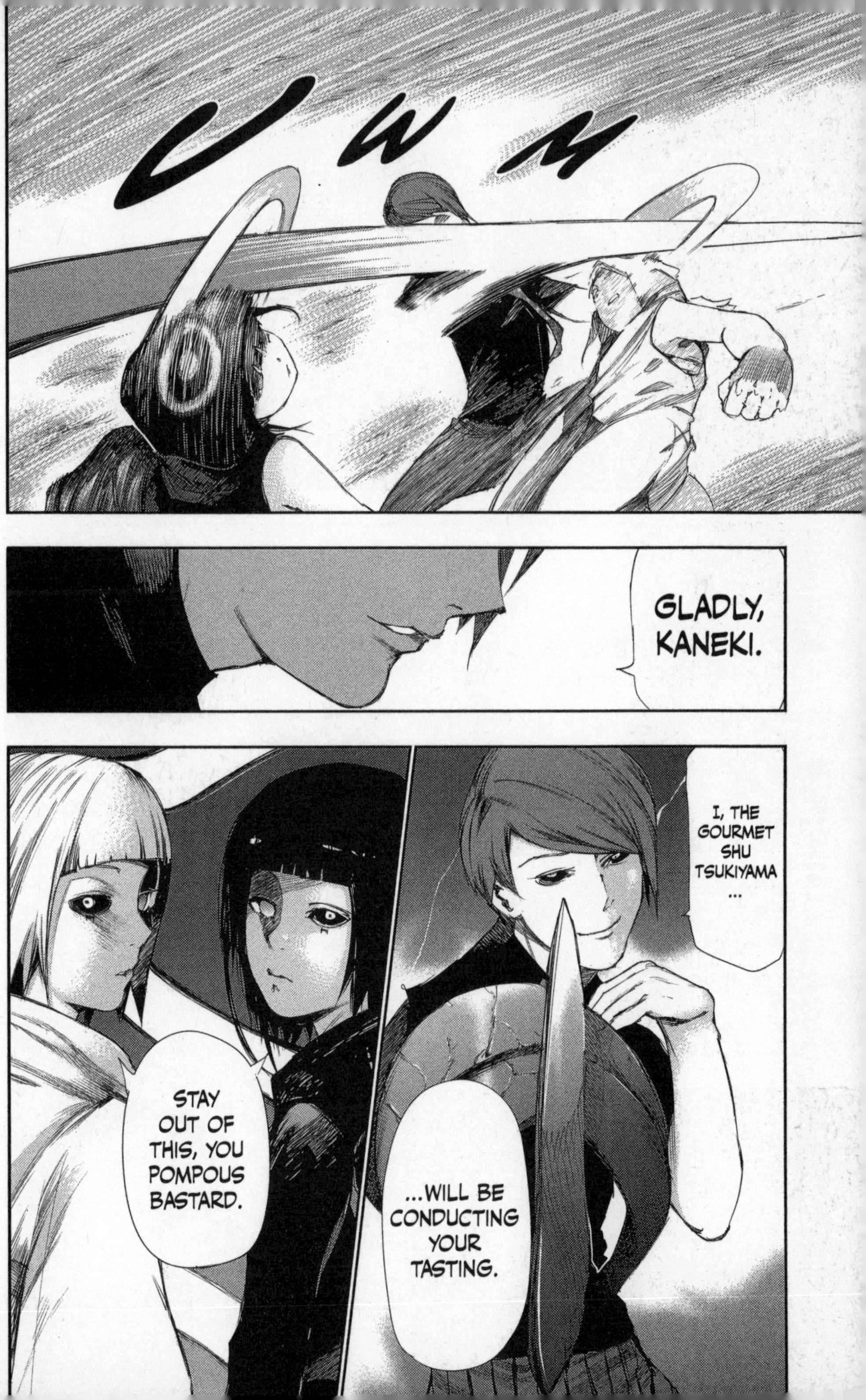
GLADLY, KANEKI.
I, THE GOURMET SHU TSUKIYAMA ...
...WILL BE CONDUCTING YOUR TASTING.
STAY OUT OF THIS, YOU POMPOUS BASTARD.

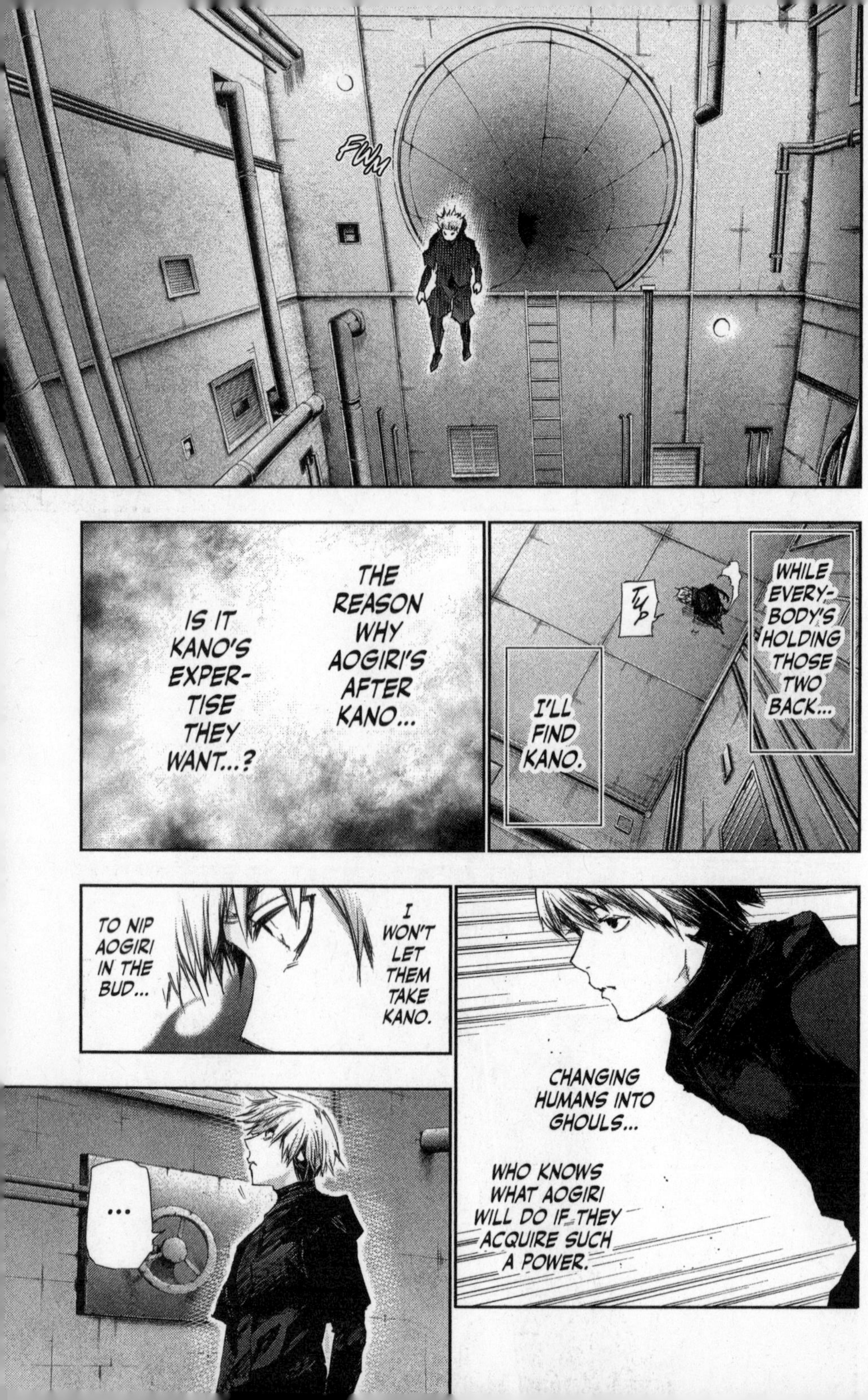
FWM
WHILE EVERY-BODY'S HOLDING THOSE TWO BACK...
TUP
I'LL FIND KANO.
THE REASON WHY AOGIRI'S AFTER KANO...
IS IT KANO'S EXPER-TISE THEY WANT...?
CHANGING HUMANS INTO GHOULS...
WHO KNOWS WHAT AOGIRI WILL DO IF THEY ACQUIRE SUCH A POWER.
I WON'T LET THEM TAKE KANO.
TO NIP AOGIRI IN THE BUD...
...

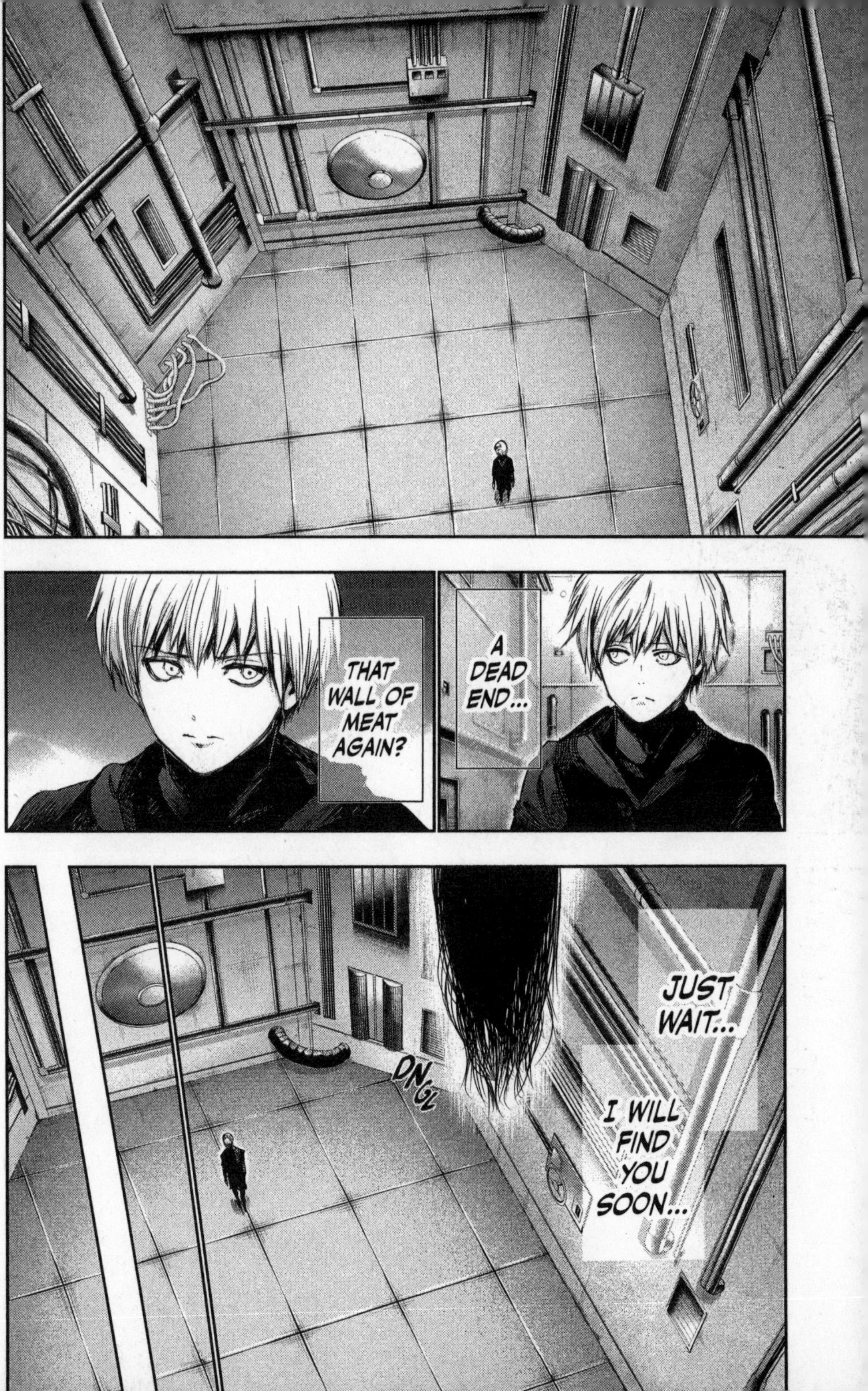
A DEAD END...
THAT WALL OF MEAT AGAIN?
JUST WAIT...
I WILL FIND YOU SOON...
DNGL

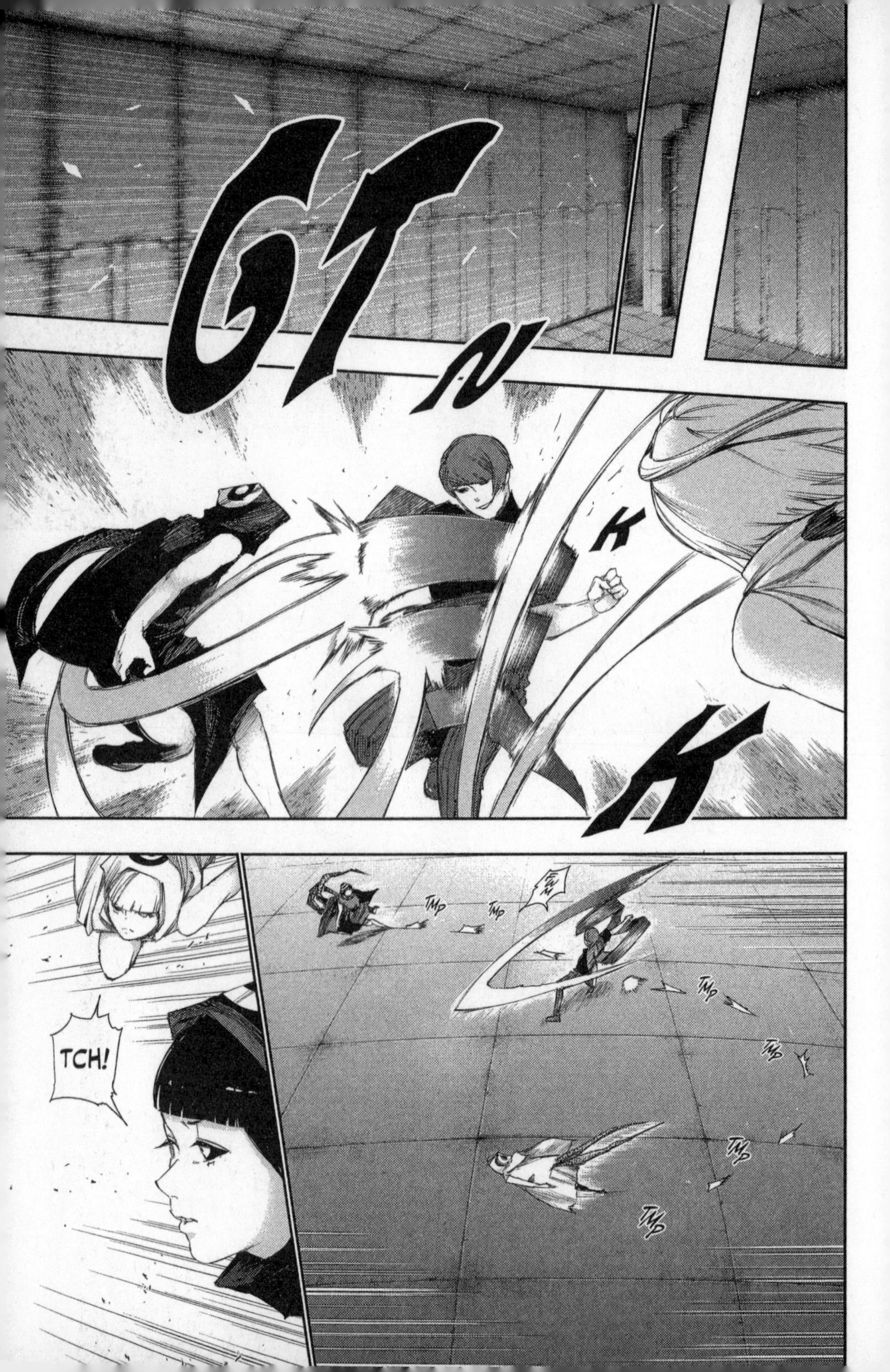
GTNKK
FWM
TMP
TMP
TMP
TMP
TMP
TMP
TCH!

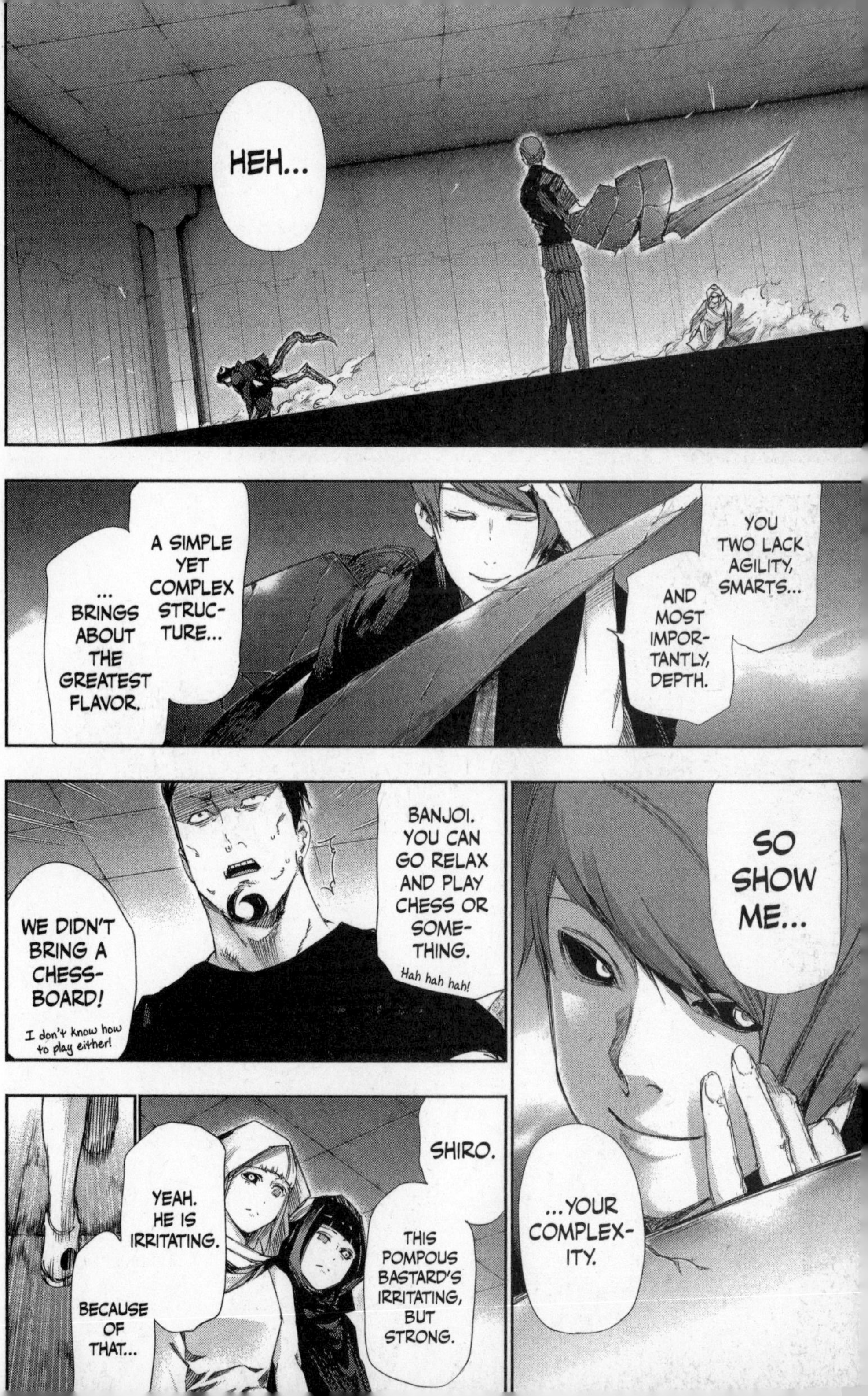
HEH...
YOU TWO LACK AGILITY, SMARTS...
AND MOST IMPORTANTLY, DEPTH.
A SIMPLE YET COMPLEX STRUCTURE...
...BRINGS ABOUT THE GREATEST FLAVOR.
SO SHOW ME...
...YOUR COMPLEXITY.
BANJOI. YOU CAN GO RELAX AND PLAY CHESS OR SOMETHING.
Hah hah hah!
WE DIDN'T BRING A CHESSBOARD!
I don't know how to play either!
SHIRO.
THIS POMPOUS BASTARD'S IRRITATING, BUT STRONG.
YEAH. HE IS IRRITATING.
BECAUSE OF THAT...

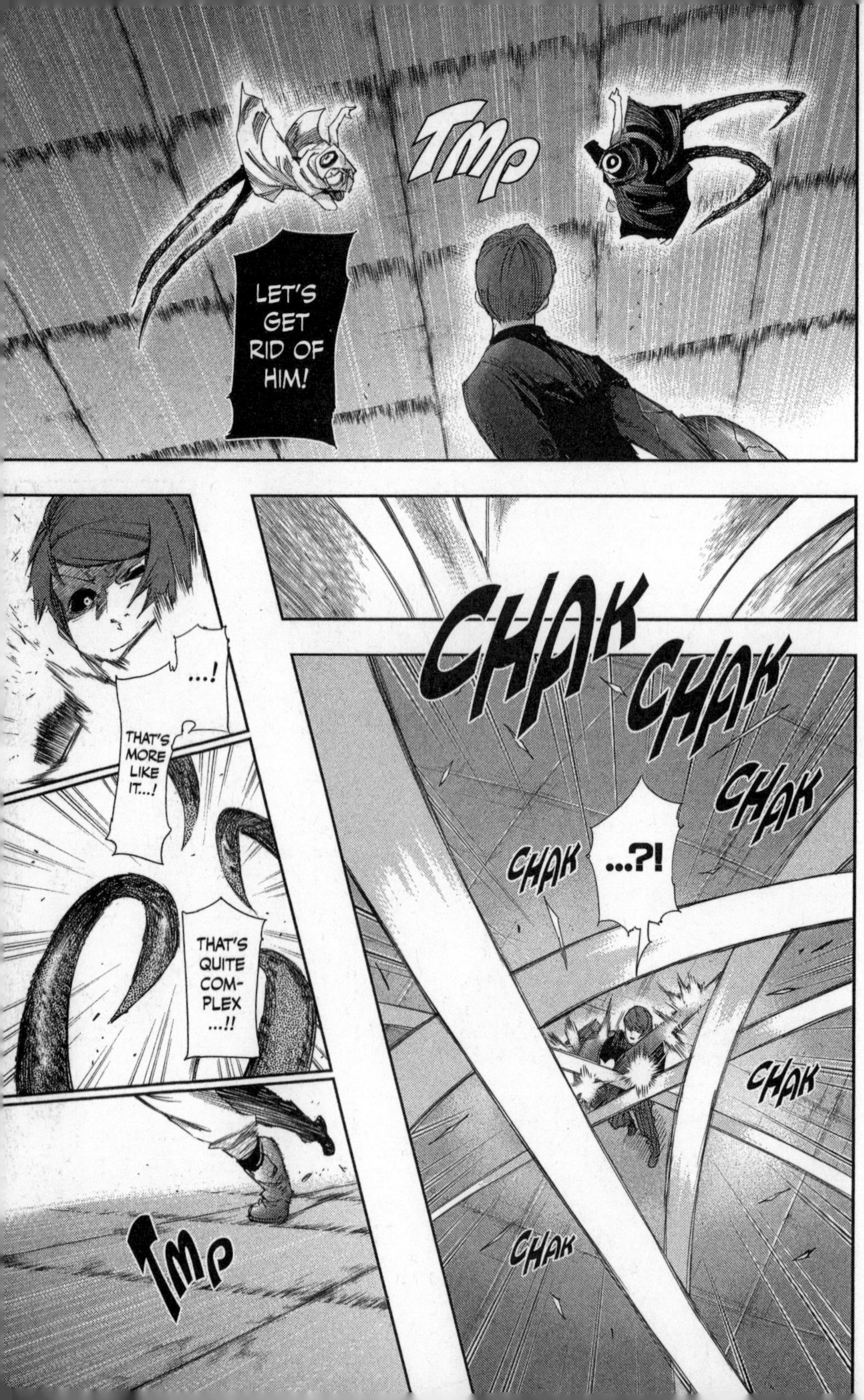
TMP
LET'S GET RID OF HIM!
CHAK
CHAK
CHAK
CHAK
...?!
CHAK
CHAK
...!
THAT'S MORE LIKE IT...!
THAT'S QUITE COMPLEX...!!
TMP

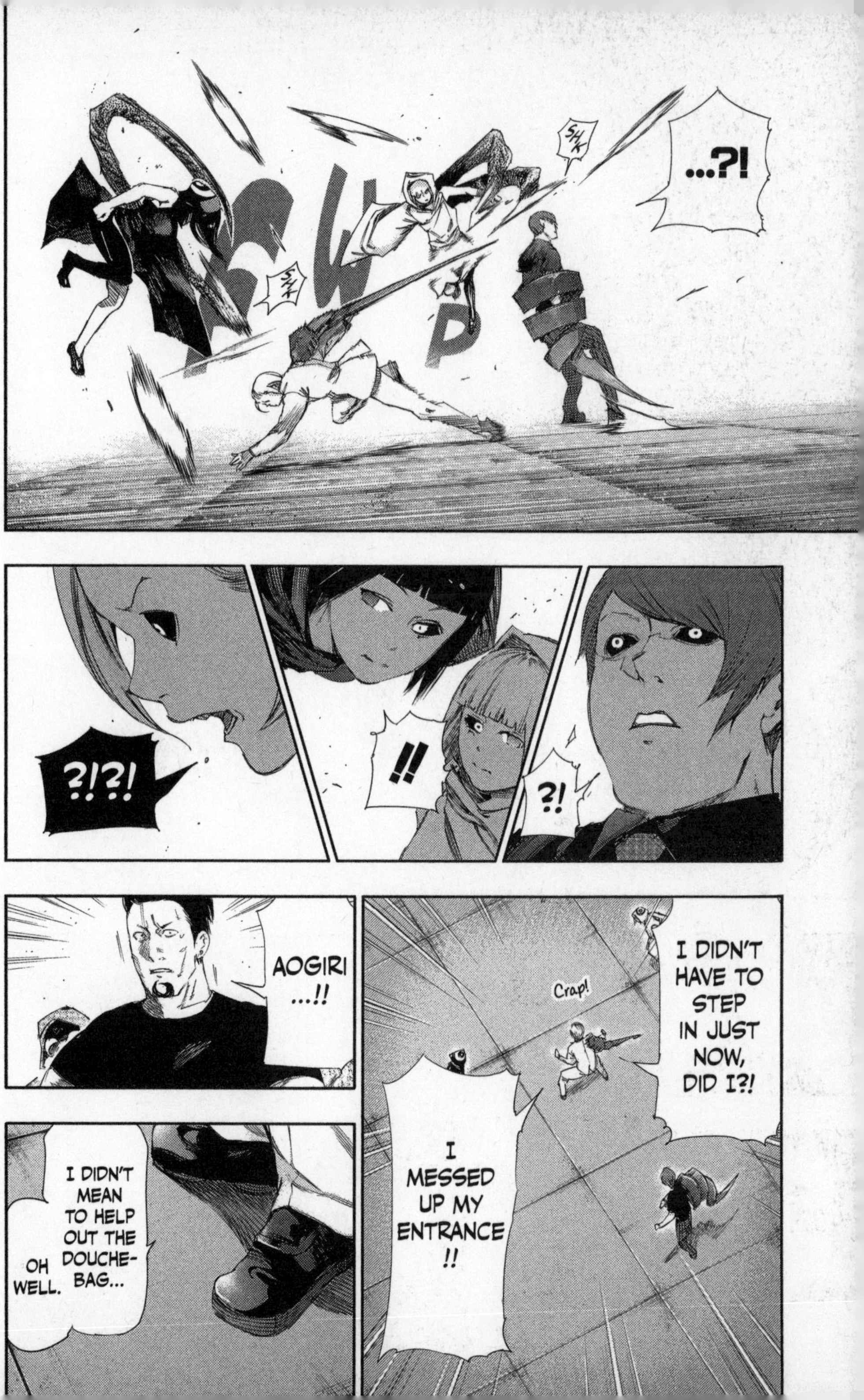
...?!
SHK
SHK
?!
!!
?!?!
I DIDN'T HAVE TO STEP IN JUST NOW, DID I?!
Crap!
I MESSED UP MY ENTRANCE !!
AOGIRI ...!!
I DIDN'T MEAN TO HELP OUT THE DOUCHE-BAG...
OH WELL.

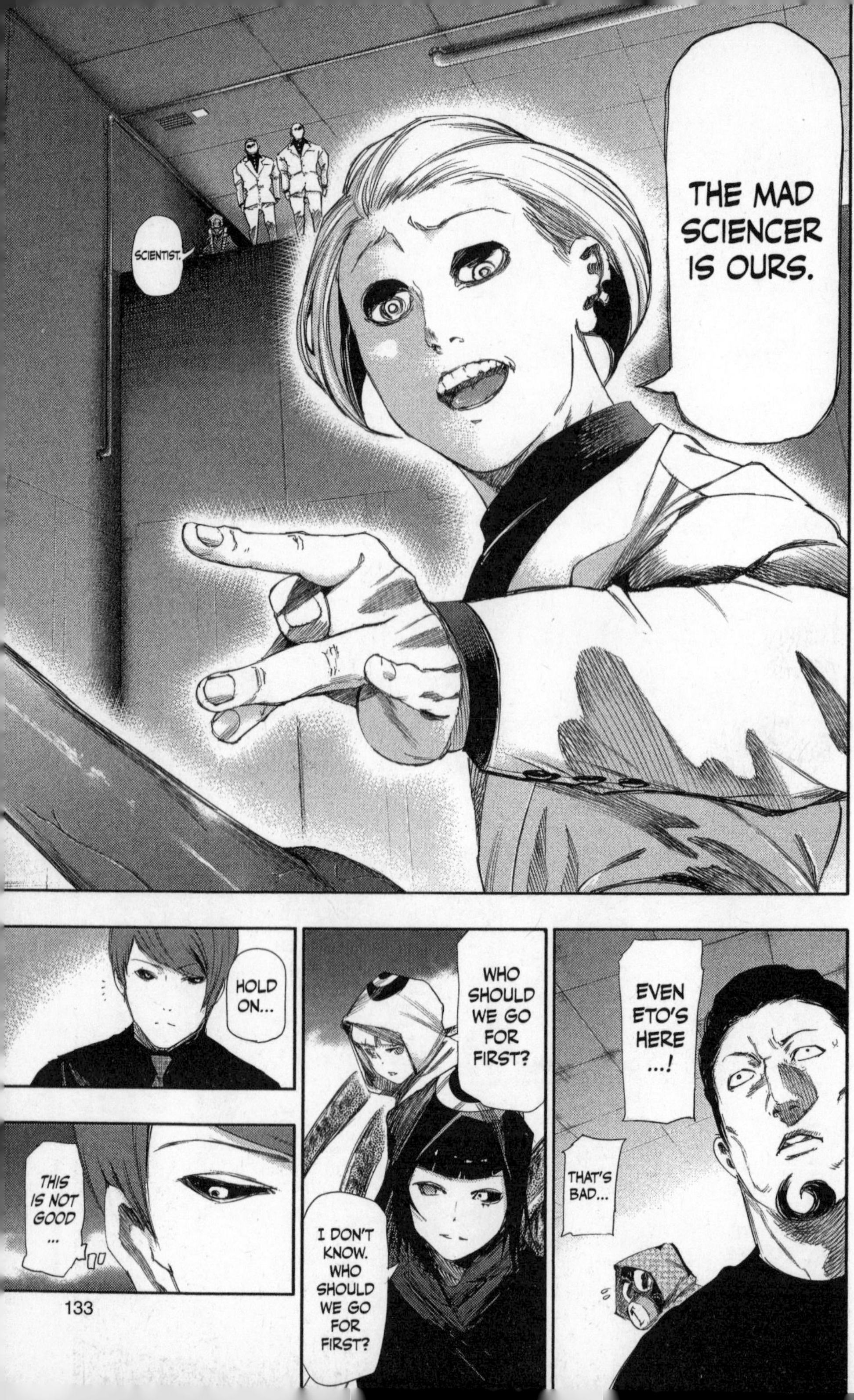
THE MAD SCIENCER IS OURS.
SCIENTIST.
EVEN ETO'S HERE ...!
THAT'S BAD...
WHO SHOULD WE GO FOR FIRST?
I DON'T KNOW. WHO SHOULD WE GO FOR FIRST?
HOLD ON...
THIS IS NOT GOOD ...

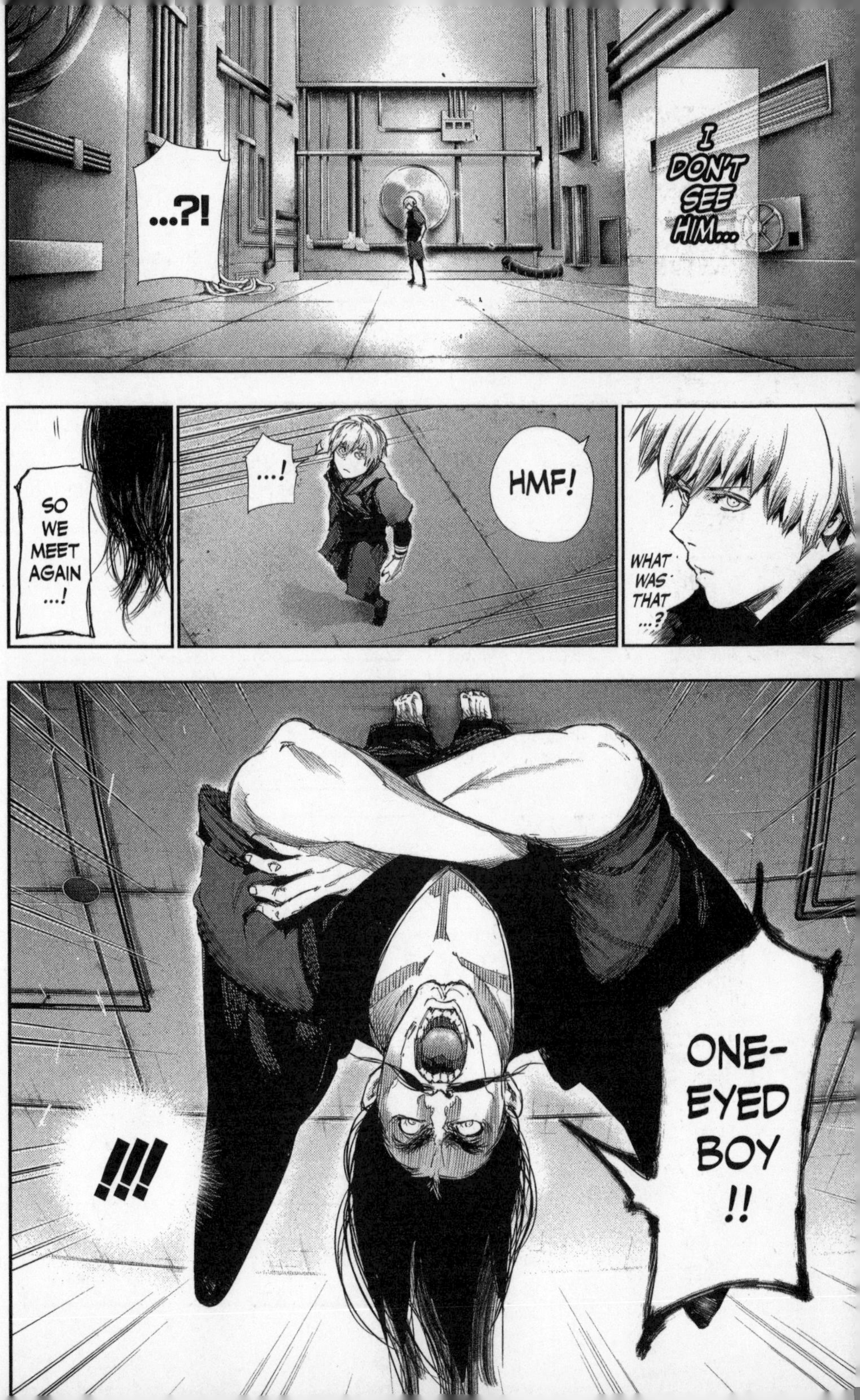
I DON'T SEE HIM...
...?!
WHAT WAS THAT ...?
HMF!
...!
SO WE MEET AGAIN ...!
ONE-EYED BOY !!
!!!

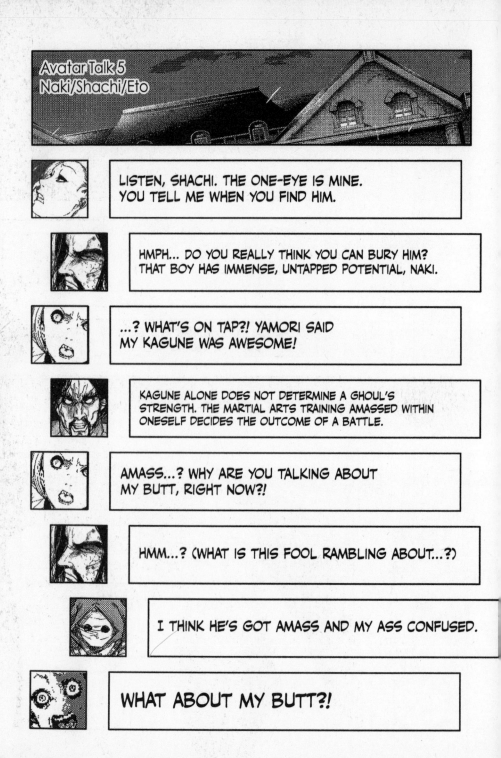

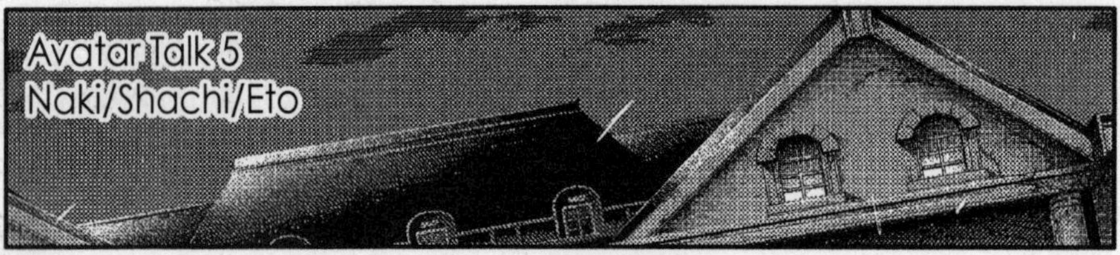
Avatar Talk 5
Naki/Shachi/Eto

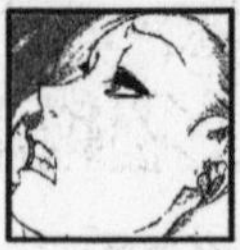

LISTEN, SHACHI. THE ONE-EYE IS MINE.
YOU TELL ME WHEN YOU FIND HIM.

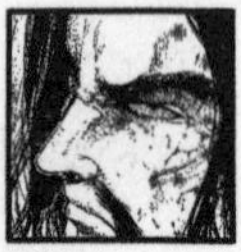

HMPH... DO YOU REALLY THINK YOU CAN BURY HIM?
THAT BOY HAS IMMENSE, UNTAPPED POTENTIAL, NAKI.

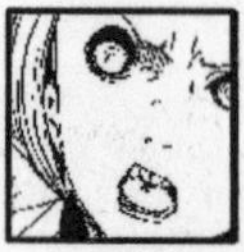

...? WHAT'S ON TAP?! YAMORI SAID
MY KAGUNE WAS AWESOME!

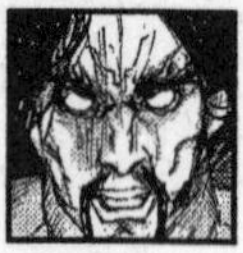

KAGUNE ALONE DOES NOT DETERMINE A GHOUL'S
STRENGTH. THE MARTIAL ARTS TRAINING AMASSED WITHIN
ONESELF DECIDES THE OUTCOME OF A BATTLE.

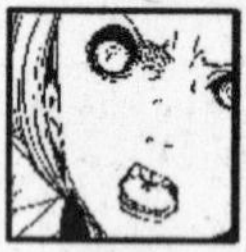

AMASS...? WHY ARE YOU TALKING ABOUT
MY BUTT, RIGHT NOW?!

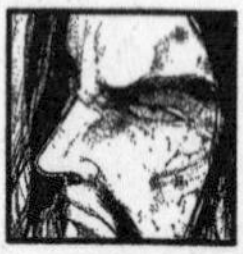

HMM...? (WHAT IS THIS FOOL RAMBLING ABOUT...?)

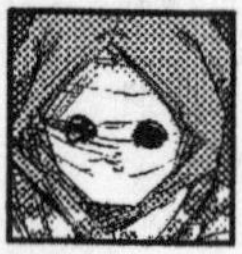

I THINK HE'S GOT AMASS AND MY ASS CONFUSED.

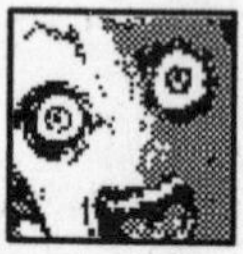

WHAT ABOUT MY BUTT?!

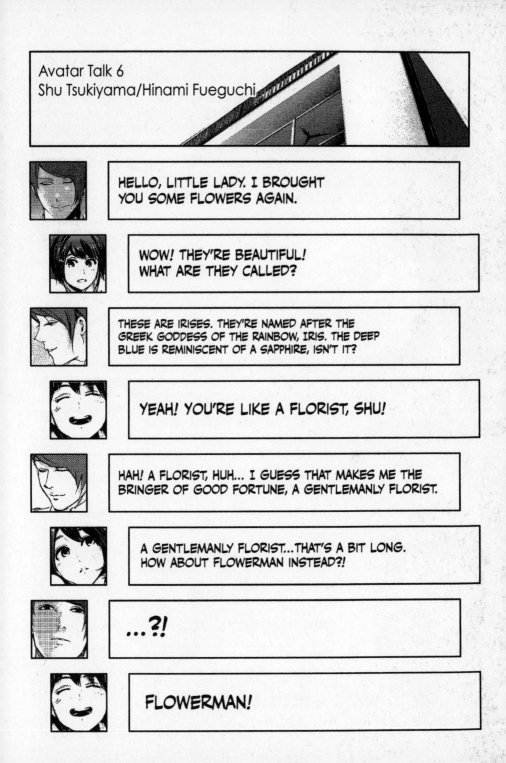

Avatar Talk 6
Shu Tsukiyama/Hinami Fueguchi

HELLO, LITTLE LADY. I BROUGHT YOU SOME FLOWERS AGAIN.

WOW! THEY'RE BEAUTIFUL! WHAT ARE THEY CALLED?

THESE ARE IRISES. THEY'RE NAMED AFTER THE GREEK GODDESS OF THE RAINBOW, IRIS. THE DEEP BLUE IS REMINISCENT OF A SAPPHIRE, ISN'T IT?

YEAH! YOU'RE LIKE A FLORIST, SHU!

HAH! A FLORIST, HUH... I GUESS THAT MAKES ME THE BRINGER OF GOOD FORTUNE, A GENTLEMANLY FLORIST.

A GENTLEMANLY FLORIST...THAT'S A BIT LONG. HOW ABOUT FLOWERMAN INSTEAD?!

...?!

FLOWERMAN!

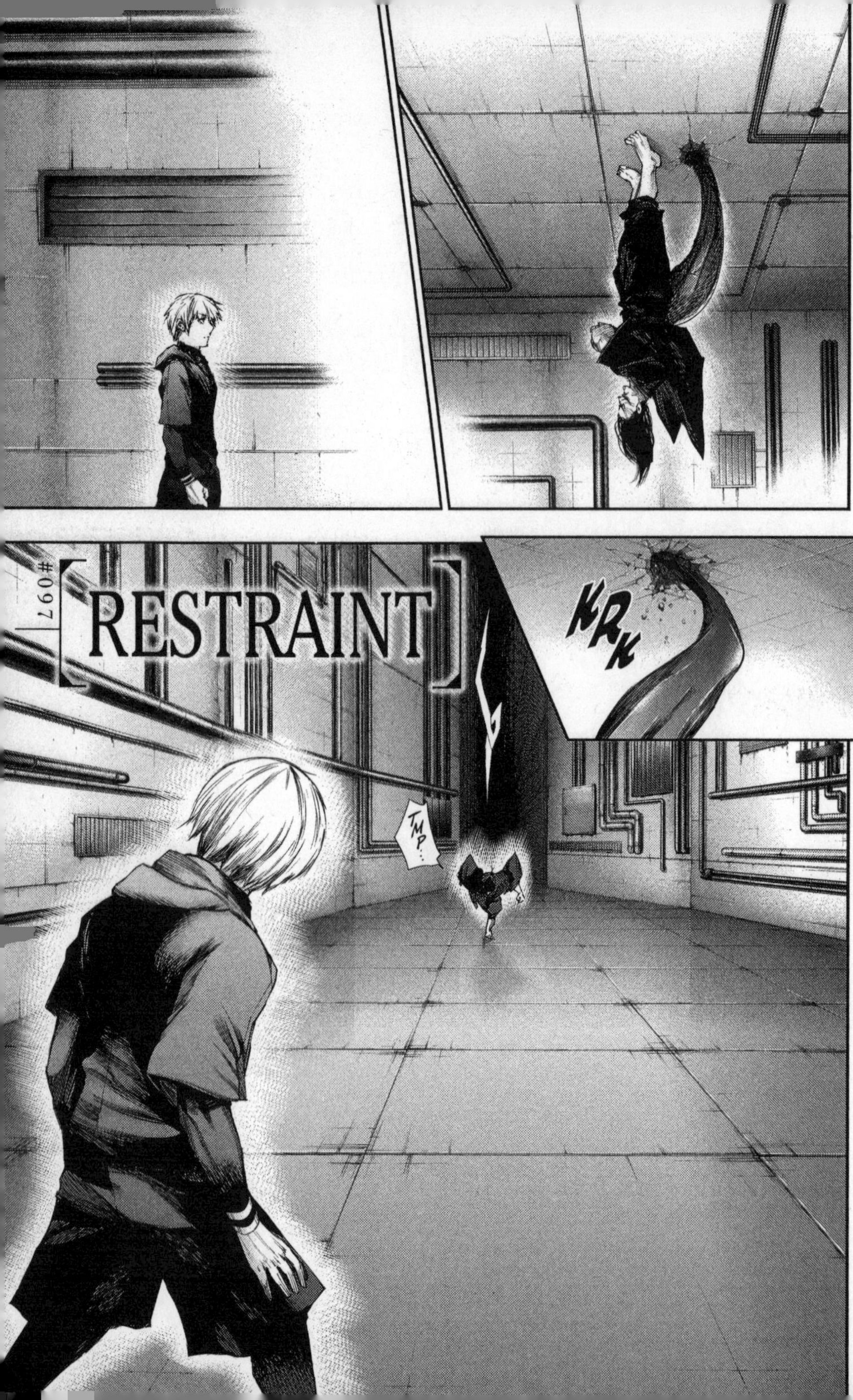
#097
RESTRAINT
KRK
TMP...

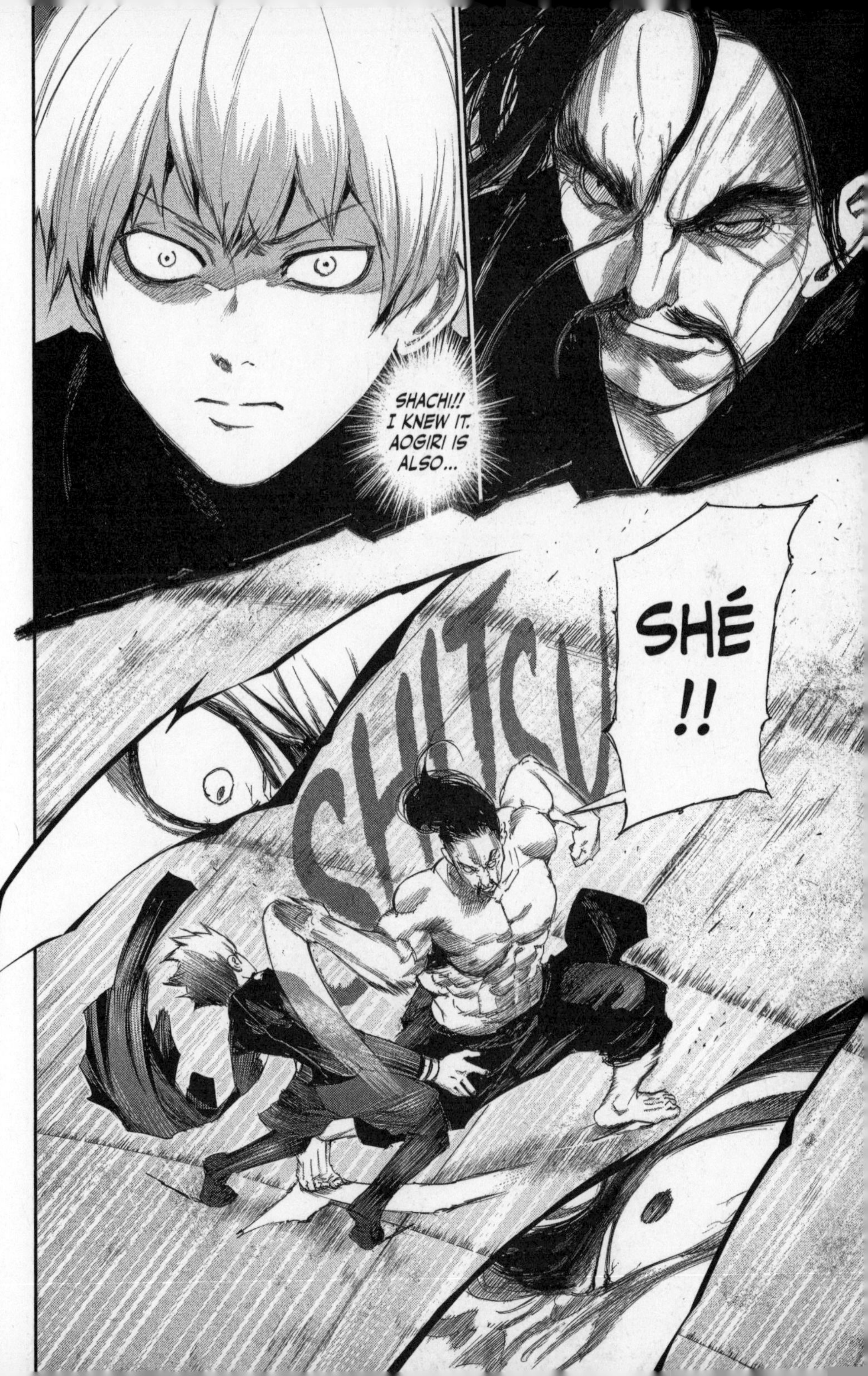
SHACHI!! I KNEW IT. AOGIRI IS ALSO...
SHÉ !!
CHITSU

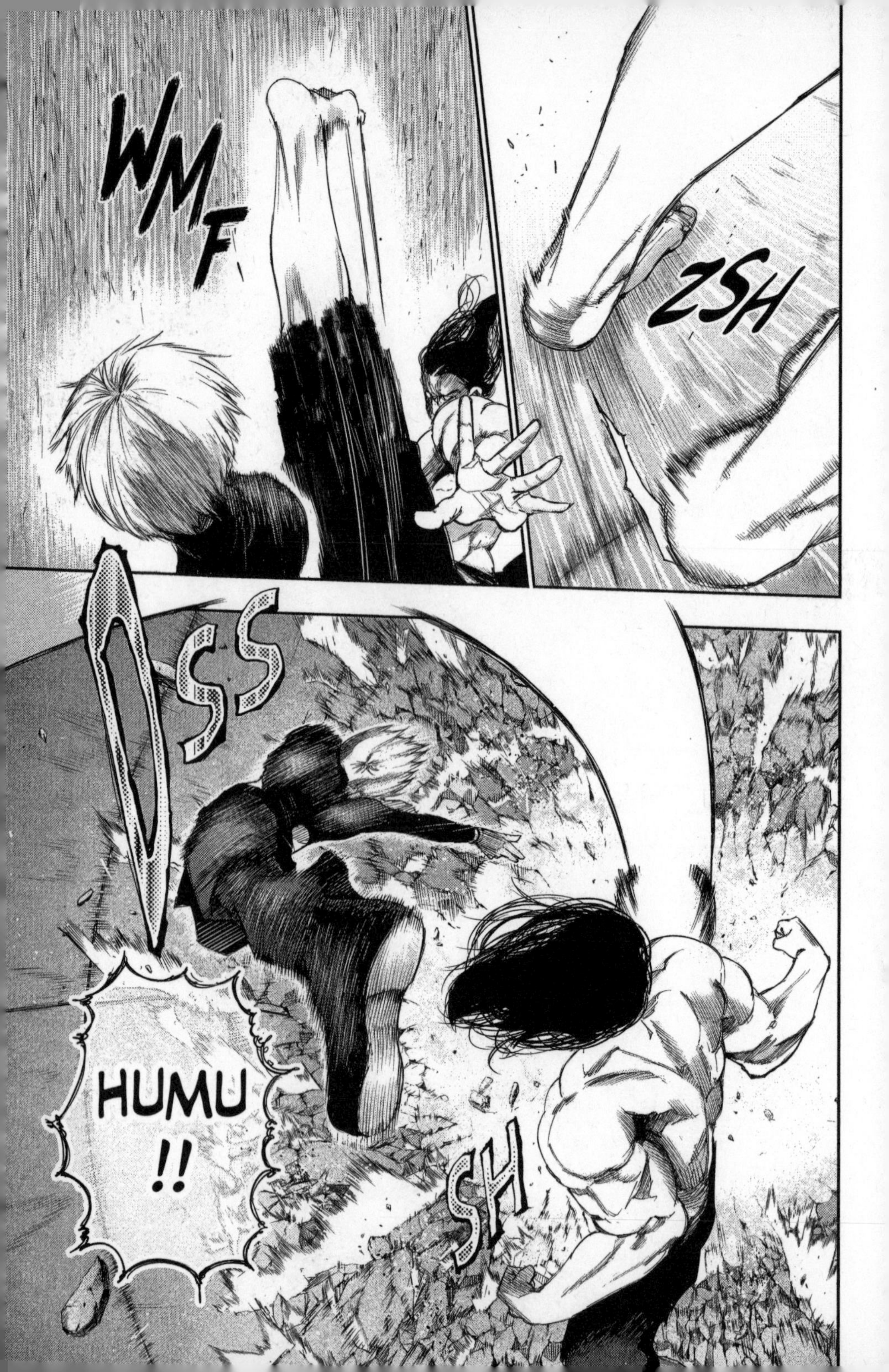
ZSH
WMF
DOSS
HUMU!!
SH

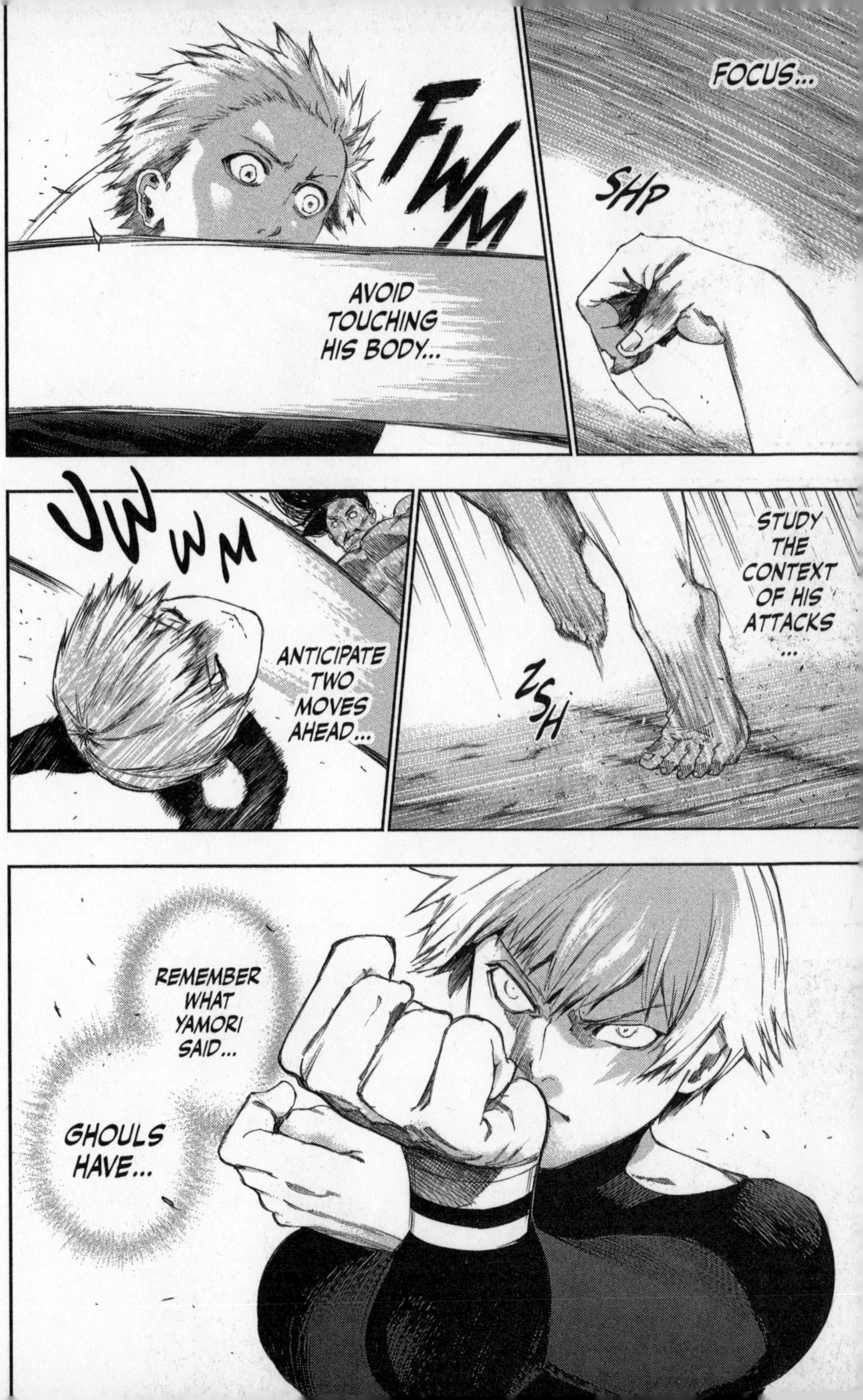
FOCUS...
SHP
FWM
AVOID TOUCHING HIS BODY...
STUDY THE CONTEXT OF HIS ATTACKS ...
ZSH
ANTICIPATE TWO MOVES AHEAD...
REMEMBER WHAT YAMORI SAID...
GHOULS HAVE...

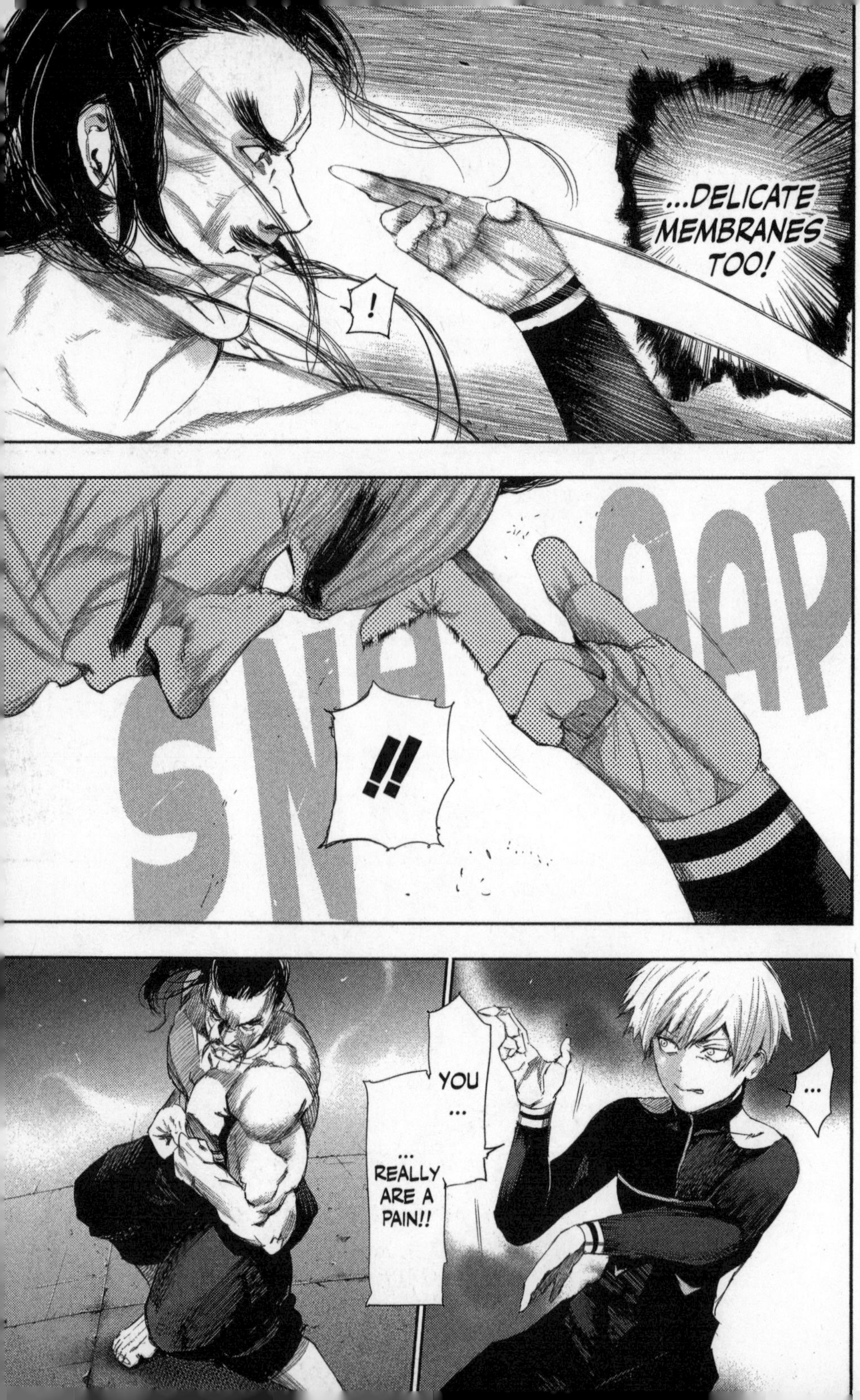
...DELICATE MEMBRANES TOO!
!
SNAP
!!
...
YOU ...
... REALLY ARE A PAIN!!

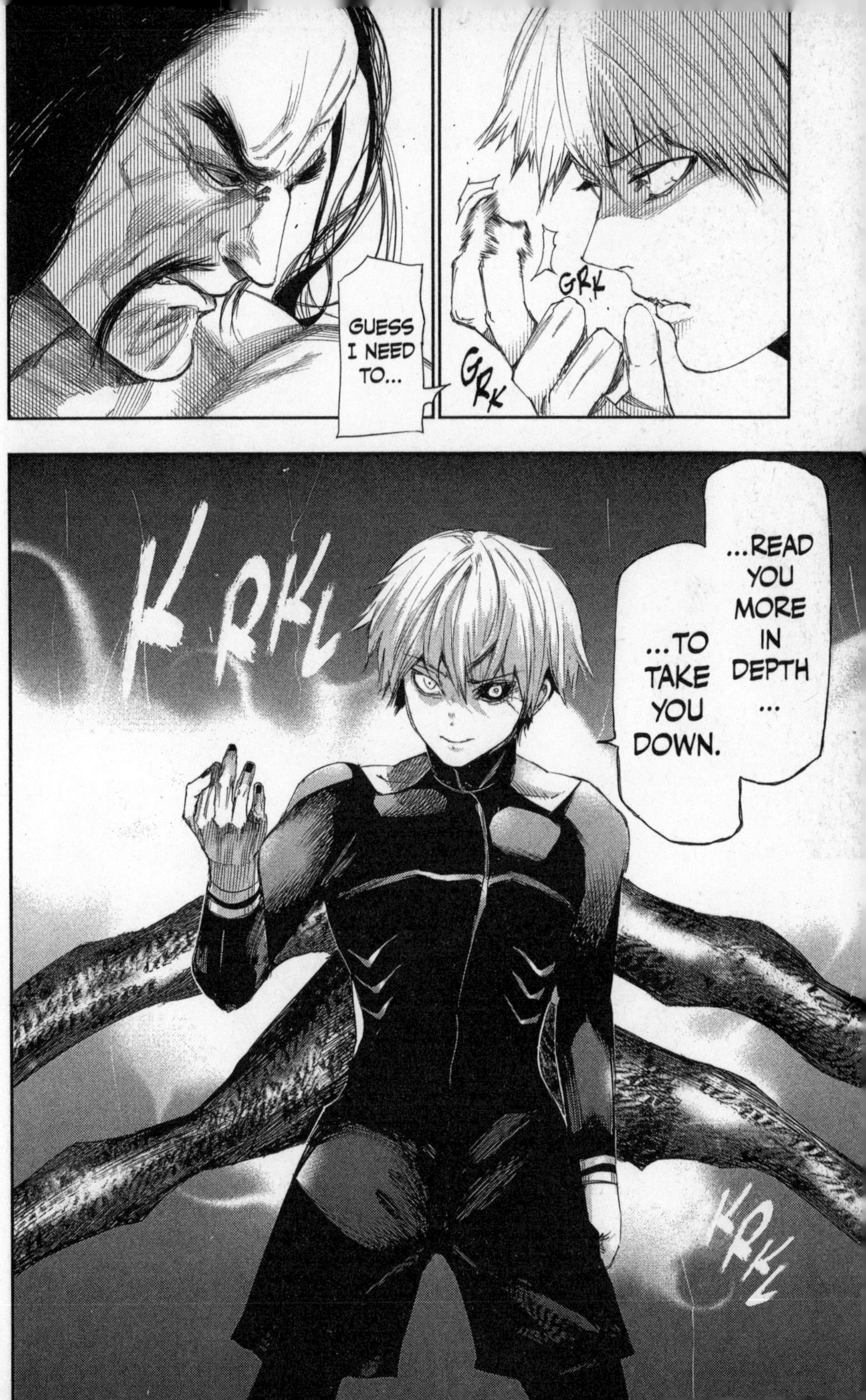
GRK
GRK
GUESS I NEED TO...
...READ YOU MORE IN DEPTH ...
...TO TAKE YOU DOWN.
KRKL
KRKL

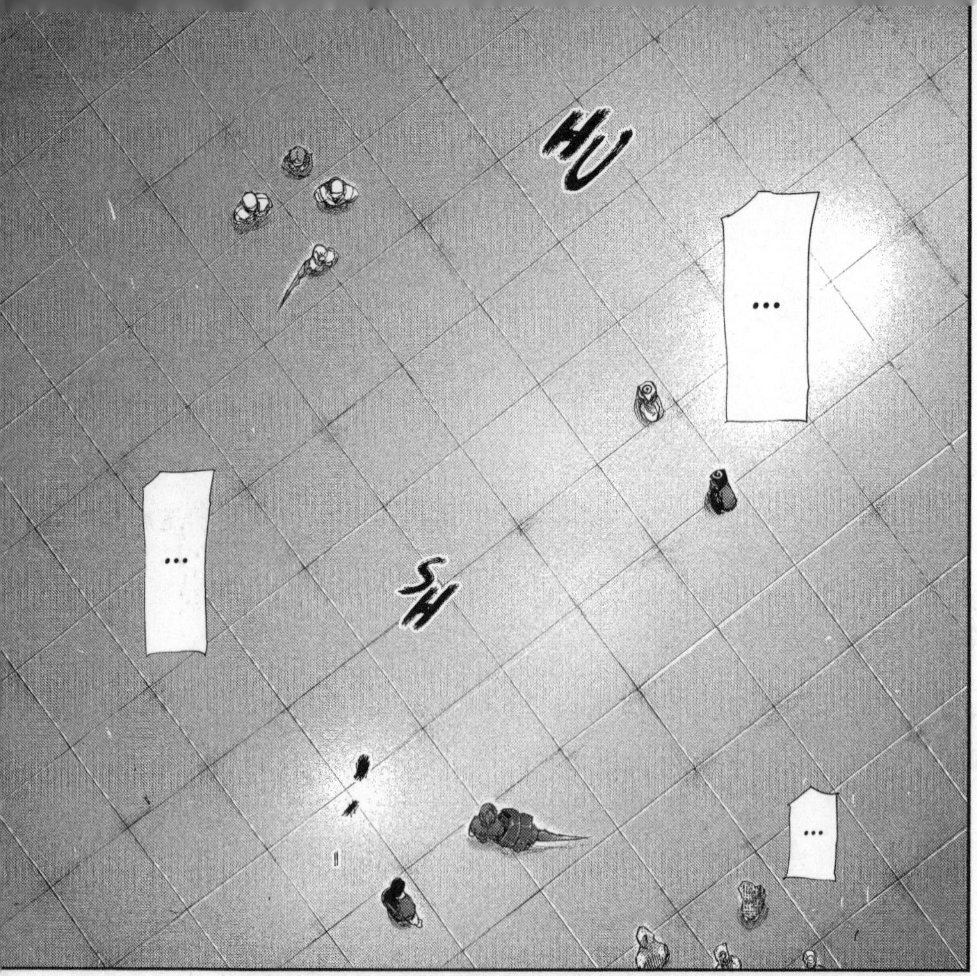
HU
...
...
SH
...

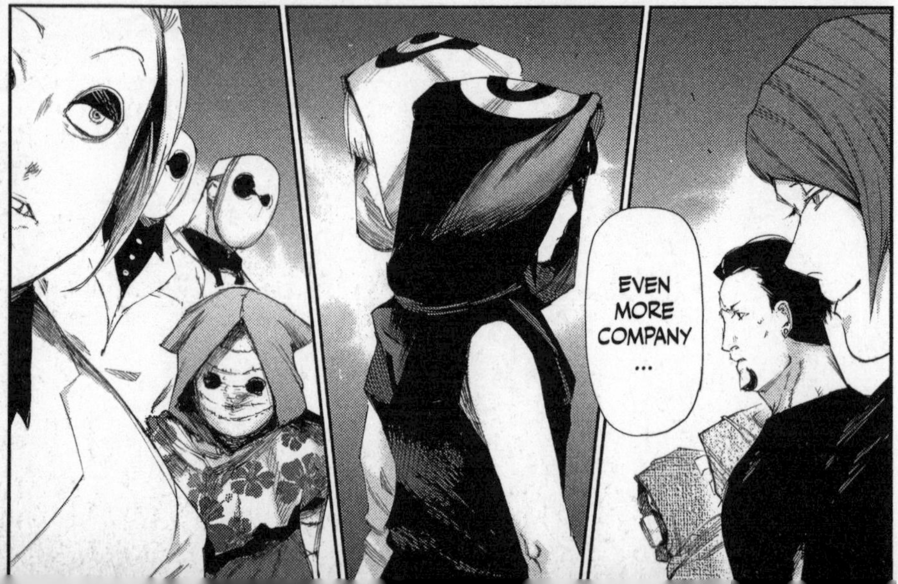
EVEN MORE COMPANY ...

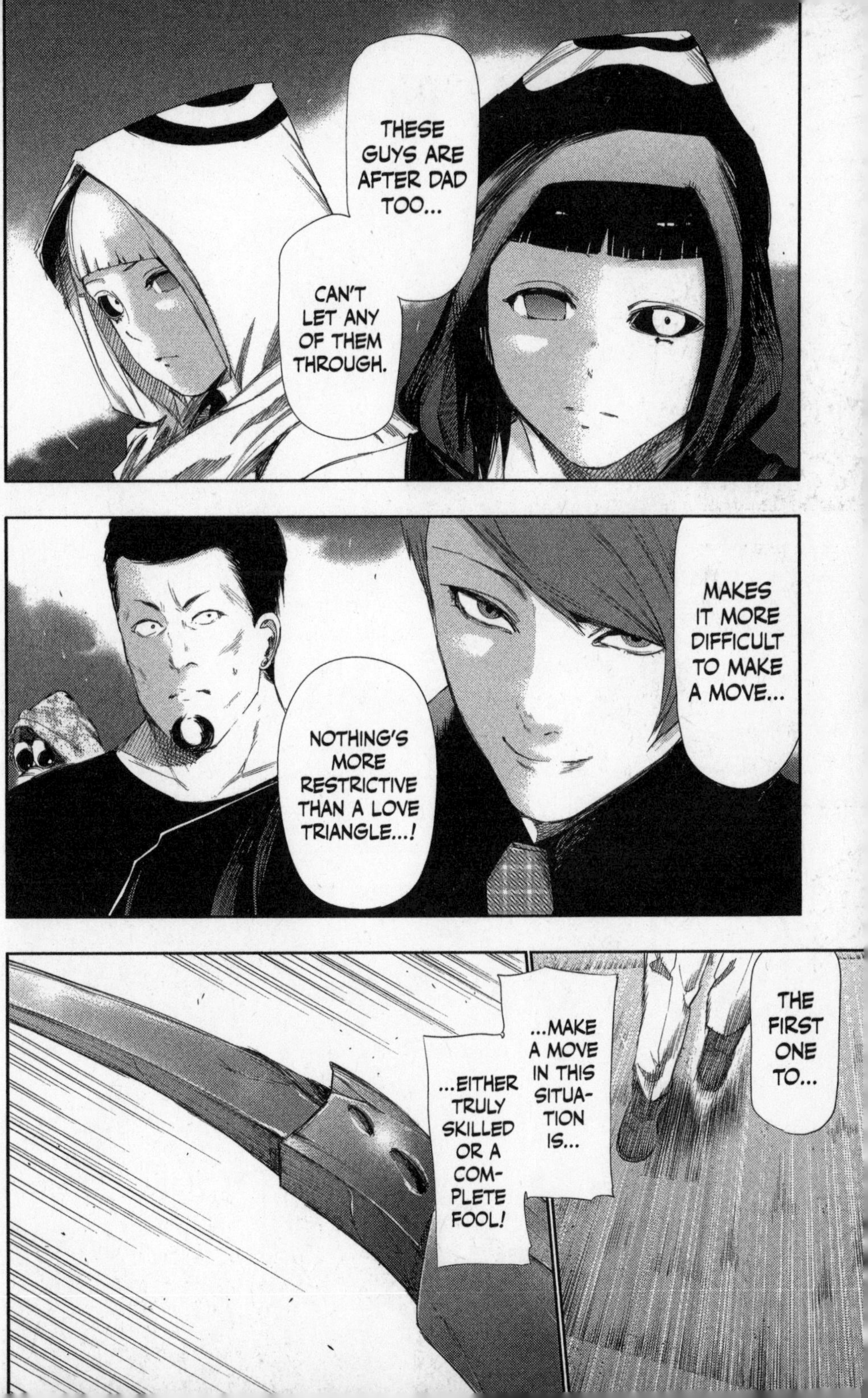
THESE GUYS ARE AFTER DAD TOO...
CAN'T LET ANY OF THEM THROUGH.
MAKES IT MORE DIFFICULT TO MAKE A MOVE...
NOTHING'S MORE RESTRICTIVE THAN A LOVE TRIANGLE...!
THE FIRST ONE TO...
...MAKE A MOVE IN THIS SITUATION IS...
...EITHER TRULY SKILLED OR A COMPLETE FOOL!

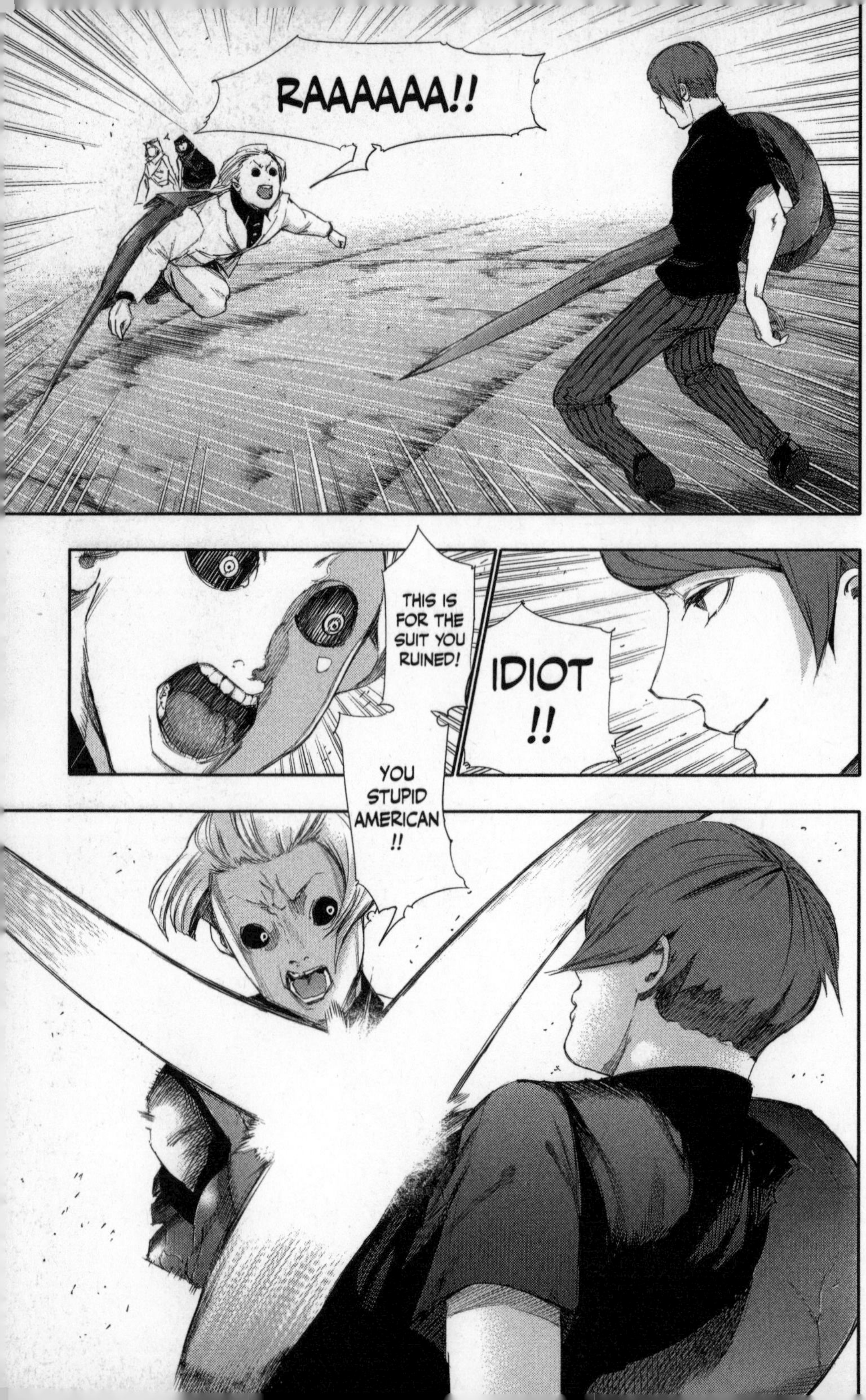
RAAAAAA!!
IDIOT !!
THIS IS FOR THE SUIT YOU RUINED!
YOU STUPID AMERICAN !!

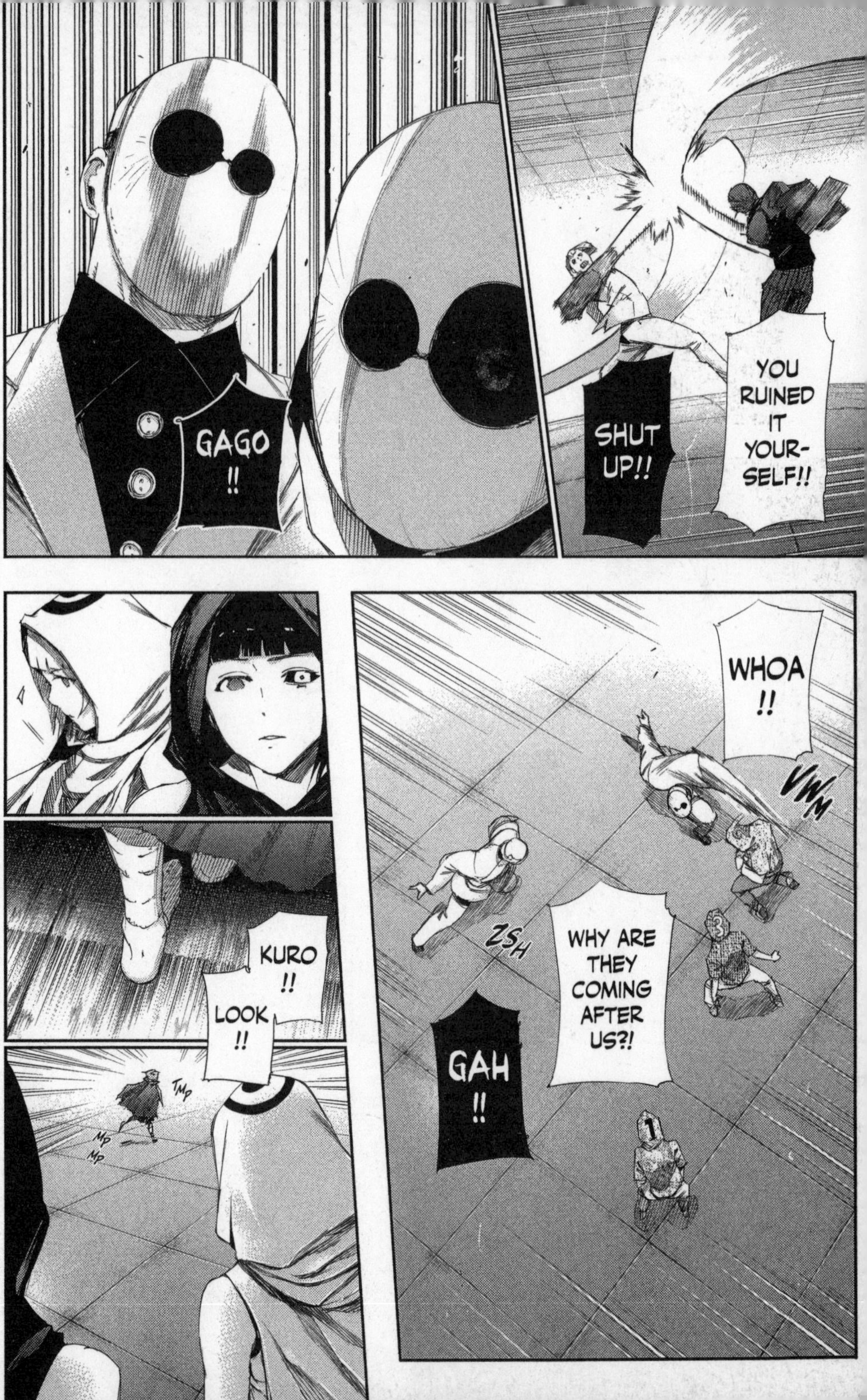
YOU RUINED IT YOUR-SELF!!
SHUT UP!!
GAGO !!
WHOA !!
VWM
WHY ARE THEY COMING AFTER US?!
ZSH
GAH !!
KURO !!
LOOK !!
TMP
MP MP

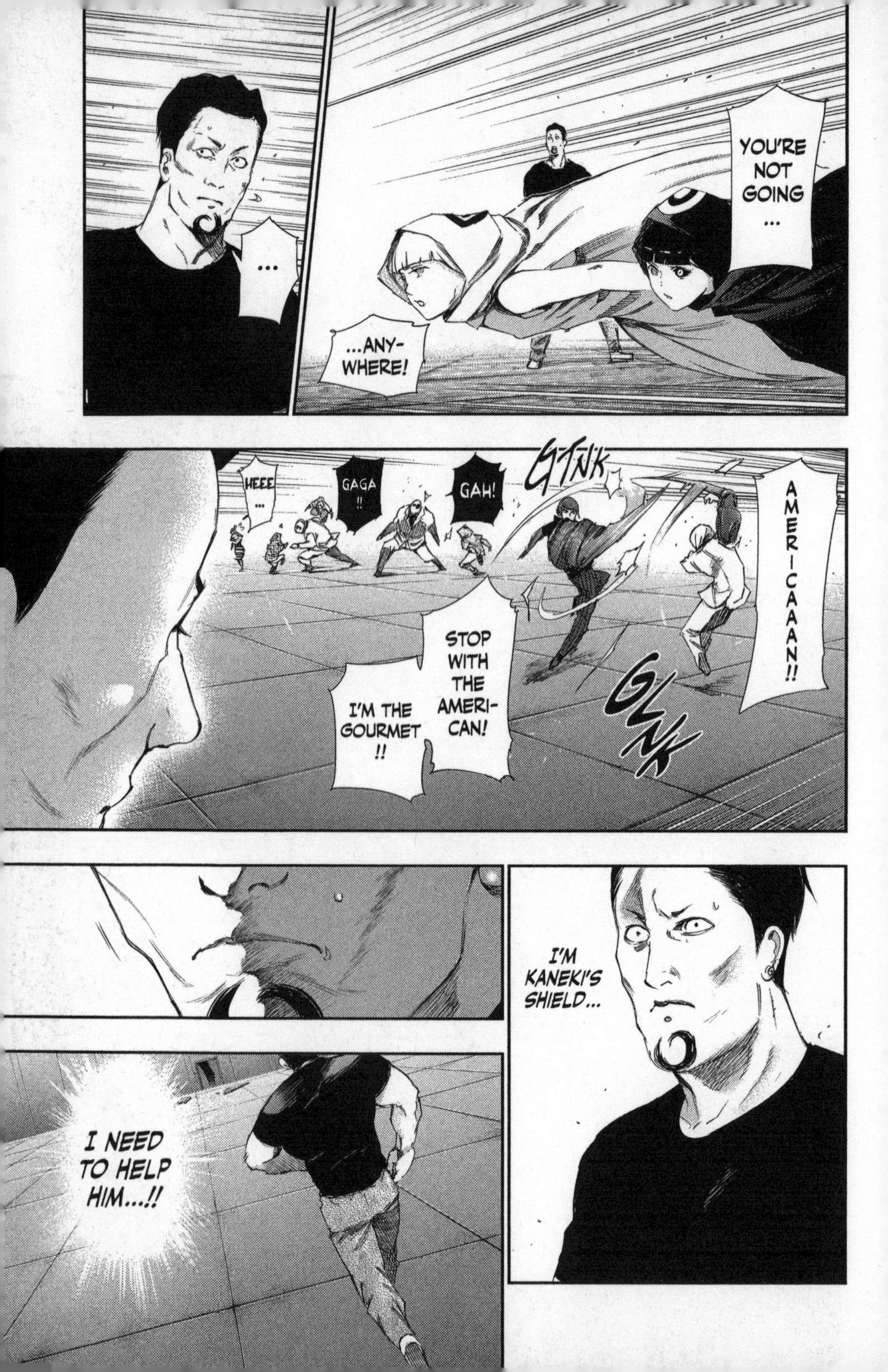
YOU'RE NOT GOING ...
...ANY-WHERE!
...
AMERICAAAAN!!
GLNK
STOP WITH THE AMERI-CAN!
I'M THE GOURMET !!
GAH!
GAGA !!
HEEE ...
I'M KANEKI'S SHIELD...
I NEED TO HELP HIM...!!

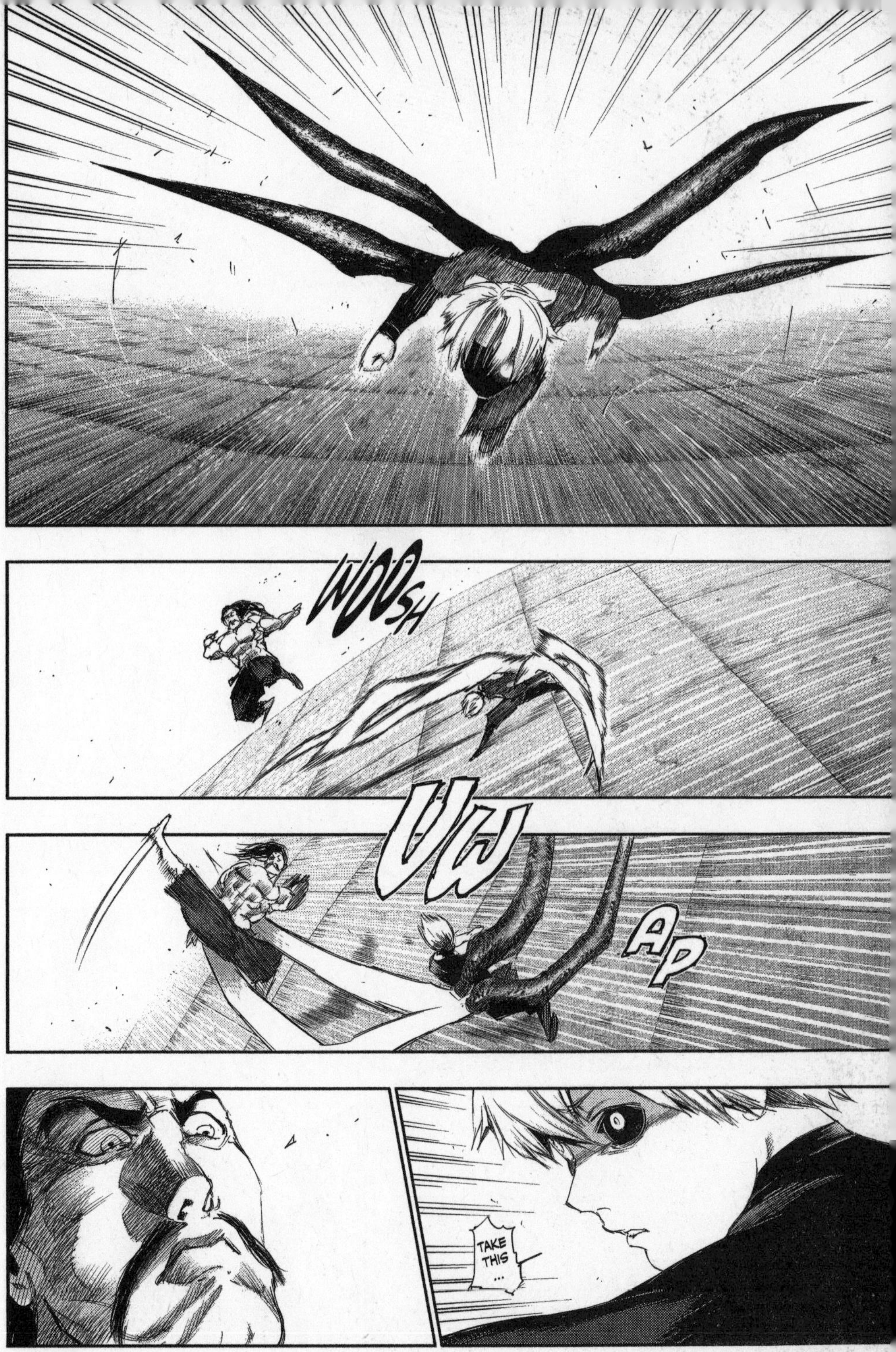
WOOSH
WH
AP
TAKE THIS ...

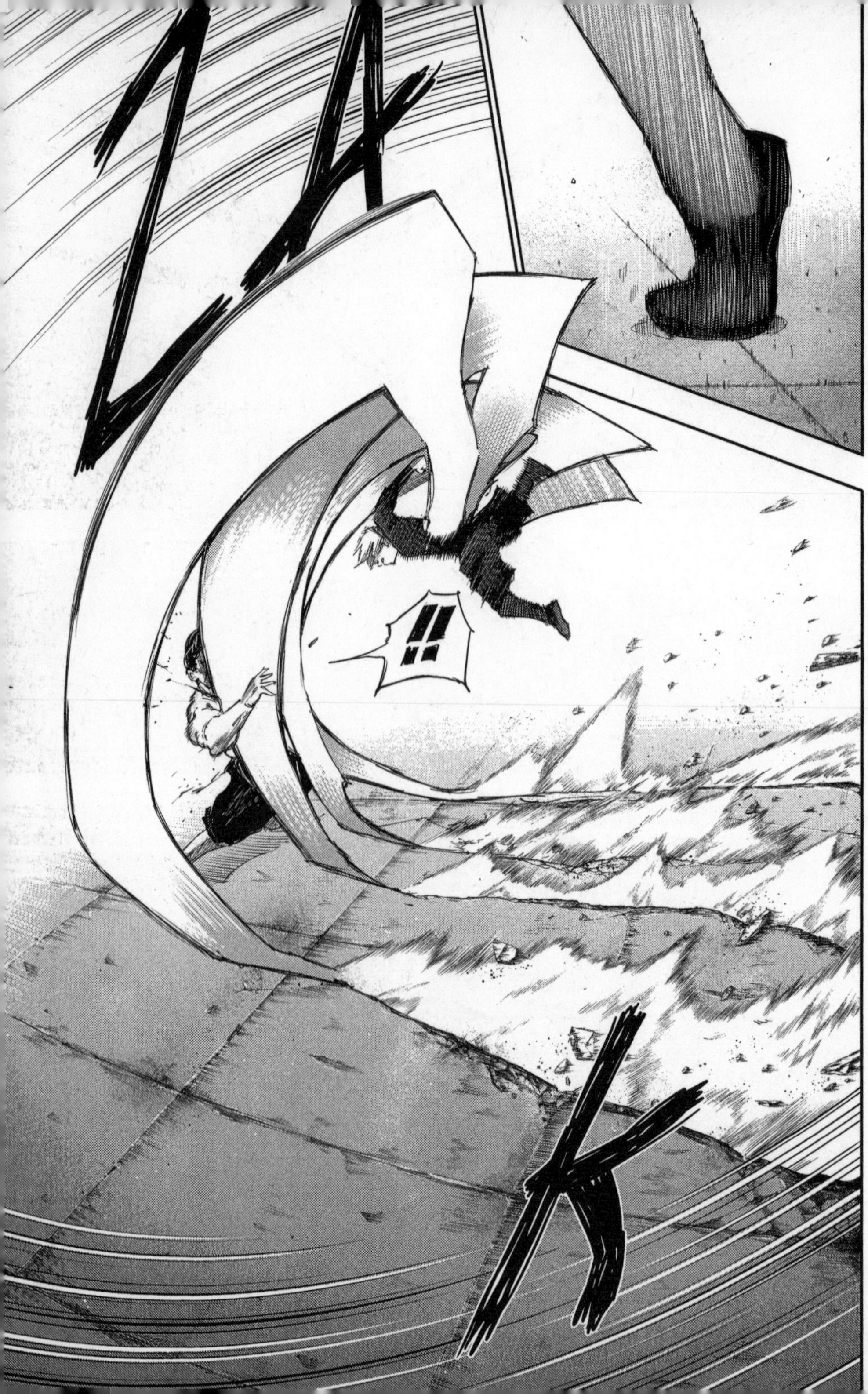
ZAK
!!

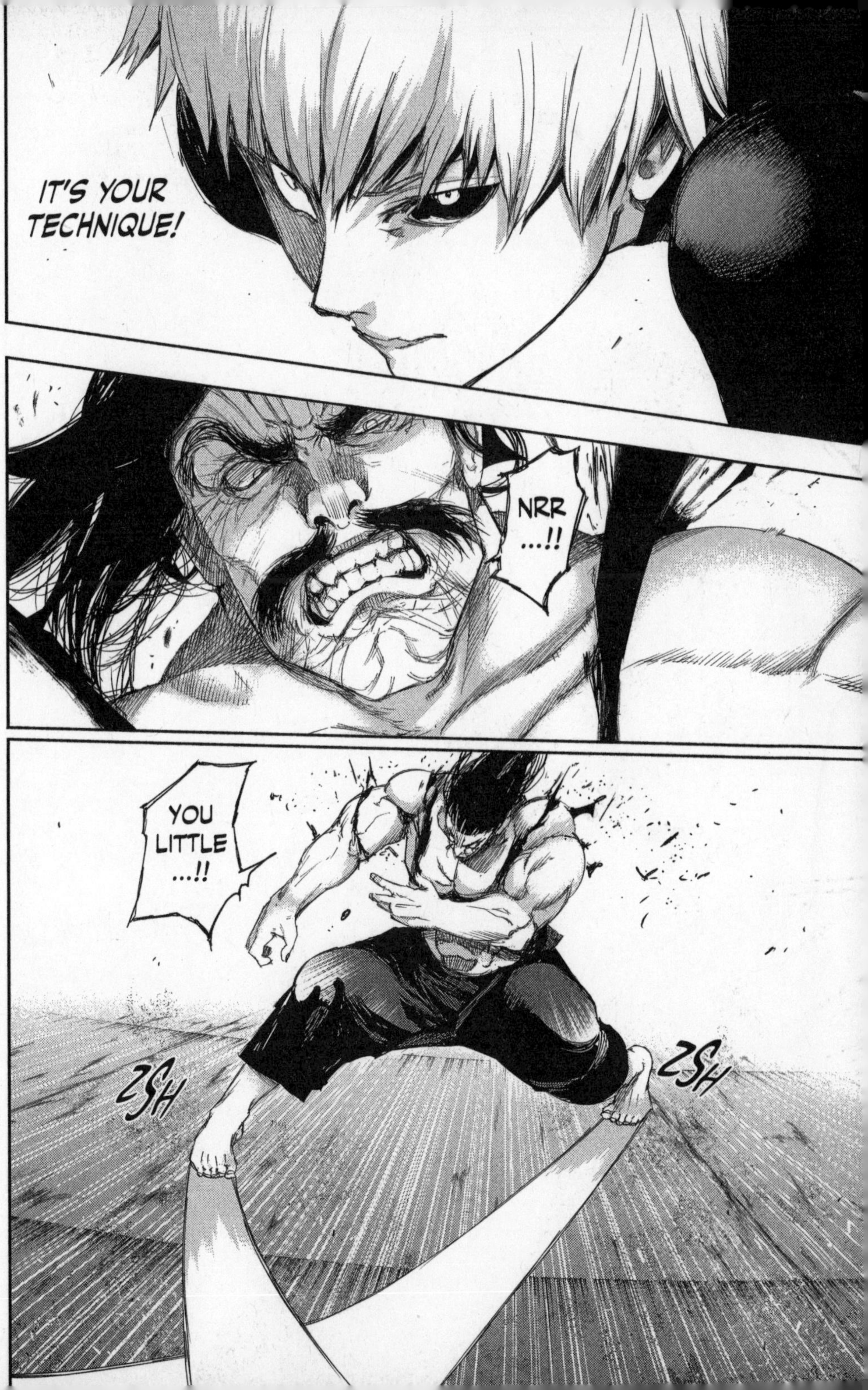
IT'S YOUR TECHNIQUE!
NRR ...!!
YOU LITTLE ...!!
ZSH
ZSH

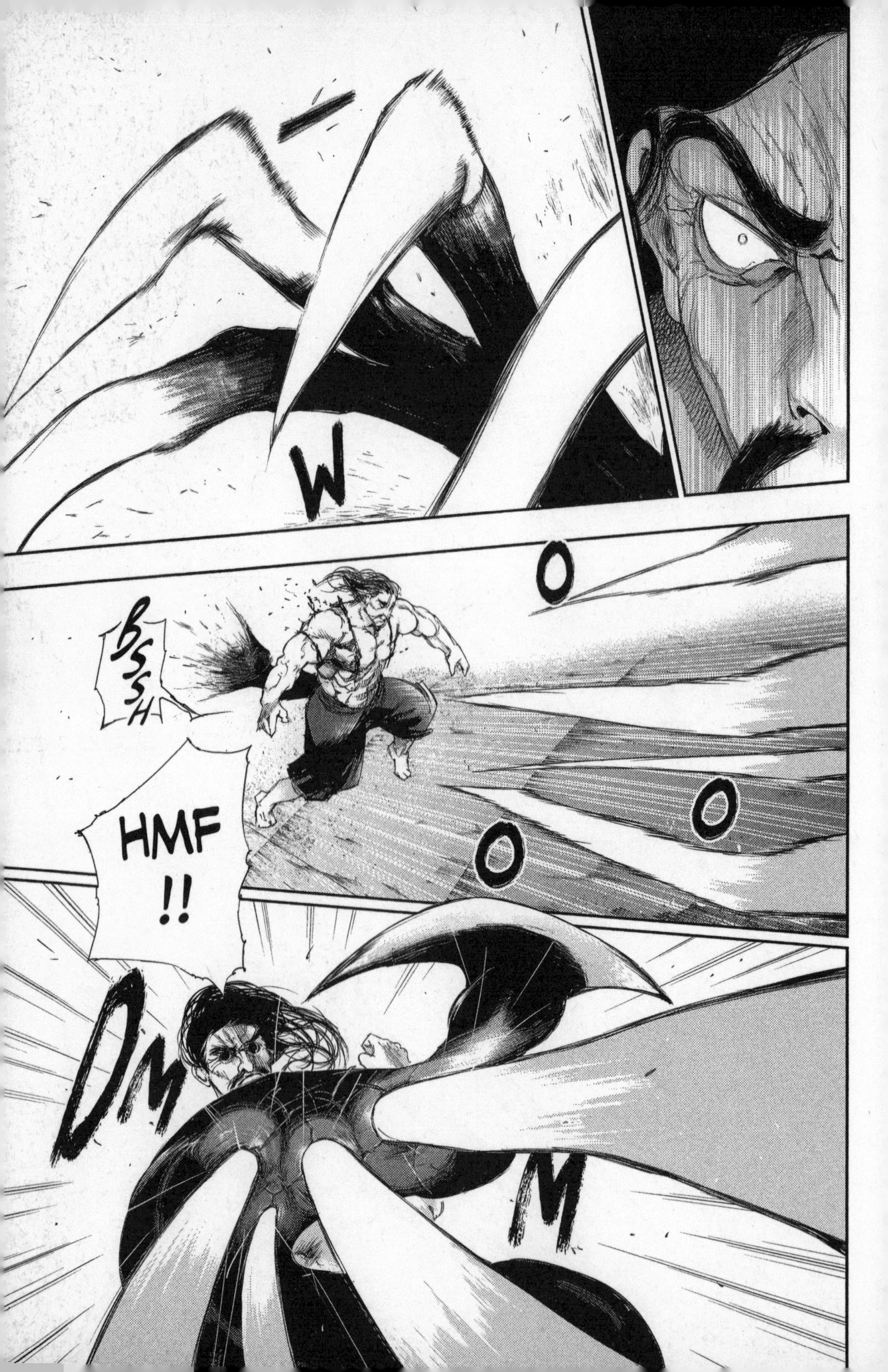
W
O
O
O
BSSH
HMF !!
DM
M

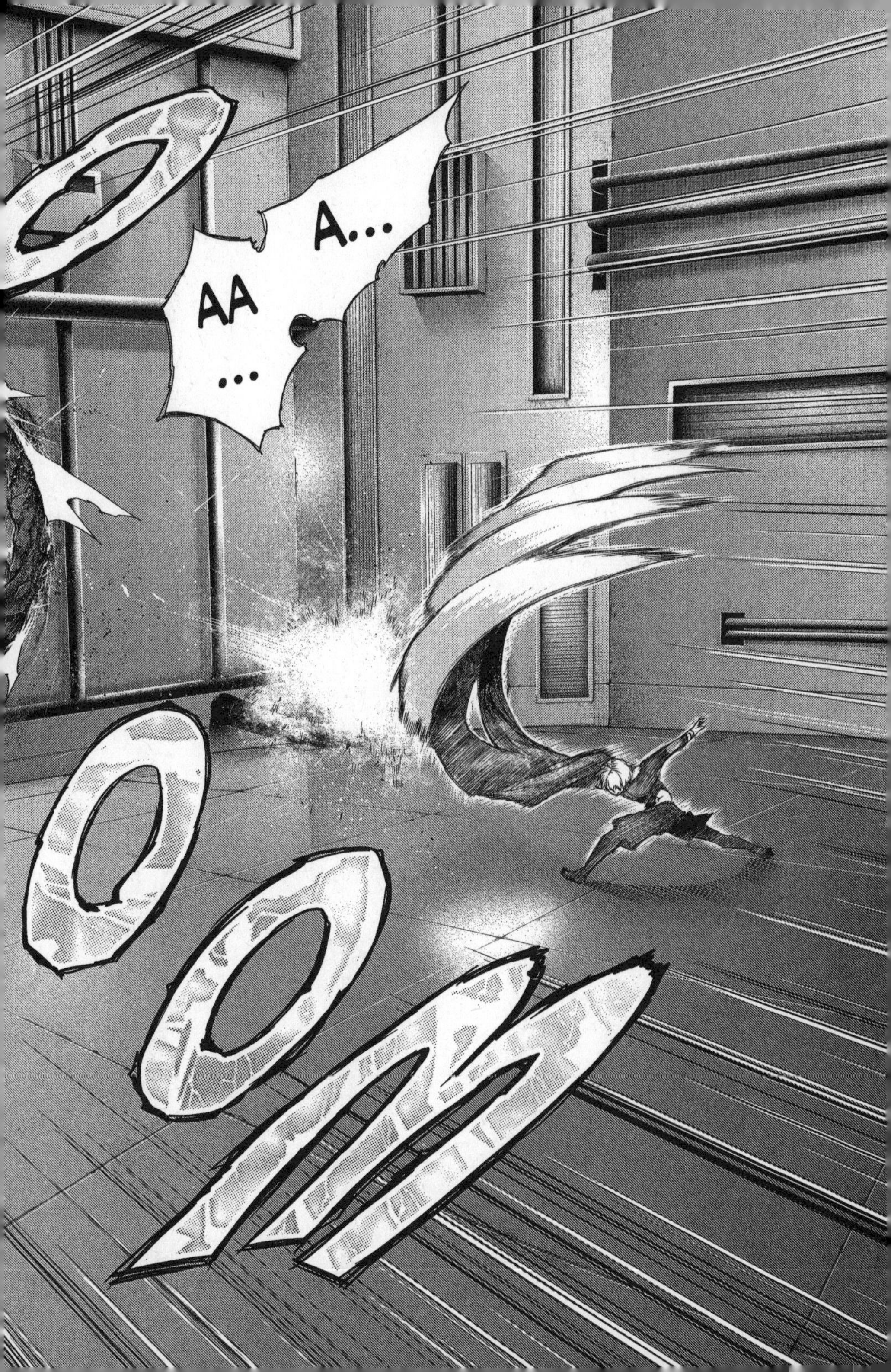
A... AA...
OOOM

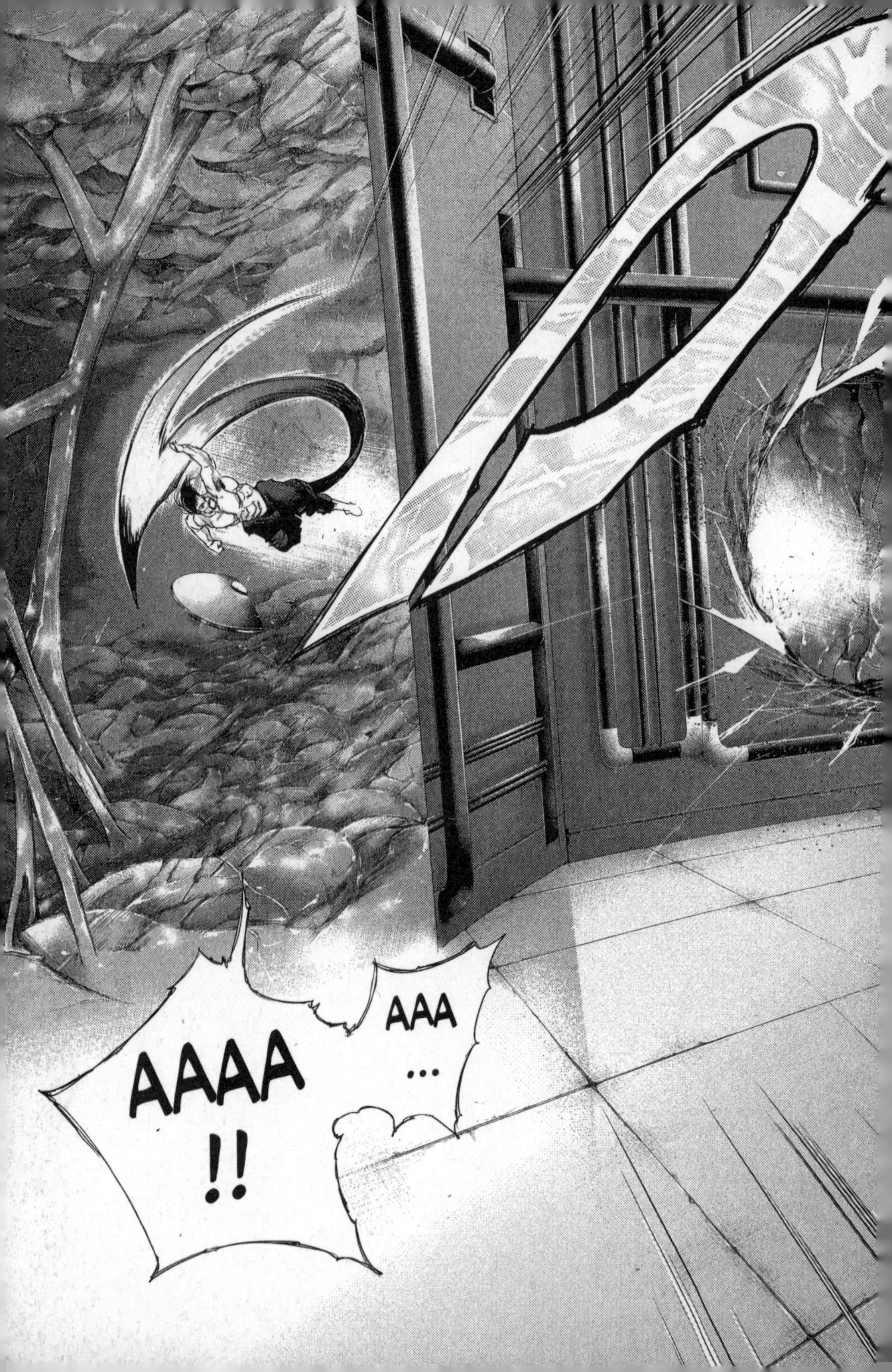
AAA...
AAAA!!

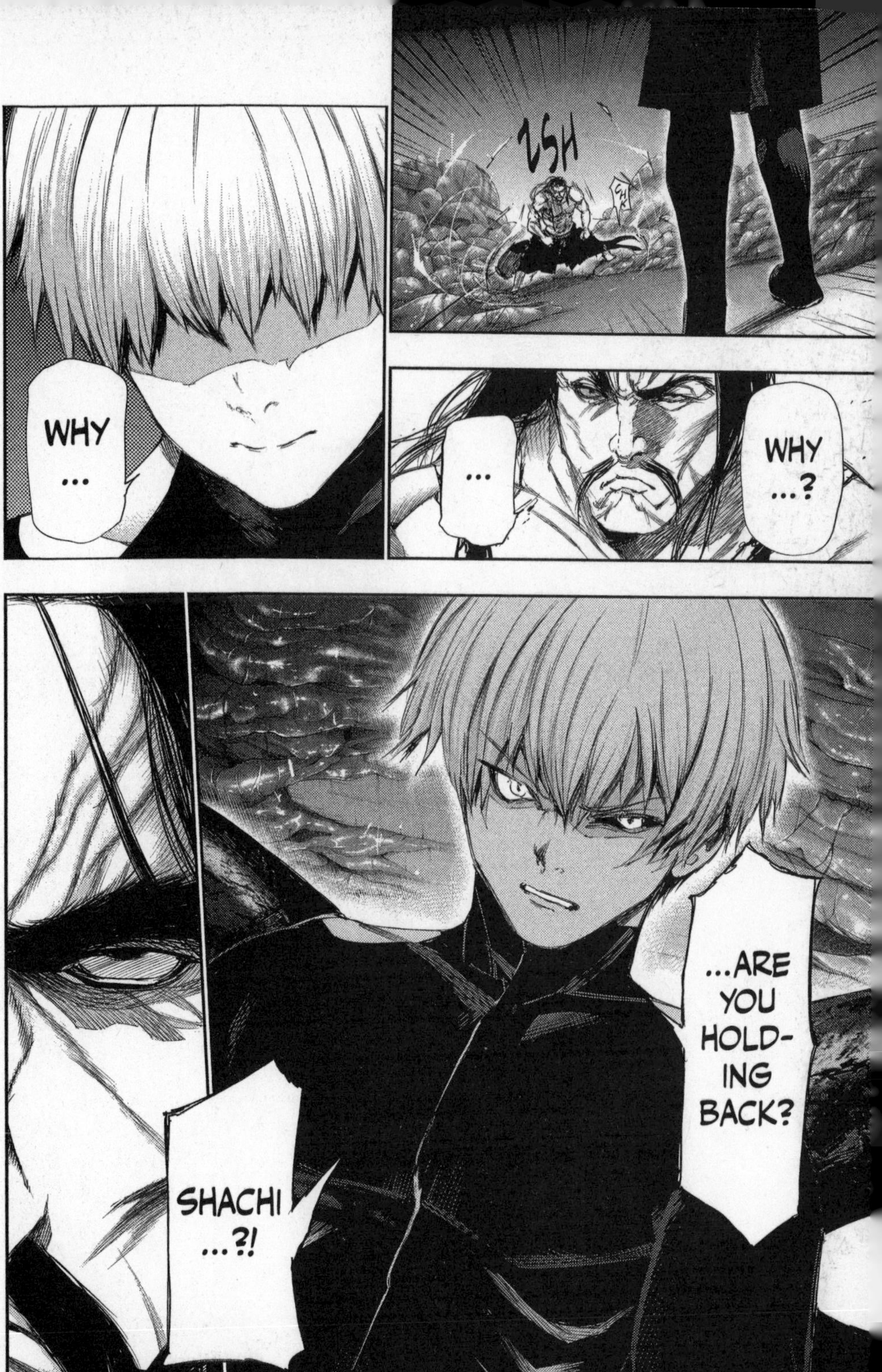
ZSH
CHK
WHY ...?
...
WHY ...
...ARE YOU HOLDING-ING BACK?
SHACHI ...?!

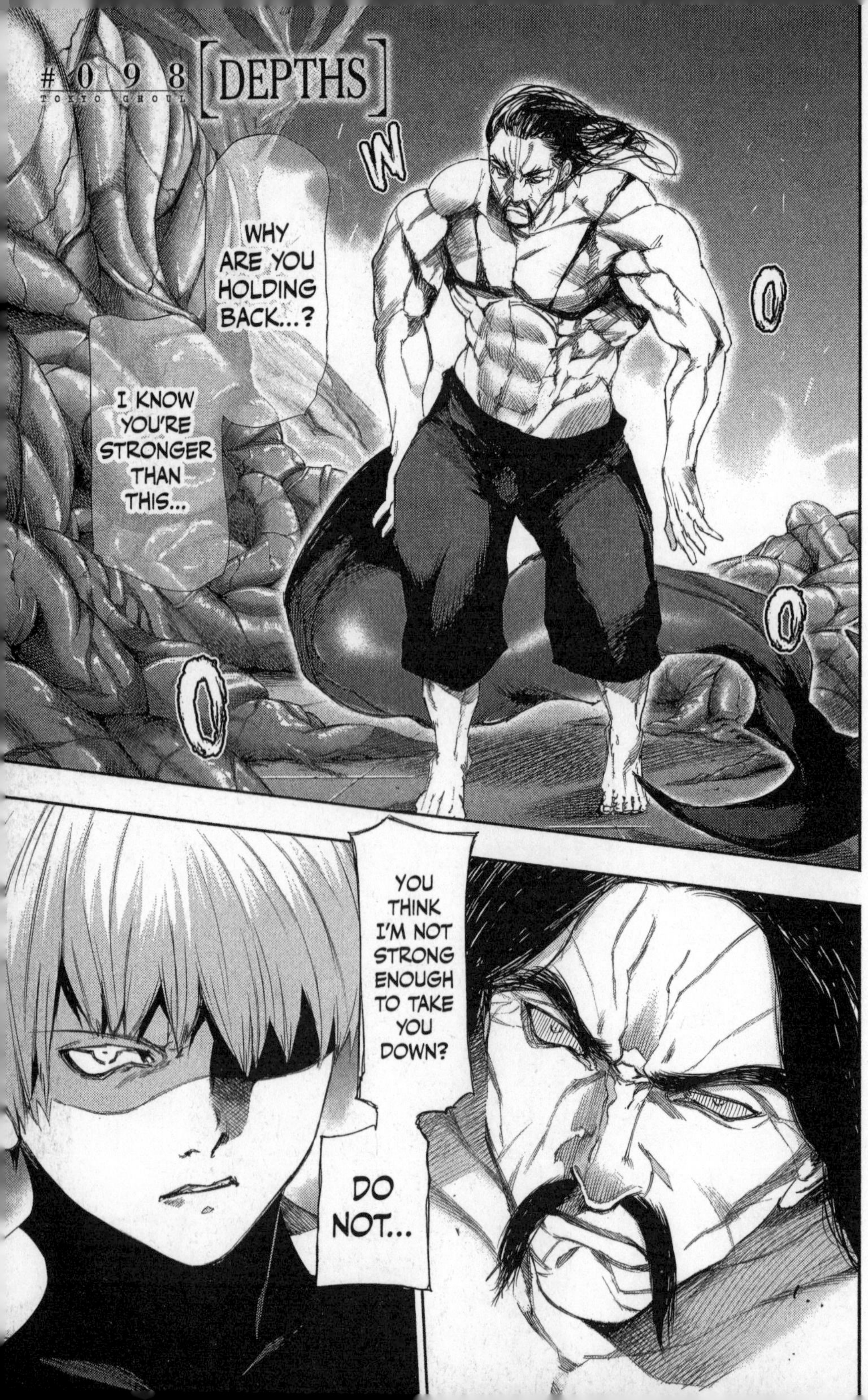
#098 [DEPTHS]
TOKYO GHOUL
WHY ARE YOU HOLDING BACK...?
I KNOW YOU'RE STRONGER THAN THIS...
YOU THINK I'M NOT STRONG ENOUGH TO TAKE YOU DOWN?
DO NOT...

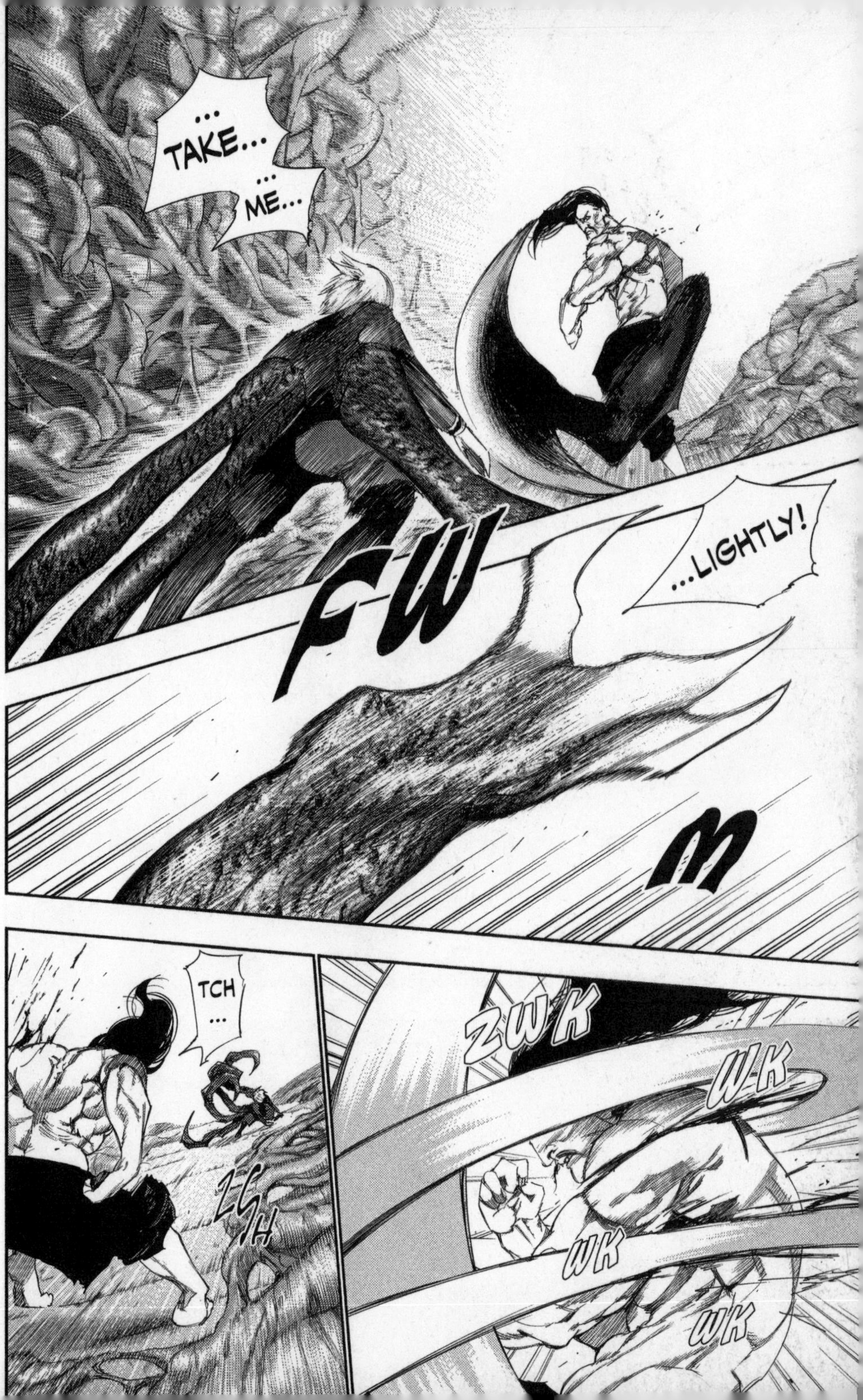
... TAKE... ... ME...
FW
...LIGHTLY!
M
ZWK
WK
WK
WK
TCH ...
ZGSH

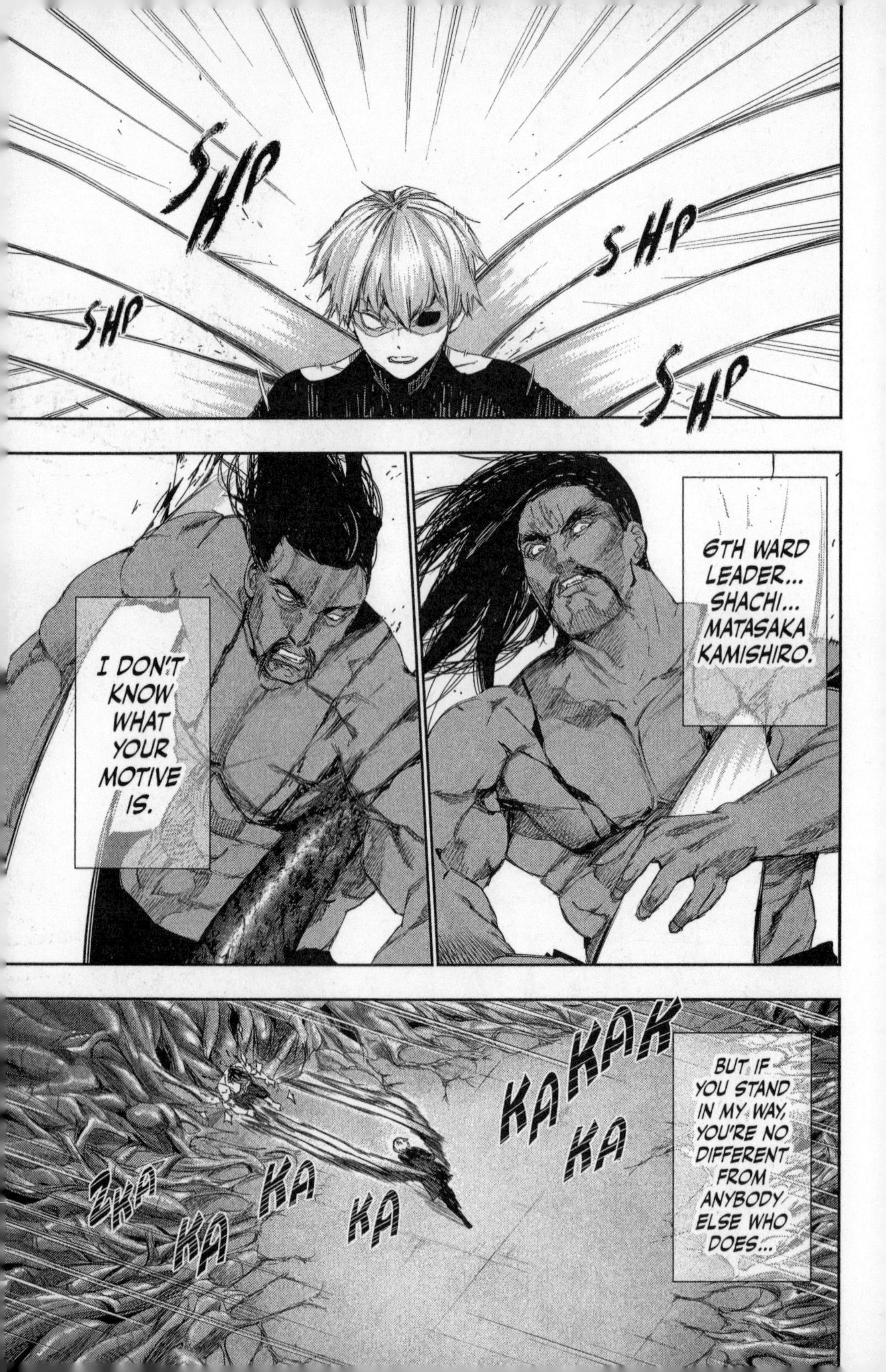
SHP
SHP
SHP
SHP
6TH WARD LEADER... SHACHI... MATASAKA KAMISHIRO.
I DON'T KNOW WHAT YOUR MOTIVE IS.
BUT IF YOU STAND IN MY WAY, YOU'RE NO DIFFERENT FROM ANYBODY ELSE WHO DOES...
KAKAK
KA
KA
ZKA
KA
KA
KA

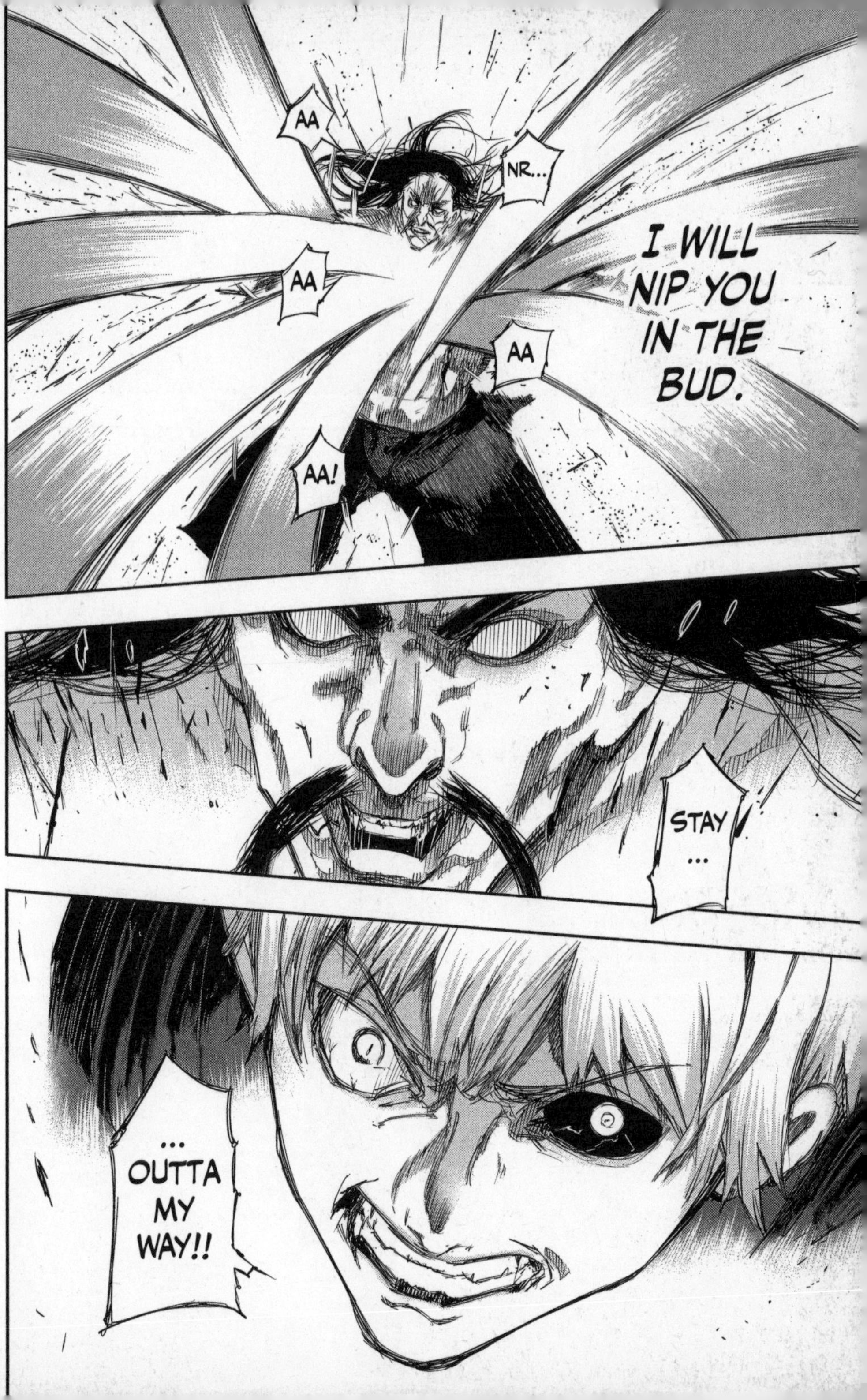

NR...
AA
AA
AA
AA!
I WILL NIP YOU IN THE BUD.
STAY ...
... OUTTA MY WAY!!

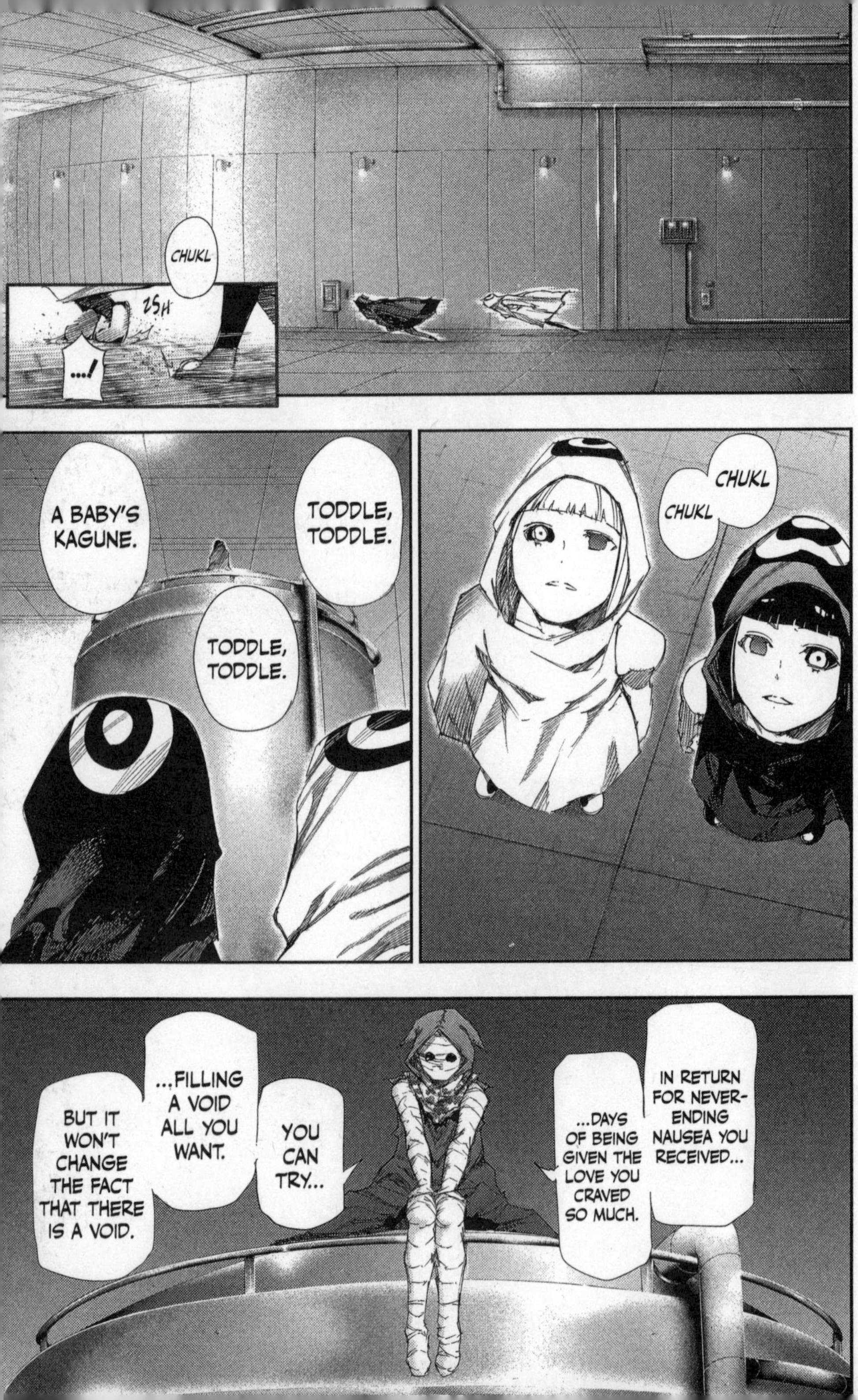
CHUKL
ZSH
...!
CHUKL
CHUKL
TODDLE, TODDLE.
A BABY'S KAGUNE.
TODDLE, TODDLE.
IN RETURN FOR NEVER-ENDING NAUSEA YOU RECEIVED...
...DAYS OF BEING GIVEN THE LOVE YOU CRAVED SO MUCH.
YOU CAN TRY...
...FILLING A VOID ALL YOU WANT.
BUT IT WON'T CHANGE THE FACT THAT THERE IS A VOID.

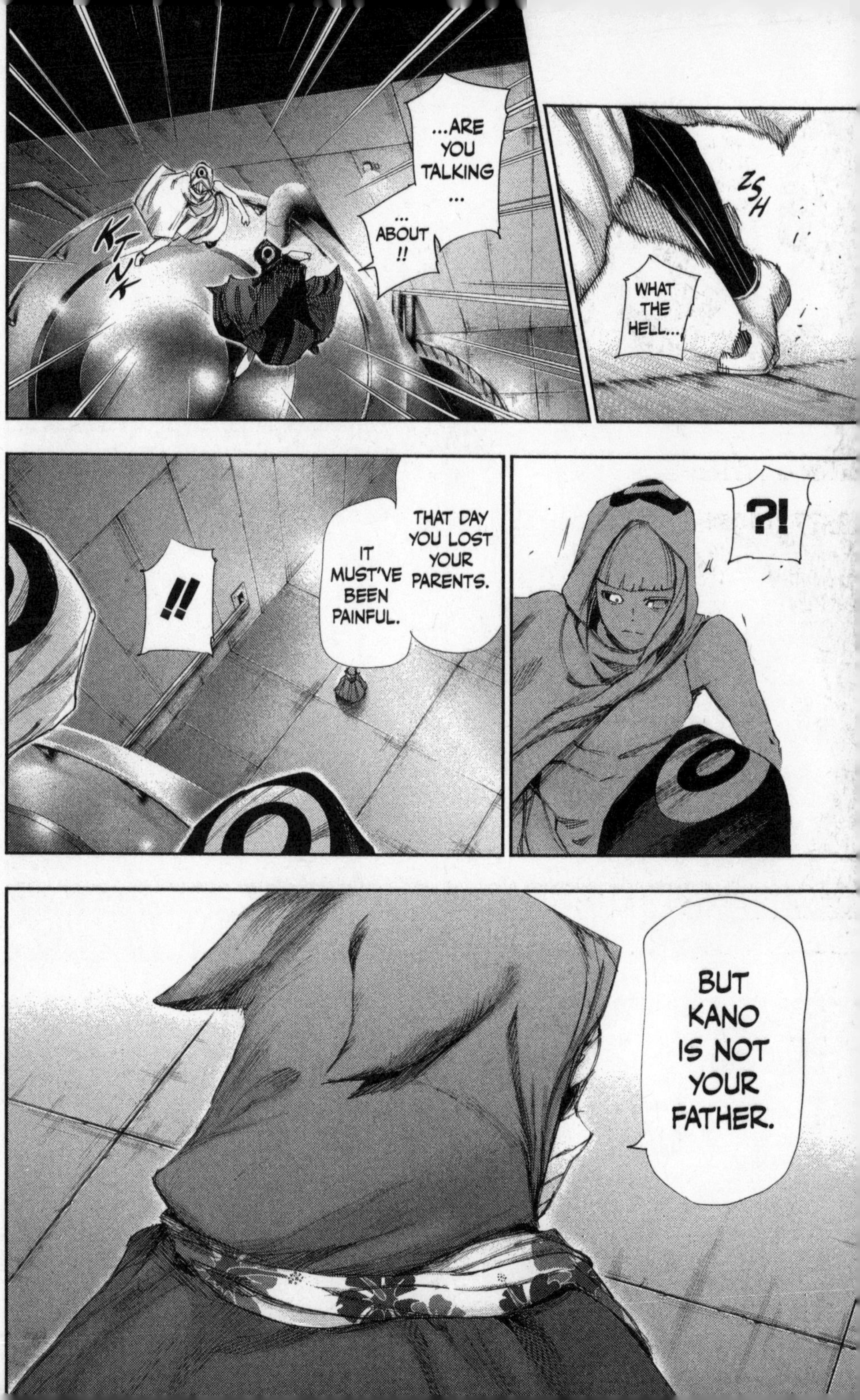
ZSH
WHAT THE HELL...
...ARE YOU TALKING ...
...ABOUT !!
KTINK
?!
THAT DAY YOU LOST YOUR PARENTS.
IT MUST'VE BEEN PAINFUL.
!!
BUT KANO IS NOT YOUR FATHER.

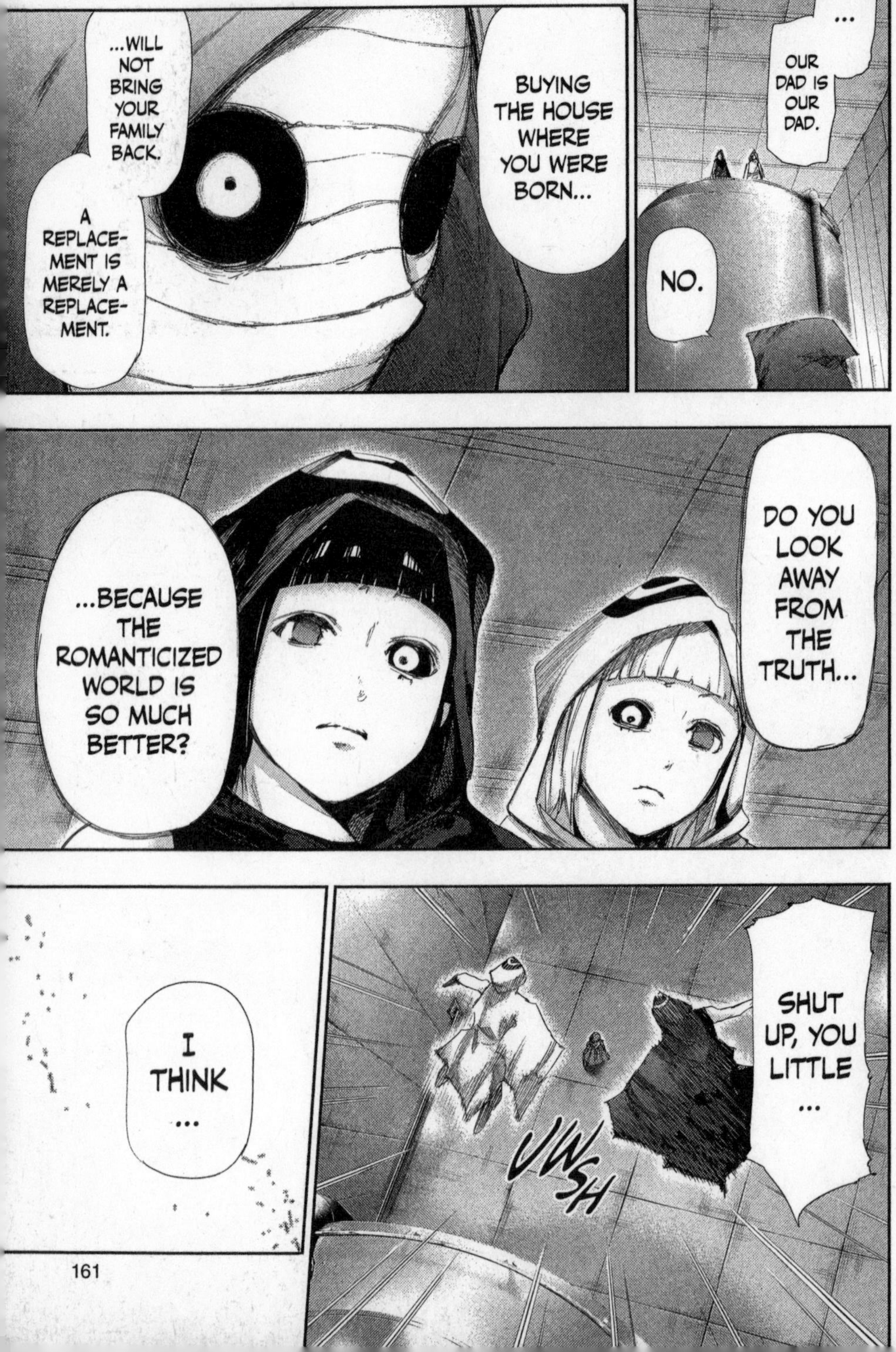
...
OUR DAD IS OUR DAD.
NO.
BUYING THE HOUSE WHERE YOU WERE BORN...
...WILL NOT BRING YOUR FAMILY BACK.
A REPLACEMENT IS MERELY A REPLACEMENT.
DO YOU LOOK AWAY FROM THE TRUTH...
...BECAUSE THE ROMANTICIZED WORLD IS SO MUCH BETTER?
SHUT UP, YOU LITTLE ...
VWSH
I THINK ...

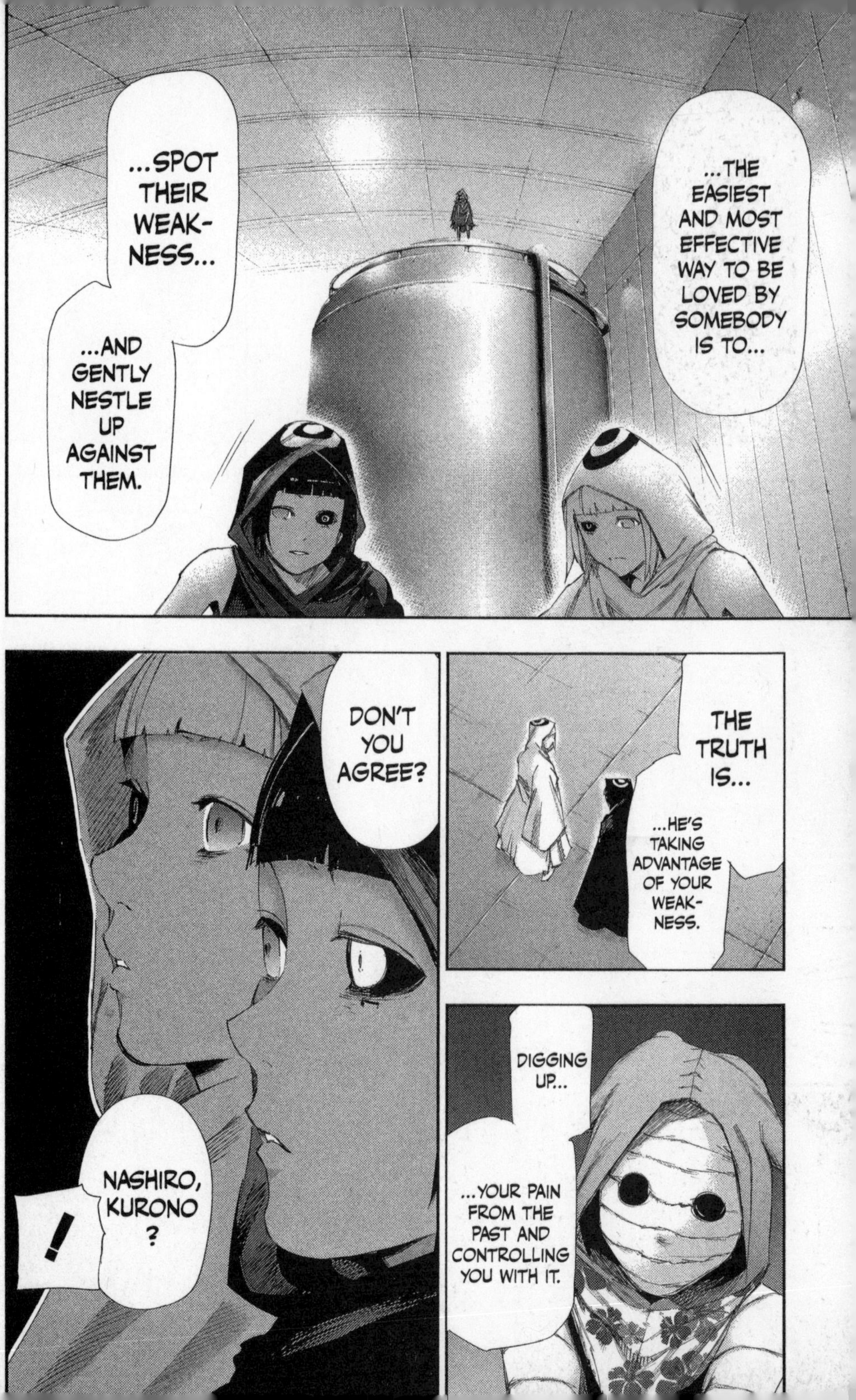
...THE EASIEST AND MOST EFFECTIVE WAY TO BE LOVED BY SOMEBODY IS TO...
...SPOT THEIR WEAKNESS...
...AND GENTLY NESTLE UP AGAINST THEM.
THE TRUTH IS...
...HE'S TAKING ADVANTAGE OF YOUR WEAKNESS.
DIGGING UP...
...YOUR PAIN FROM THE PAST AND CONTROLLING YOU WITH IT.
DON'T YOU AGREE?
NASHIRO, KURONO?
!

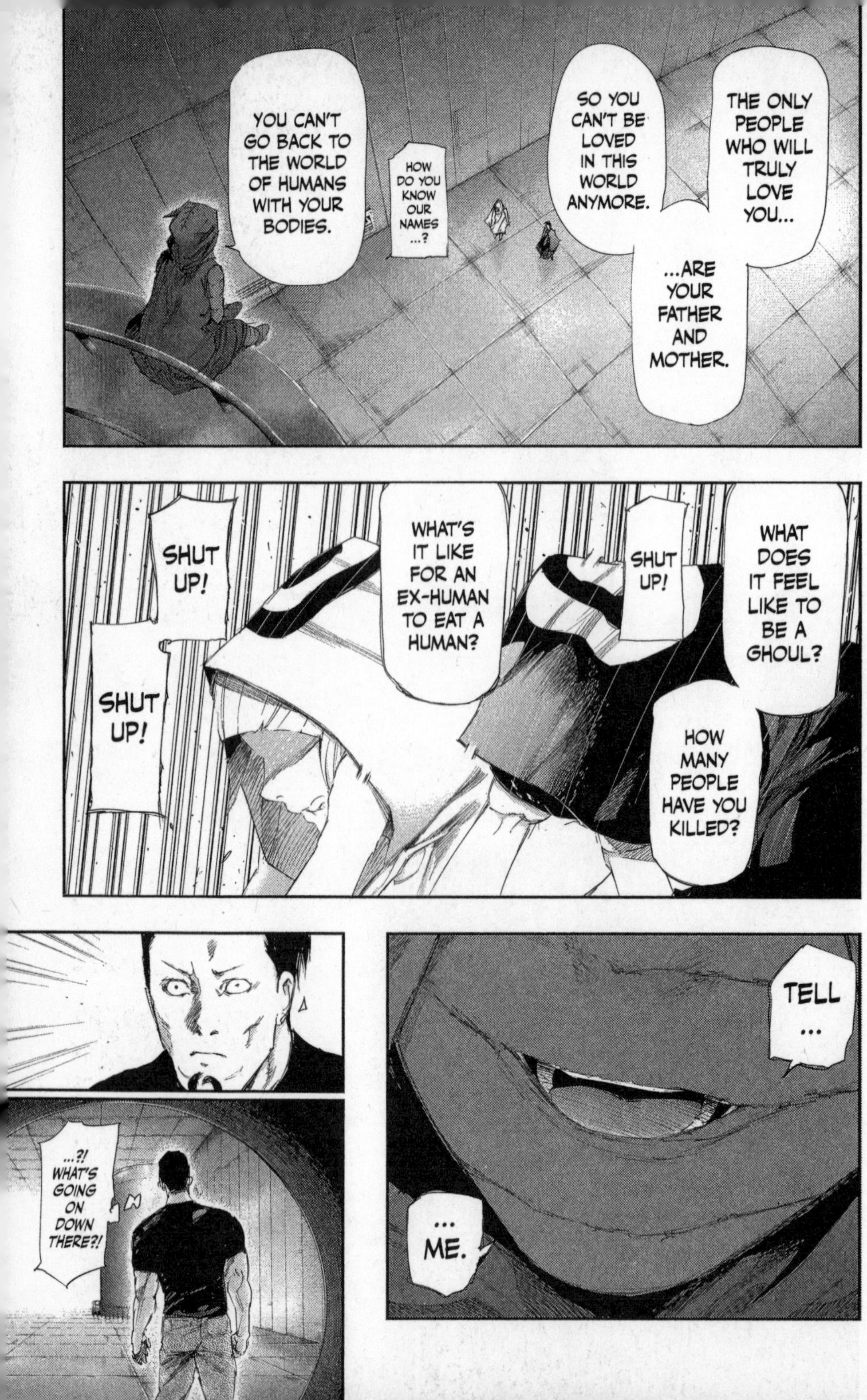
THE ONLY PEOPLE WHO WILL TRULY LOVE YOU...
...ARE YOUR FATHER AND MOTHER.
SO YOU CAN'T BE LOVED IN THIS WORLD ANYMORE.
HOW DO YOU KNOW OUR NAMES ...?
YOU CAN'T GO BACK TO THE WORLD OF HUMANS WITH YOUR BODIES.
WHAT DOES IT FEEL LIKE TO BE A GHOUL?
SHUT UP!
HOW MANY PEOPLE HAVE YOU KILLED?
WHAT'S IT LIKE FOR AN EX-HUMAN TO EAT A HUMAN?
SHUT UP!
SHUT UP!
TELL ...
... ME.
...?! WHAT'S GOING ON DOWN THERE?!

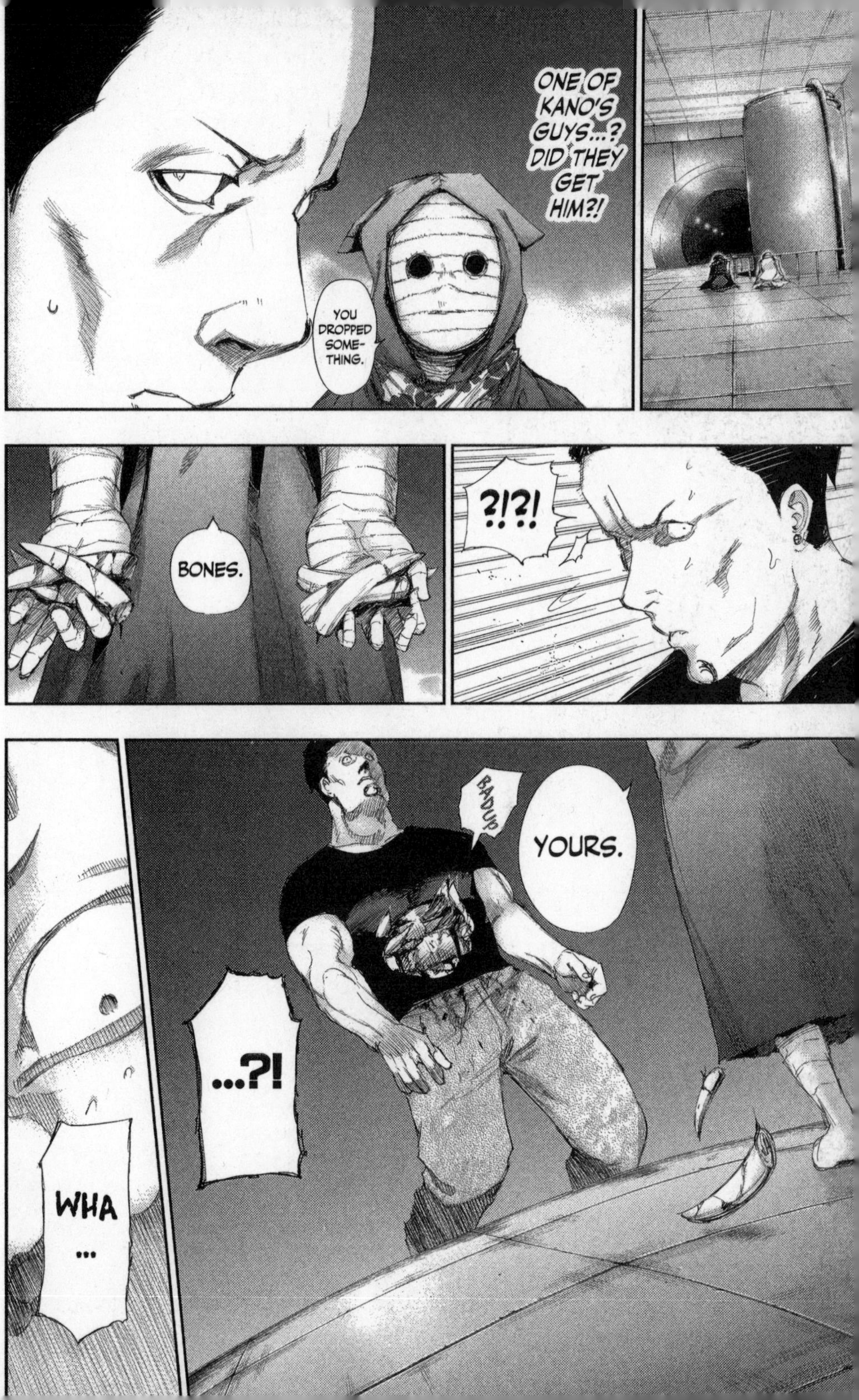
ONE OF KANO'S GUYS...? DID THEY GET HIM?!
YOU DROPPED SOME-THING.
?!?!
BONES.
BADUP
YOURS.
...?!
WHA ...

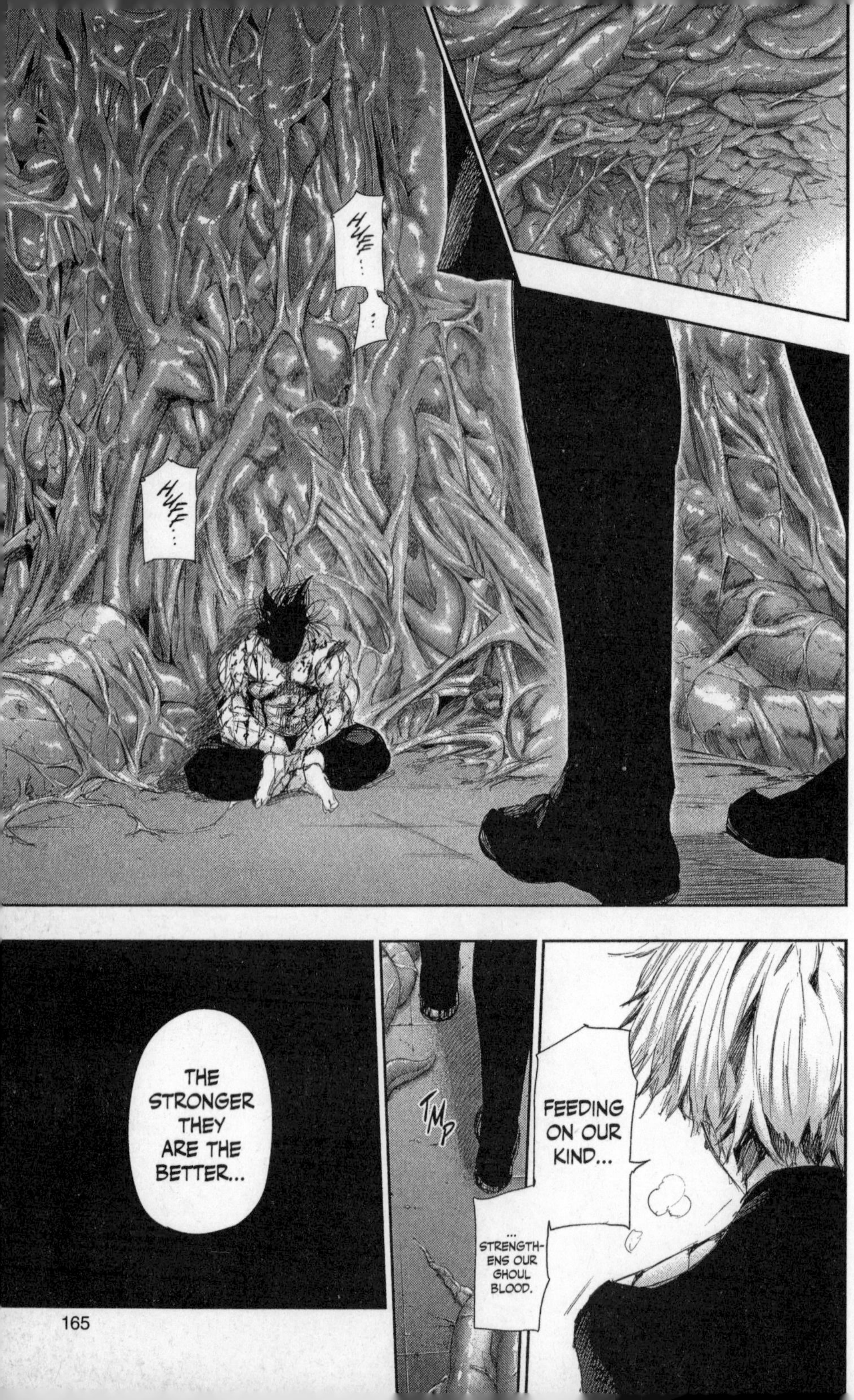
HUFF... ...
HUFF...
FEEDING ON OUR KIND...
... STRENGTHENS OUR GHOUL BLOOD.
TMP
THE STRONGER THEY ARE THE BETTER...

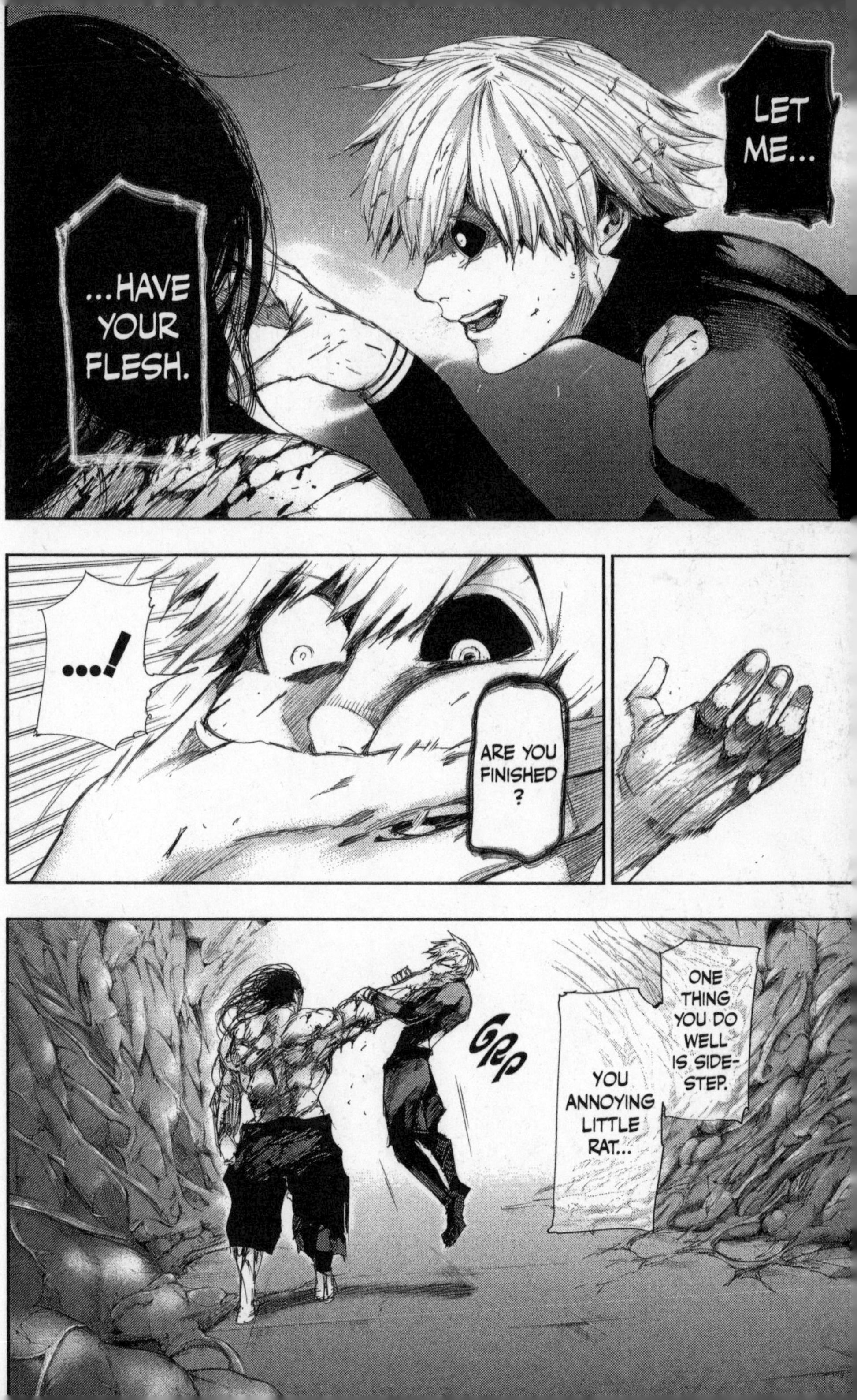
LET ME...
...HAVE YOUR FLESH.
ARE YOU FINISHED ?
...!
ONE THING YOU DO WELL IS SIDE-STEP.
YOU ANNOYING LITTLE RAT...
GRP

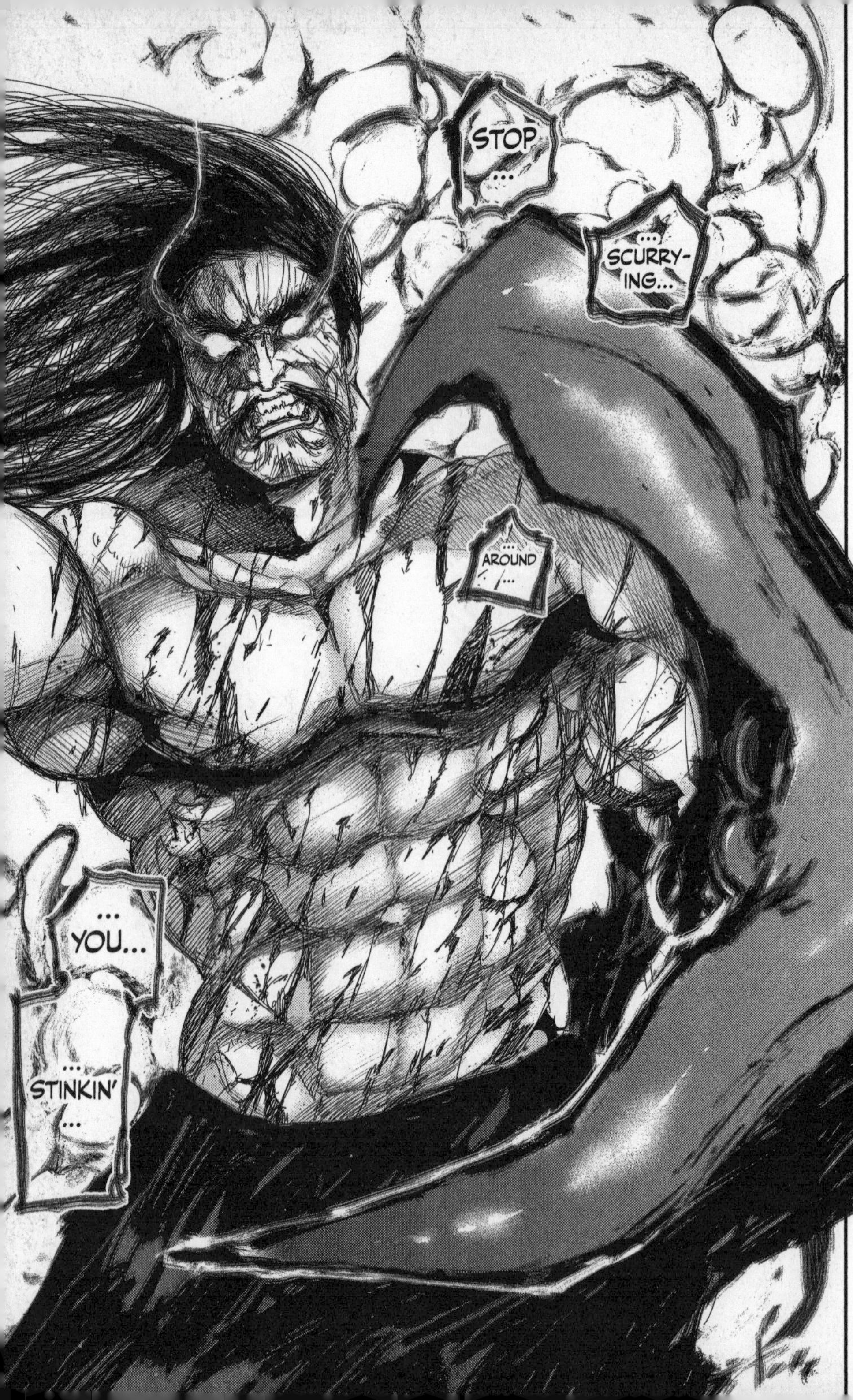
STOP ...
... SCURRY-ING...
... AROUND ...
... YOU...
... STINKIN' ...

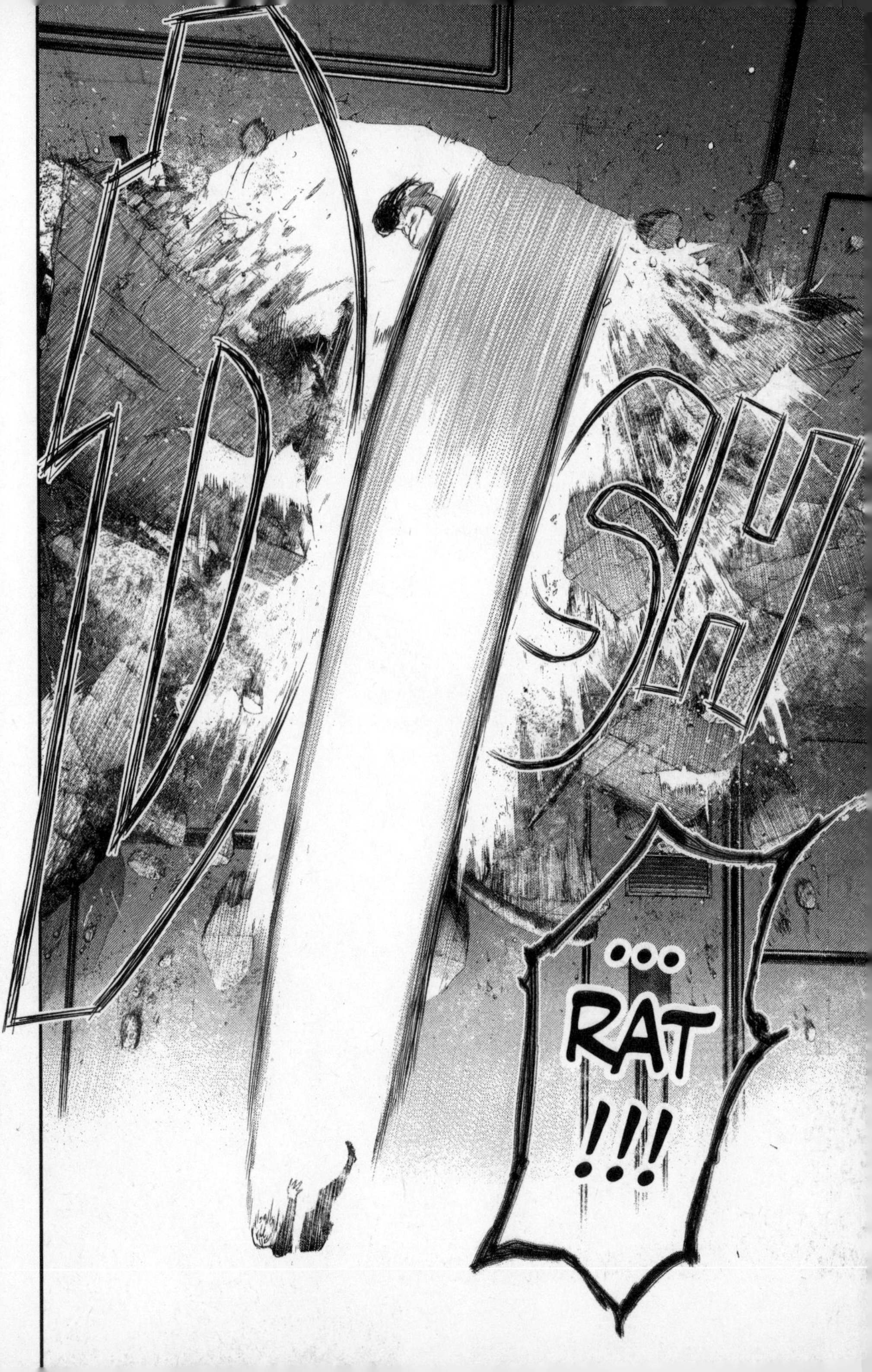
...RAT!!!

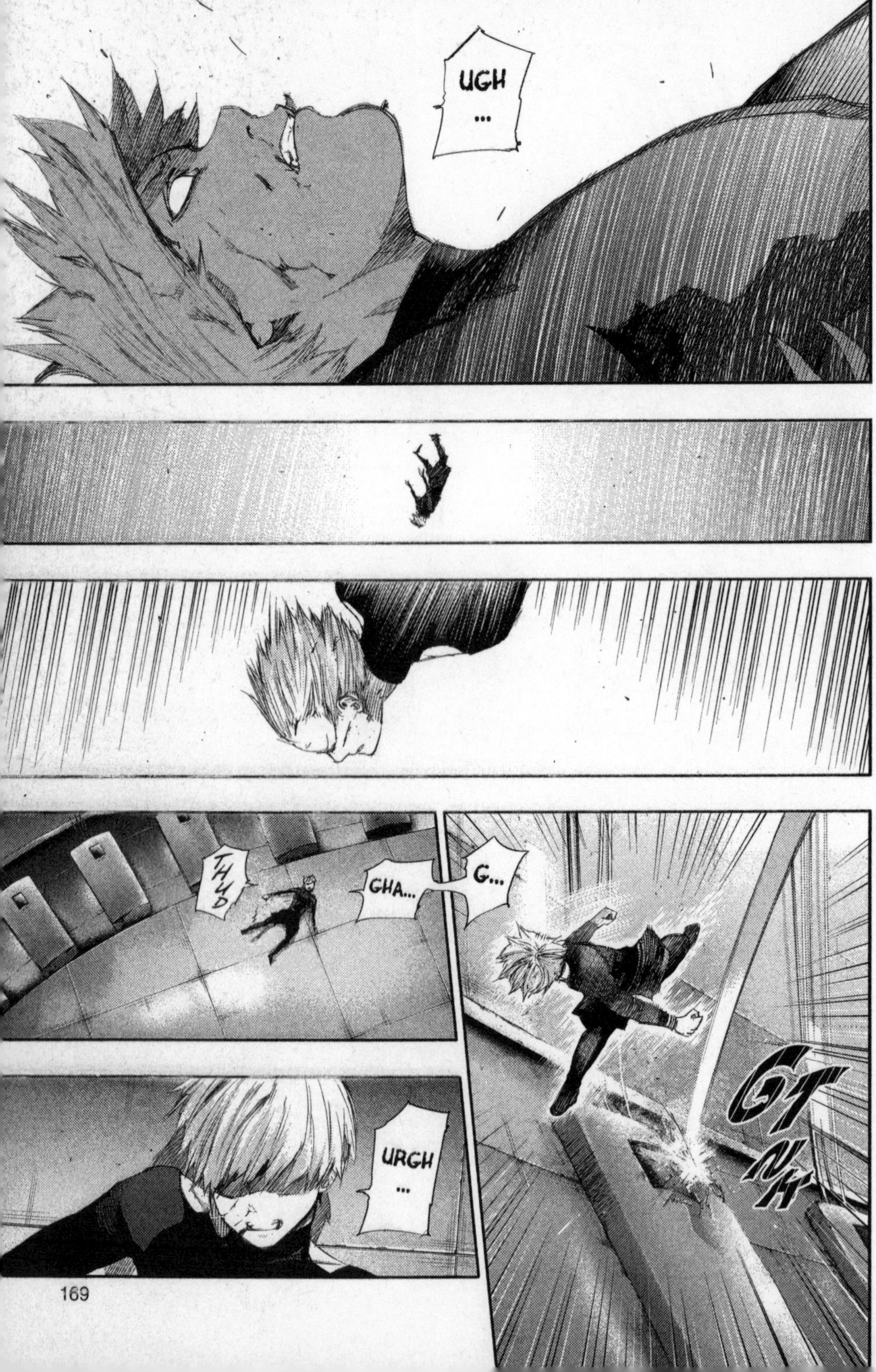
UGH ...
G...
THUD
GHA...
URGH ...

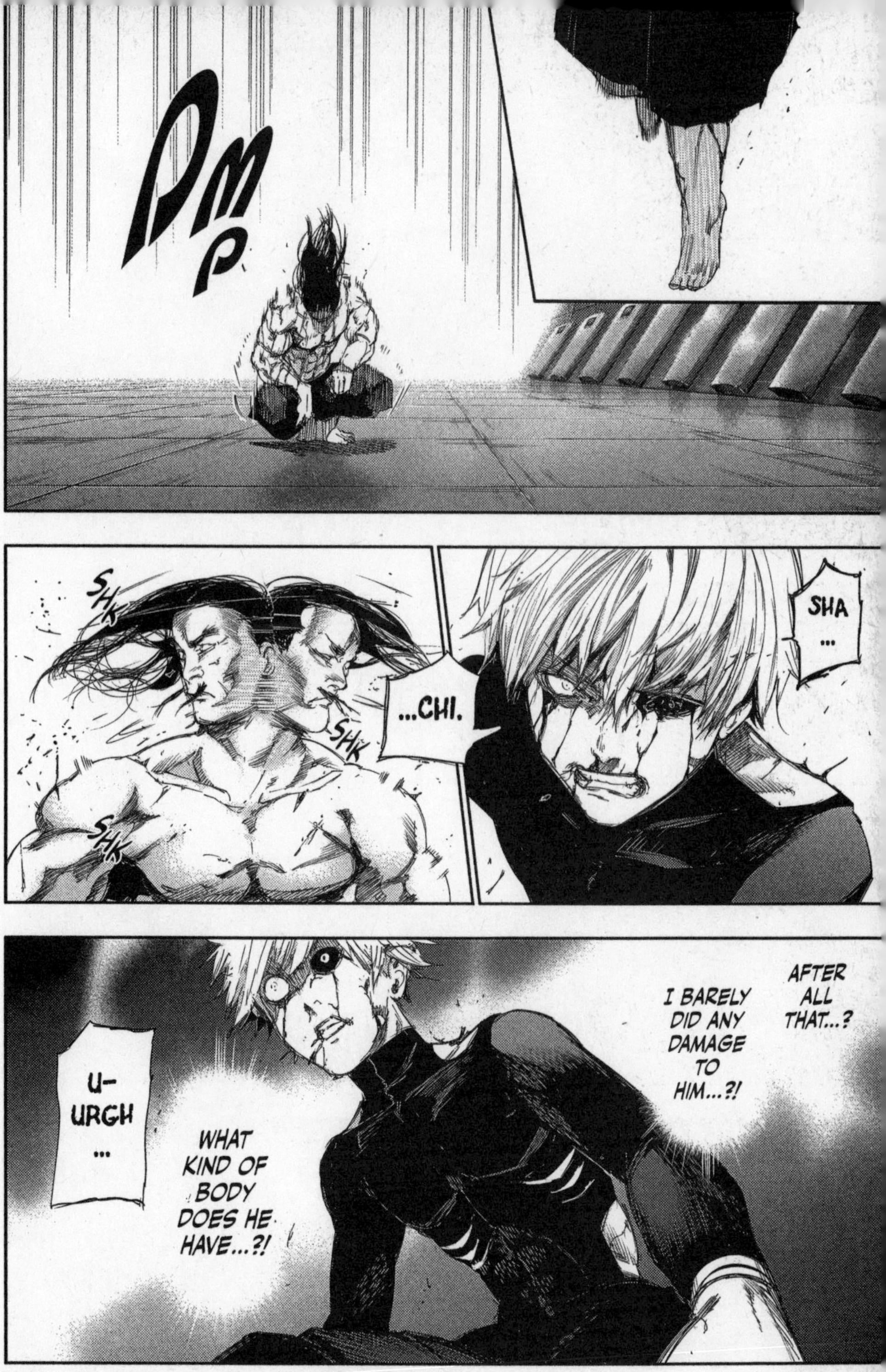
DMP
SHA...
...CHI.
SHK
SHK
SHK
AFTER ALL THAT...?
I BARELY DID ANY DAMAGE TO HIM...?!
WHAT KIND OF BODY DOES HE HAVE...?!
U-URGH...

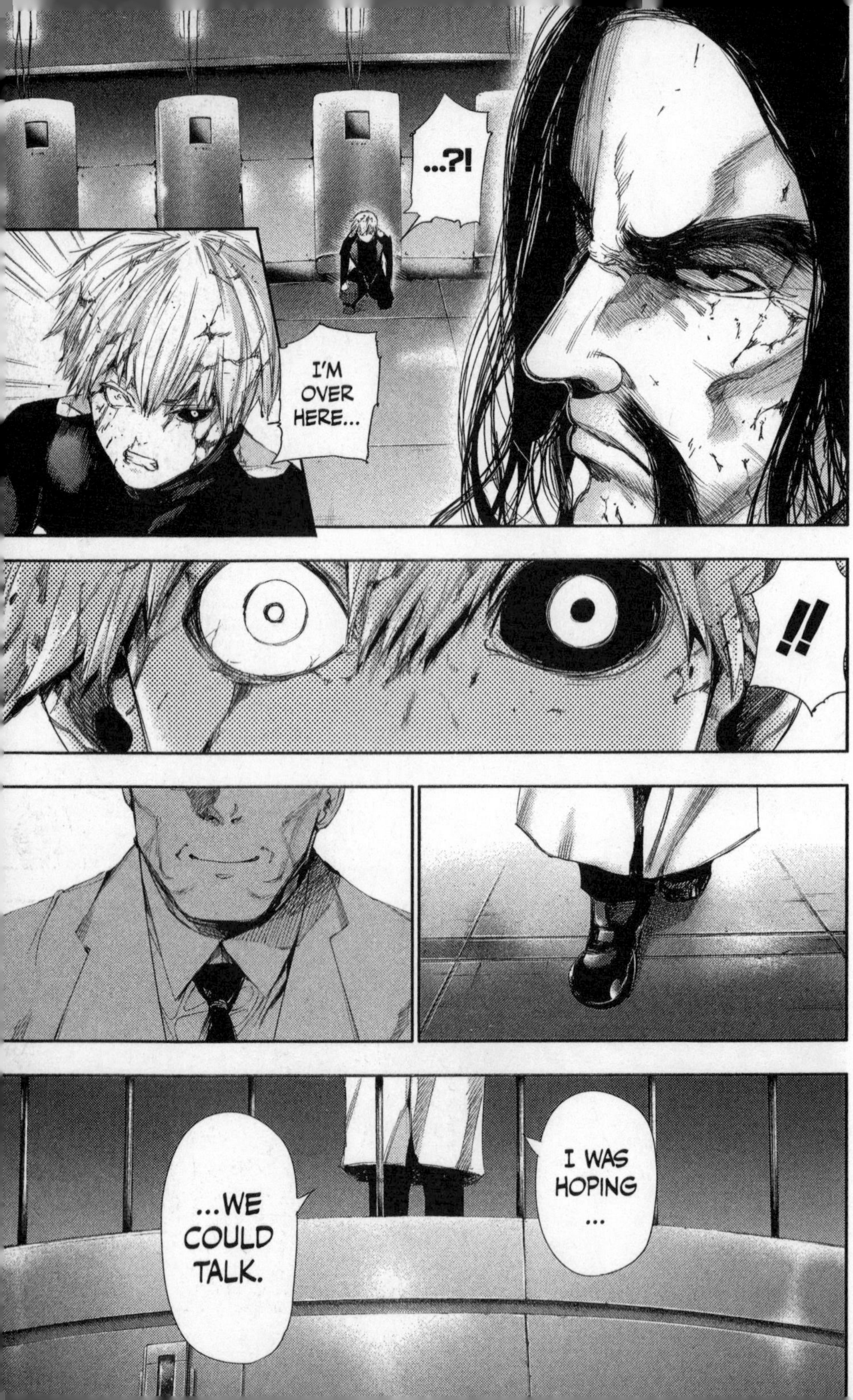
...?!
I'M OVER HERE...
!!
I WAS HOPING ...
...WE COULD TALK.

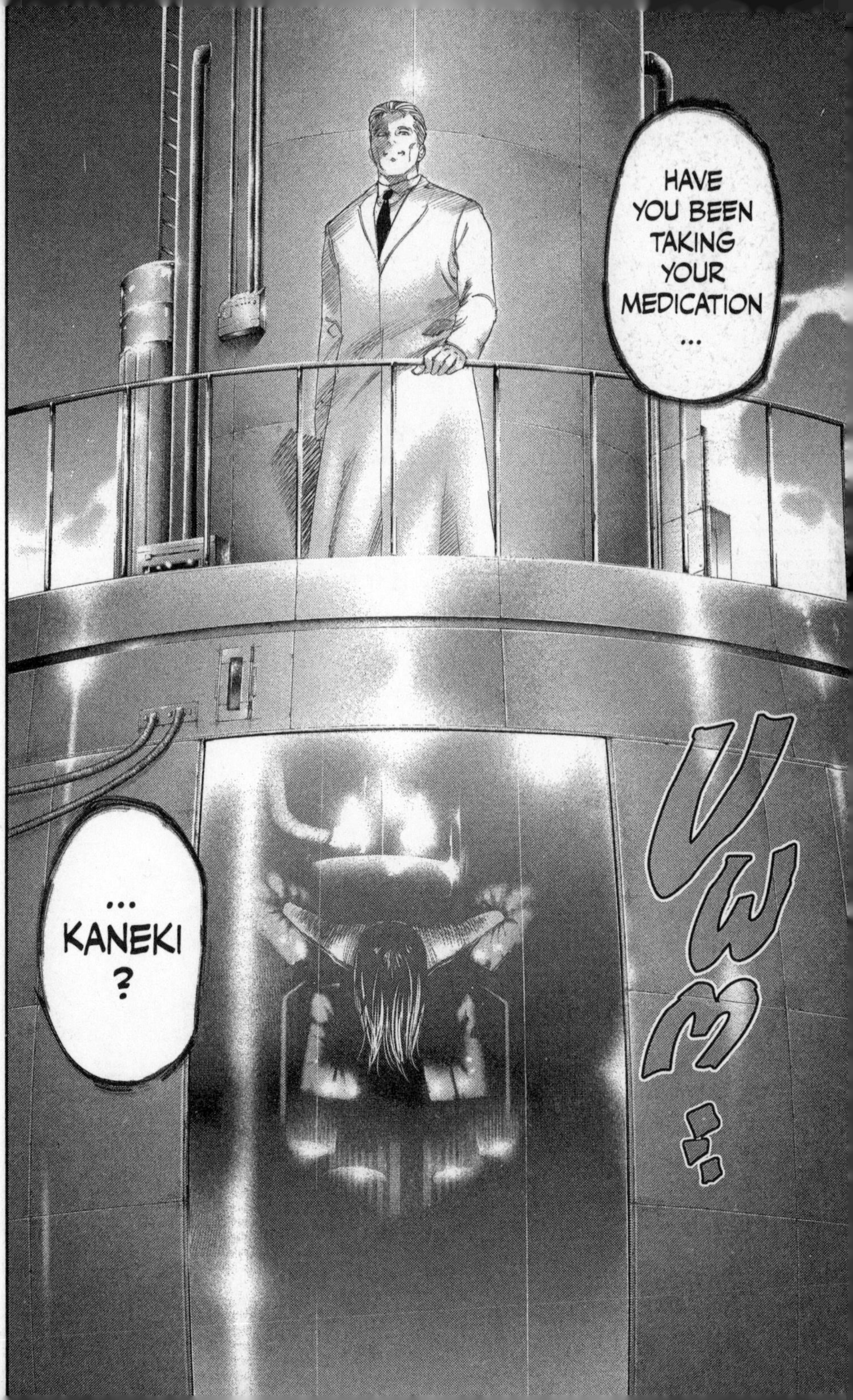
HAVE YOU BEEN TAKING YOUR MEDICATION ...
VWM...
... KANEKI ?

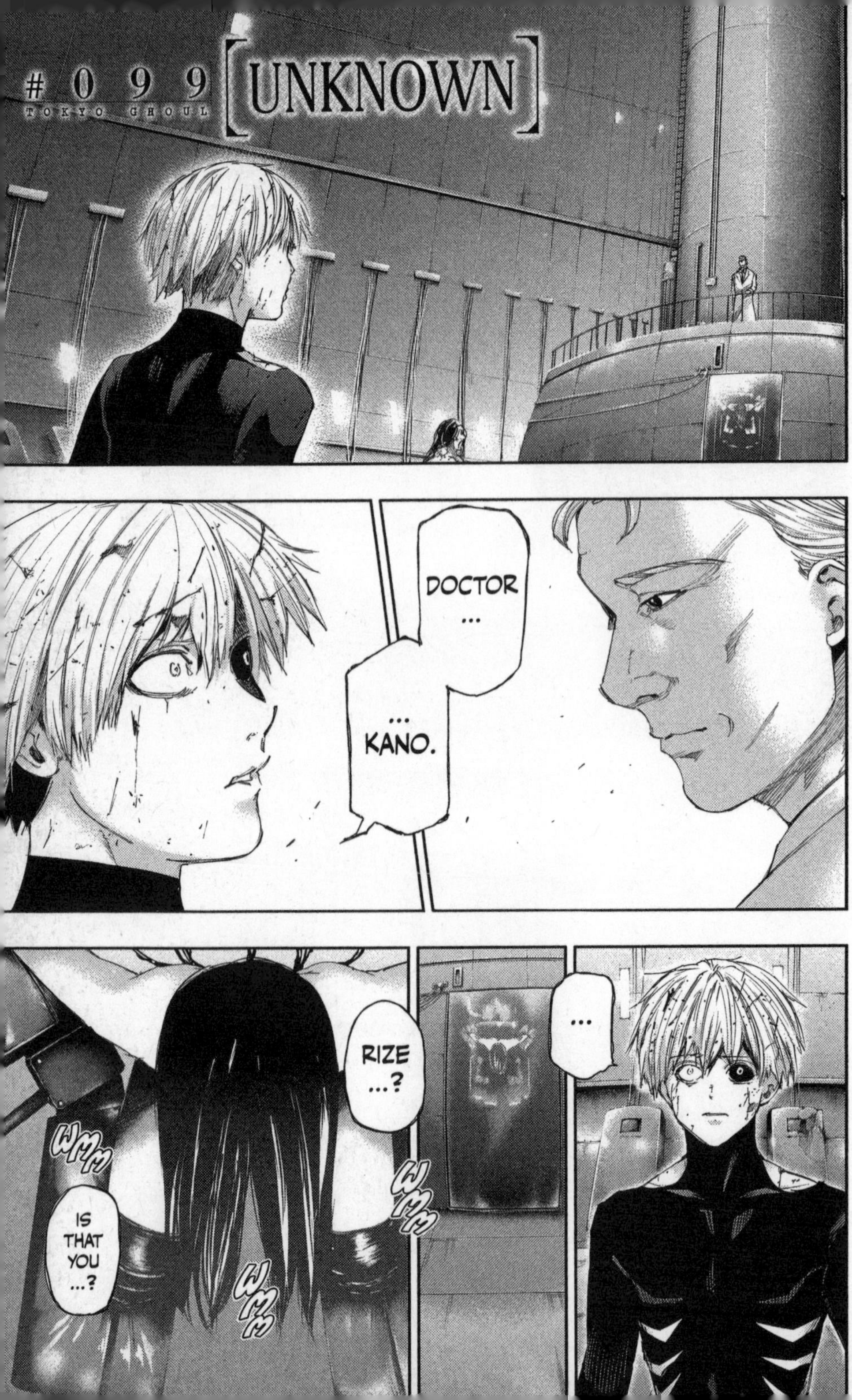
#099 [UNKNOWN]
TOKYO GHOUL
DOCTOR ...
... KANO.
...
RIZE ...?
WMM
WMM
IS THAT YOU ...?
WMM

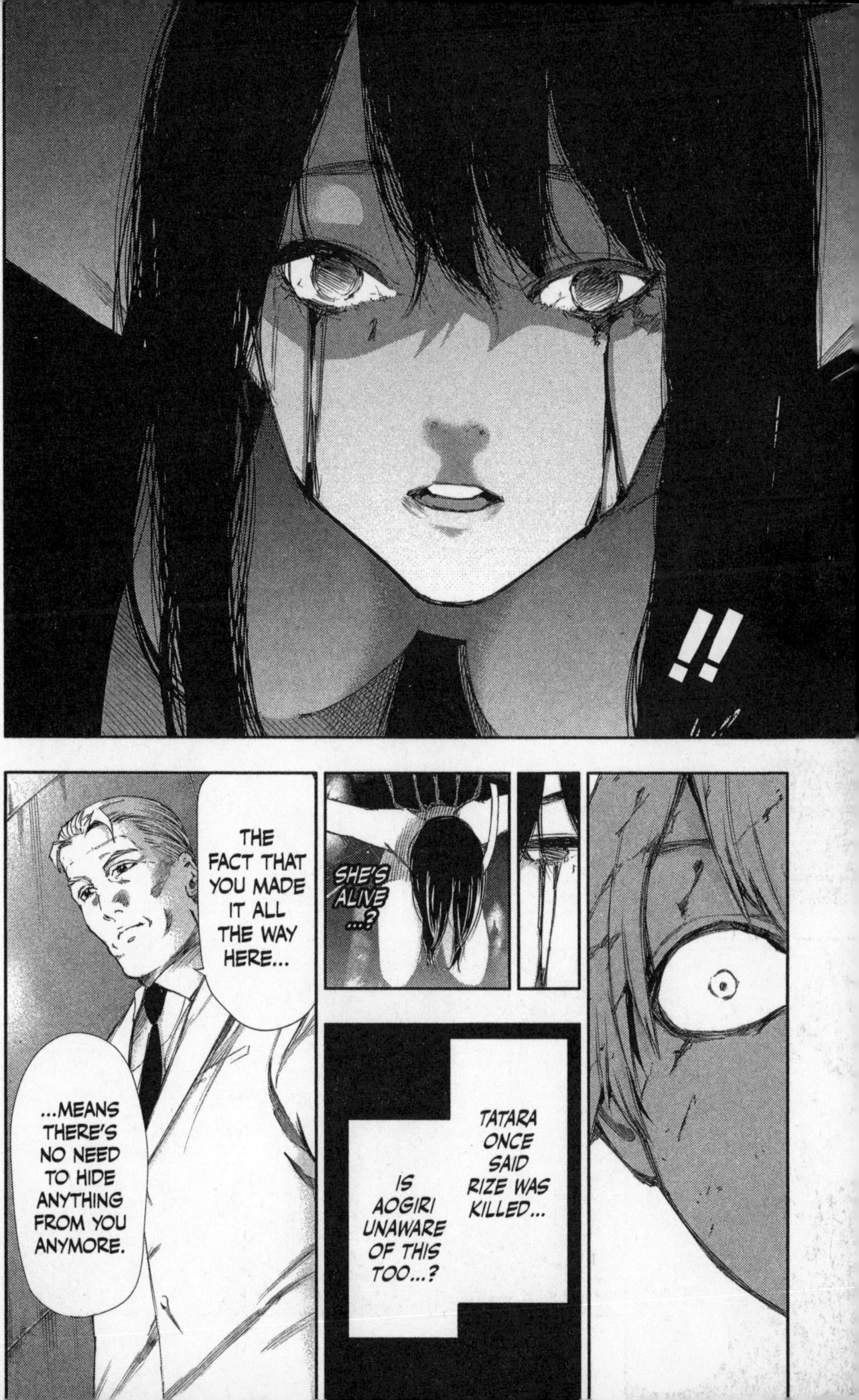
!!
SHE'S ALIVE ...?
TATARA ONCE SAID RIZE WAS KILLED...
IS AOGIRI UNAWARE OF THIS TOO...?
THE FACT THAT YOU MADE IT ALL THE WAY HERE...
...MEANS THERE'S NO NEED TO HIDE ANYTHING FROM YOU ANYMORE.

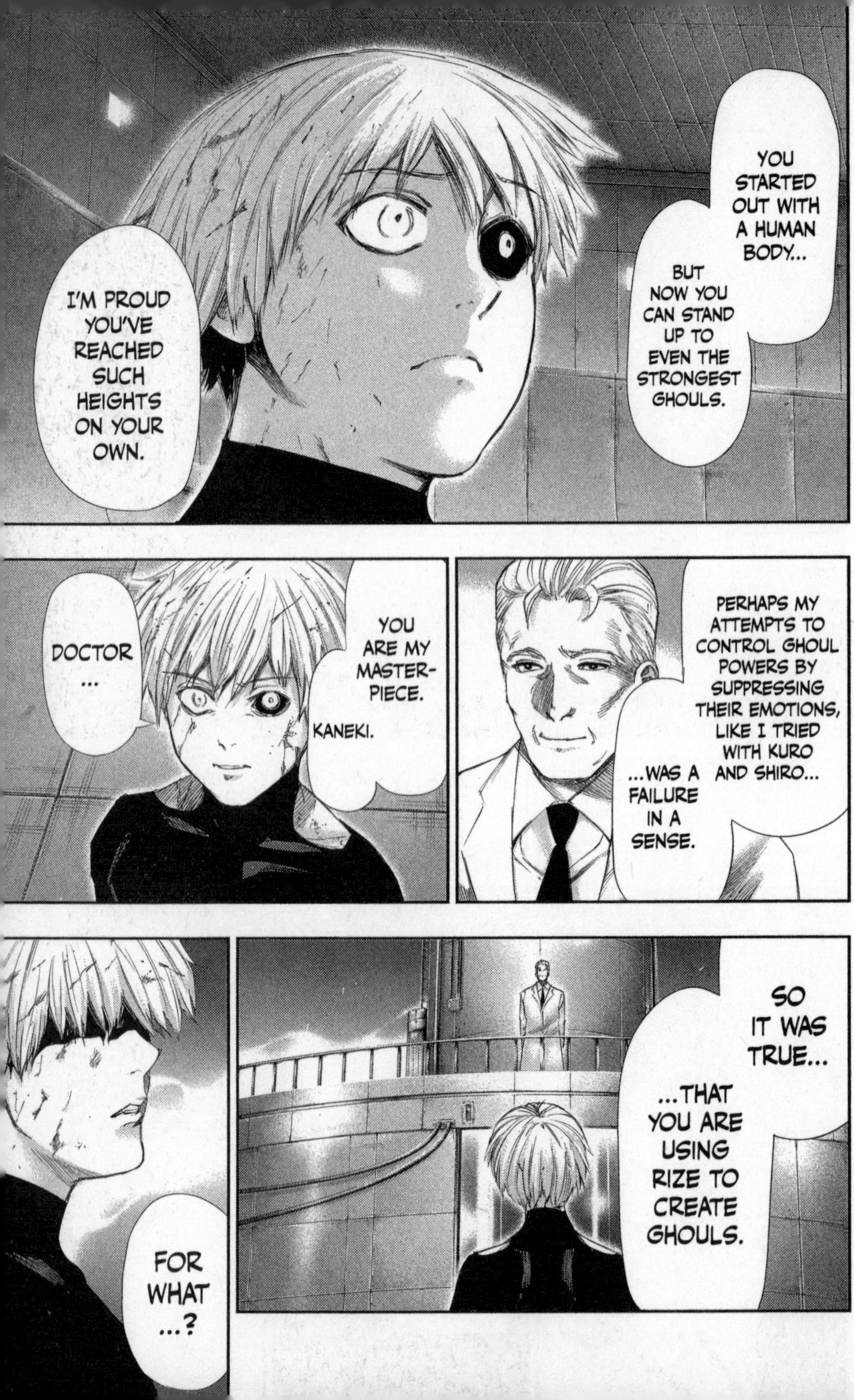
YOU STARTED OUT WITH A HUMAN BODY...
BUT NOW YOU CAN STAND UP TO EVEN THE STRONGEST GHOULS.
I'M PROUD YOU'VE REACHED SUCH HEIGHTS ON YOUR OWN.
PERHAPS MY ATTEMPTS TO CONTROL GHOUL POWERS BY SUPPRESSING THEIR EMOTIONS, LIKE I TRIED WITH KURO AND SHIRO...
...WAS A FAILURE IN A SENSE.
YOU ARE MY MASTER-PIECE.
KANEKI.
DOCTOR ...
SO IT WAS TRUE...
...THAT YOU ARE USING RIZE TO CREATE GHOULS.
FOR WHAT ...?

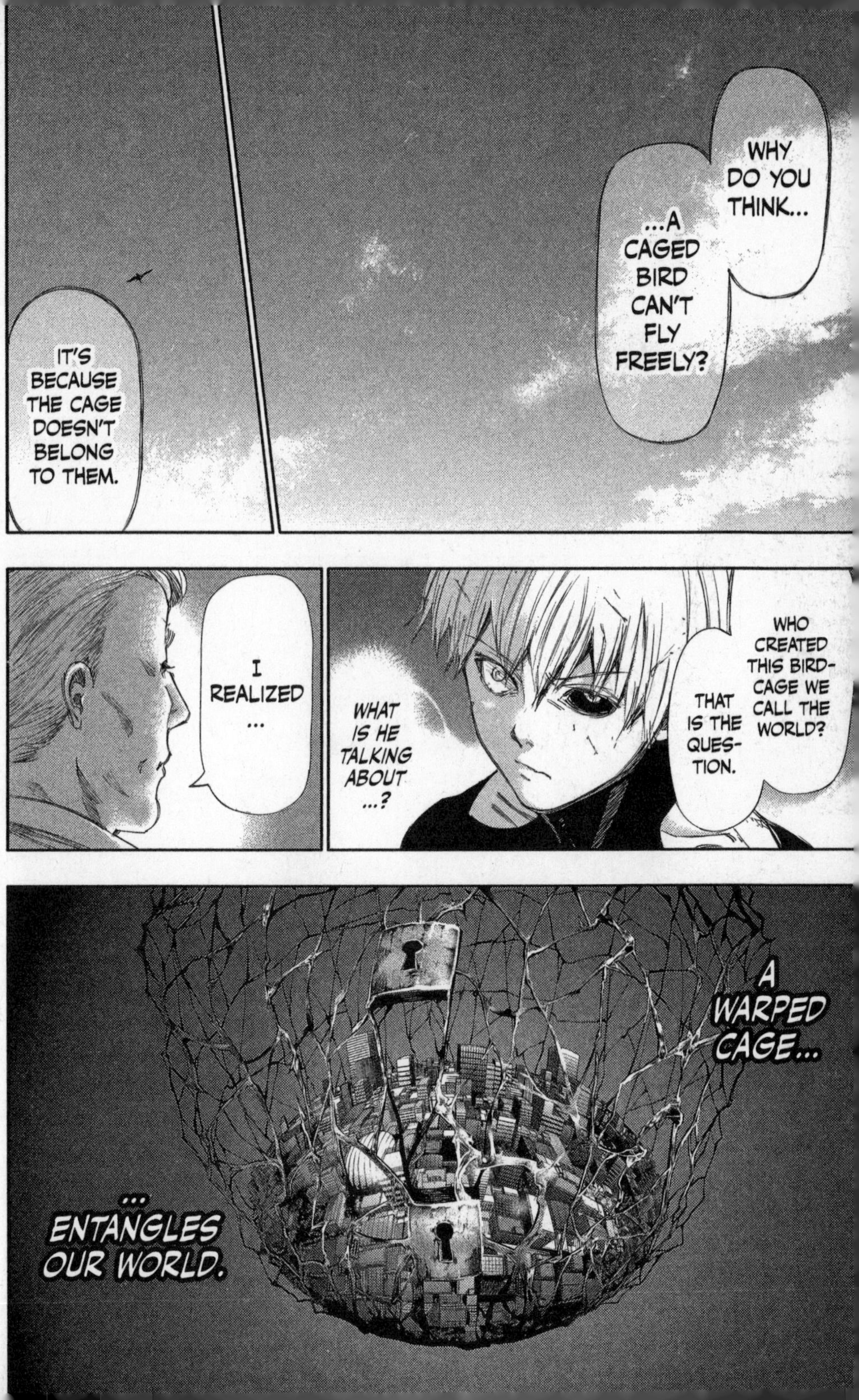
WHY DO YOU THINK...
...A CAGED BIRD CAN'T FLY FREELY?
IT'S BECAUSE THE CAGE DOESN'T BELONG TO THEM.
WHO CREATED THIS BIRD-CAGE WE CALL THE WORLD?
THAT IS THE QUES-TION.
WHAT IS HE TALKING ABOUT ...?
I REALIZED ...
A WARPED CAGE...
...ENTANGLES OUR WORLD.

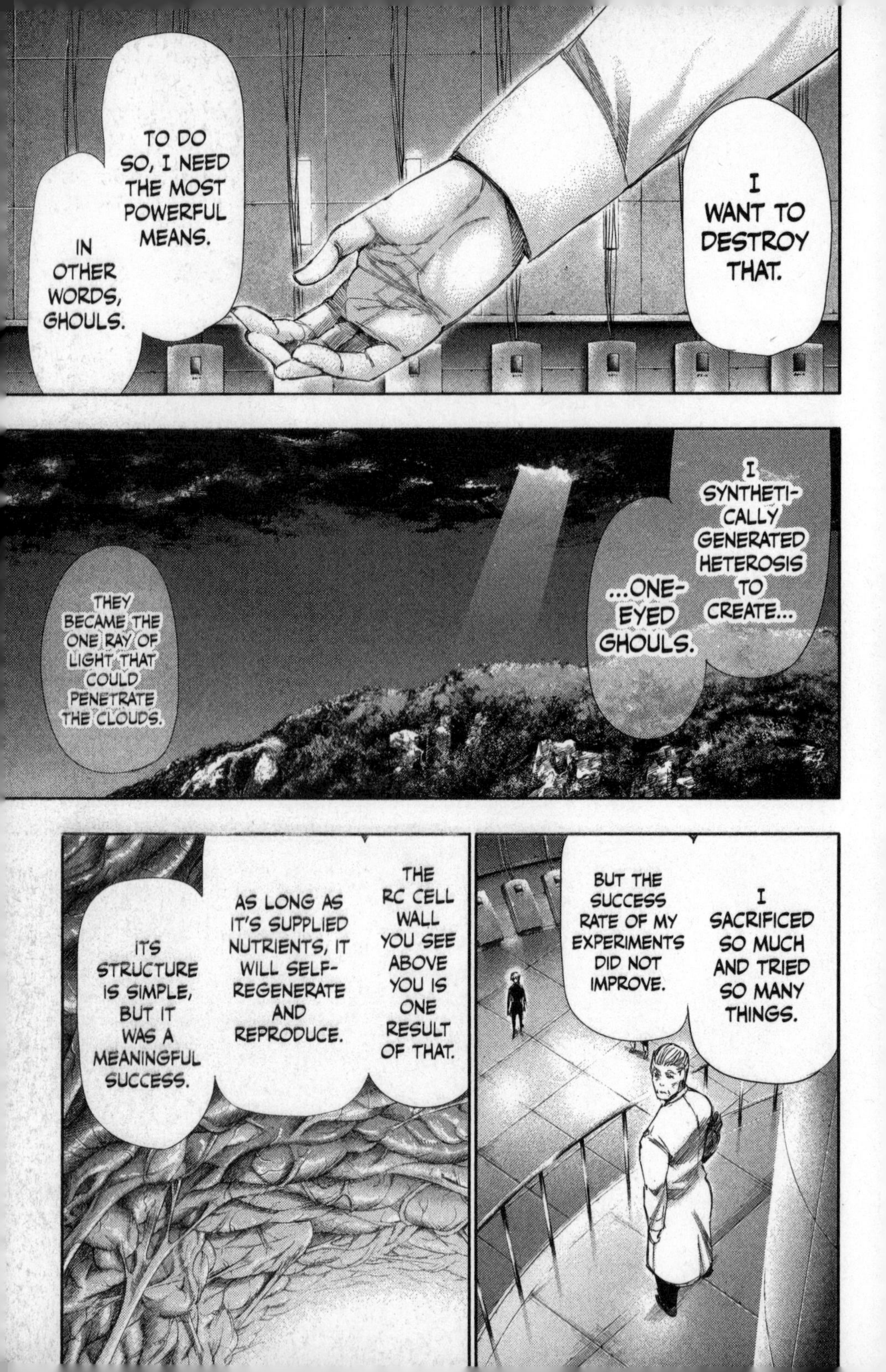
I WANT TO DESTROY THAT.
TO DO SO, I NEED THE MOST POWERFUL MEANS.
IN OTHER WORDS, GHOULS.
I SYNTHETICALLY GENERATED HETEROSIS TO CREATE...
...ONE-EYED GHOULS.
THEY BECAME THE ONE RAY OF LIGHT THAT COULD PENETRATE THE CLOUDS.
I SACRIFICED SO MUCH AND TRIED SO MANY THINGS.
BUT THE SUCCESS RATE OF MY EXPERIMENTS DID NOT IMPROVE.
THE RC CELL WALL YOU SEE ABOVE YOU IS ONE RESULT OF THAT.
AS LONG AS IT'S SUPPLIED NUTRIENTS, IT WILL SELF-REGENERATE AND REPRODUCE.
ITS STRUCTURE IS SIMPLE, BUT IT WAS A MEANINGFUL SUCCESS.

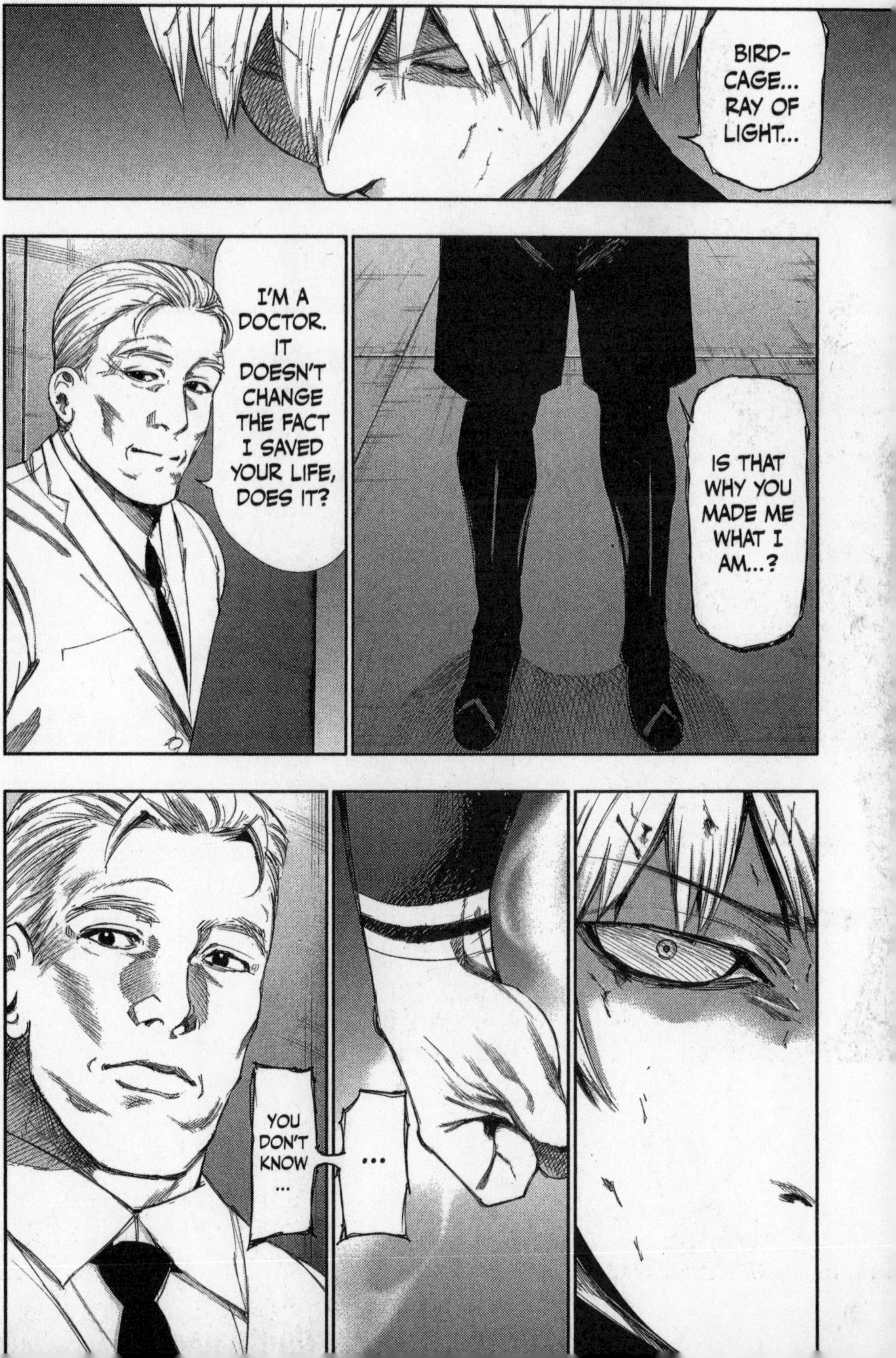
BIRD-CAGE... RAY OF LIGHT...
IS THAT WHY YOU MADE ME WHAT I AM...?
I'M A DOCTOR. IT DOESN'T CHANGE THE FACT I SAVED YOUR LIFE, DOES IT?
...
YOU DON'T KNOW ...

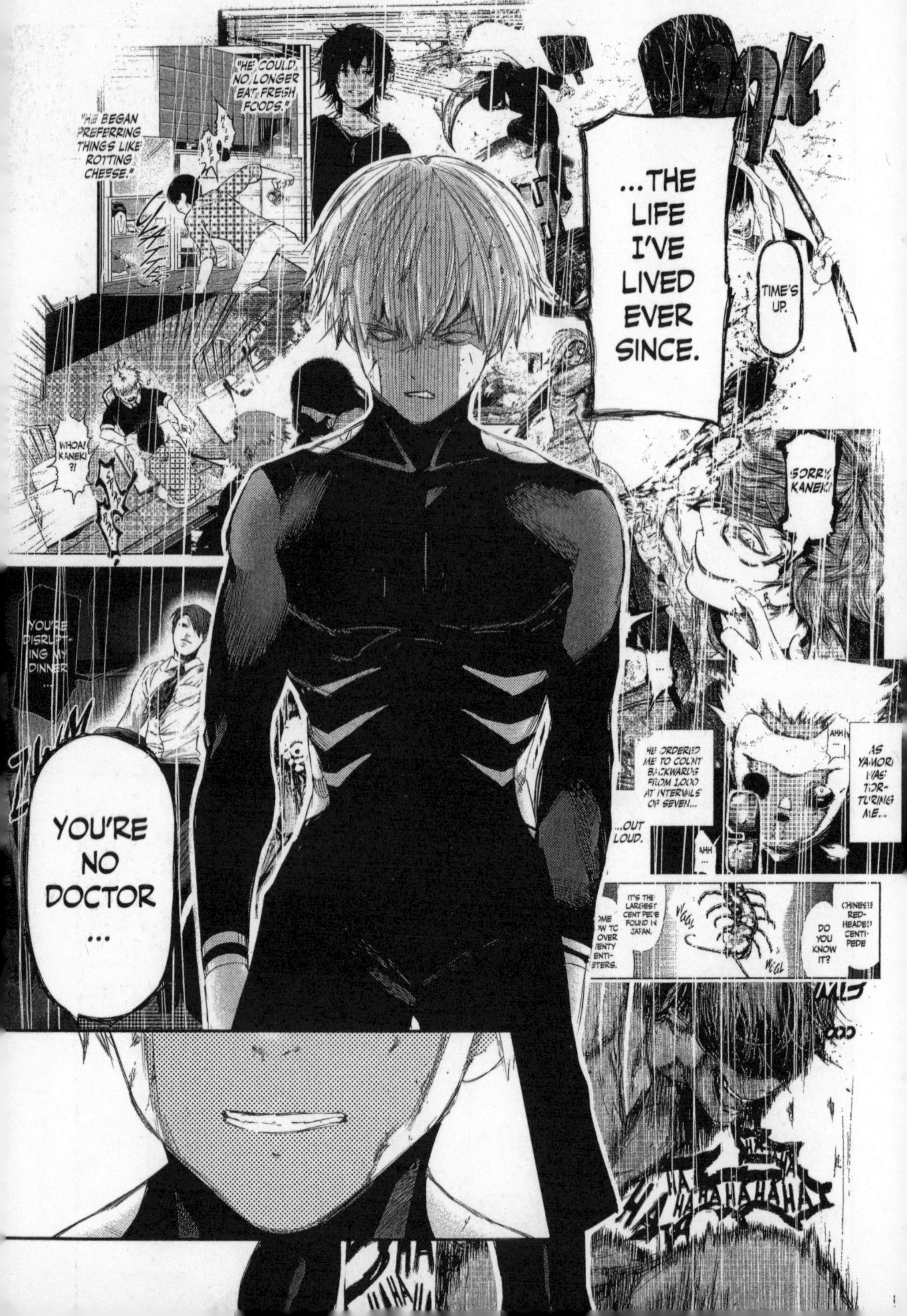
...THE LIFE I'VE LIVED EVER SINCE.
TIME'S UP.
"HE COULD NO LONGER EAT FRESH FOODS."
"HE BEGAN PREFERRING THINGS LIKE ROTTING CHEESE."
SORRY, KANEKI!
WHOA! KANEKI?!
...
AS YAMORI WAS TORTURING ME...
AHH...
HE ORDERED ME TO COUNT BACKWARDS FROM 1000 AT INTERVALS OF SEVEN...
...OUT LOUD.
AHH...
CHINESE RED-HEADED CENTIPEDE
DO YOU KNOW IT?
IT'S THE LARGEST CENTIPEDE FOUND IN JAPAN.
YOU'RE DISRUPTING MY DINNER...
YOU'RE NO DOCTOR...
HAHAHAHAHA

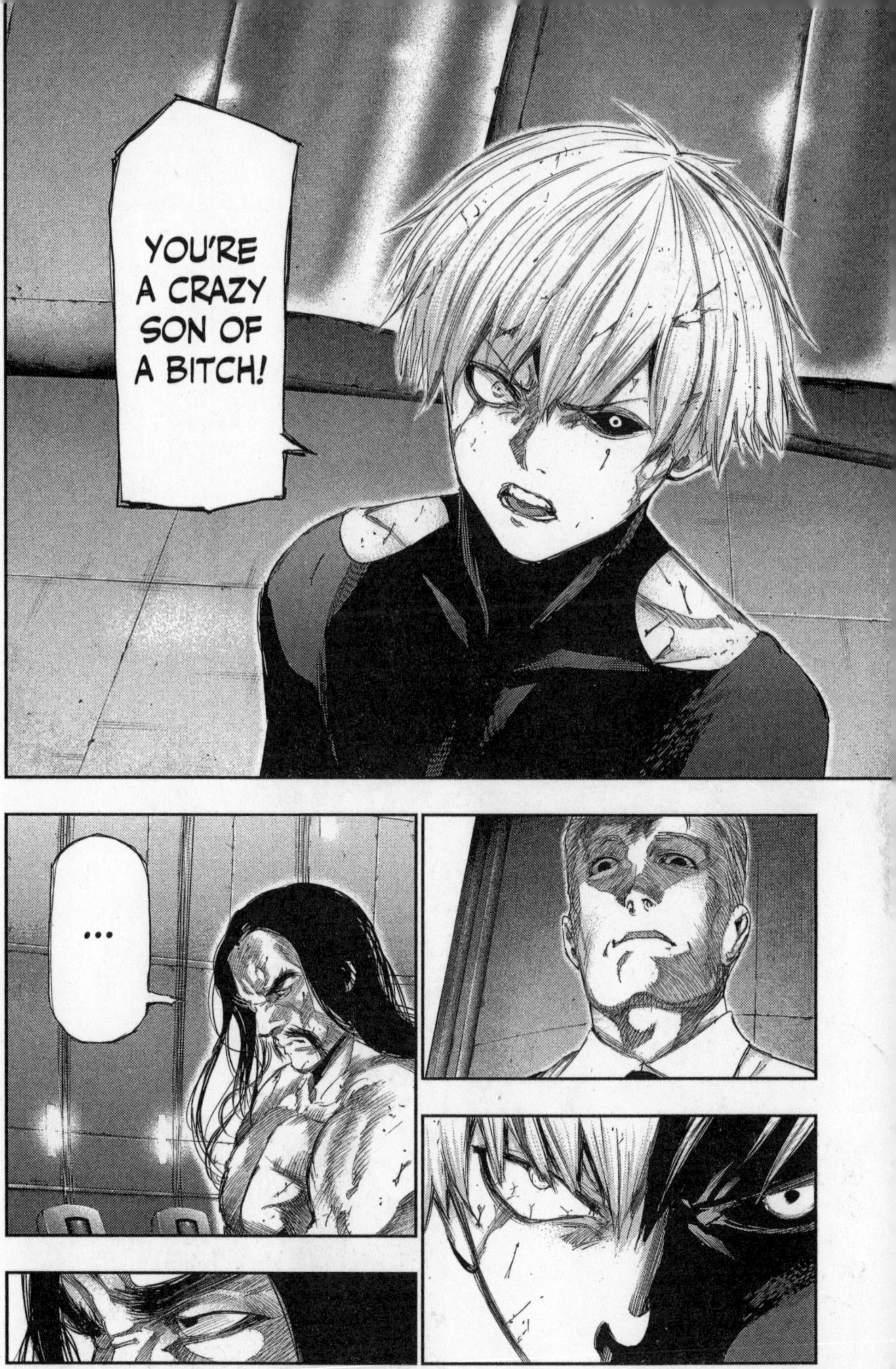
YOU'RE A CRAZY SON OF A BITCH!
...

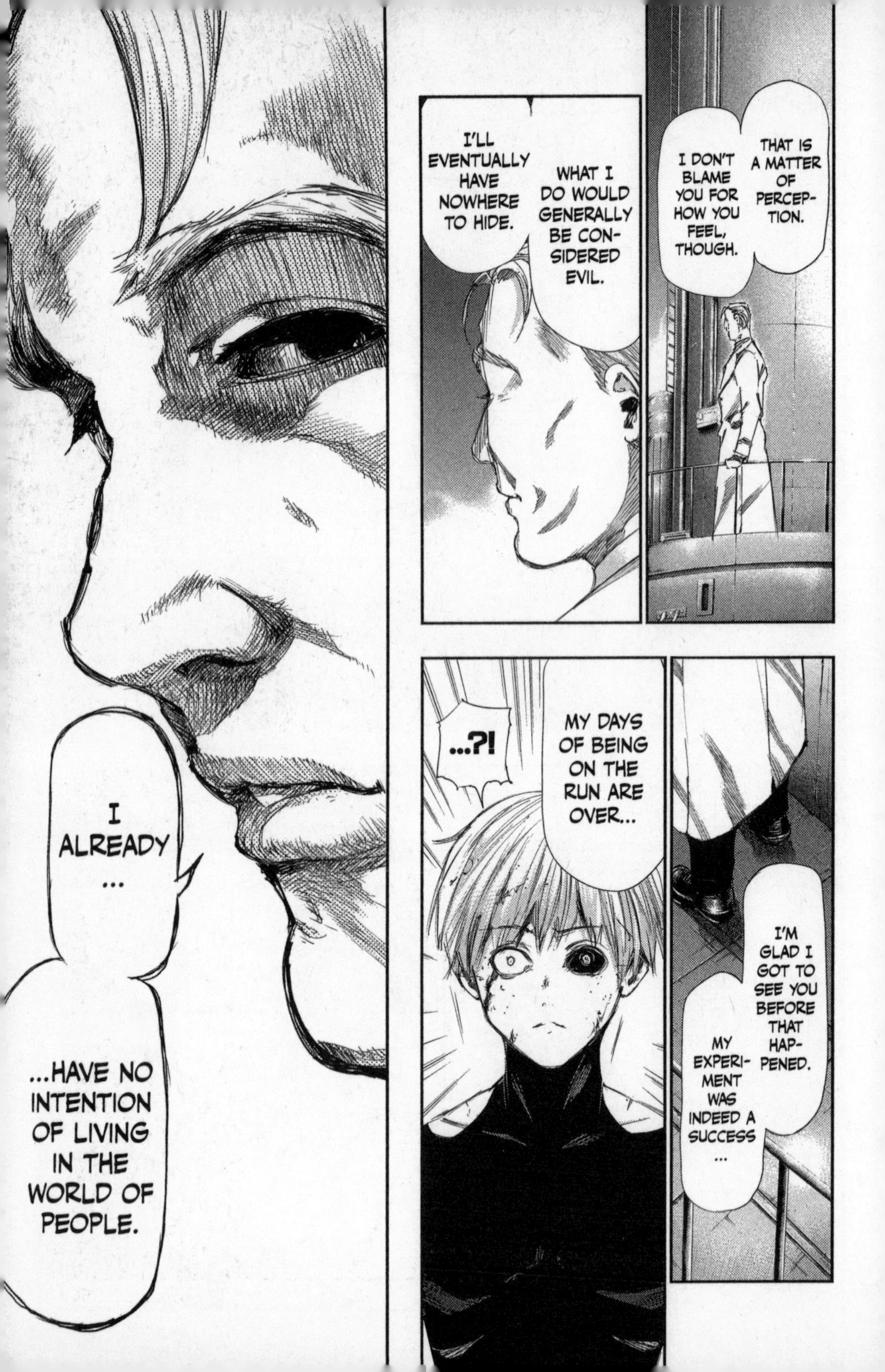
THAT IS A MATTER OF PERCEP-TION.
I DON'T BLAME YOU FOR HOW YOU FEEL, THOUGH.
WHAT I DO WOULD GENERALLY BE CON-SIDERED EVIL.
I'LL EVENTUALLY HAVE NOWHERE TO HIDE.
I'M GLAD I GOT TO SEE YOU BEFORE THAT HAP-PENED.
MY EXPERI-MENT WAS INDEED A SUCCESS ...
MY DAYS OF BEING ON THE RUN ARE OVER...
...?!
I ALREADY ...
...HAVE NO INTENTION OF LIVING IN THE WORLD OF PEOPLE.

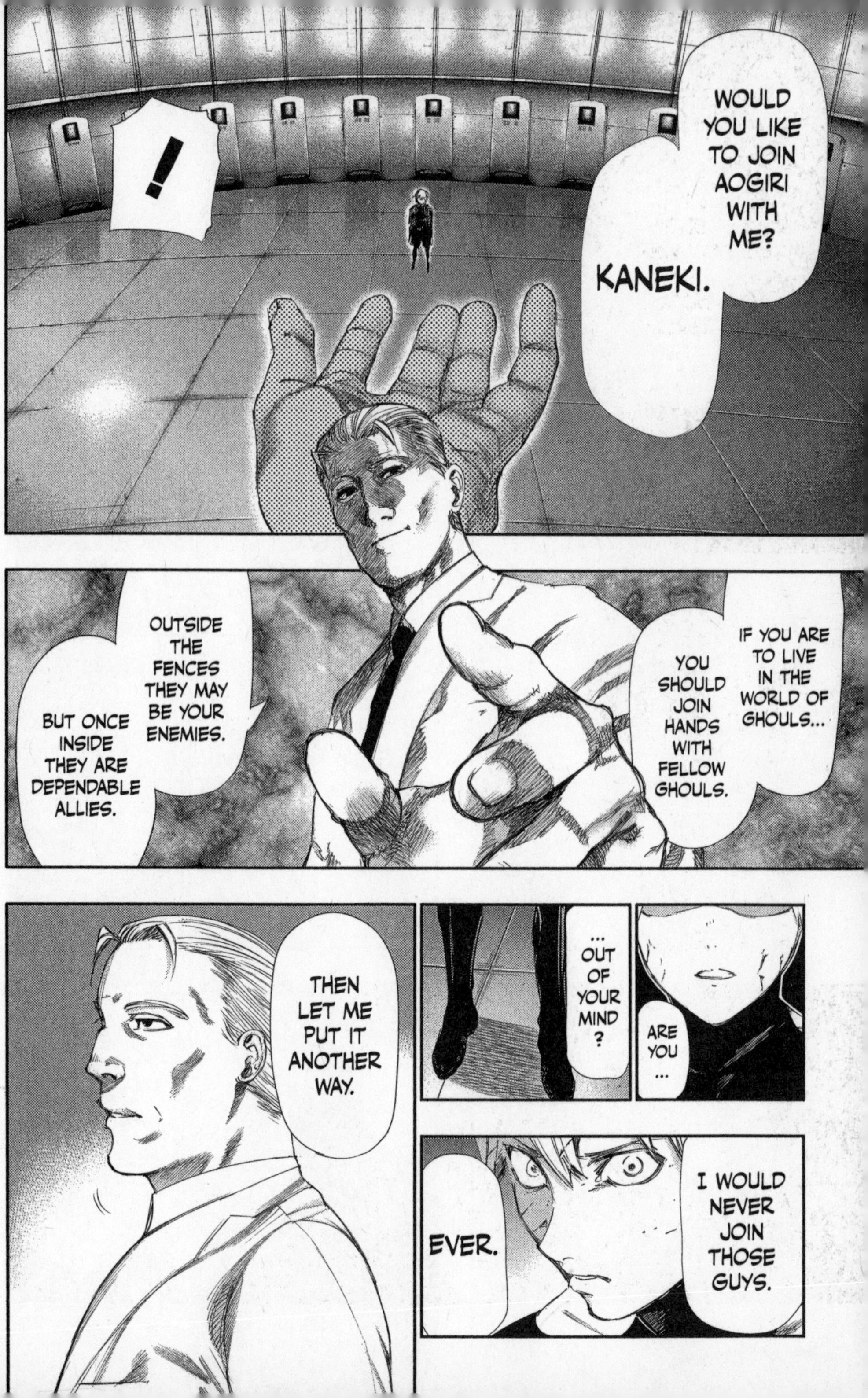
WOULD YOU LIKE TO JOIN AOGIRI WITH ME?
KANEKI.
!
IF YOU ARE TO LIVE IN THE WORLD OF GHOULS...
YOU SHOULD JOIN HANDS WITH FELLOW GHOULS.
OUTSIDE THE FENCES THEY MAY BE YOUR ENEMIES.
BUT ONCE INSIDE THEY ARE DEPENDABLE ALLIES.
ARE YOU ...
... OUT OF YOUR MIND ?
I WOULD NEVER JOIN THOSE GUYS.
EVER.
THEN LET ME PUT IT ANOTHER WAY.

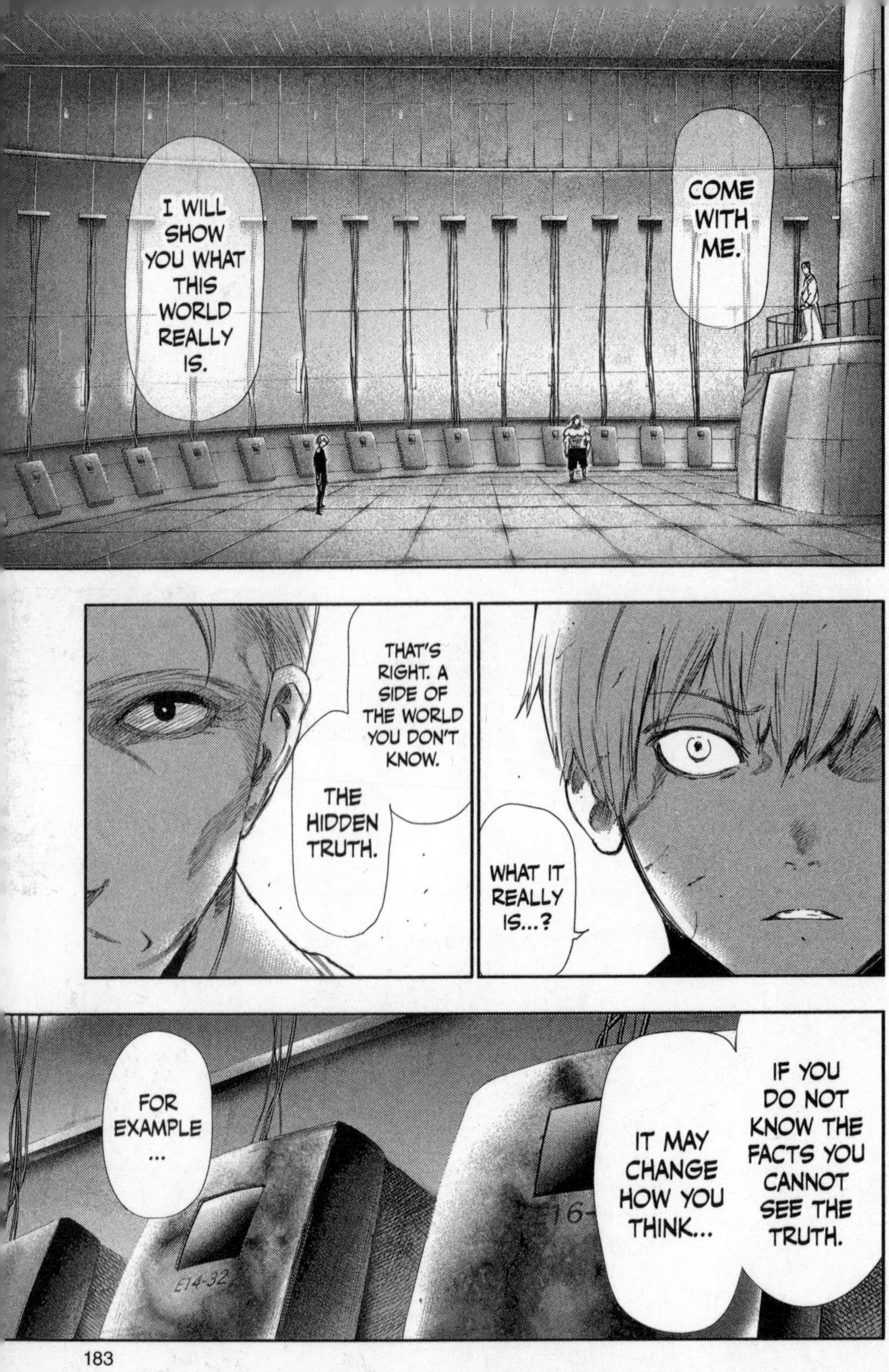
COME WITH ME.
I WILL SHOW YOU WHAT THIS WORLD REALLY IS.
WHAT IT REALLY IS...?
THAT'S RIGHT. A SIDE OF THE WORLD YOU DON'T KNOW.
THE HIDDEN TRUTH.
IF YOU DO NOT KNOW THE FACTS YOU CANNOT SEE THE TRUTH.
IT MAY CHANGE HOW YOU THINK...
FOR EXAMPLE ...

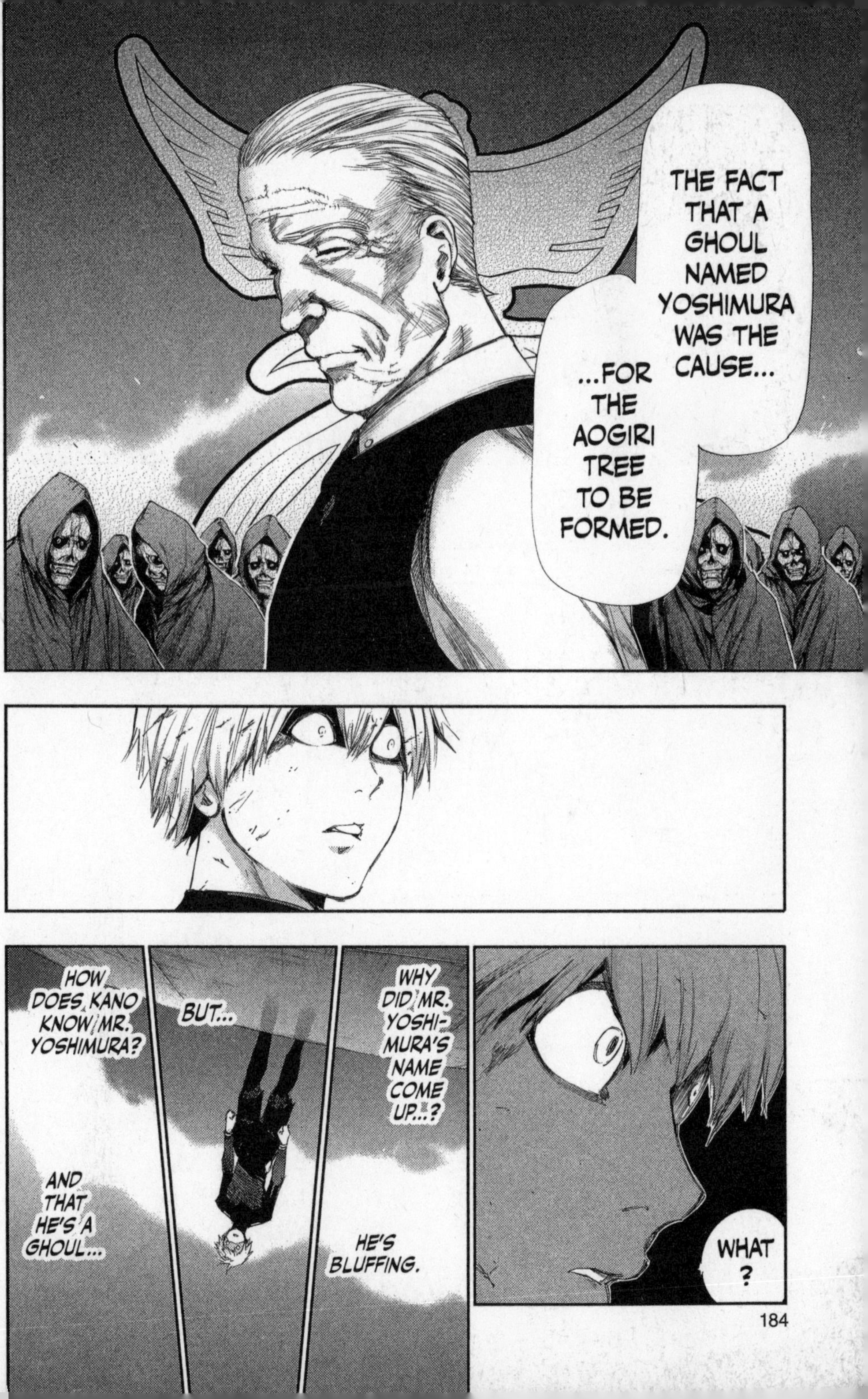

THE FACT THAT A GHOUL NAMED YOSHIMURA WAS THE CAUSE...
...FOR THE AOGIRI TREE TO BE FORMED.
WHAT?
WHY DID MR. YOSHIMURA'S NAME COME UP...?
HE'S BLUFFING.
BUT...
HOW DOES KANO KNOW MR. YOSHIMURA?
AND THAT HE'S A GHOUL...

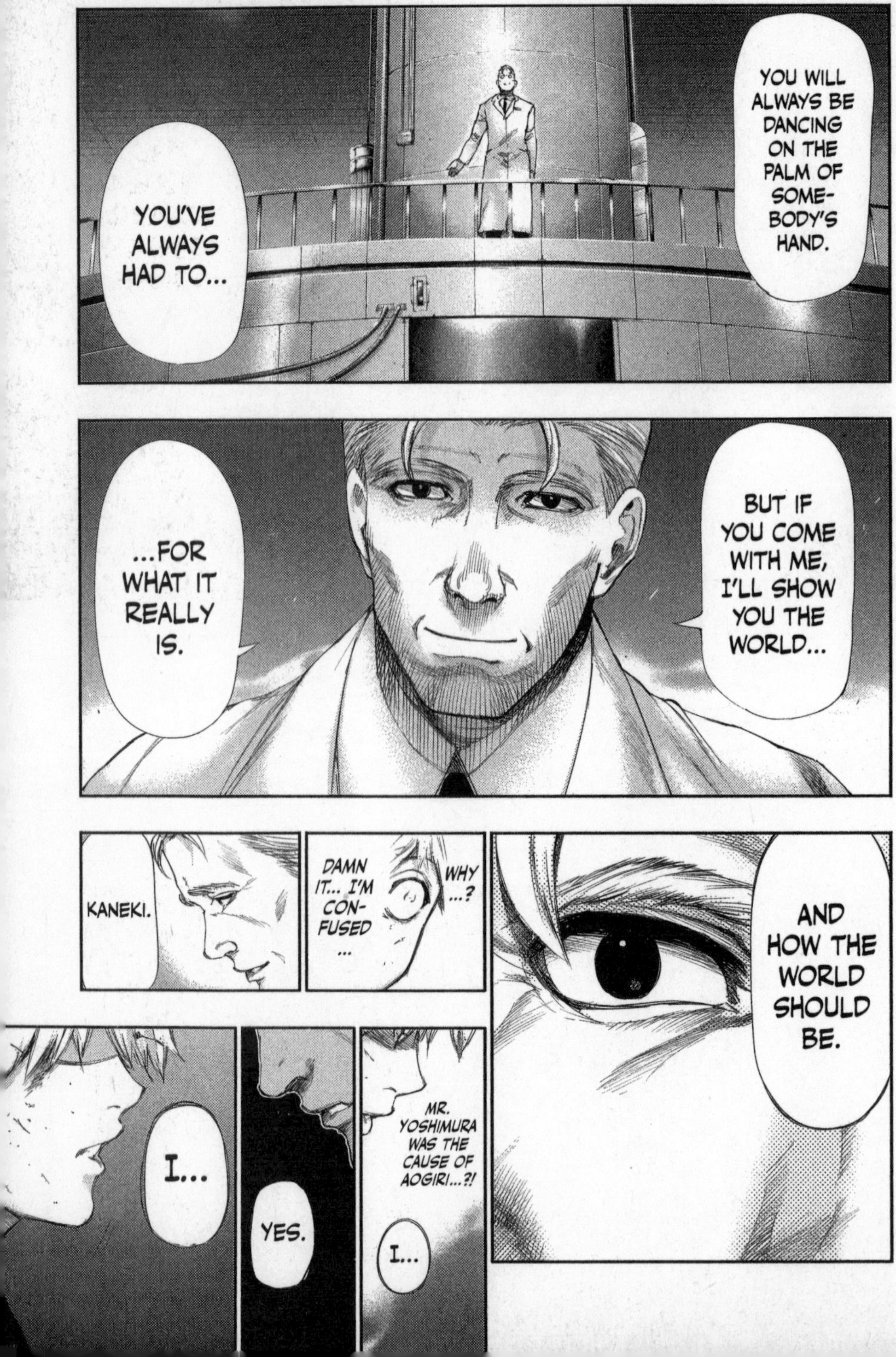
YOU WILL ALWAYS BE DANCING ON THE PALM OF SOME-BODY'S HAND.
YOU'VE ALWAYS HAD TO...
BUT IF YOU COME WITH ME, I'LL SHOW YOU THE WORLD...
...FOR WHAT IT REALLY IS.
AND HOW THE WORLD SHOULD BE.
WHY ...?
DAMN IT... I'M CON-FUSED ...
KANEKI.
MR. YOSHIMURA WAS THE CAUSE OF AOGIRI...?!
I...
YES.
I...

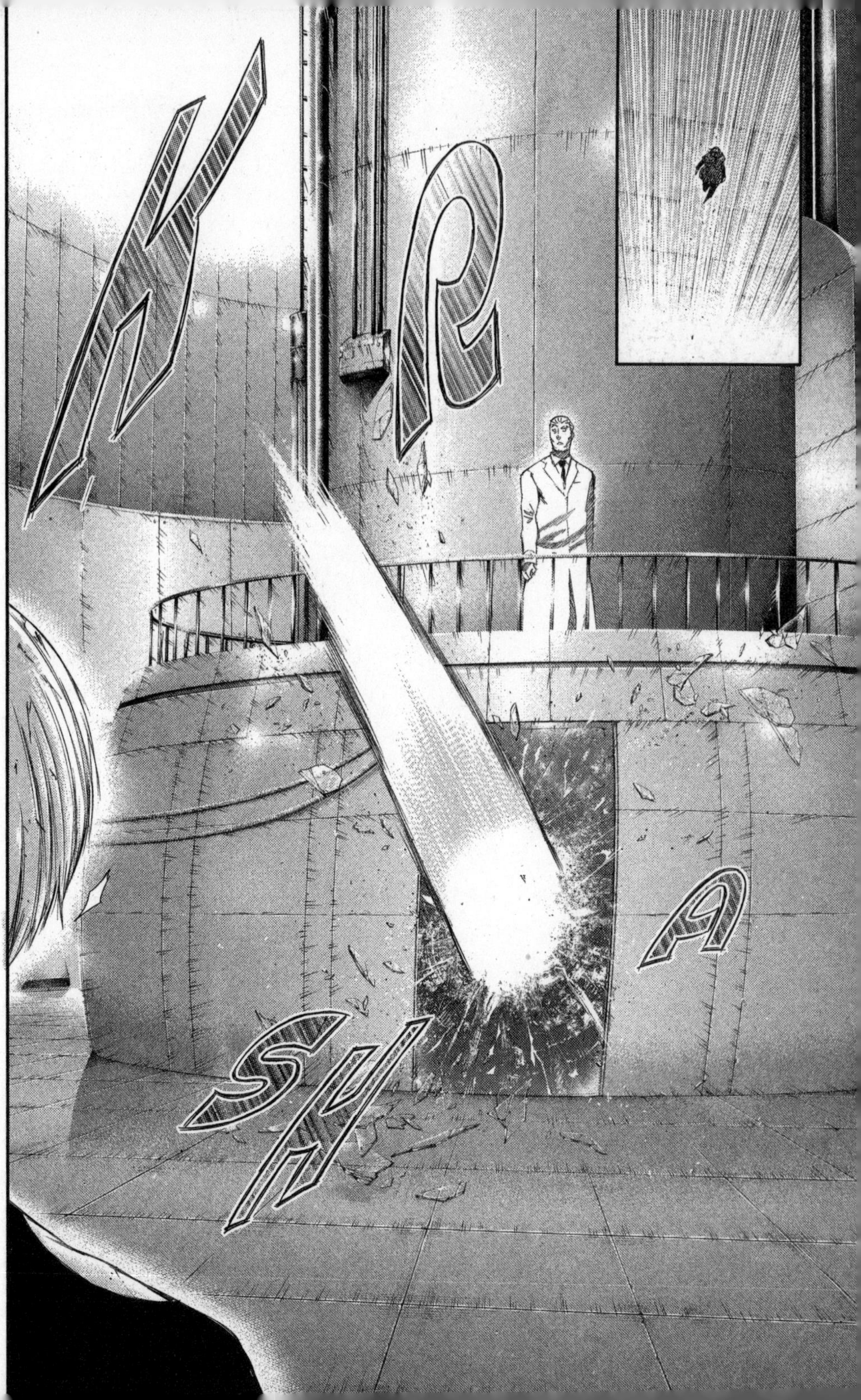
KRASH

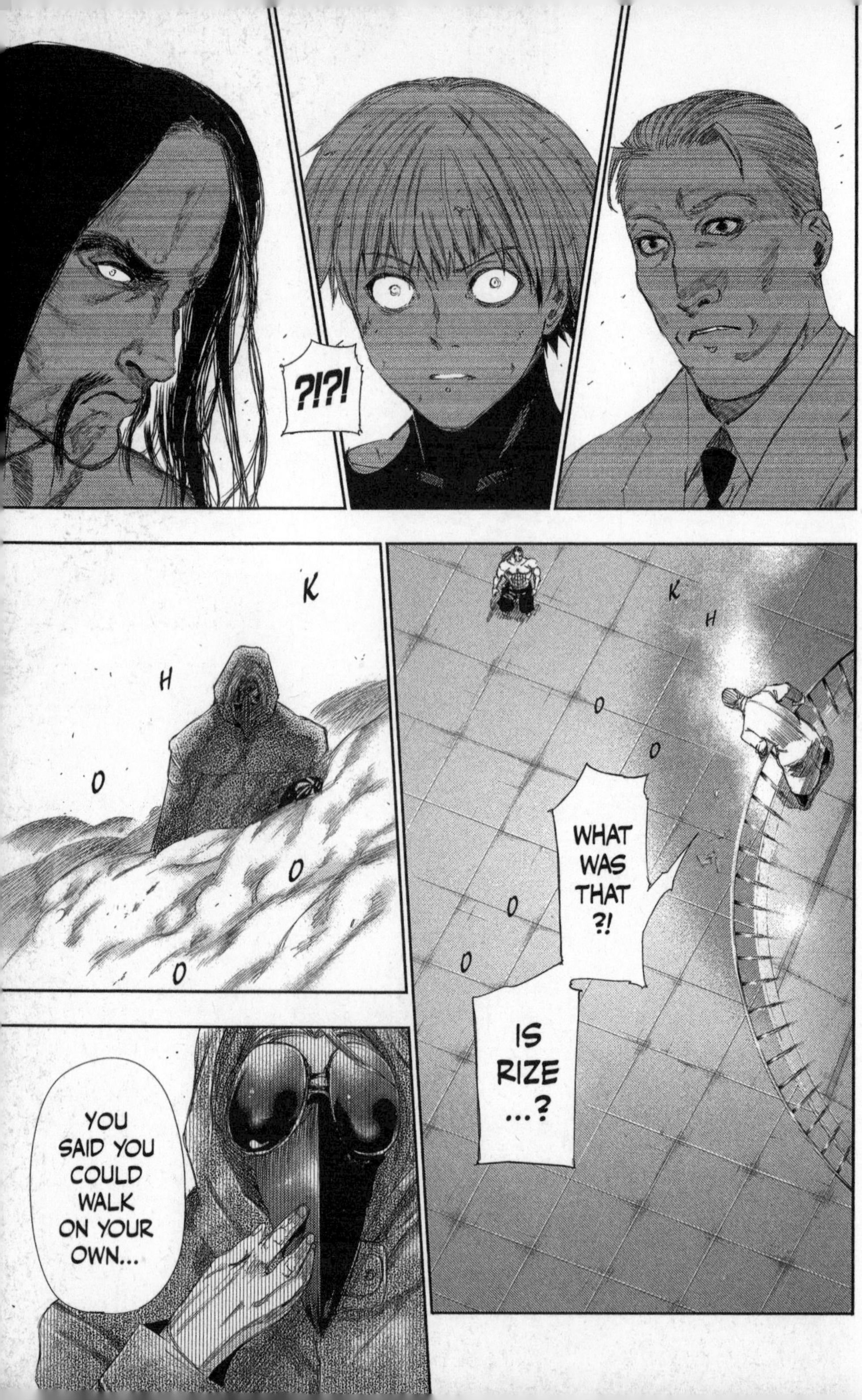
?!?!
KHOOOO
WHAT WAS THAT ?!
IS RIZE ...?
KHOOO
YOU SAID YOU COULD WALK ON YOUR OWN...

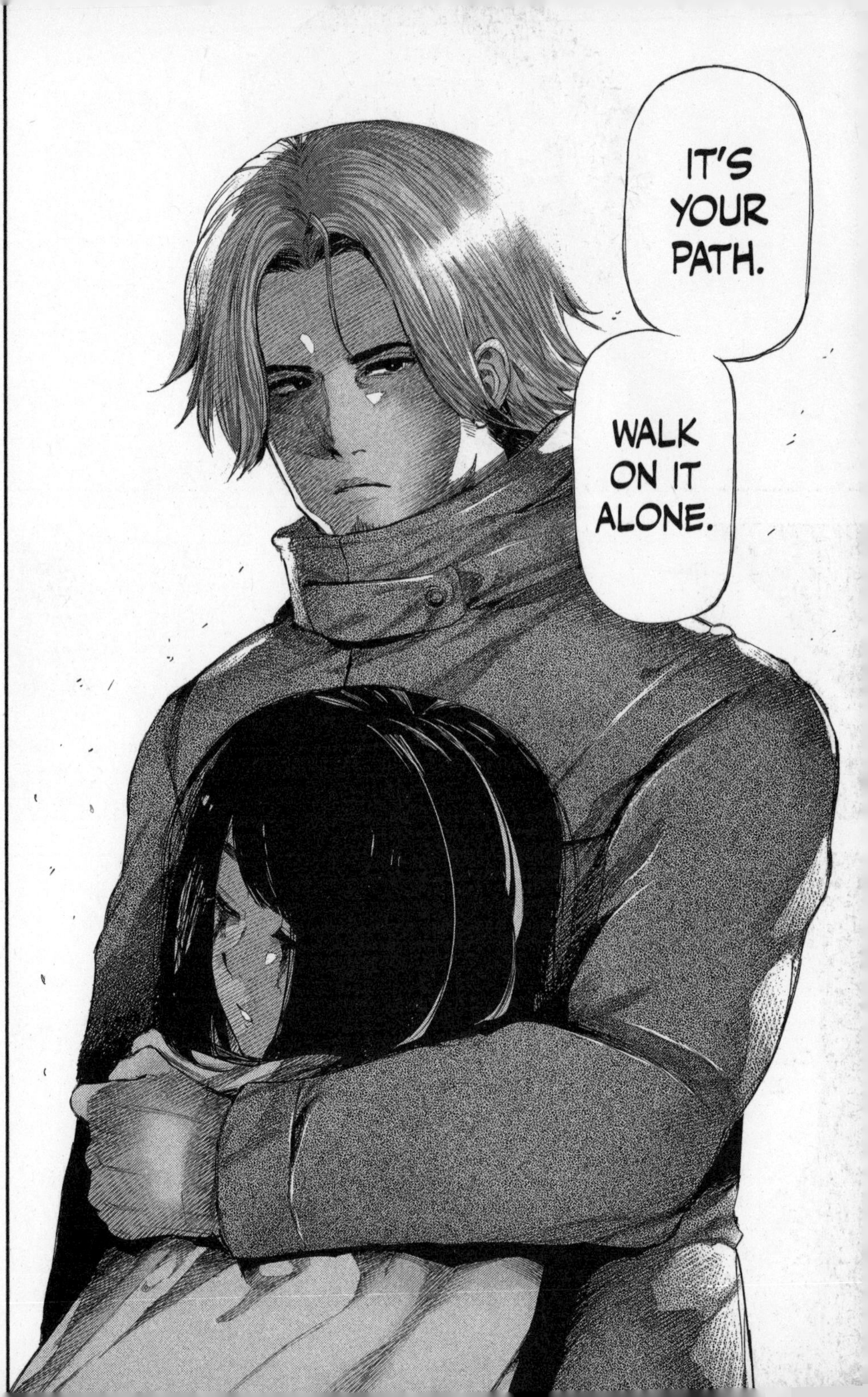
IT'S YOUR PATH.
WALK ON IT ALONE.

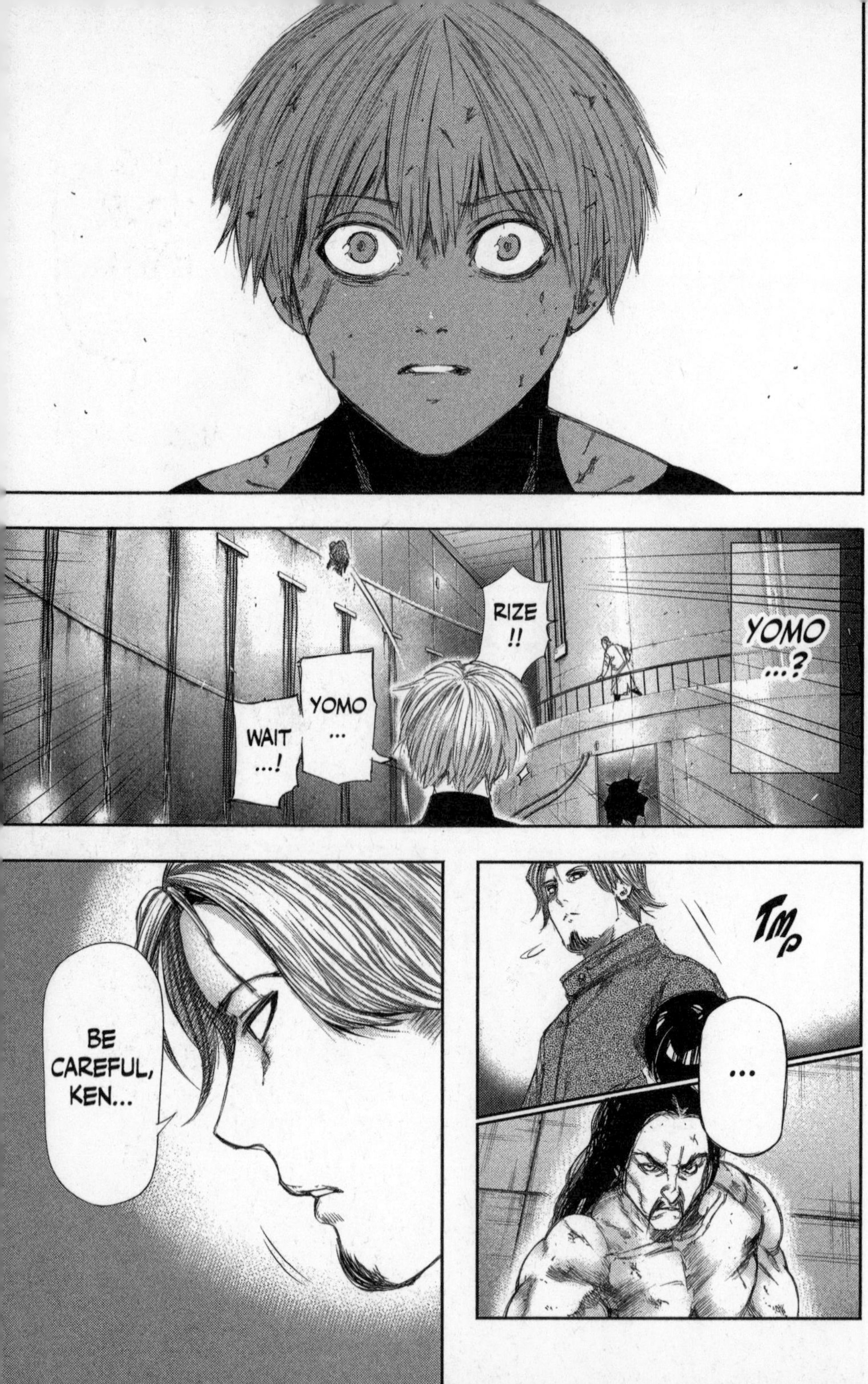
YOMO ...?
RIZE !!
YOMO ...
WAIT ...!
TMP
...
BE CAREFUL, KEN...

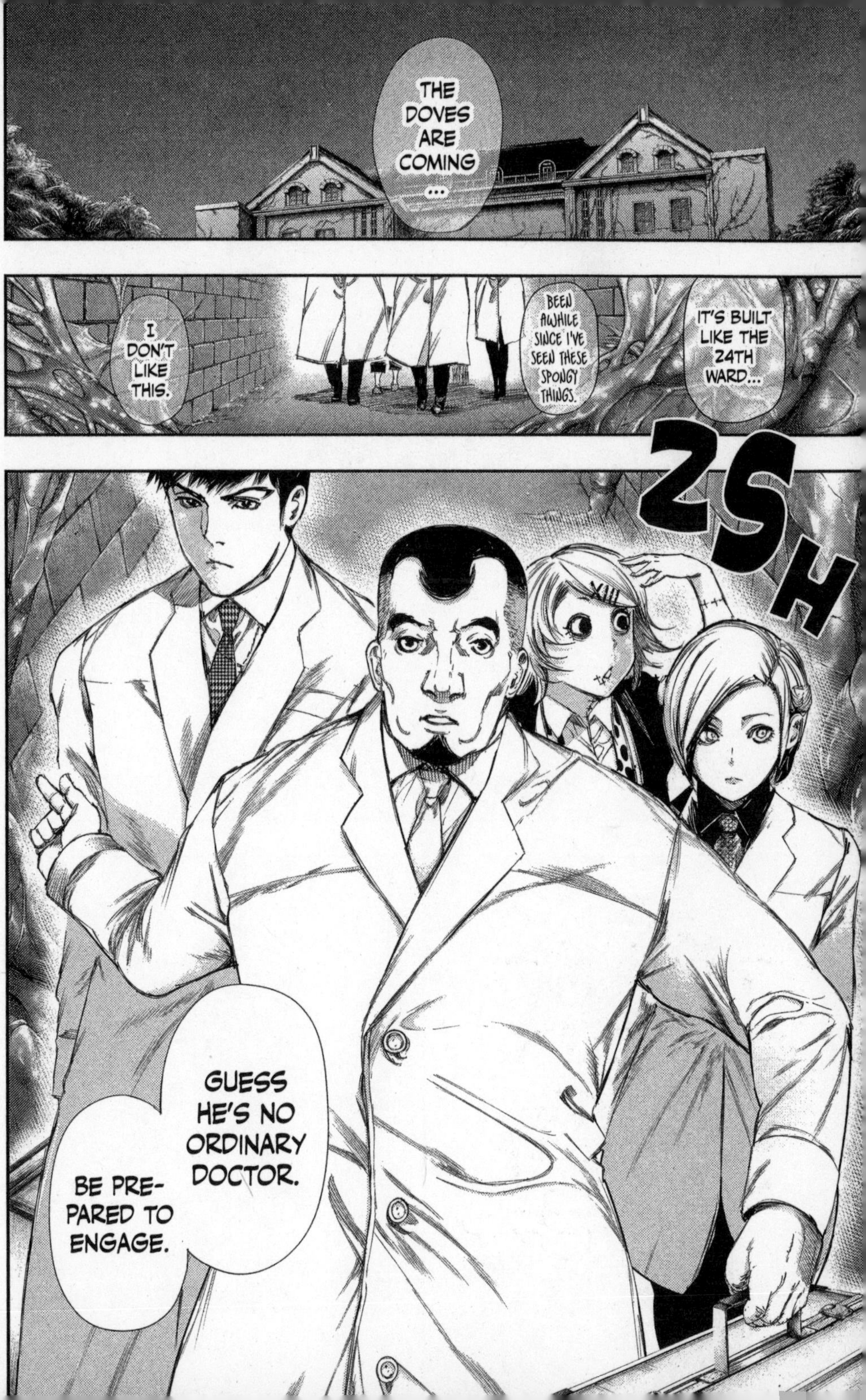
THE DOVES ARE COMING ...
IT'S BUILT LIKE THE 24TH WARD...
BEEN AWHILE SINCE I'VE SEEN THESE SPONGY THINGS.
I DON'T LIKE THIS.
ZSH
GUESS HE'S NO ORDINARY DOCTOR.
BE PRE-PARED TO ENGAGE.

東京
トーキョーグール
喰種
Tokyo
Ghoul

Avatar Talk 7
Touka Kirishima/Nishiki Nishio

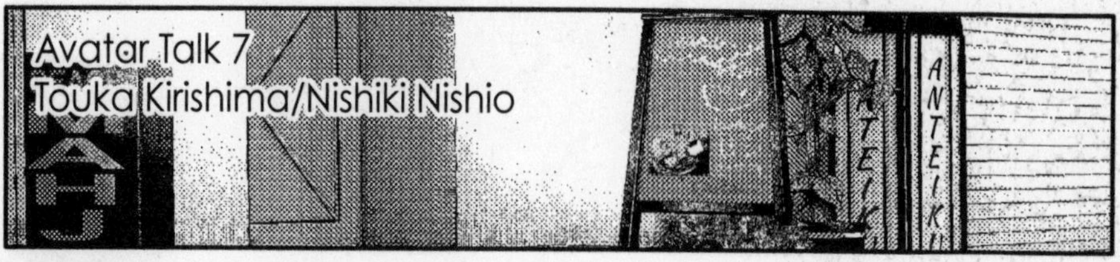
ANTEIKU
ANTEIKU

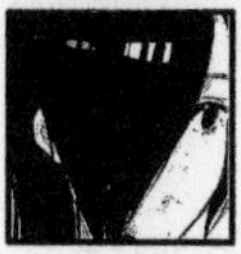

STUPID-ASS NISHIKI...

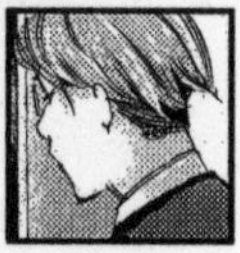

WHAT, STUPID-ASS TOUKA?

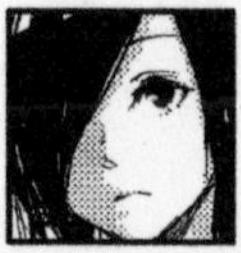

YOUR GIRL... WAS IT MIKI? YOU GONNA GET HER A GIFT OR WHAT?

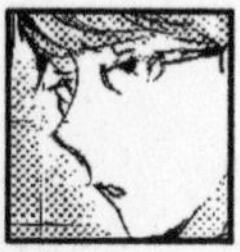

I DO WHEN I HAVE TO. LIKE ON HER BIRTHDAY OR WHATEVER...

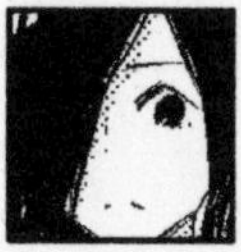

LIKE A KEY CHAIN?

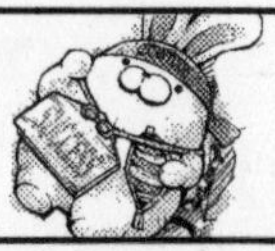

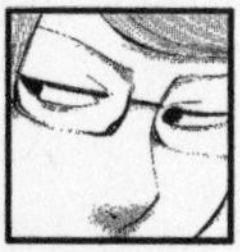

OH, I GIVE THAT KINDA THING TO PEOPLE NOT WORTH SPENDING MONEY ON OR PEOPLE I DON'T REALLY CARE ABOUT.

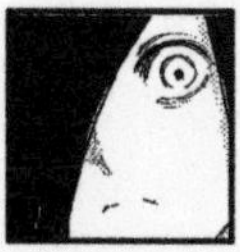

...YOU WANNA DIE?

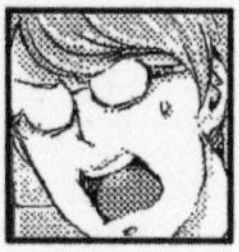

WHAT THE HELL...?!

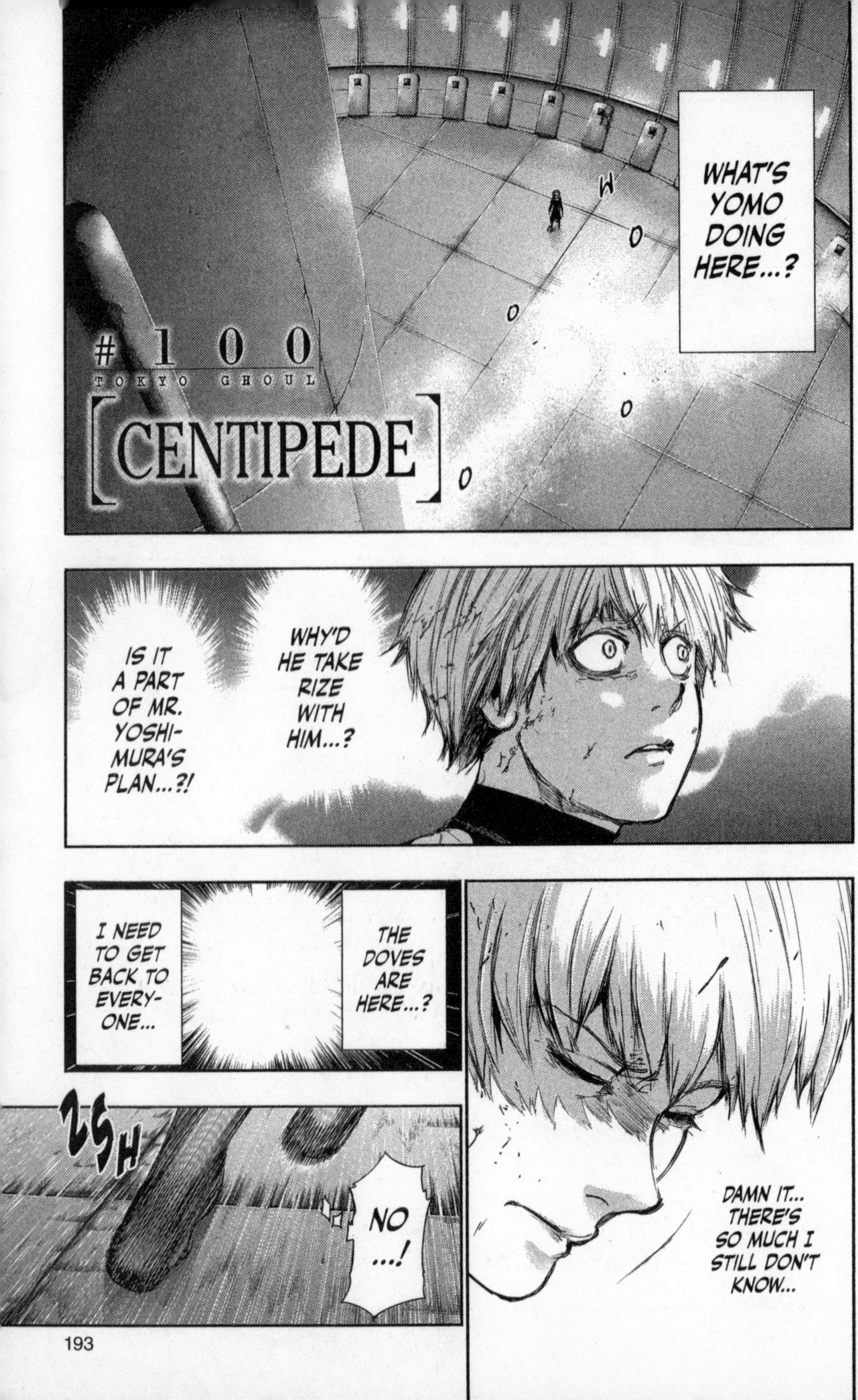
#100
TOKYO GHOUL
[CENTIPEDE]
WHAT'S YOMO DOING HERE...?
WOOOO
WHY'D HE TAKE RIZE WITH HIM...?
IS IT A PART OF MR. YOSHI-MURA'S PLAN...?!
DAMN IT... THERE'S SO MUCH I STILL DON'T KNOW...
THE DOVES ARE HERE...?
I NEED TO GET BACK TO EVERY-ONE...
ZSH
NO ...!

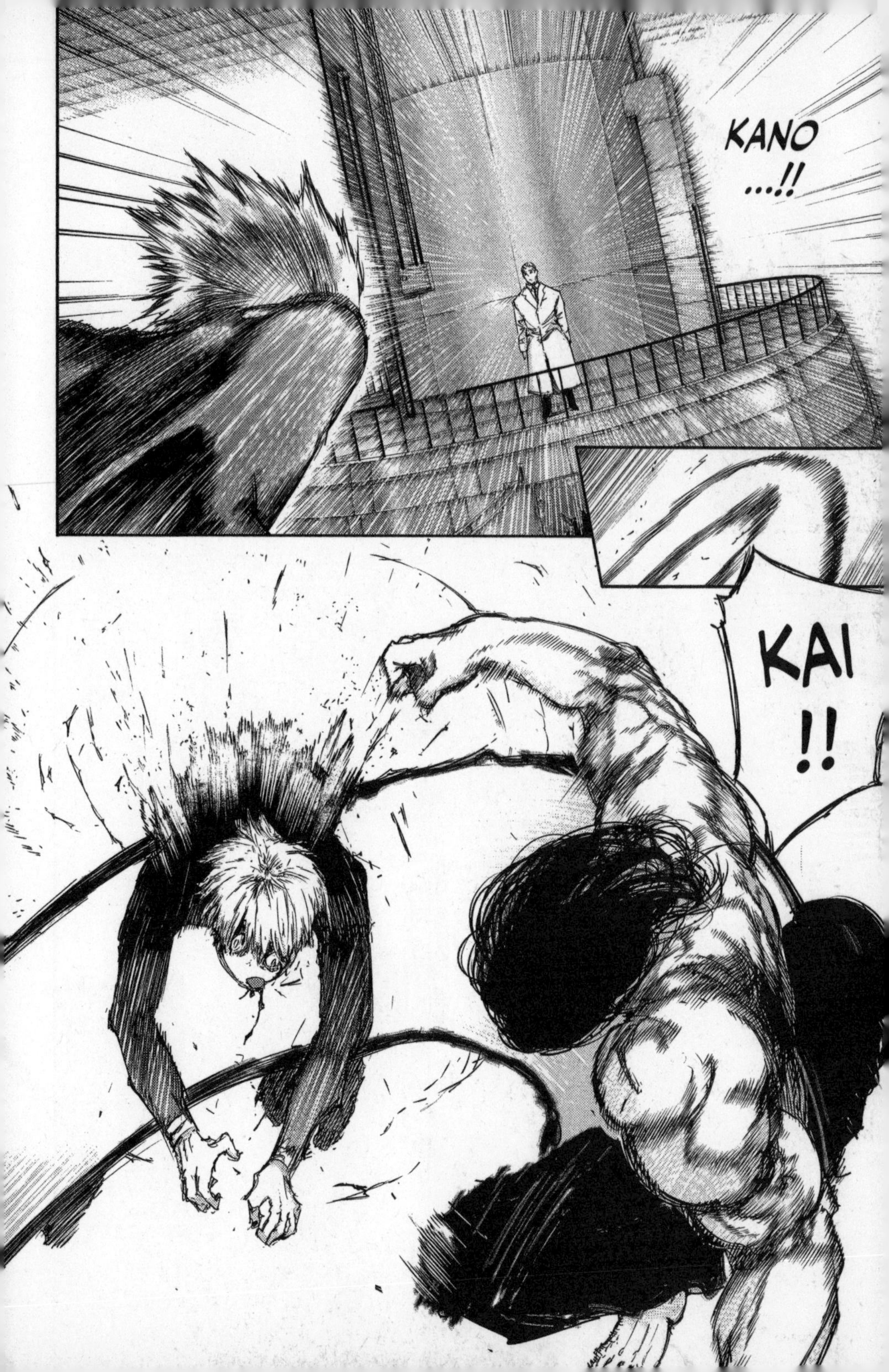
KANO ...!!
KAI !!

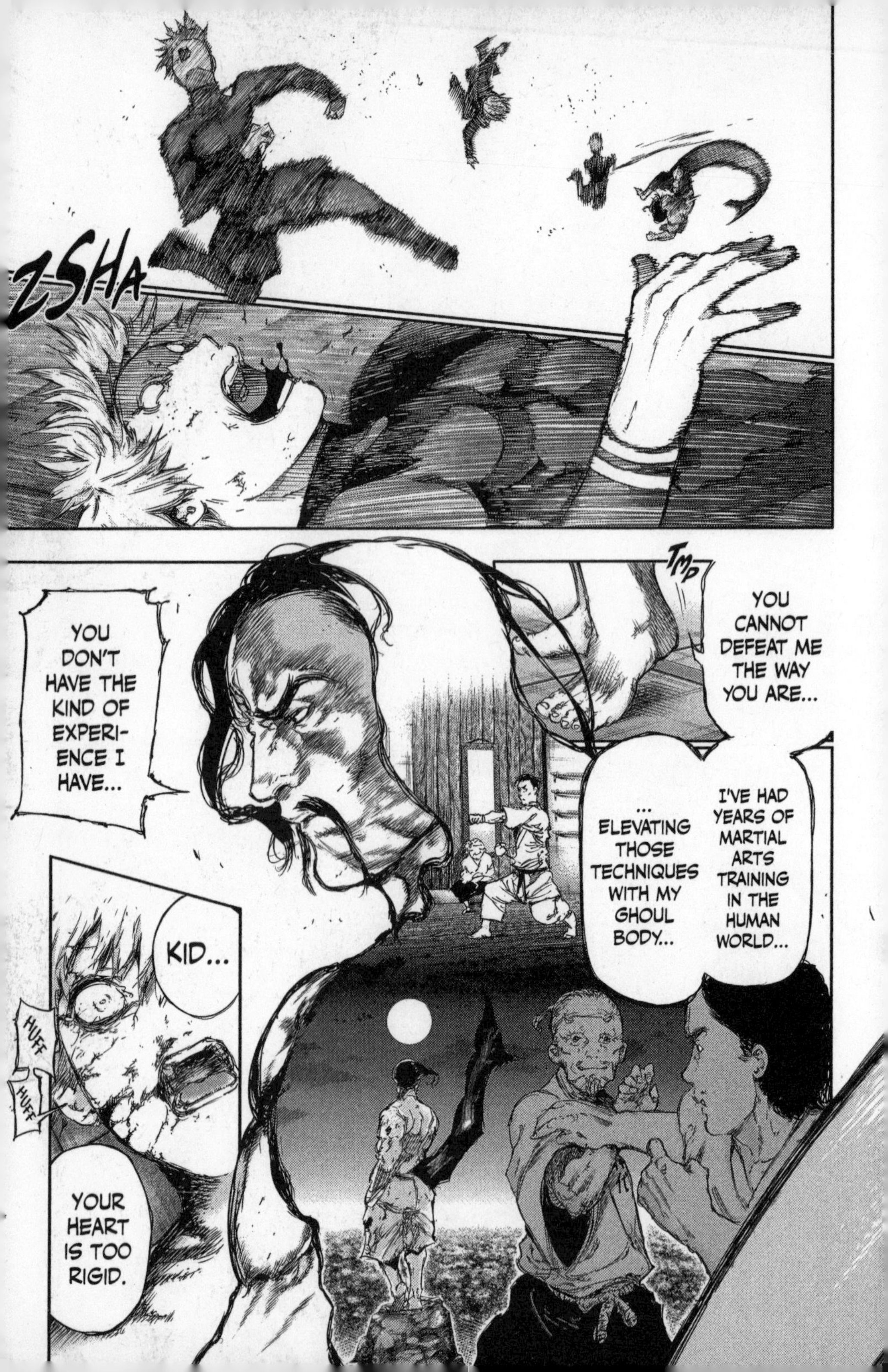
ZSHA
TMP
YOU CANNOT DEFEAT ME THE WAY YOU ARE...
YOU DON'T HAVE THE KIND OF EXPERIENCE I HAVE...
I'VE HAD YEARS OF MARTIAL ARTS TRAINING IN THE HUMAN WORLD...
...ELEVATING THOSE TECHNIQUES WITH MY GHOUL BODY...
KID...
HUFF
HUFF
YOUR HEART IS TOO RIGID.

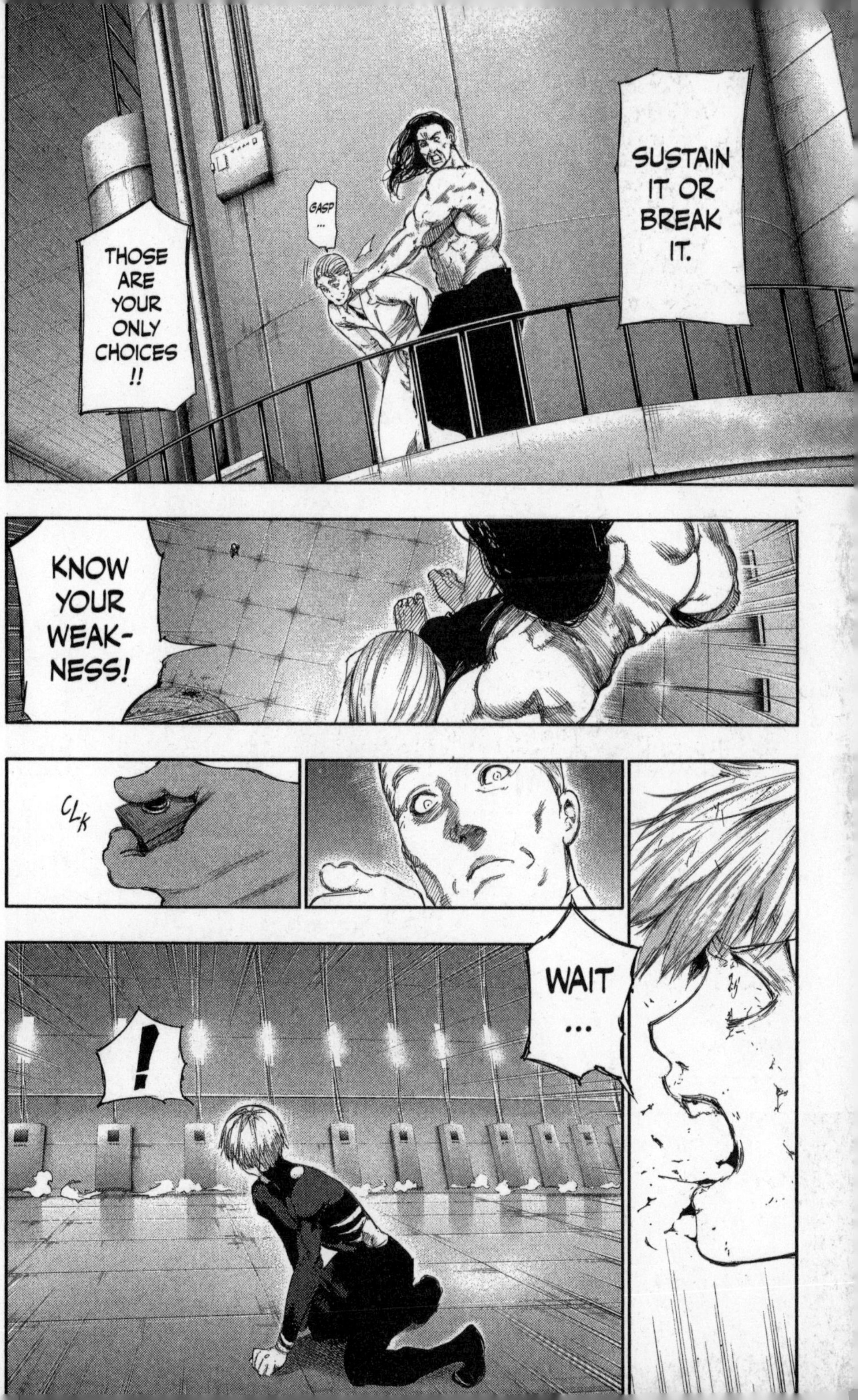
SUSTAIN IT OR BREAK IT.
GASP ...
THOSE ARE YOUR ONLY CHOICES !!
KNOW YOUR WEAK-NESS!
WAIT ...
CLK
!

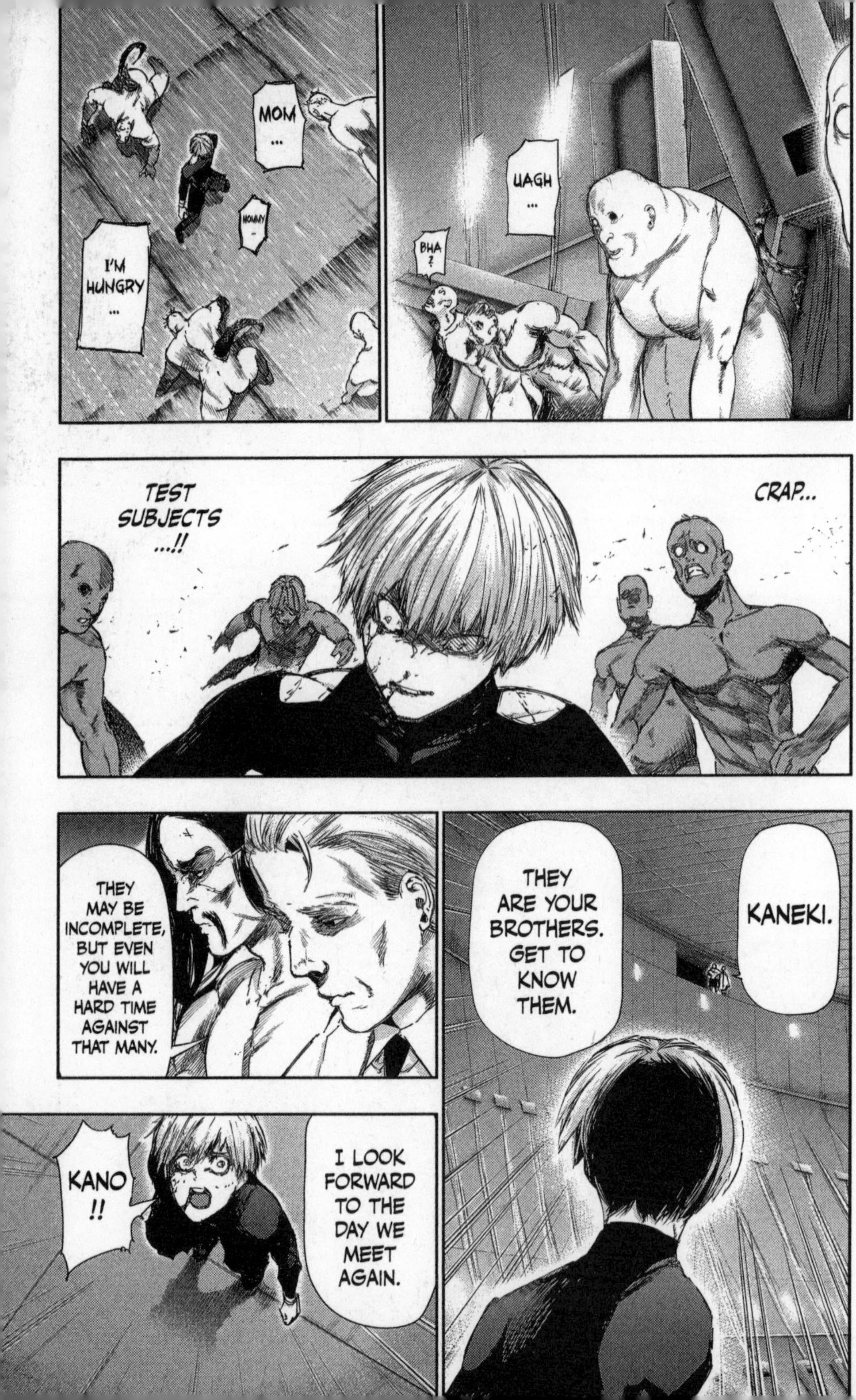
UAGH ...
BHA ?
MOM ...
MOMMY ...
I'M HUNGRY ...
CRAP...
TEST SUBJECTS ...!!
KANEKI.
THEY ARE YOUR BROTHERS. GET TO KNOW THEM.
THEY MAY BE INCOMPLETE, BUT EVEN YOU WILL HAVE A HARD TIME AGAINST THAT MANY.
I LOOK FORWARD TO THE DAY WE MEET AGAIN.
KANO !!

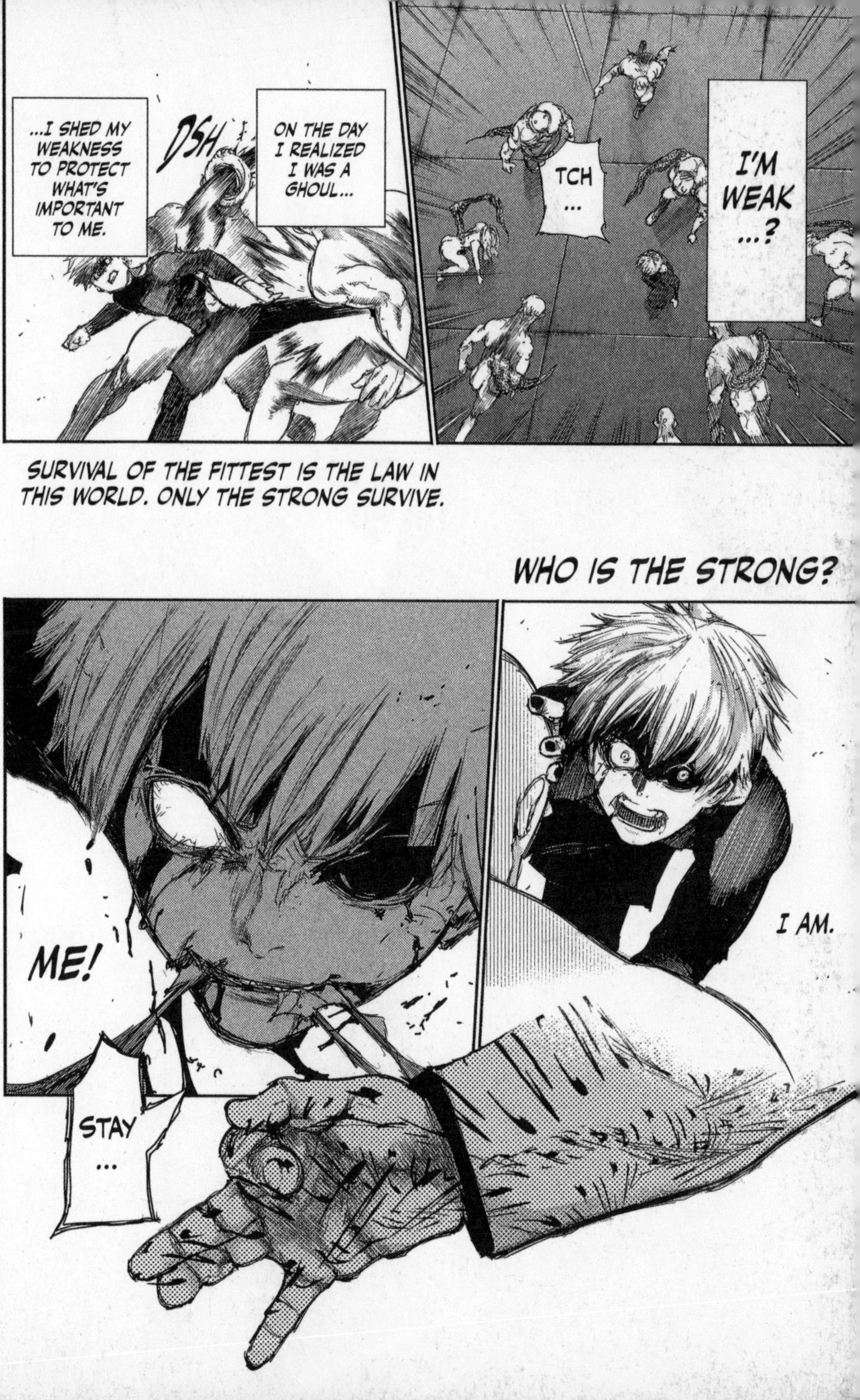
I'M WEAK ...?
TCH ...
DSH
ON THE DAY I REALIZED I WAS A GHOUL...
...I SHED MY WEAKNESS TO PROTECT WHAT'S IMPORTANT TO ME.
SURVIVAL OF THE FITTEST IS THE LAW IN THIS WORLD. ONLY THE STRONG SURVIVE.
WHO IS THE STRONG?
I AM.
ME!
STAY ...

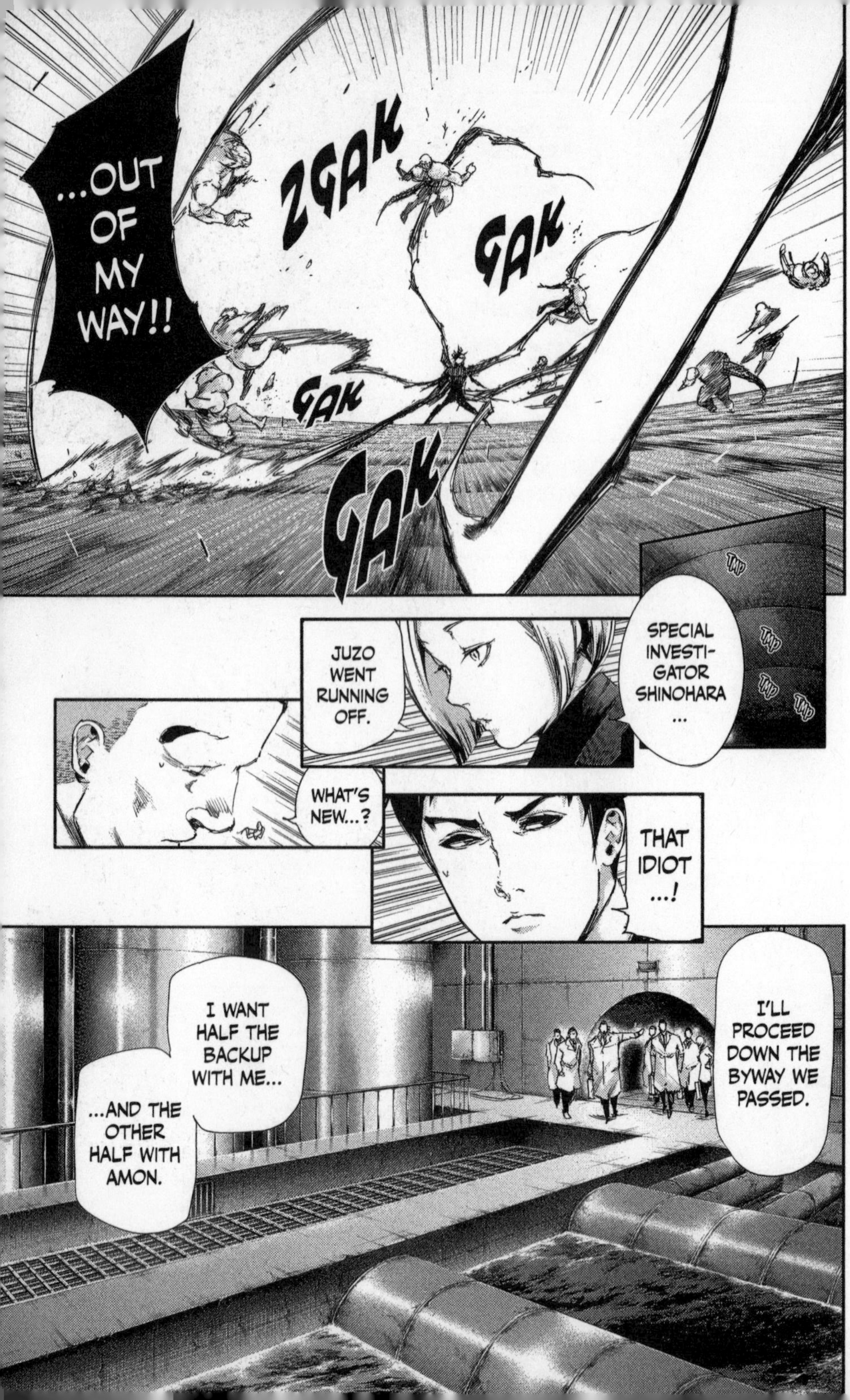
ZGAK
GAK
...OUT OF MY WAY!!
GAK
GAK
TMP
TMP
TMP
TMP
SPECIAL INVESTIGATOR SHINOHARA...
JUZO WENT RUNNING OFF.
WHAT'S NEW...?
THAT IDIOT...!
I'LL PROCEED DOWN THE BYWAY WE PASSED.
I WANT HALF THE BACKUP WITH ME...
...AND THE OTHER HALF WITH AMON.

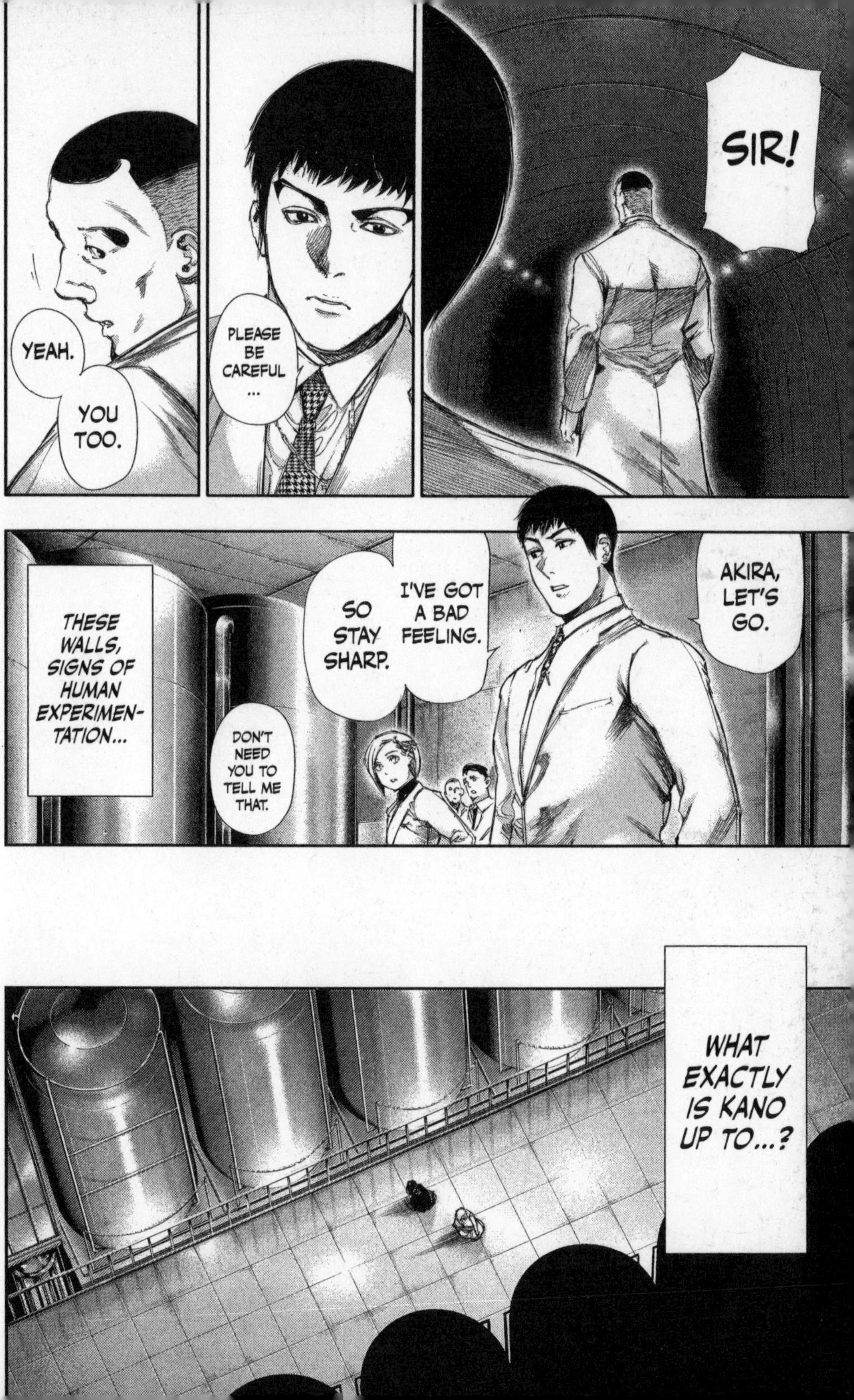
SIR!
PLEASE BE CAREFUL ...
YEAH.
YOU TOO.
AKIRA, LET'S GO.
I'VE GOT A BAD FEELING.
SO STAY SHARP.
DON'T NEED YOU TO TELL ME THAT.
THESE WALLS, SIGNS OF HUMAN EXPERIMENTATION...
WHAT EXACTLY IS KANO UP TO...?

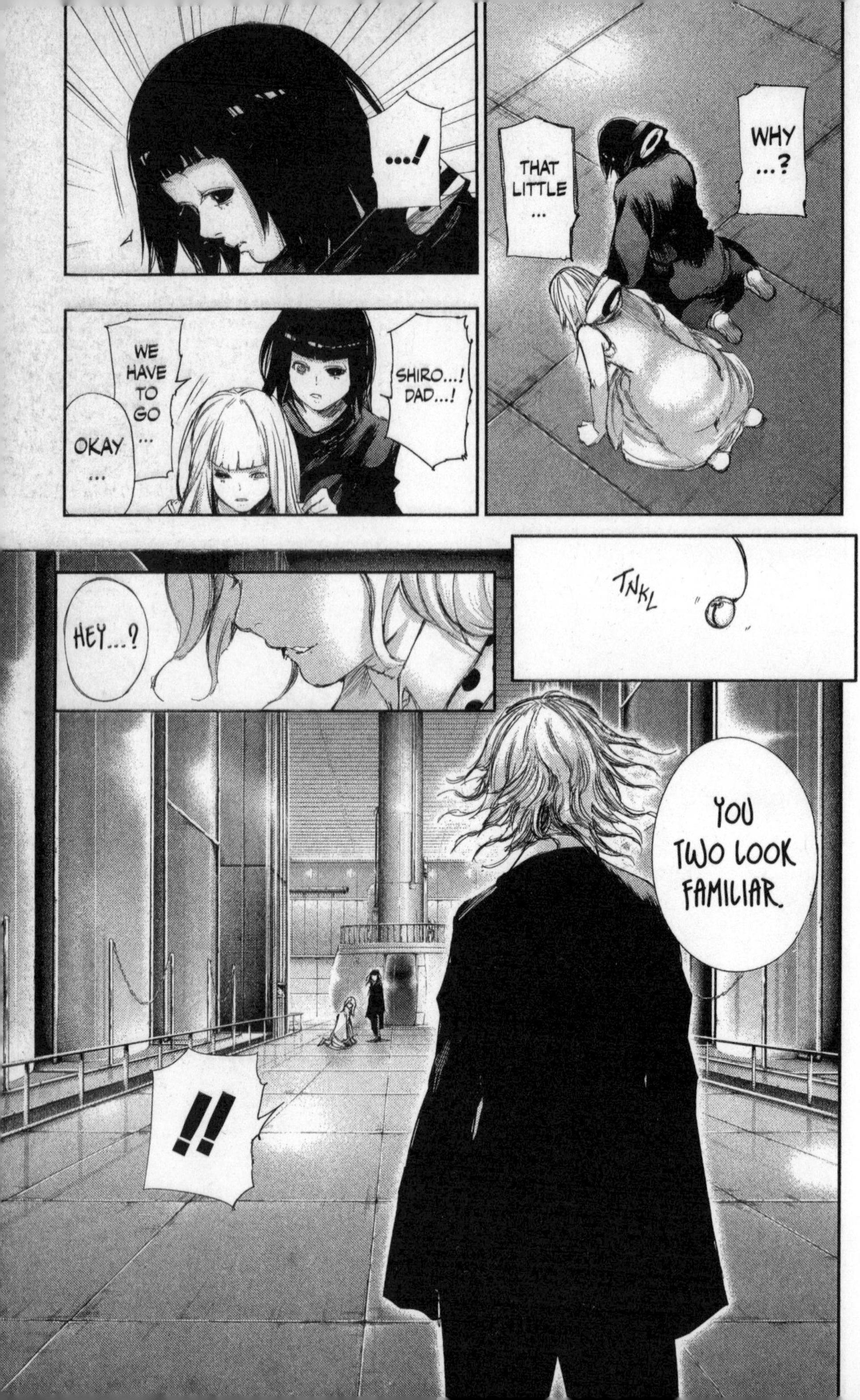
WHY ...?
THAT LITTLE ...
...!
SHIRO...! DAD...!
WE HAVE TO GO ...
OKAY ...
TNKL
HEY...?
YOU TWO LOOK FAMILIAR.
!!

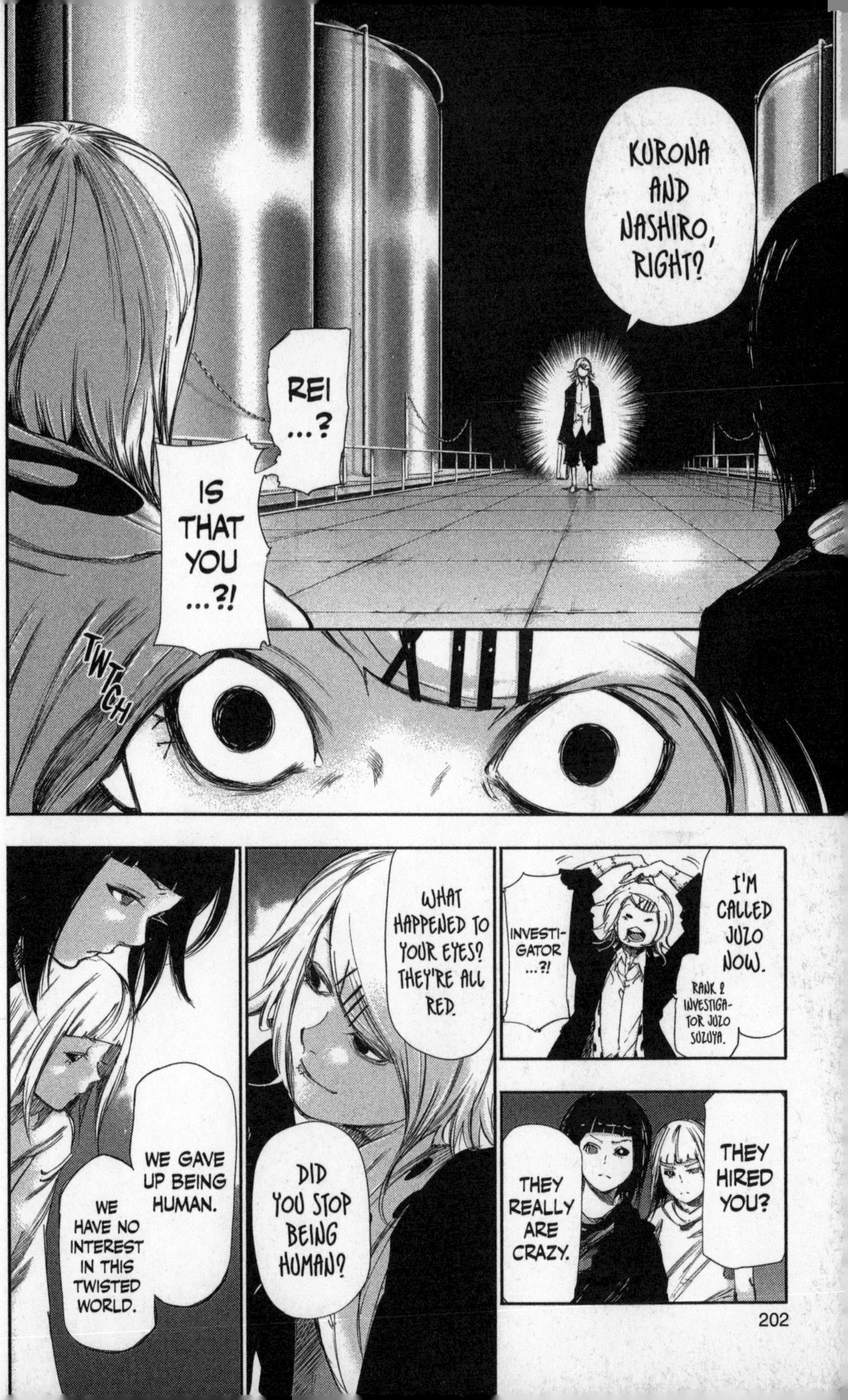
KURONA AND NASHIRO, RIGHT?
REI ...?
IS THAT YOU ...?!
TWITCH
I'M CALLED JUZO NOW.
RANK 2 INVESTIGATOR JUZO SUZUYA.
INVESTIGATOR ...?!
THEY HIRED YOU?
THEY REALLY ARE CRAZY.
WHAT HAPPENED TO YOUR EYES? THEY'RE ALL RED.
DID YOU STOP BEING HUMAN?
WE GAVE UP BEING HUMAN.
WE HAVE NO INTEREST IN THIS TWISTED WORLD.

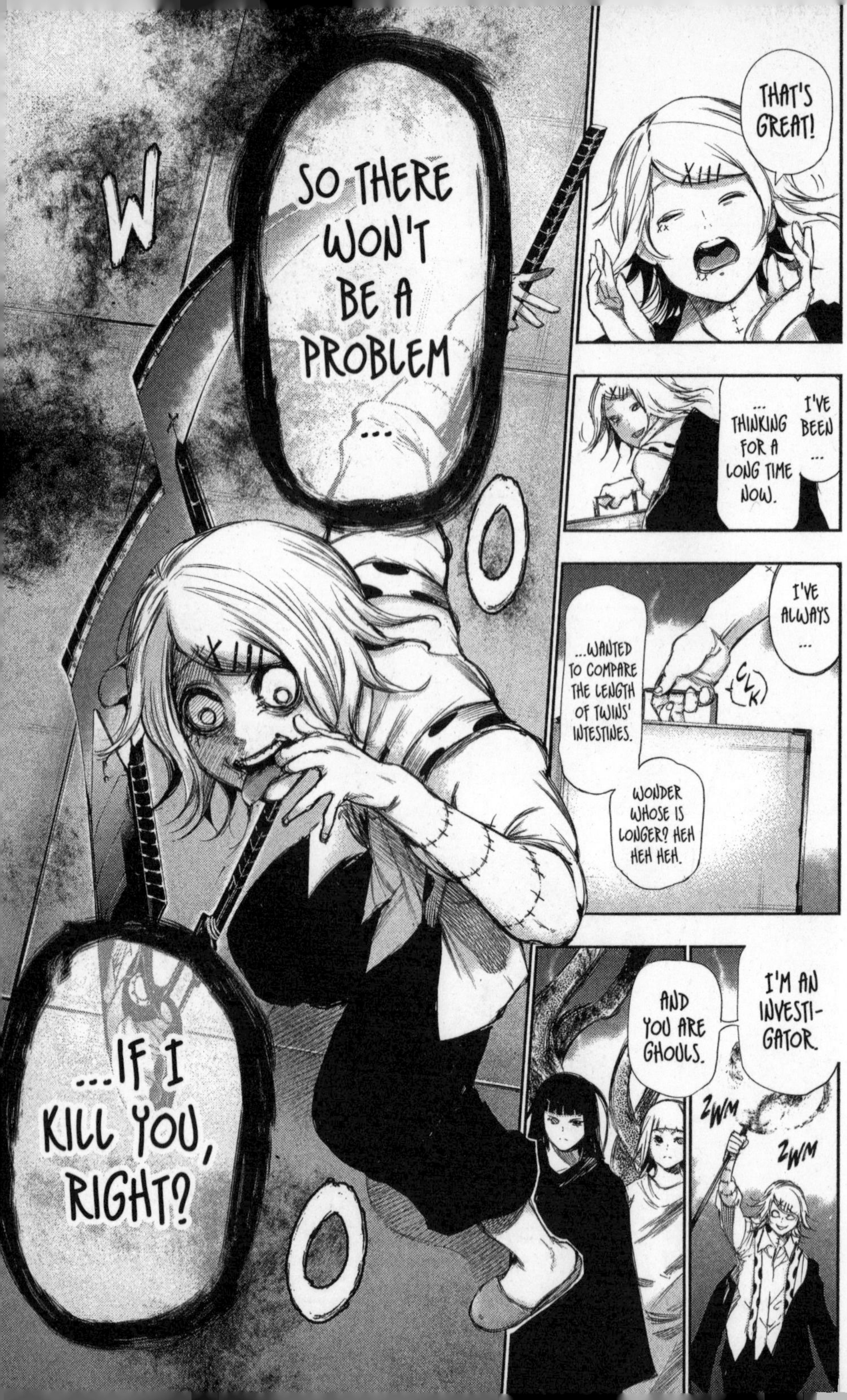
THAT'S GREAT!
I'VE BEEN...
...THINKING FOR A LONG TIME NOW.
I'VE ALWAYS...
CLIK
...WANTED TO COMPARE THE LENGTH OF TWINS' INTESTINES.
WONDER WHOSE IS LONGER? HEH HEH HEH.
I'M AN INVESTI-GATOR.
AND YOU ARE GHOULS.
ZWM
ZWM
W
SO THERE WON'T BE A PROBLEM...
...IF I KILL YOU, RIGHT?

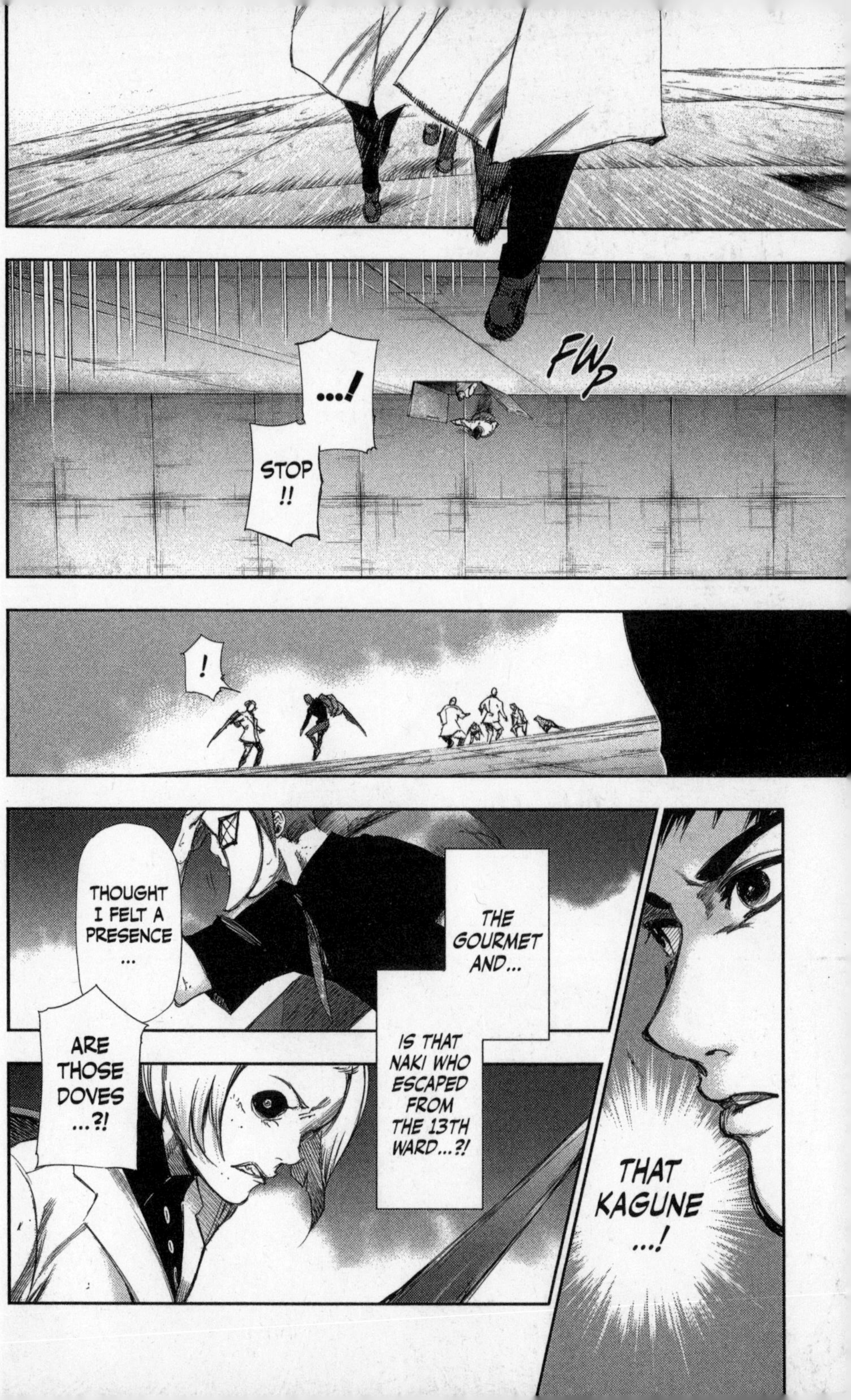
FWP
...!
STOP !!
!
THAT KAGUNE ...!
THE GOURMET AND...
THOUGHT I FELT A PRESENCE ...
IS THAT NAKI WHO ESCAPED FROM THE 13TH WARD...?!
ARE THOSE DOVES ...?!

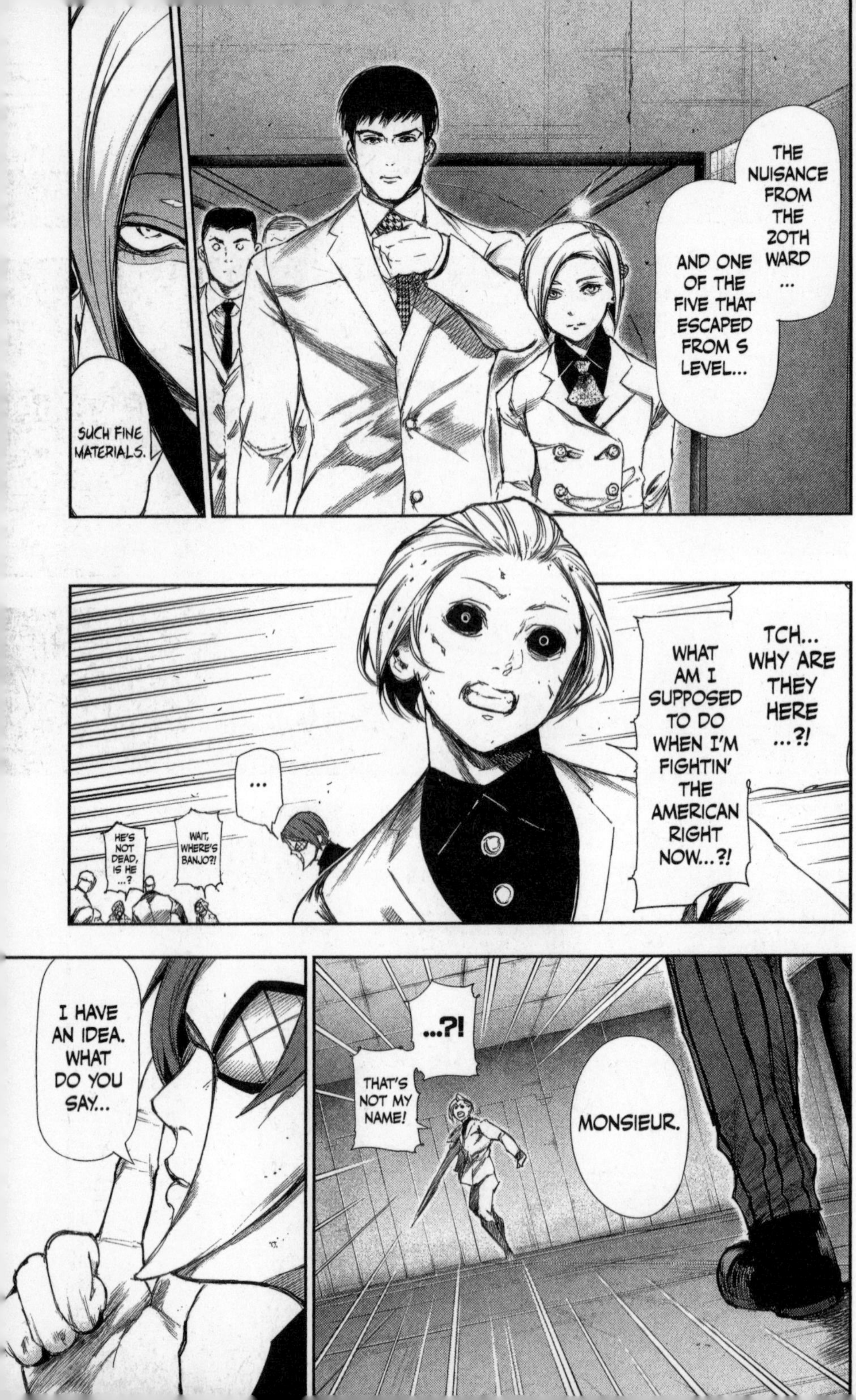
THE NUISANCE FROM THE 20TH WARD ... AND ONE OF THE FIVE THAT ESCAPED FROM S LEVEL...
SUCH FINE MATERIALS.
TCH... WHY ARE THEY HERE ...?!
WHAT AM I SUPPOSED TO DO WHEN I'M FIGHTIN' THE AMERICAN RIGHT NOW...?!
...
WAIT, WHERE'S BANJO?!
HE'S NOT DEAD, IS HE ...?
MONSIEUR.
...?!
THAT'S NOT MY NAME!
I HAVE AN IDEA. WHAT DO YOU SAY...

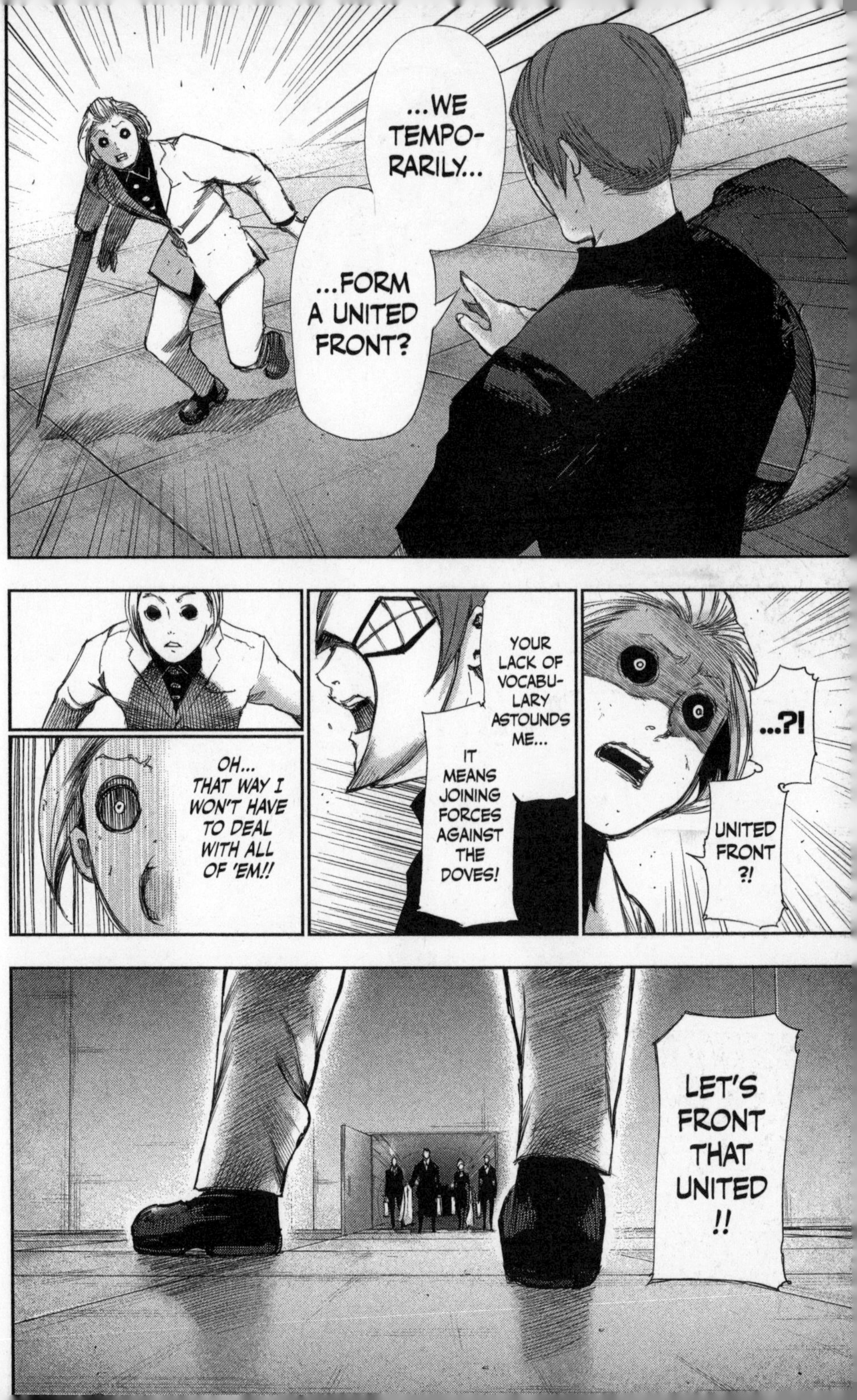
...WE TEMPO-RARILY...
...FORM A UNITED FRONT?
...?!
UNITED FRONT ?!
YOUR LACK OF VOCABU-LARY ASTOUNDS ME...
IT MEANS JOINING FORCES AGAINST THE DOVES!
OH... THAT WAY I WON'T HAVE TO DEAL WITH ALL OF 'EM!!
LET'S FRONT THAT UNITED !!

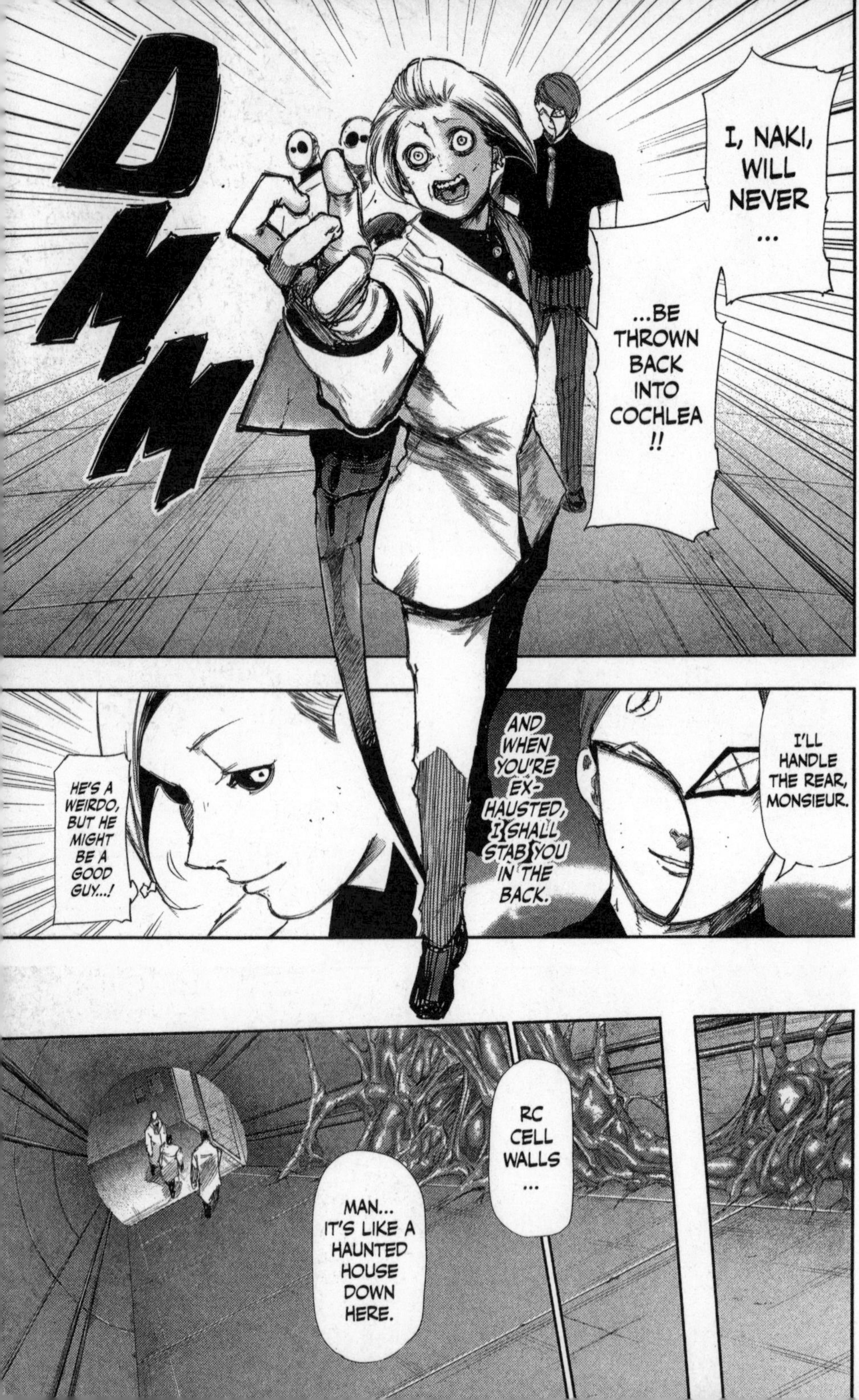
I, NAKI, WILL NEVER ...
...BE THROWN BACK INTO COCHLEA !!
DMM
I'LL HANDLE THE REAR, MONSIEUR.
AND WHEN YOU'RE EX-HAUSTED, I SHALL STAB YOU IN THE BACK.
HE'S A WEIRDO, BUT HE MIGHT BE A GOOD GUY...!
RC CELL WALLS ...
MAN... IT'S LIKE A HAUNTED HOUSE DOWN HERE.

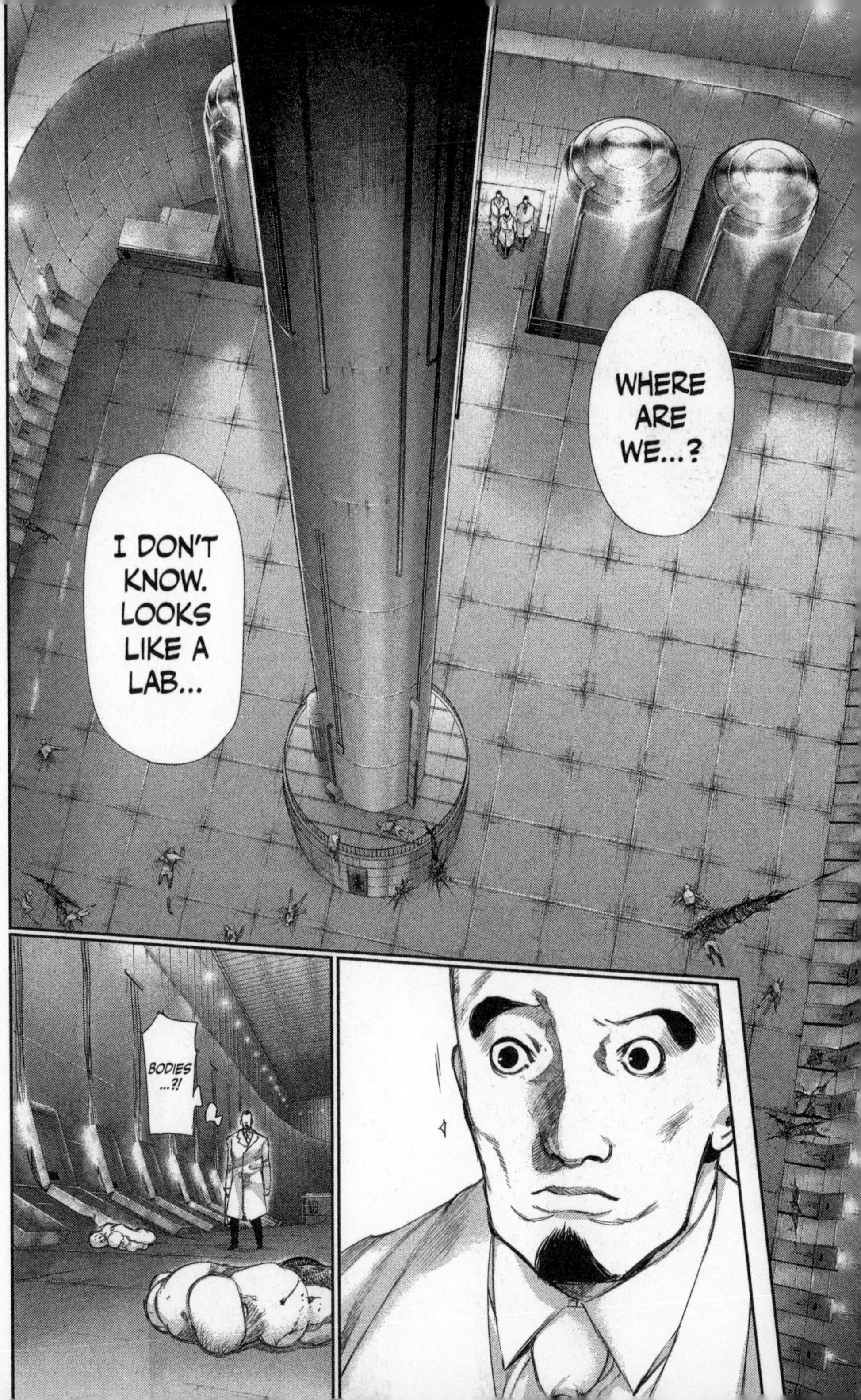
WHERE ARE WE...?
I DON'T KNOW. LOOKS LIKE A LAB...
BODIES ...?!

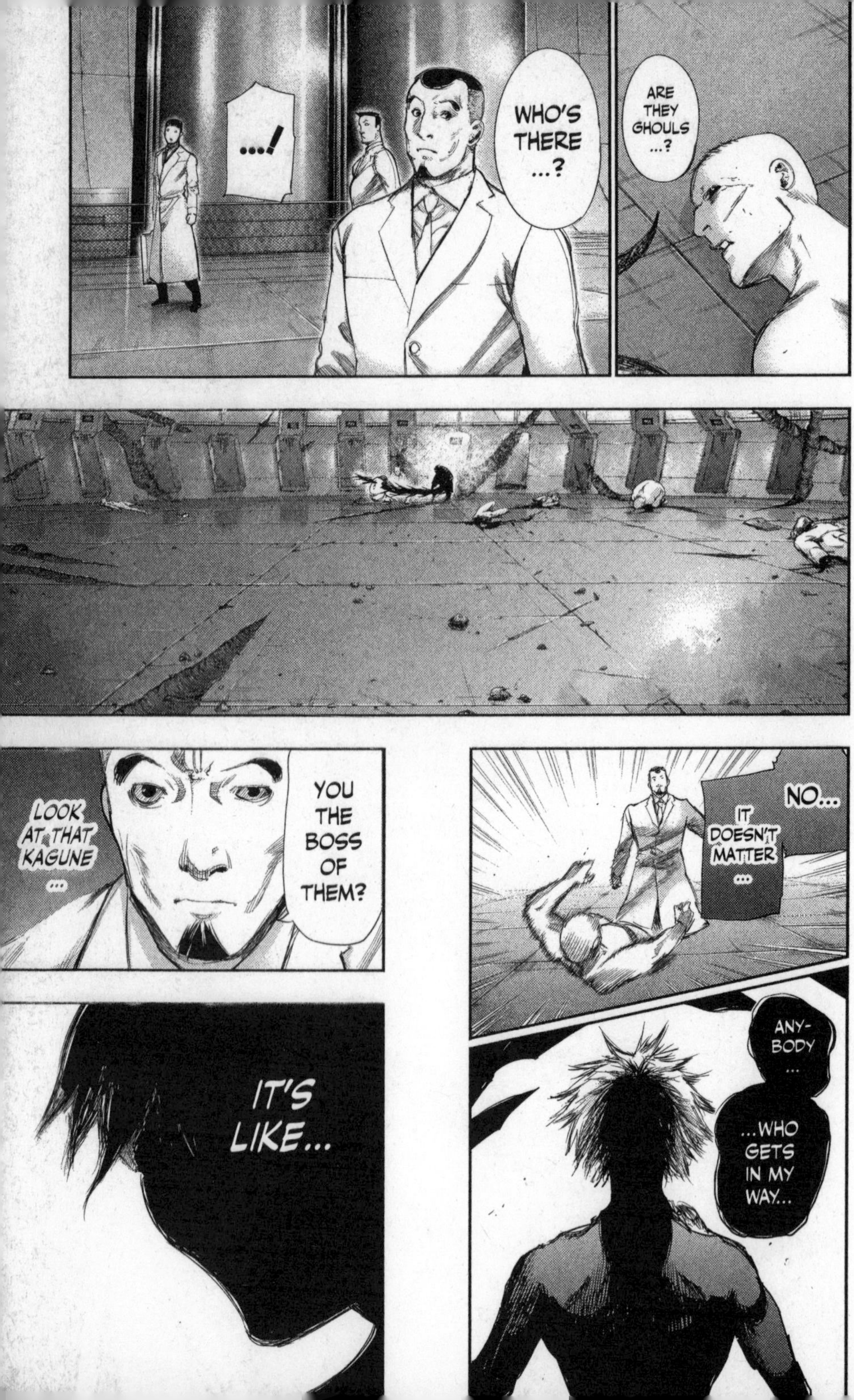

ARE THEY GHOULS ...?
WHO'S THERE ...?
...!
NO...
IT DOESN'T MATTER ...
YOU THE BOSS OF THEM?
LOOK AT THAT KAGUNE ...
ANY-BODY ...
...WHO GETS IN MY WAY...
IT'S LIKE...

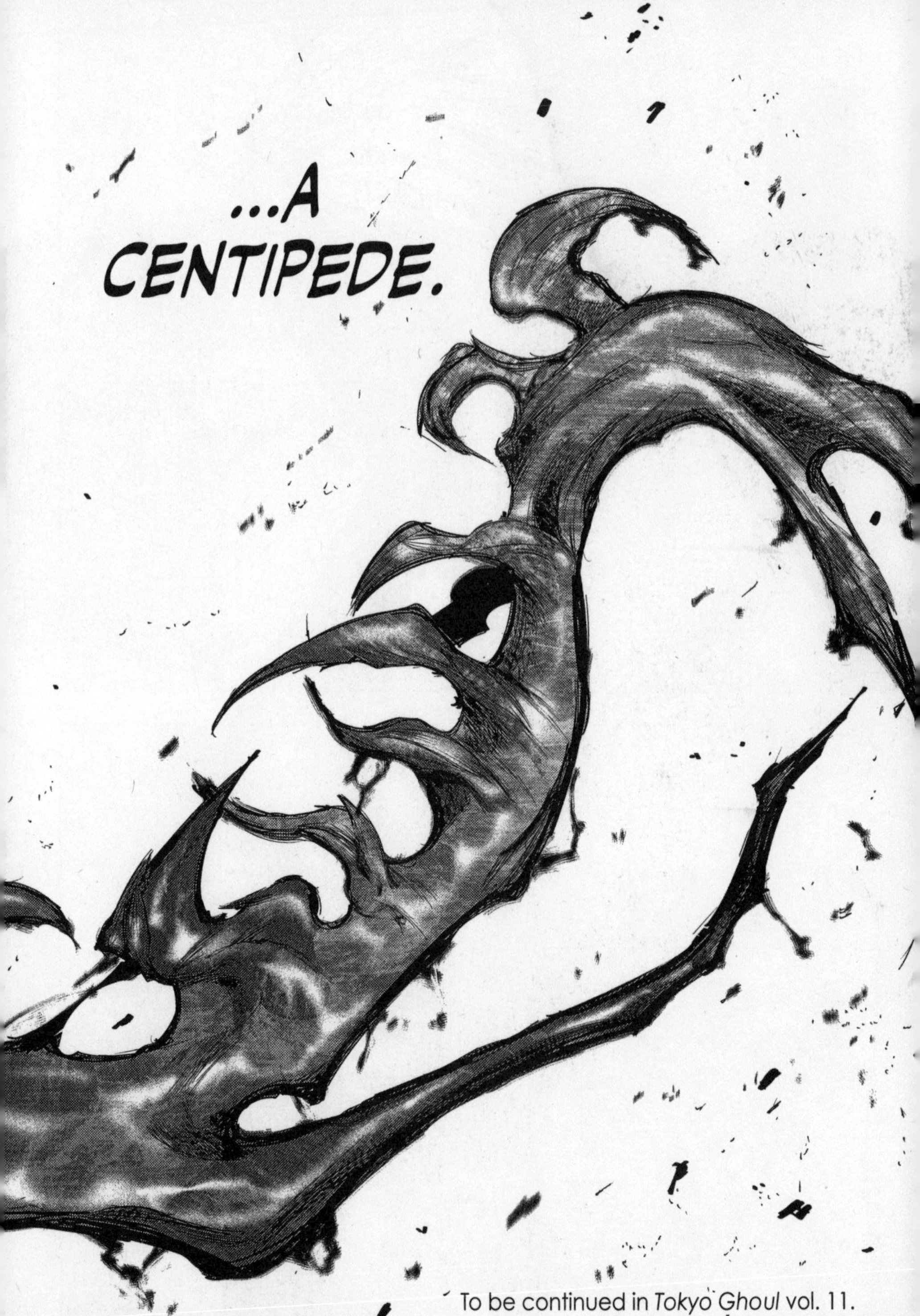
...A CENTIPEDE.

To be continued in *Tokyo Ghoul* vol. 11.

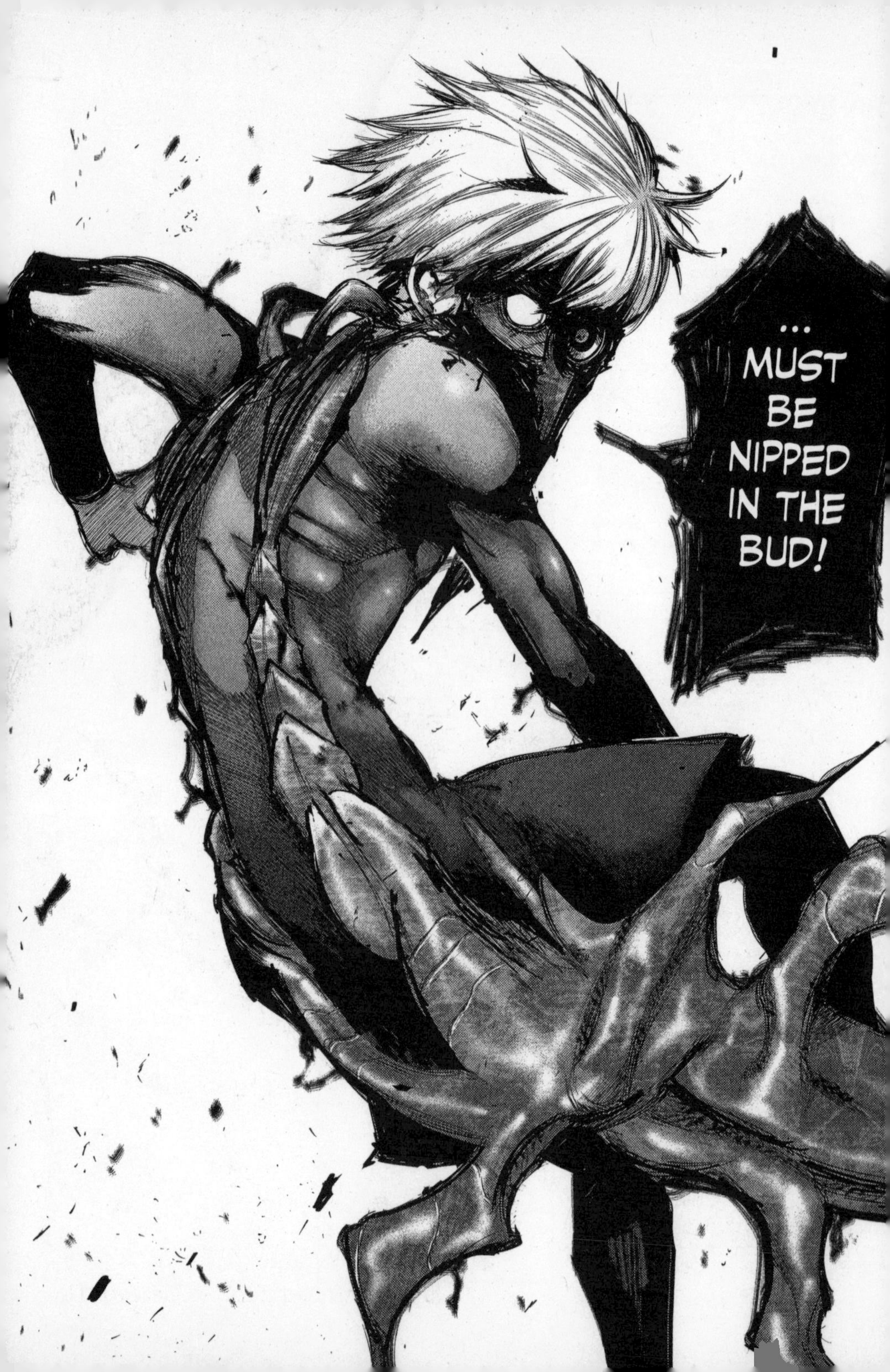
...MUST BE NIPPED IN THE BUD!

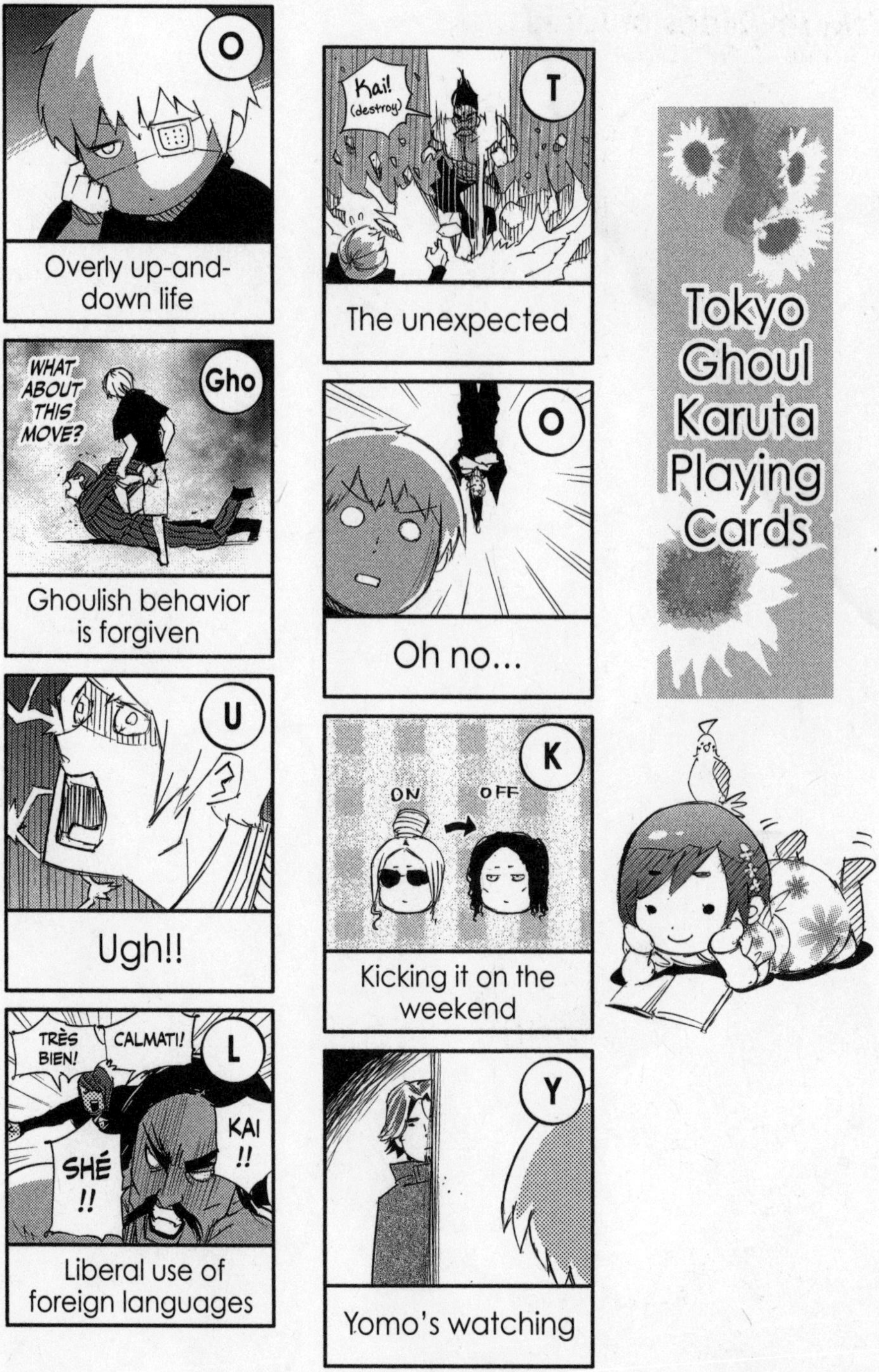

Tokyo Ghoul Karuta Playing Cards
T
Kai! (destroy)
The unexpected
O
Oh no...
K
ON
OFF
Kicking it on the weekend
Y
Yomo's watching
O
Overly up-and-down life
Gho
WHAT ABOUT THIS MOVE?
Ghoulish behavior is forgiven
U
Ugh!!
L
TRÈS BIEN!
CALMATI!
KAI !!
SHÉ !!
Liberal use of foreign languages

Many Sides of Touka

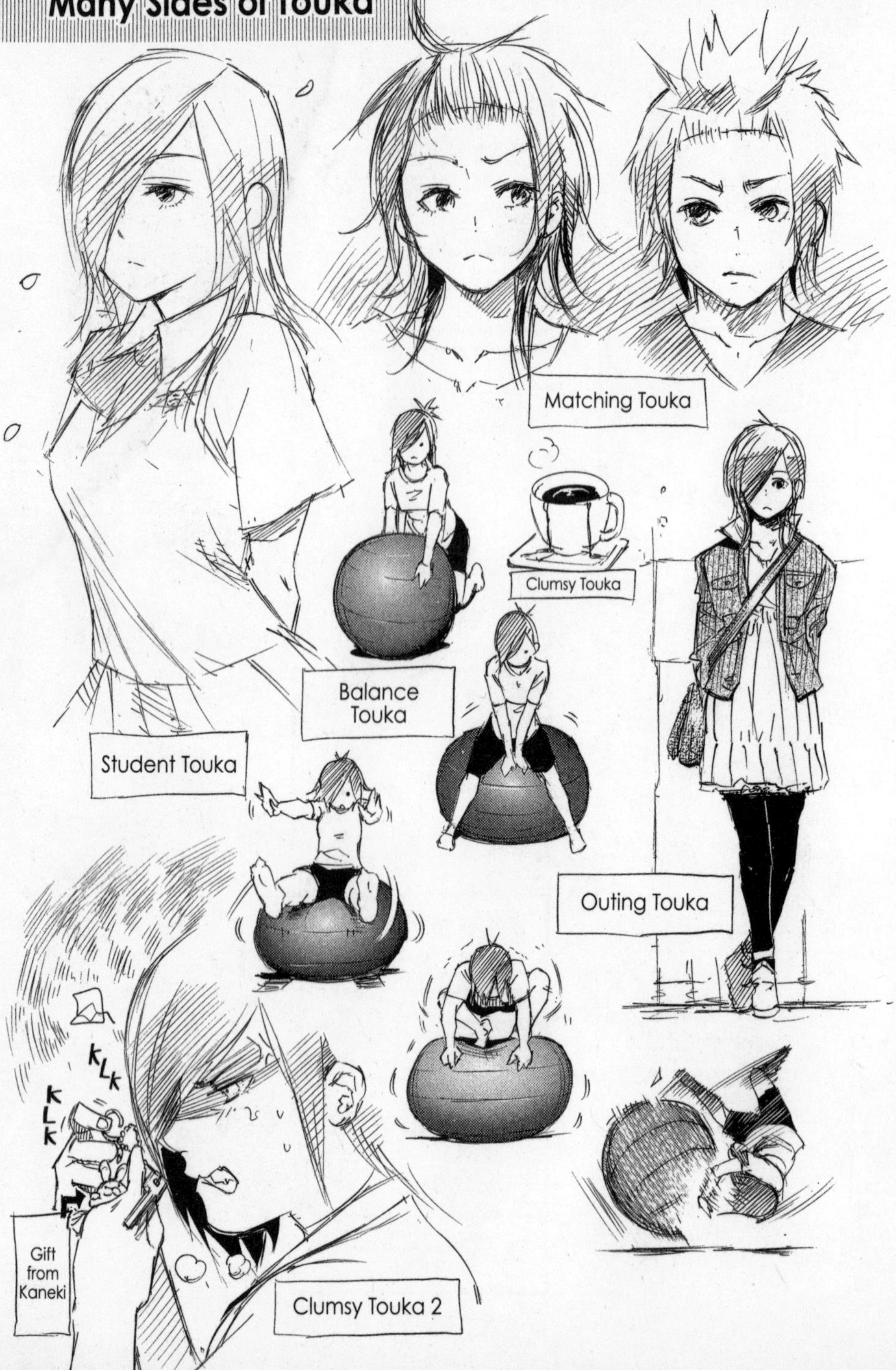
Matching Touka
Student Touka
Clumsy Touka
Balance Touka
Outing Touka
KLK
KLK
Gift from Kaneki
Clumsy Touka 2

Many Sides of Shachi

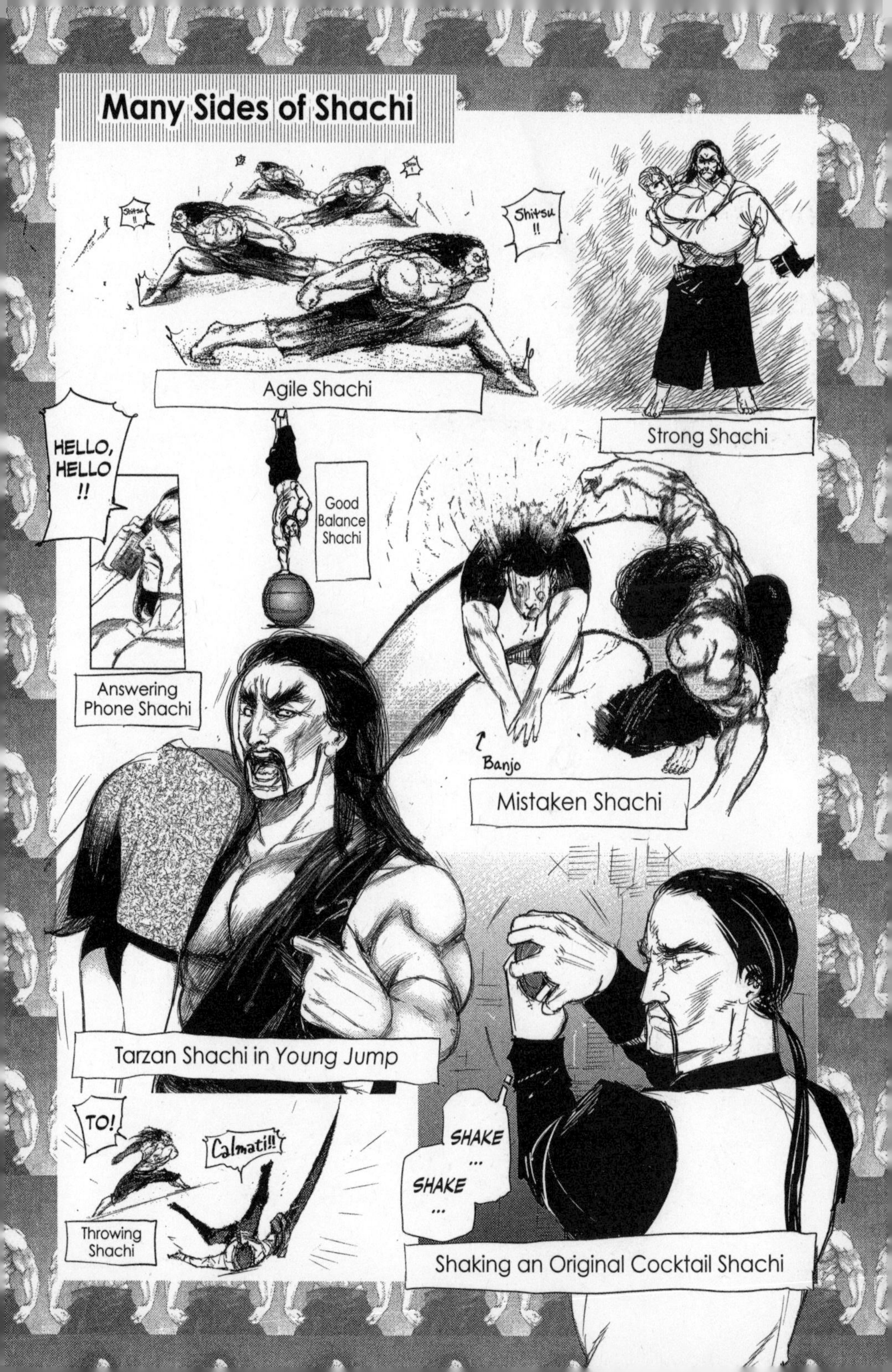

Shitsu !!
Strong Shachi
Shitsu !!
Agile Shachi
Banjo
Mistaken Shachi
Good Balance Shachi
HELLO, HELLO !!
Answering Phone Shachi
Tarzan Shachi in *Young Jump*
SHAKE ... SHAKE ...
Shaking an Original Cocktail Shachi
Calmati!!
TO!
Throwing Shachi

THANKS

Ryuji Miyamoto
Mizuki Ide
Matsuzaki
Nakano
Kouta Shugyo
Hashimoto

Design
Hideaki Shimada (L.S.D.)

Cover
Miyuki Takaoka (POCKET)

Editor
Jumpei Matsuo

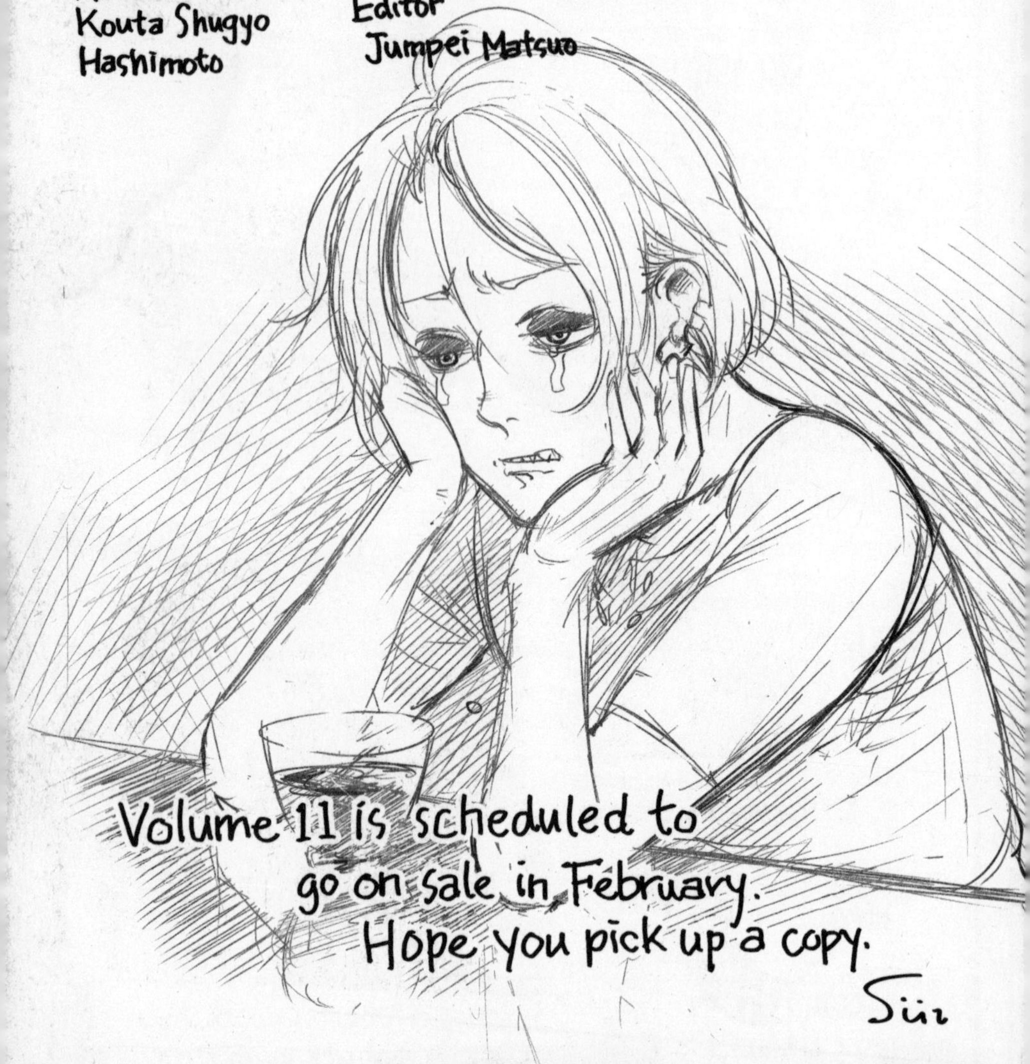

Volume 11 is scheduled to go on sale in February. Hope you pick up a copy.

Suu

TOKYO GHOUL

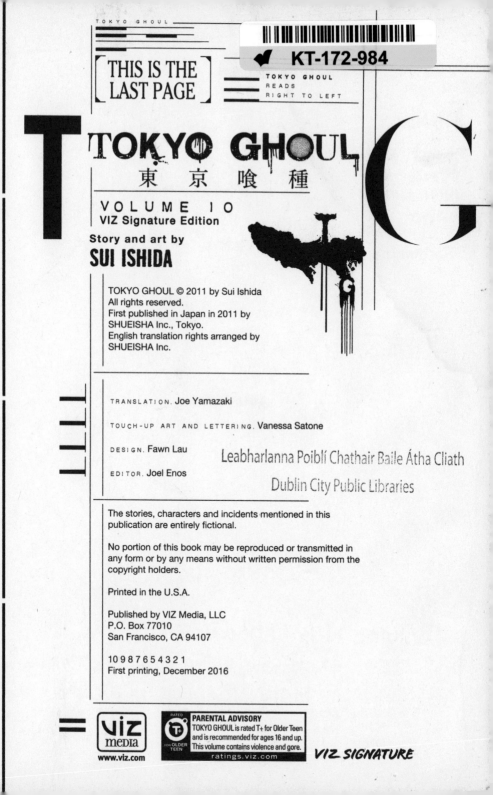

THIS IS THE LAST PAGE

TOKYO GHOUL READS RIGHT TO LEFT

TOKYO GHOUL
東京喰種

VOLUME 10
VIZ Signature Edition

Story and art by
SUI ISHIDA

First published in Japan in 2011 by
SHUEISHA Inc., Tokyo.
English translation rights arranged by
SHUEISHA Inc.

TRANSLATION. Joe Yamazaki

TOUCH-UP ART AND LETTERING. Vanessa Satone

DESIGN. Fawn Lau

EDITOR. Joel Enos

Printed in the U.S.A.

Published by VIZ Media, LLC
P.O. Box 77010
San Francisco, CA 94107

10 9 8 7 6 5 4 3 2 1
First printing, December 2016

www.viz.com

RATED T+ FOR OLDER TEEN

PARENTAL ADVISORY
TOKYO GHOUL is rated T+ for Older Teen and is recommended for ages 16 and up. This volume contains violence and gore.
ratings.viz.com

VIZ SIGNATURE